MW00604381

is due at the WALTER R. DAVIS LIBRARY on
e stamped under "D te
bringing it

Social Psychology and the Unconscious

FRONTIERS OF SOCIAL PSYCHOLOGY

Series Editors:
Arie W. Kruglanski, *University of Maryland at College Park*
Joseph P. Forgas, *University of New South Wales*

Frontiers of Social Psychology is a new series of domain-specific handbooks. The purpose of each volume is to provide readers with a cutting-edge overview of the most recent theoretical, methodological, and practical developments in a substantive area of social psychology, in greater depth than is possible in general social psychology handbooks. The Editors and contributors are all internationally renowned scholars, whose work is at the cutting edge of research.

Scholarly, yet accessible, the volumes in the *Frontiers* series are an essential resource for senior undergraduates, postgraduates, researchers, and practitioners, and are suitable as texts in advanced courses in specific subareas of social psychology.

Published titles

Affect in Social Thinking and Behavior, Forgas
Evolution and Social Psychology, Schaller, Simpson, & Kenrick
Close Relationships, Noller & Feeney
Negotiation Theory and Research, Thompson

Forthcoming titles

Culture, Chiu & Mallorie
Personality and Social Behavior, Rhodewalt
Political Psychology, Krosnick
Science of Social Influence, Pratkanis
Social Cognition, Strack & Förster
Social Communication, Fiedler
The Self, Sedikides & Spencer

For continually updated information about published and forthcoming titles in the *Frontiers of Social Psychology* series, please visit: **www.psypress.com/frontiers**

Discarded by University of
North Carolina Library

BF 315
.S58
2007

Social Psychology and the Unconscious

The Automaticity of Higher Mental Processes

Edited by

John A. Bargh

R

4-4-07

Ψ Psychology Press
Taylor & Francis Group

NEW YORK AND HOVE

UNIVERSITY LIBRARY
UNIVERSITY OF NORTH CAROLINA
AT CHAPEL HILL

Published in 2007
by Psychology Press
270 Madison Avenue
New York, NY 10016
www.psypress.com

Published in Great Britain
by Psychology Press
27 Church Road
Hove, East Sussex BN3 2FA
www.psypress.co.uk

Copyright © 2007 by Psychology Press

Psychology Press is an imprint of the Taylor & Francis Group, an informa business

Typeset by RefineCatch Limited, Bungay, Suffolk, UK
Printed in the United States of America on acid-free paper by Edwards Brothers, Inc.
Cover design by Lisa Dynan

All rights reserved. No part of this book may be reprinted or reproduced or utilized in any form or by any electronic, mechanical, or other means, now known or hereafter invented, including photocopying and recording, or in any information storage or retrieval system, without permission in writing from the publishers.

10 9 8 7 6 5 4 3 2 1

Library of Congress Cataloging in Publication Data

Social psychology and the unconscious : the automaticity of higher mental processes / edited by John A. Bargh.
    p. cm. – (Frontiers of social psychology)
    Includes bibliographical references and index.
    ISBN-13:. 978-1-84169-472-6 (hardback : alk. paper) 1. Subconsciousness. 2. Social psychology. I. Bargh, John A.
BF315.S58 2006
154.2 – dc22

    2006024733

ISBN13: 978-1-84169-472-6 (hbk)

ISBN10: 1-84169-472-X (hbk)

UNIVERSITY LIBRARY
UNIVERSITY OF NORTH CAROLINA
AT CHAPEL HILL

Contents

About the Editor

John Bargh has spent his research career studying the necessity of conscious intentions in social judgment, motivation, and behavior, and along the way has been as surprised as anyone else by how many complex psychological and behavioral phenomena operate just fine without them.

Bargh received his undergraduate degree, summa cum laude, from the University of Illinois in 1977 and then completed his Ph.D. in Psychology at the University of Michigan in 1981. His thesis on "Automatic social perception," under the supervision of R. B. Zajonc, won the annual Dissertation Award from the Society for Experimental Social Psychology in 1982. For the next 22 years he served on the faculty of the Psychology Department at New York University and was the Silver Chair in Psychology from 2001 to 2003; in 2003 he moved to Yale University.

Bargh is also the recipient of the Early Career Contribution Award from the American Psychological Association in 1989, and the Donald T. Campbell Career Award from the Society for Personality and Social Psychology in 2007; he was named a Guggenheim Fellow in 2001, and has been a Fellow at the Center for Advanced Study in the Behavioral Sciences (2001–2002).

Contributors

Henk Aarts
Department of Psychology
University of Utrecht
Heidelberglaan 1
3584 CS Utrecht, The Netherlands

Susan M. Andersen
Department of Psychology
New York University
6 Washington Place, Seventh Floor
New York, NY 10003, USA

Mahzarin R. Banaji
Department of Psychology
Harvard University
William James Hall
33 Kirkland Street
Cambridge, MA 02138, USA

John A. Bargh
Department of Psychology
Yale University
POB 208205
New Haven, CT 06520–8205, USA

Lisa Feldman Barrett
Department of Psychology
427 McGuinn Building
Boston College
Chestnut Hill, MA 02167, USA

Tanya L. Chartrand
Fuqua School of Business
Duke University
1 Towerview Drive, Room A304
Durham, NC 27708, USA

Serena Chen
University of California
Department of Psychology
3413 Tolman Hall
Berkeley, CA 94720–1650, USA

Ap Dijksterhuis
Professor of Psychology
University of Amsterdam
Roetersstraat 15
1018 WB
Amsterdam, The Netherlands

Melissa J. Ferguson
Department of Psychology
Cornell University
250 Uris Hall
Ithaca, NY 14853–7601, USA

Gràinne M. Fitzsimons
University of Waterloo
Department of Psychology
200 University Drive
Waterloo, ON
Canada N2L 1G5

Anthony G. Greenwald
Department of Psychology
University of Washington
Box 351525
Seattle, WA 98195–1525, USA

James J. Gross
Department of Psychology
Jordan Hall, Building 420
Stanford University
Stanford, CA 94305–2130, USA

Jan De Houwer
Department of Psychology
Ghent University
Henri Dunantlaan 2
9000 Ghent, Belgium

Agnes Moors
Department of Psychology
Ghent University
Henri Dunantlaan 2
9000 Ghent, Belgium

Brian A. Nosek
University of Virginia
Department of Psychology
Gilmer Hall
Charlottesville, VA 22904, USA

Kevin N. Ochsner
Department of Psychology
Columbia University
1190 Amsterdam Avenue
New York City, NY 10027, USA

B. Keith Payne
Department of Psychology
University of North Carolina
CB# 3270 Davie Hall
Chapel Hill, NC 27599, USA

Brandon D. Stewart
Ohio State University
Department of Psychology
1835 Neil Avenue
Columbus, OH 43210, USA

Introduction

JOHN A. BARGH

Research on the automaticity of higher mental processes (i.e., judgment, motivation, social behavior) has come a long way over the past 25 years. As Dijksterhuis, Chartrand, and Aarts (Chapter 2) note, had they been asked to contribute a chapter back then on the automaticity of social behavior, there would not have been much to write about. The rich detail provided in the seven chapters of the present volume attests to the fact that the situation has certainly changed. From a handful of relevant studies (see Bargh, 1984) – nearly all of them concerned with social perception and judgment – there are now hundreds of published experiments bearing not only on automatic influences on social perception (e.g., stereotyping, behavior categorization) but on evaluation, social behavior, and goal pursuit as well. Moreover, traditional domains of psychological research such as emotional expression and experience, and the formation and maintenance of close relationships, are beginning to apply concepts of automaticity and control to better understand their focal phenomena.

When social psychology began to "go cognitive" in the 1970s it was nearly universally assumed that the cognition in question was conscious and deliberate, that people were aware of how they made judgments, and aware as well of the influential inputs into those judgments. This assumption seemed so intuitively obvious and "commonsensical" that few thought to question it – but fortunately, some did (i.e., the seminal early works by Hamilton, Taylor & Fiske, Langer, and others; see Bargh 1984). Barrett, Ochsner, and Gross (Chapter 4) argue that emotion research has now reached a similar point in its history, that it is now time to move beyond commonsense models of emotion and the intuitively appealing assumptions that – when scrutinized – are without much empirical support after all. Common sense, or what "feels" to be the case based on our personal experience, is a mine in the harbor of research progress when it comes to automatic phenomena, because by definition many of those phenomena operate outside of our awareness or knowledge. I can recall trying, many years ago, to explain some of the early automaticity findings to my brother-in-law, a successful engineer, only to be met with incredulity and the counterargument that he could not recall even one time that he did something for reasons he was not aware of (!). As Wegner (2002) has shown, even feelings of agency, of intending a given action, are themselves attributions or inferences one makes – they are not veridical readouts of actual personal causation. (Baron, 1995, has argued against the validity of "thought experiments" in philosophy on similar grounds.)

The initial forays into the automaticity of higher mental processes were tentative. Under the mainstream assumption that mental and behavioral processes were under an individual's conscious control, carrying out the early research was akin to sticking one's toes in the water cautiously to see if it was warm enough to swim. But those early results were encouraging, confidence began to grow, and soon classic, mainstream domains of social psychological research such as the attention–behavior relation, causal attribution, and stereotyping and prejudice were shown to possess significant automatic components. Encouraged, researchers held their breath and pushed the envelope still further – could we experimentally cause people to behave in one way versus another without their intention or awareness? Could we trigger motivations and goal pursuits in the same manner, such that the multiple psychological processes needed for goal pursuit – attention, perception, judgment, behavior – could all be put into play outside of awareness, and then operate that way for extended periods of time? The answer kept coming back: yes, we could. As Dijksterhuis et al. (Chapter 2) conclude, it seems like everything can be primed, conscious intent and guidance is not necessary for even the highest of higher mental processes to operate. The pendulum has now swung so far in the other direction that Chen, Fitzsimons, and Andersen (Chapter 3) point out to us that assumptions of automaticity are now held so widely in social psychology that many of the experimental hurdles one used to have to jump to make the claim that a process was automatic are hardly ever seen any more.

This may well prove to be a mixed blessing: untested and widely held assumptions work against progress in a field unless they are put to the test. For example, in the 1980s some initial demonstrations of automatic stereotype influences on information processing led many to assume that stereotyping was unavoidable and uncontrollable as well. As Moors and De Houwer (Chapter 1) make clear, the original assumption of a simple dichotomy between automatic and controlled mental processes was largely to blame for this. If a process can be only one or the other type, then as evidence comes in researchers can quickly switch from one assumption to the other. But, of course, things are not and never were that simple: the features that have been traditionally associated with a conscious or controlled process – awareness, intentionality, controllability, limited capacity – do not always or even usually hang together in an all-or-none fashion, and neither do the features normally attributed to an automatic process (lack of awareness, unintentional, uncontrollable, and efficiency). Rather, the complex, higher mental processes of most interest to social psychologists were usually mixtures or combinations of these features – for example, the commonly accepted "automaticity" of my typing at the keyboard right now pertains only to how my hands and fingers are moving in response to the handwritten notes in front of me – without my having to consciously decide each time to hit a particular key and then guide my movements to do so. That is fine as far as it goes, but one should not go further and assume (as the field did back then, under the "one process or the other" assumption) that my typing is also "unintentional" or "uncontrollable."

Payne and Stewart (Chapter 7) describe an experimental "process dissociation" paradigm (PDP; Jacoby, 1991) that was developed for precisely this reason. All sufficiently complex psychological phenomena are comprised of both automatic and controlled components; as they show, even for those processes we believe "are automatic" there can be significant controlled aspects, and vice versa. For example, we may be intentionally and effortfully engaging in a given process (e.g., classifying the objects that people are holding as to whether they are guns or hand-tools) but our responses can be influenced by automatic assumptions or associations (e.g., that members of certain social groups are more likely than others to be carrying a gun). The PDP paradigm helps us get around the oversimplifying dichotomous thinking about automatic vs. controlled processes by measuring both types of process within a given task or behavior.

The present chapters were designed to be comprehensive reviews and state-of-the-art analyses of automatic phenomena in the realm of the higher mental processes – such as those involved in social perception and judgment, emotion, close interpersonal relationships, attitudes and evaluation, and social behavior and goal pursuits. Each chapter, in its given domain, gives careful attention to terminology and definitions; each also provides a thoughtful, painstaking analysis of the key concepts and how they are related to each other. Because the book was intended to serve as a sourcebook for researchers, especially those new to the notion of automatic information processing or of nonconscious, implicit influences, two chapters are devoted to the new methodological approaches developed in the past decade: the Implicit Association Test (Nosek, Greenwald, & Banaji, Chapter 6) and the aforementioned Process Dissociation Paradigm (Payne & Stewart, Chapter 7). The book will therefore be a useful resource for researchers who wish to get involved in this vital and vibrant research area.

Automaticity is one of those phenomena that look simple on the surface but become more complicated upon closer and further inspection. In the opening chapter, Moors and De Houwer provide a detailed analysis of the concept of automaticity and its component features. First, as have previous such analyses (e.g., Bargh, 1994; more recently Conrey, Sherman, Gawronski, Hugenberg, & Groom, 2005), they argue against a simple automatic vs. controlled processes dichotomy, in which a given process of interest is considered either entirely automatic or entirely controlled. Instead, on both empirical and theoretical grounds, Moors and De Houwer conclude in favor of deconstructing the process in terms of its component features (i.e., intentional or not, controllable or not, efficient vs. consumptive of limited attentional capacity, in awareness or not), because many, perhaps most, processes of interest are actually mixtures of automatic and controlled features.

In harmony with the deconstruction approach, the authors provide an analysis of the concept of automaticity in terms of its component features, but they go further to analyze each component feature as well – such as whether it is a gradual or absolute quality, and whether it is conceptually distinct from the others. But the authors do not leave their deconstructed Humpty Dumpty just sitting there on the pavement in pieces, they try to put him back together again, by addressing the important next question of whether there might be some combinations of features which are more likely than others, and further, whether *any* combination of these features is possible. For example, processes we are aware of are also more likely to be controllable, and those we are not aware of are unlikely to be intentional. Their chapter discusses which of these combinations are more versus less likely to co-occur. Overall it provides much needed clarity as to the basic conceptual issues at stake in contemporary automaticity research.

Chapter 2 by Dijksterhuis, Chartrand, and Aarts covers the rapidly growing research area of automaticity in social perception, social behavior, and goal pursuit. Their chapter puts several different research areas in social cognition together for the first time – carefully fitting them together like a jigsaw puzzle. Much of this research has utilized *priming* procedures which cause the activation of various complex social knowledge structures – for example, representations of social groups, significant individuals in our life, stereotypes and role concepts, stock situations – in a passive, unobtrusive manner, with the researchers then assessing the covert influence of these activated representations. Dijksterhuis et al. conclude from their review that in principle nearly every type of social psychological phenomena can be primed in this way: that is, shown to be capable of operating automatically without the individual's intent or awareness. More generally, however, they argue that this research demonstrates that social behavior does not normally or even usually originate with a conscious intention, but instead with impulses that are sparked by recent experience as well as by one's own internal imaginings (see also Wegner, 2002).

In their analysis of the mechanisms mediating these automatic effects on social behavior, Dijksterhuis et al. trace three main routes leading from the triggering environmental stimuli and events to their culmination in social behavior: one through natural mimicry and imitation processes, another through the activation of trait concepts (such as aggressive or intelligent), and a third through the activation of goals to be pursued within that situation. There is now considerable evidence of unconscious mimicry in speech, facial expressions, postures, gestures, mannerisms – yet the new research described in Chapter 2 by Chartrand and her colleagues goes beyond such demonstrations to examine how these tendencies are moderated by one's current goals regarding the interaction partner. For example, this research suggests that there are important positive benefits of the natural ways we tend to mimic our interaction partners: it produces more altruistic behavior in the other person and influences persuasion/liking for behavior being imitated (choosing or consuming one product vs. another); also better subsequent self-regulation if they had themselves been mimicked by another person.

Another especially valuable feature of Dijksterhuis et al.'s chapter is their distinction between the trait and goal routes, and their discussion of the differences between them, because both routes produce similar outcomes (e.g., automatic social behavior) but do so through presumably different mechanisms. They conclude that automatic behavioral effects via the trait activation route (as when these concepts are activated in the natural course of social perception; see Uleman, Newman, & Moskowitz, 1996) occur because the activated trait concept adjusts ongoing behavior, not because the trait activation instigates a new course of action – the latter effect, in their view, is the exclusive province of the goal route. The goal route, in turn, is analyzed into three phases: goal setting, goal adoption, and goal implementation, and the authors give consideration to the nature of the underlying cognitive and neurological processes that support automatic goal pursuit.

In life outside the psychology laboratory, one important environmental context in which all of these automatic effects on perception and behavior really come into play is in our close relationships. In Chapter 3, Chen, Fitzsimons, and Andersen review the growing evidence of automaticity in relationship cognition, including effects on information processing, affective responses and evaluations, expectancy generation, self-concepts and self-worth, self-regulation, as well as interpersonal behavior. Close relationships are where everything we study in social cognition matters the most in real life – these are the people we encounter most frequently, whose opinions of us matter the most to our feelings of self-worth, and with whom we pursue many of our most important life tasks and goals. The sheer frequency and consistency with which we interact with our close partners in itself makes the relationship domain a potentially fruitful place to study automatic phenomena; in addition, demonstrations of automatic processes in close relationships are also demonstrations that automatic processes are not merely artificial laboratory phenomena concerning stimuli the participant does not really care about, but instead do have considerable real world significance.

Many automatic phenomena can be understood as natural and unintended effects of our past upon our present, and this is the common theme of the research reviewed by Chen et al. – the perpetuation of prior relationships and relationship experiences and their re-emergence in present-day encounters. Their chapter covers such automatic effects as transference (how significant others from the past affect present relationships and impressions of new acquaintances); the influence of relational schemas (consisting of notions of the individuals involved along with their interpersonal script); how the close relationship partner comes to be included as a key feature of one's self-concept, and the consequences of this for affect and behavior within the relationship; and secure versus insecure attachment working models.

The authors argue that people pursue today the goals and strategies that worked in the past (or at least on which they relied in the past) to provide them with feelings of closeness and security, regardless of whether those are the most appropriate strategies for the current environment. As they acknowledge, the notion that early attachment experiences play themselves out in adolescent and adult relationships is not a new one, being a prominent theme of Bowlby's original work on attachment theory. What is new is the conceptualization of close relationships as corresponding to cognitive structures; once that assumption is made, one can then apply to them the cognitive principles of accessibility, applicability, association, priming, as well as automaticity and control. This is the tack taken by many researchers in the relationship domain over the past 10–15 years and it has led to a fast pace of important new discoveries – just as the reconceptualization of motives and goals as knowledge structures at about the same time led to a similar explosion of provocative new findings in the domain of motivation and goal pursuit (see Chapter 2).

If there is any one domain of psychological phenomena that is easier for the lay public to accept as operating automatically, it is emotional experience. Barrett, Ochsner, and Gross (Chapter 4) address this consensual, commonsense view that emotions just play themselves out in us, that to a large extent at least we are under their control (e.g., the reduced sentences handed out for "crimes of passion"). They note the traditional, historical nature of this view that emotions are part of our "animal nature" and are thus something to be controlled. Two main approaches to the study of emotions over the years are distinguished: "basic emotion" research in which constellations or patterns of packages of associated responses distinguish one emotion from another, and "appraisal" research, which has focused on how environmental stimuli are perceived and evaluated that cause or give rise to the emotional response in question. Automatic processes of social perception and interpretation (see also Ferguson, Chapter 5) are especially relevant to appraisal models, as they are concerned with the cognitive processes that are involved in producing the underlying "direct experience" that automatically produces emotions.

Barrett et al. sketch out and then critically examine what they term the "modal model" of emotion research over the past 100 years, consisting of two major assumptions that have guided research: first, that there is only a small, limited set of distinct or "basic" emotions, and second, that these emotions occur automatically and not as a result of any controlled process. The authors argue that this modal model has problems – it focuses on only a narrow range or limited set of emotions (leaving a lot out, potentially), and the existing evidence, even after a century of looking for it, is not very supportive. For one thing, they point out, much research has shown that behavior is too sensitive to the current situational context, and the requirements/constraints of that situation, than the modal model assumes. For another, there is no, or at most poor, evidence that emotional states have specific and unique physiological signatures.

Importantly, Barrett et al. also join the other authors in urging us away from the too-simple automatic–controlled dichotomy, specifically from the assumption that emotions are always due to an automatic process and their regulation is always due to a controlled process. In doing so, they advance the intriguing argument that because controlled processing can itself operate outside of awareness (see especially Chapter 2), then a lot of emotion may be produced (or not) by the operation of these "hidden" controlled processes. For example, emotions such as anger might not even be experienced in the first place (say, upon a perceived insult) if they conflict with a nonconsciously operating goal, such as ingratiating oneself to one's boss or an attractive potential romantic partner. Fortunately, as do Moors and De Houwer, Barrett et al. do not leave us with only the shattered remains of our former assumptions, but help put Humpty Dumpty back together again at the end of their chapter. This they do by offering new approaches to the study of emotion such as parallel distributed processing, or constraint satisfaction models.

Another form of affective experience that research suggests is automatically generated concerns one's preferences and evaluations. Ferguson (Chapter 5) reviews the body of research on automatic evaluation or automatic attitude activation that has accrued since the seminal theoretical and empirical work of Fiske (1982) and Fazio (1986). Those researchers conceptualized automatic affective responses not as produced by a separate psychological system, as did Zajonc (1980), but as summary evaluations that become, over time, strongly associated with, or incorporated within, the concept in question. In Fiske's (1982) original "category based affect" model, immediate and automatic affective responses could occur in the mundane course of object or social perception if the evaluation also became active when the perceptual representation itself became active.

Ferguson analyzes the cognitive architecture of evaluation, describing and discussing models of how evaluations are represented mentally – the main theoretical question at present being whether evaluations correspond to relatively permanent representations in memory, or as cognitive constructions made on the spot, when and where needed. Some of the evidence pointing to an automatic construction process are recent studies showing that automatic evaluations are modified by the current context. Ferguson then makes a potentially quite useful distinction between two different kinds of "context" that have been conflated in prior theoretical treatments: one involving the past, and another involving the future. Some contextual effects are due to one's recent experience, such as when prior exposure to Black churchgoers reduces the manifestation of implicit or automatic negative stereotype influences; but other contextual influences come from *prospective* memory, as when stimuli are evaluated on the basis of ongoing goal pursuits – that is, whether the stimulus in question will help or hinder that pursuit.

In her review, Ferguson remarks on how the study of attitudes and evaluations has profited hugely from the methodological advances of the past quarter century that enable us now to go beyond self-report of attitudes on questionnaires and surveys, to implicit measures of those attitudes that the individual is unable to manage strategically for self-presentational purposes. There are now a variety of methods to get at these implicit attitudes, discussed here as well as in the final two chapters of the volume. Ferguson notes that the advent of these new measures raises important new questions for research, such as: What is the relation between implicit and explicit attitudes? Is the underlying attitude the same and just measured in different ways or are there two separate attitudes? How do automatic evaluations develop in the first place?

The final two chapters deal in great detail with two "next generation" methodologies for assessing automatic influences (see Bargh & Chartrand, 2000, for a description of the older methods, still very much in use, such as subliminal and sequential priming techniques, cognitive load, and divided attention). In Chapter 6, Nosek, Greenwald, and Banaji provide a comprehensive and state-of-the-art review of the Implicit Association Test (IAT), which is easily the most commonly used technique today to assess the presence and strength of automatic or implicit associations among various concepts (e.g., *smoking* and *good; Republicans* and *bad*). Given its current popularity, the authors – who developed the IAT and implemented it on the Internet so that over a million people around the world now have taken it in one form or another – provide the interested researcher with detailed practical advice on how to use it effectively, the conclusions that can/ cannot be legitimately drawn from it, and whether it is a reliable and valid measure compared to other implicit measures.

In Chapter 7, Payne and Stewart describe another major advance in the study of automatic and controlled processes: the Process Dissociation Paradigm (PDP) developed originally by Jacoby (1991). This method has the unique advantage of being able to separate out the automatic from the controlled processing components of the task in question, and to provide numerical estimates of the contribution of each type of processing. This paradigm helps move us past the either–or automatic–controlled process dichotomy by assuming that both types of processing, not just one or the other, are present in most real-world psychological phenomena. The basic strategy is to compare the extent of automatic influences when one is not told about them (allowing them free rein to operate) to their extent when the participant is explicitly told about their possibility and instructed to not let them occur if at all possible. Task performance is then compared between these *inclusion* and *exclusion* conditions.

Payne and Stewart argue that whereas the PDP technique was developed to study the implicit or unconscious influences of memory on judgment (such as when one attributes the experienced familiarity of a name actually caused by its prior presentation in the experimental setting to the popular "fame" of that person), it can profitably be used in contexts outside of memory research – indeed to any situation that involves both automatic and controlled processing components. A highly topical and socially relevant situation of this sort to which the PDP approach has been applied is the "shooter" paradigm, in which participants role-play police officers who have to make very quick decisions about whether to shoot at a crime suspect or not. These experimental situations were set up to simulate the tragic case of Amadou Diallo who was shot on his apartment doorstep over 40 times by police in Brooklyn despite being unarmed himself (he had held up his wallet to the officers in order to show that he lived in the building; officers then began firing as if he had raised a gun instead). The intentional or controlled component of this process would be to base the shooting decision on whether the stimulus person on a given trial was holding a gun or not; the automatic component would be to base the decision on the target person's race. Using the PDP approach, one can measure both the strength of the automatic influence under certain, manipulated conditions, as well as the ability to engage in executive control under those same conditions. Payne and Stewart describe the basics of the PDP approach and the experimental questions to which it can be applied – essentially, any phenomenon for which the researcher is interested in disentangling the intentional from the unintentional influences.

Anyone who reads this book has to be impressed by the significant and substantial advances in automaticity research that have been made over the past 25 years. What is especially rewarding and encouraging to me personally is that all of the principal authors of the present chapters are of the next generation of researchers.

Their chapters reflect the same sense of excitement and thrill of discovery that was true of their "elders" in the 1970s and 80s. The methodological and theoretical advances they are making are impressive – reading these chapters leaves little doubt that progress will continue to be made, at an ever accelerating rate, over the next quarter century.

REFERENCES

Bargh, J. A. (1984). Automatic and conscious processing of social information. In R. S. Wyer, Jr., & T. K. Srull (Eds.), *Handbook of social cognition* (Vol. 3, pp. 1–43). Hillsdale, NJ: Erlbaum.

Bargh, J. A. (1994). The Four Horsemen of automaticity: Awareness, efficiency, intention, and control in social cognition. In R. S. Wyer, Jr., & T. K. Srull (Eds.), *Handbook of social cognition* (2nd ed., pp. 1–40). Hillsdale, NJ: Erlbaum.

Bargh, J. A., & Chartrand, T. L. (2000). A practical guide to priming and automaticity research. In H. Reis & C. Judd (Eds.), *Handbook of research methods in social psychology* (pp. 253–285). New York: Cambridge University Press.

Baron, J. (1995). A psychological view of moral intuition. *Harvard Review of Philosophy, 5,* 36–40.

Conrey, F. R., Sherman, J. W., Gawronski, B., Hugenberg, K., & Groom, C. (2005). Separating multiple processes in implicit social cognition: The Quad model of implicit task performance. *Journal of Personality and Social Psychology, 89,* 469–487.

Damasio, A. R. (1994). *Descartes' error: Emotion, reason, and the human brain.* New York: Grosset/Putnam.

Fazio, R. H. (1986). How do attitudes guide behavior? In R. M. Sorrentino & E. T. Higgins (Eds.), *The handbook of motivation and cognition: Foundations of social behavior* (Vol. 1, pp. 204–243). New York: Guilford Press.

Fiske, S. T. (1982). Schema-triggered affect: Applications to social perception. In M. S. Clark & S. T. Fiske (Eds.), *Affect and Cognition: The 17th Annual Carnegie Symposium on Cognition* (pp. 55–78). Hillsdale, NJ: Erlbaum.

Jacoby, L. L. (1991). A process dissociation framework: Separating automatic from intentional uses of memory. *Journal of Memory and Language, 30,* 513–541.

Uleman, J. S., Newman, L. S., & Moskowitz, G. B. (1996). People as flexible interpreters: Evidence and issues from spontaneous trait inference. In M. P. Zanna (Ed.), *Advances in experimental social psychology* (Vol. 28, pp. 211–279). San Diego, CA: Academic Press.

Wegner, D. M. (2002). *The illusion of conscious will.* Cambridge, MA: MIT Press.

Zajonc, R. B. (1980). Feeling and thinking: Preferences need no inferences. *American Psychologist, 35,* 151–175.

1

What is Automaticity? An Analysis of Its Component Features and Their Interrelations

AGNES MOORS and JAN DE HOUWER

The concept of automaticity is becoming increasingly important across nearly all subareas of psychology. Investigators who search for guidelines to asses the automatic nature of a certain task performance or process are faced with a multitude of views of automaticity. The variety of views is largely due to the topic studied (e.g., perception, memory, skill development, attention), the research paradigm employed (e.g., direct vs. indirect), the characteristics of the underlying information processing model (e.g., instance-based vs. rule-based), and the characteristics of the larger framework in which the information processing model fits (e.g., computational vs. connectionist). Many views define the concept of automaticity in terms of a number of features, but they differ with regard to the features they put most emphasis on, as well as with regard to the coherence they assume among the features. One contemporary account is the gradual and decompositional view, which proposes to investigate each automaticity feature separately and determine the degree to which it is present. In this chapter, we engage in a detailed analysis of the most important features in order to examine whether they can indeed be regarded as gradual, and whether they can be conceptually and logically separated.

Before embarking on a discussion of some prominent views of automaticity, we must specify what the word automatic can be a predicate of and stipulate the research questions that prevail in the study of automaticity. The word automatic can be used to describe performances or effects, which are observable, or to describe the processes underlying the performance, which are not observable and hence need to be inferred. We take it as a general rule that when the performance is classified as automatic, so can the process underlying the performance. It may be good to keep in mind that processes can be described at different levels of analysis. Marr (1982), for example, distinguished between three levels of process understanding: the computational level, the algorithmic level, and the hardware level. The computational level articulates the functional relation between input and output, whereas the algorithmic level contains information about the formal properties of the processes involved in transforming input into output (i.e., what is actually in the black box). For example, the higher-level functional process of stimulus evaluation (i.e., is a stimulus good or bad) may be further specified at the algorithmic level as a process of direct memory retrieval (activation of a stored valence label in memory) or as a process of algorithm computation (comparison between a desired and an actual state). The hardware level is concerned with the physical implementation of processes in the brain. Other theorists (e.g., Anderson, 1987; Pylyshyn, 1984) have proposed a different number of levels and have placed the boundaries between the levels at somewhat different heights, but the important lesson is that processes described at higher levels can be explained by processes described at lower levels. Similarly, performances or effects can be explained by higher-level processes and further down by lower-level processes. It should be clear that we use the term explanation here in the sense of an explanation that specifies the underlying mechanism.

Now that we have clarified our use of the terms performance, process, and explanation, we can distinguish between two types of research purposes that automaticity researchers have been concerned with. A first purpose is to diagnose the automatic nature of a task performance or a higher-level process. For example, skill-development researchers have tried to assess whether the performance on certain tasks has reached an automatic level. Affective priming researchers have tried to find out whether the affective priming effect (i.e., the fact that responses to a target are faster when preceded by a prime with the same valence; see Fazio, 2001, for a review) occurs automatically, and, by inference, whether the higher-level process of the evaluation of the primes can take place automatically. A second purpose is to explain automaticity in general. This purpose amounts to investigating which type of lower-level processes can lead to automatic performance or automatic higher-level processes, and can be rephrased as the purpose to diagnose the automatic nature of these lower-level processes. Researchers may manipulate the lower-level process that participants will use for a certain task, and they may then assess which type of lower-level process leads to automatic performance. For example, affective priming studies may be designed to encourage the retrieval of a valence label from memory (e.g., Fazio, Sanbonmatsu, Powell, & Kardes, 1986) or, alternatively, the comparison between a desired and an actual state (e.g., Moors, De Houwer, & Eelen, 2004). It may then be assessed which of these lower-level processes produces automatic affective priming effects. Both research purposes can be rephrased as being about diagnosis: the first concerns the diagnosis of the automatic nature of a task performance or a higher-level process, and the second concerns the diagnosis of the automatic nature of a lower-level process. The diagnosis of a phenomenon is usually closely related to the way in which it is defined. We therefore start with an overview of different views (of the definition) of automaticity.

VIEWS OF AUTOMATICITY

Most theories of automaticity are feature-based, defining automaticity in terms of one or more features. Different feature-based theories vary with regard to the features they select as the crucial ones, as well as with regard to the degree of coherence they assume among the features. Another proposal is to define and diagnose automaticity, not in terms of features, but in terms of the underlying process. This view is called the mechanism-based approach.

Feature-based Approach

Features have been clustered into two modes, into three (or more) modes, or they have been considered to be entirely independent. The first view to be discussed is the dual mode view. Although this view is now largely abandoned, several researchers seem to still implicitly rely on it, as is sometimes revealed in unguarded moments.

Dual Mode View   According to a dual mode view, there are two modes of processing that are each characterized by a fixed set of features. Automatic processes are characterized as unintentional, unconscious, uncontrollable, efficient, and fast. Nonautomatic processes are supposed to possess all the opposite features. The dual mode view is also an all-or-none view. Such a view combines the idea of a perfect correlation among the features of each mode with the idea that both modes are mutually exclusive and that they exhaust the universe of possible cognitive processes. In this way, any performance or process holds all of the features of one, and none of the features of the other mode. According to this all-or-none view, one can diagnose a performance or process as automatic (or nonautomatic) by assessing the presence of one feature belonging to the automatic (or the nonautomatic) mode. The presence of the remaining features of that mode can then be logically inferred (Bargh, 1992).

Two historical research traditions have been appointed as responsible for the creation of the dual mode view (Bargh, 1996; Bargh & Chartrand, 2000; Wegner & Bargh 1998). The first tradition developed from the single capacity view of attention (Shiffrin & Schneider, 1977), a view that originated from early research on skill development (Bryan & Harter, 1899) and dual tasks (Solomons & Stein, 1896; see review by Shiffrin, 1988). This tradition was also inspired by the writings of James (1890) and Jastrow (1906) on habit formation. The second research tradition grew out of the New Look program in perception research (e.g., Bruner, 1957).

Capacity view   The single capacity view of attention regarded attention as a limited amount of energy that can flexibly be allocated to different stages of processing (e.g., Kahneman, 1973). It was assumed that the early stages in the processing sequence (sensory analysis) require less attention (i.e., pre-attentive) than the later stages. In virtue of extensive (consistent) practice, processes that are initially capacity-demanding can progressively develop to operate without attention. Automatic processing was defined as processing without or with minimal attention (i.e., efficient), and automatization was defined as the gradual withdrawal of attention involvement due to practice (Hasher & Zacks, 1979; Posner & Snyder, 1975a, b; Shiffrin & Schneider, 1977). We call this view the capacity view of automaticity.

Initially, proponents of the capacity view conceived of the criterion of attentional requirements as a continuum (see Hasher & Zacks, 1979), with automatic processes depleting only a minimal amount (efficient) and nonautomatic processes drawing on a substantial amount of attentional capacity (nonefficient). Other functional feature pairs (such as unintentional vs. intentional, unconscious vs. conscious, uncontrollable vs. controllable, fast vs. slow, parallel vs. serial) were derived from the feature pair efficient–nonefficient, and eventually this led to the view that automatic and nonautomatic processes represent two opposite modes of processing, each characterized by a fixed set of features. In this way, the initial conception of automaticity as a continuum developed into a dichotomous view.

New Look   The second research tradition that contributed to a dual mode view was the New Look movement in perception (Bruner, 1957). The original focus in this tradition was on the constructivist nature of perception, that is, the interaction between person variables (needs, expectancies, values, knowledge) and information available in the environment (Bartlett, 1932). Because of the hidden character of the influence of person variables on perception, the focus shifted toward unconscious perception (Erdelyi, 1992). The dual mode models that developed from this research tradition put most emphasis on the features *unconscious* and *unintentional* (e.g., Fodor, 1983).

To summarize, the first research tradition took the feature pair efficient–nonefficient as a starting point and added other feature pairs to this distinction. The second research tradition added other feature pairs to a dual mode model based on the feature pair conscious–unconscious. This different emphasis on individual features of automaticity stems for a large part from the type of research paradigms employed in both traditions. For example, Shiffrin and Schneider (1977) used search tasks, which are a special type of skill development task. In these tasks, participants are explicitly instructed to engage in the process under study (e.g., to detect a target). After extended (consistent) practice, the process becomes impervious to variations in task load, and this is taken as an indication that it has become efficient (Shiffrin & Schneider, 1977). Investigators from the New Look tradition used tasks in which participants were instructed to engage in a process that is different from the process under study or in which the process under study was concealed. For example, Bruner and Goodman (1947) asked participants to draw the physical size of coins and equally sized discs and they observed an overestimation of the size of coins compared to discs. This effect was larger for coins with a higher monetary value and for poor participants. The fact that participants processed the monetary value of coins even when they were not instructed to do so, yields support for the unintentional nature of this processing. In other studies, tachistoscopic presentations were used to establish thresholds for conscious recognition of desired and undesired words (e.g., Postman, Bruner, & McGinnies, 1948).

Despite these differences, researchers of both traditions have proposed very similar dual mode models for information processing in which perception, attention, and memory are intertwined. Both consider information processing as based on the activation of a sequence of nodes from long-term memory. Nodes can be activated in two distinct ways: by stimulus input alone, in which case activation is spread further to connected nodes with little attentional demand; or by a non-automatic process, through the allocation of attention. The dual mode model developed by these early researchers appears to be a tenacious one. Despite criticism and recent evolutions, it is still popular in various domains of research (e.g., emotion, social cognition). One of the reasons why the dual mode view seems so difficult to shake off is that it is strongly ingrained in the classic, computational metaphor of cognition on which most dual mode models rest. The computational metaphor of cognition can thus be considered as a third factor that is responsible for the creation and persistence of the dual mode view.

Computational framework   There are several elements in the computational framework that render it more susceptible to a dual mode view than the connectionist framework (see also Cleeremans, 1997). First, in computational models, knowledge is represented symbolically in long-term memory. This knowledge may consist of data (concepts, exemplars) stored in declarative memory, and programs (procedures, rules, algorithms) stored in procedural memory. Processing amounts to combining data and programs in working memory. The system takes data as its input, runs a program on it, and produces new data as its output. One commonly voiced concern is that symbolic representations, because they are abstract, need an external *interpreter* in order to inject them with meaning (i.e., symbol grounding problem; Searle, 1992). Further, the conception of processing as symbol manipulation presupposes an external *manipulator* or processor. In most classic models, the interpreter (in charge with providing conscious meaning) and the manipulator (or controller) are united in one single entity, for example, a central executive (Baddeley, 1986). This central executive is also charged with directing the attention window. Hence, it is no surprise to find that the features *conscious*, *controlled*, and *nonefficient* are often mentioned in the same breath.

Not many classic models are strictly computational. The declarative database is often depicted as an associative network, and activation can travel through the network without help from the executive. Automatic processing is equated with everything that is done without the central executive. This explains why the features *unconscious*, *uncontrolled*, and *efficient* are often glued together. In the majority of the classic models, the retrieval of single facts from a declarative database is all that can be done automatically (cf. Logan, 1988). In some classic models, algorithms can also be stored according to associative principles and they can be activated and fired without the help of an external manipulator (cf. Anderson, 1996).

In connectionist models, a concept is represented subsymbolically, by a pattern of activation that is distributed among many nodes or units in a network, instead of being tied to a single unit. Different representations show more or less resemblance in pattern activity as a function of the semantic resemblance of their concepts. In this way, the intrinsic properties of subsymbolic representations reflect the meaning of their concepts, and there is no need for an external interpreter.[1] Similarly, rules are represented subsymbolically, in the connection weights between units. The system is thus able to behave in a rule-like manner without actually possessing the rule as a symbolic representation (Cleeremans, 1997). Processing in the connectionist framework does not amount to combining data and rules, but to dynamic patterns of activation. Note that no distinction is made between representations (of both data and programs) and processing: both are defined in terms of patterns of activation. There is equally no distinction between a storage place and a working space, nor between encoding (or learning) and deployment (or processing). Each encounter with a stimulus both activates previously established patterns and increments the connection weights. Both the lack of a distinction between representations and processing, and the unanimous idea that activation can travel through the network without external help, render superfluous the intervention of a central executive. Because of the fact that connectionist models have spelled out the homunculus in charge of conscious interpretation, manipulation, and the orienting of attention, there is nothing that provides the glue for the features *conscious*, *controlled*, and *nonefficient*. In most connectionist models, it is the quality of the nodes or the quality of the activity between the nodes that determines their fate in terms of consciousness (Cleeremans & Jiménez, 2002). It is not always clear how control and attention must be shaped in a strictly connectionist system. Control is sometimes dispelled as an illusion, or it is taken care of by non-connectionist goal modules. Attention is sometimes translated in a biasing of connection weights. The idea that attention or selectivity is not a cause but rather a passive by-product of natural priming effects is an old idea (James, 1890, p. 447; Neisser, 1976; Johnston & Dark, 1986; Fernandez-Duque & Johnson, 2002).[2]

The Dual Mode View Challenged

The dual mode view came under attack when empirical studies showed a lack of co-occurrence among some of the central features listed for automatic processes (e.g., Bargh, 1992; Kahneman & Treisman, 1984; Logan, 1985, 1988, 1989; Logan & Cowan, 1984). For example, several studies demonstrated that the occurrence of the Stroop interference effect, which was generally thought to be unintentional and uncontrollable, was not independent of attention because it could be diluted when attention was directed away from the targets (e.g., Francolini & Egeth, 1980; Kahneman & Chajczyk, 1983; Kahneman & Henik, 1981). Uleman and Moskowitz (1994) found that trait inference processes were unintentional, unconscious, but not uncontrollable because they could be disrupted. Thus, it was concluded that the dual mode view was no longer tenable.

Several solutions can be proposed in response to the problems raised by these studies. A first solution is to distinguish between different types of automatic processes, resulting in a triple mode or a quadruple mode view. However, such views are likely to run into the same problems as the dual mode view. Ultimately, it may turn out that for any random combination of features (some automatic, others nonautomatic) a process can be found that fits the description (Bargh, 1992). A second solution is to dismiss the concept of automaticity and to investigate individual features of automaticity in their own right. A third, more cautious, solution is to investigate features separately but to preserve the term automatic and consider it as a gradual concept (e.g., Logan, 1985). A fourth alternative is to pick out one feature that is shared by all automatic processes and to allow processes to differ with regard to all features except the chosen one (e.g., Bargh, 1992). A fifth solution is to abandon the feature-based approach of automaticity altogether and to embrace a mechanism-based approach. Several authors have turned to one or a combination of the above solutions. In the next sections, we shed light on these solutions and evaluate some of their merits and problems.

Imp .
Summary

Triple Mode View

Several theorists have proposed a triple mode view instead of a dual mode view: in addition to the nonautomatic mode, they have postulated two automatic modes. Bargh (1996; Bargh & Chartrand, 2000; Wegner & Bargh 1998) suggested that the New Look movement and the skill development tradition were each concerned with a different type of automatic process: the New Look with preconscious automaticity and the skill development tradition with goal-dependent automaticity. Both types of automatic processes possess a different sample of automaticity features. Preconscious processes are almost purely stimulus-driven. Goal-dependent automatic processes require a processing goal and a conscious input in order to get started, but once they are triggered they run off autonomously. Examples of goal-dependent automatic processes are those involved in skilled activities such as knitting and walking down the stairs.

Carver and Scheier (1999, 2002) and Moskowitz (2001) distinguished between two types of automaticity that arise at different stages in the evolution of a process. Initially, emergent bottom-up processes are elicited by stimulus input alone. These processes are so weak that they remain hidden to consciousness and therefore cannot be intentionally employed or controlled in other ways. With more repetition, these processes become consolidated in memory so that they can be recognized by a conscious processor, which may invoke them as a guide to behavior and adjust them. With still more top-down use, these processes become so well-established and accurate that top-down control is no longer required and that they drop out of consciousness again (although they remain potentially accesssible to consciousness). Other authors have distinguished between the same set of processing stages, but they have reserved the term *automatic* exclusively for processes in the third stage (e.g., Cleeremans & Jiménez, 2002).

Several attention researchers have distinguished between pre-attentive and learned automatic processes (Treisman, Vieira, & Hayes, 1992). Pre-attentive processes are those involved in the early stages of the processing sequence (e.g., sensory analysis). Learned automatic processes are those that become impervious to attentional capacity as a result of practice. Attention researchers who adhere to the distinction between both types of automatic processes have rejected the idea that the learned type eventually develops to behave as a pre-attentive type (Gibson, 1969; LaBerge, 1973). They argued that pre-attentive and learned automatic processes differ not only with respect to the origin of their capacity independence (innate or acquired), but also with respect to certain functional properties. Logan (1992) recognized the distinction between the pre-attentive and the learned type, but he reserved the term *automatic* exclusively for the learned type.

Although the taxonomies proposed by these authors show certain resemblance, they are not entirely overlapping. Bargh's (1996) taxonomy is based on features; Carver and Scheier's (2002) taxonomy is based on stages of learning; and Treisman et al.'s (1992) taxonomy is based on stages in the processing chain. Preconscious processes do not equate with pre-attentive ones because they include both pre-attentive and learned automatic processes. Pre-attentive processes occur prior to any attentional involvement whereas learned preconscious processes may require that some spatial attention be directed at the triggering stimulus. Further, given that preconscious processes include learned ones, they also do not equate with emergent ones. Finally, emergent processes are also not identical to pre-attentive ones. The former occur in the first stages of learning, whereas the latter occur in the first stages of the processing sequence. The first stages in learning may comprise all stages of the processing sequence.

Gradual View   Bargh (1989, 1992, 1997) has proposed three (instead of two) classes in which most automatic processes fit: preconscious, postconscious, and goal-dependent automatic processes. Roughly, preconscious processes require no conscious input and no intention. Postconscious processes require conscious input but no intention. Goal-dependent processes require both conscious input and an intention or another goal to get started, but no goal to run to completion. These categories should not be taken as all-or-none categories, but rather as heuristic devices. Bargh (1992) suggested that any random combination of features (some automatic, others nonautomatic) is, in principle, possible. Certain researchers went one step further and reasoned that due to the lack of co-ocurrence among features of automaticity, the concept of automaticity is inherently inconsistent and may just as well be abandoned (Pashler, 1998; Regan, 1981). Logan (1985) argued that the lack of momentary co-occurrence among features does not necessarily threaten the internal consistency of the automaticity concept. He took up the initial idea of capacity theorists that automaticity is a continuum and that the degree of automaticity is determined by the amount of practice. He also suggested that "each property has its own time-course of change with practice" (Logan, 1985, p. 373). For example, a process may evolve faster from conscious to unconscious than from nonefficient to efficient. Because in most studies the status of different features is measured at one point in practice, it is not surprising that a lack of co-occurrence among these features is observed. Only if it would be demonstrated that features evolve in opposite directions with practice (e.g., more efficient and more conscious) would the automaticity concept be jeopardized. The alternative that Logan proposed in 1985 is a gradual view: processes are automatic to a certain degree, possessing few or more features of automaticity. Such a view recommends the separate investigation of features. This view is also gradual with regard to individual features: features are present to a lower or higher degree. It should be noted that although a gradual view of automaticity may well prevent the rejection of the automaticity concept, it hollows it out at the same time. As a gradual concept, automaticity loses its ability to tell apart one type of process (automatic) from another type (nonautomatic), because any process can be labelled automatic to some degree.

Appointing one minimal feature of automaticity   Bargh (1992) proposed a solution to the problem posed by the gradual view by choosing the feature *autonomous* as the one feature that is true of all automatic processes. He defined an autonomous process as one that can run to completion without conscious monitoring, irrespective of whether it was started intentionally or unintentionally. This option is theoretically appealing because it provides a criterion to separate automatic from nonautomatic processes. On the other hand, one may wonder how to justify that autonomy and not any other feature should be chosen as the critical feature. It is true that autonomy allows the greatest variety of processes to be included in the realm of automatic processes, but is that justification enough? Remember that other scholars proposed other critical features of automaticity. For example, attention researchers picked out the feature *efficient*. In a sense, the choice of a minimal feature of automaticity is an arbitrary matter.

Conditional View   In addition to the idea that all automatic processes are autonomous, Bargh (1989, 1992) suggested that all automatic processes are dependent on a set of preconditions. Automaticity research should primarily be concerned with investigating these preconditions. For example, it may be examined whether a process requires the intention that it occurs (or another goal), whether a certain amount of capacity is needed, and whether the stimulus input must be consciously perceived. An assessment of these conditions permits the allocation of the features unintentional, efficient, and unconscious to the process under study. In addition to the conditions described above which are related to features of automaticity, the conditional approach also permits the investigation of other kinds of conditions, such as the salience of the stimulus material or the precise nature of the task instructions, independent of their relation with automaticity features. Investigators may also discover interdependencies between conditions. For example, it may be that a certain process does not rely on intentions provided that the stimulus input is salient enough (see later).

Mechanism-based Approach

All of the views that we discussed until now are feature-based in that they define and diagnose automaticity in terms of features. In 1988, Logan criticized the feature-based accounts arguing that they do not explain how these features were acquired. They lack an explicit learning mechanism that explains the development toward automaticity (i.e., automatization). Logan explained automatization as the transition from algorithm computation (which Logan defined as multi-step memory retrieval) to single-step memory retrieval. Nonautomatic processing is based on algorithm computation in order to produce an output. This output may subsequently be stored in memory so that future processing can bypass computation of the algorithm and rely entirely on memory retrieval to produce the same outcome. For example, to solve arithmetic problems of the type "3+4+2=?", participants initially engage in an algorithm. In a first step, they retrieve the sum of 3 and 4, leading to the intermediate outcome 7. In a next step, they retrieve the sum of 7 and 2, leading to the final outcome 9. After sufficient practice with the same set of digits, a direct association is formed in memory between the set of digits and their sum, and as a result, participants are able to produce the final outcome in a single retrieval step when presented with the set of digits.

Logan (1988, 1991) explained automat*ization* as a shift toward single-step memory retrieval and he explained automat*icity* as based on single-step memory retrieval. Moreover, he postulated that single-step memory retrieval is the only lower-level process that can lead to automatic performance or automatic higher-level processes. From there, it was a small step for Logan to also *define* automaticity as single-step memory retrieval and to propose *diagnosing* automaticity by investigating whether the performance was based on single-step memory retrieval.

Other theorists explained automatization not as a shift from one type of process to another, but rather as a change in the *same underlying process*. They emphasized the strengthening or improvement of algorithms as the main mechanism underlying automatization (e.g., Anderson, 1992; Rosenbloom & Newell, 1986). The algorithm strengthening view is a mechanism-based view in the sense that it emphasizes one learning mechanism as responsible for automatization. It does not, however, select one type of low-level process to explain automatic performance and another to explain nonautomatic performance. The algorithm strengthening view hypothesizes that the same algorithm responsible for the non-automatic stage of performance is also responsible for the automatic stage of performance, but in the latter stage, the algorithm is executed faster and more efficiently. Hence, automatic and nonautomatic algorithms only differ with regard to the features (fast, efficient) they possess. In sum, the algorithm strengthening view is a mechanism-based view with regard to the *explanation* of automat*ization*, but a feature-based view with regard to the *definition* and *diagnosis* of automat*icity*.

The learning mechanisms proposed by Logan (1988) and Anderson (1992) are both dependent on consistent practice. A shift toward single-step memory retrieval benefits from practice on consistent data, whereas algorithm strengthening requires algorithms to remain consistent during practice but not the data on which these algorithms operate. Anderson (1992, 1996) distinguished between a declarative and a procedural subsystem of memory, suggesting that extended practice of algorithms results in the storage of these algorithms in the procedural subsystem. The matter in discussion is thus not whether memory is involved in automaticity, but whether the system is able to store and automatically retrieve algorithms in addition to single facts.

Although Anderson's (1992) model includes other learning mechanisms such as a reduction of procedural steps to a single step, and the strengthening of declarative facts, automaticity is mainly attributed to the strengthening of algorithms. Tzelgov and colleagues (Tzelgov, Henik, Sneg & Baruch, 1996; Tzelgov,

Yehene, Kotler, & Alon, 2000) advocated a reconciling approach, maintaining that both mechanisms of algorithm improvement and a shift toward direct memory retrieval are equivalent mechanisms underlying automatization.

The debate between the direct memory retrieval view and the reconciling view is a debate about which lower-level processes can lead to automatic performance (or automatic higher-level processes) (i.e., second research purpose, see above). The direct memory retrieval view predicts that only single-step memory retrieval can lead to automatic performance, whereas the reconciling view predicts that, in addition to single-step memory retrieval, there are also certain algorithms that can lead to automatic performance.

Support for algorithm-based automaticity has come mainly from skill development tasks in which it was shown that the benefits of practice with consistent algorithms transferred to data that were never encountered during practice (Carlson & Lundy, 1992; Kramer, Strayer, & Buckley, 1990; Schneider & Fisk, 1984; Smith & Lerner, 1986). These benefits consisted in an increased speed and efficiency. Recent studies using Stroop-like and priming tasks also support the unintentional (Moors et al., 2004; Tzelgov et al., 2000) nature of algorithm computation. During a practice phase, Tzelgov et al. (2000) displayed pairs of meaningless symbols, which they presented as artificial digits, and they asked participants to decide which symbol represented the larger magnitude. Due to feedback about the correctness of their decisions, participants eventually learned to make correct magnitude comparisons of these artificial digits. During a Stroop phase, participants had to indicate as fast as possible which symbol was physically larger from a pair of artificial digits (of which one was physically large, the other small) and to ignore the magnitude that was represented by the digits. Size congruity effects were obtained, with faster response times for pairs in which the physically larger stimulus also represented the larger magnitude compared to pairs in which the physically larger stimulus represented the smallest magnitude. Importantly, this effect occurred also for pairs that were not encountered (as a pair) during practice and for which no magnitude decision could have been stored. The occurrence of a size congruity effect for these pairs suggests that participants compared their magnitudes during the Stroop phase. Because making magnitude comparisons was not part of the instructions of the Stroop task, it can be concluded that participants made these comparisons unintentionally.

Conclusion

Logan (1988) proposed to replace the feature-based approach of automaticity by a mechanism-based approach equating automaticity with single-step memory retrieval. Partisans of the reconciling approach found this proposal to be unsatisfactory because it cannot integrate findings supporting algorithm-based automaticity. The choice between the direct memory retrieval view and the reconciling view is a matter of empirical evidence, which has not been settled in favor of either view yet. Because we prefer to keep all options open at this stage, we do not believe it to be fruitful to proceed from a view that excludes certain (lower-level) processes from the realm of automatic processes on an a priori basis. As a consequence, we have no choice but to return to an approach that uses features as diagnostic criteria for automaticity, such as a gradual, decompositional approach, which proposes to investigate each automaticity feature separately to determine the degree to which it is present.

Before we can choose for a gradual and decompositional approach to the study of automaticity, two questions need to be answered. The first question is whether features of automaticity can be seen as gradual. The second question is whether these features can be conceptually and logically separated, because only then is it useful to devote effort to their separate investigation. Before addressing these questions, we will consider the definitions that authors have given for the most important features of automaticity. Our aim is to analyse these definitions and to come up with a list of central ingredients for each feature. In a second part, we examine to what extent these features can be considered as gradual. In a third part, we explore whether our analysis in central ingredients provides ways to keep features conceptually and logically separated.

DEFINING FEATURES

In the present section, we consider definitions for the goal-related features (un)intentional, goal-(in)dependent, (un)controlled/(un)controllable, and autonomous. In addition, we consider definitions for the features "purely stimulus-driven", (un)conscious, (non)efficient, and fast(slow).

(Un)Intentional and Goal-(in)dependent

Most of the thinking about intentionality has been done with respect to overt behavior. Assuming important parallels between overt acts or actions, and covert/mental acts or processes, we will use the general term "act" throughout this section (as well as throughout the sections of the other goal-related features and the feature "purely stimulus-driven"). At least three different views can be discussed under the heading of intentionality. The first two views vie for the definition of intentionality; the third view doubts that much of our behavior and processing is intentional.

Causal View   The causal view of intentionality states that an intentional act is an act that is caused by an intention. This definition contains three ingredients: an intention, an act, and the causal connection between intention and act. An intention is a special kind of goal,[3] which has as its content an act and not just any state of affairs. One can intend to paint the house blue, but one cannot intend the house to be blue. In other words, an intention is a goal to engage in an act.

When both the goal to act and the act are present, but the goal is not the cause of the act, the act does not qualify as an intentional act (Davidson, 1980; Searle, 1983). For example, when Little Red Cap wants to kneel down to pick a flower for grandmother and she does kneel down but not due to her goal to do so, but rather because the wind pushes her so that she falls on her knees, then the act of kneeling down does not count as an intentional act.

A qualification of the third ingredient is that the goal should cause the act *in the right way* (Davidson, 1980) or *proximally* (Brand, 1989). When the intention to act causes the act, but only indirectly, by means of other intervening factors, the act cannot be classified as intentional. For example, when Little Red Cap has the goal to kneel down to pick a flower for grandmother but the thought of this plan makes her so overcome with emotion that she suddenly feels weak and sinks to her knees, then the act of kneeling down cannot be classified as an intentional act, although it was indirectly caused by the goal to kneel down.

The same objective act sequence can be intentional under one description but unintentional under another. This means that some aspects of an act are produced intentionally, whereas other aspects are produced unintentionally. One should thus specify under which description one considers or investigates an act to be intentional or not. Consider Little Red Cap walking in the woods, thereby crushing a ladybird. Supposing that Little Red Cap had the intention to walk in the woods but not the intention to crush the ladybird, her act can be labelled intentional under the description of "walking" but not under the description of "crushing a ladybird".

Aspects that are included and aspects that are not included in one's intentions may be situated at the same level of abstraction, as in the above example, or they may be at different levels of abstraction. Vallacher and Wegner (1987) argued that acts can be described at various levels of abstraction, going from low-level descriptions containing physical details to more abstract or high-level descriptions (Vallacher & Wegner, 1987). For example, "walking" occupies a higher level of description than "bending and stretching one's legs with a certain strength". An act can be intentional under the high-level but unintentional under the low-level description (or vice versa).

In addition to specifying the aspect of an act sequence that one considers, it is also important to delineate the boundaries of the act sequence itself. Strictly speaking, an act description should not include the result or consequences of the act. For example, an act described as walking in the woods does not include the arrival at grandmother's house. It is beyond doubt that Little Red Cap can have the goal to arrive at grandmother's house, but this state of arrival does not strictly belong to the act of walking in the woods. Things become more complicated if we consider that high-level descriptions of acts often include the results of acts (Wegner & Bargh, 1998). For example, the act of "walking in the woods" may be described at a higher level as "going to grandmother's house". The latter description does include the arrival at grandmother's house.

The above paragraphs illustrate an important aspect of causation spelled out by Yablo (1992) that causes and effects must be proportional. In order for an intention and an act to stand in a causal relation, the intention should be adequate and just enough for the act. The intention to go to grandmother's house is more than enough for the act of walking in the woods and is therefore not an ideal candidate cause for the act of walking in the woods. Turning it round, the intention to walk in the woods is not adequate for the act of going to grandmother's house, because Little Red Cap may be walking in the woods without ever arriving at grandmother's house.

Other aspects of causation can be found in Mackie's (1974, 1975) proposal that a cause C of an effect E, is an **I**nsufficient but **N**ecessary part of a combination or set of conditions that is in itself **U**nnecessary but **S**ufficient for the occurrence of the effect (short, INUS condition). For example, saying that a short circuit is the cause of a house being on fire means that the short circuit, although **I**nsufficient to start the fire by itself, is a **N**ecessary part of a set of conditions (including combustible material and oxygen), that is in itself **U**nnecessary but **S**ufficient to start the fire (another set of conditions may have started the fire as well, e.g., a set in which the short circuit is replaced by the dropping of a lit cigarette). One could say that C is conditionally necessary for E, that is, necessary within this particular sufficient set (CX). This means that E does not occur when C is removed from this set; C is not unconditionally necessary for E, that is, not necessary within every sufficient set. There may be other sets in which C is also absent (e.g., KX) that do suffice for E.

An intentional act can thus be redefined as an act for which the intention to engage in the act is an INUS condition for the act. That is, the intention is a necessary part of a sufficient set of conditions for the act. The intention is not in itself sufficient for the act. Other necessary parts of the set are the stimulus input and a host of background conditions that are usually taken for granted. For example, to intentionally process a visual stimulus, the light must be on, the stimulus must be within the visual field, and the person must not be blind. There may be other sets in which the intention is not necessary that are also sufficient for the act. Many acts are intentional in some circumstances but unintentional in others. Research can thus be aimed at identifying other conditions in the set that modulate the necessity of an intention for the act.

In addition to the three ingredients of the definition of intentional acts (intention, act, and causal connection), the literature on goal striving (Gollwitzer, 1990, 1993; Heckhausen, 1991) has presented a number of conditions that must be fulfilled in order for an intention to be implemented, that is, to actually translate into an act. Given that multiple intentions compete for implementation, the strength of the critical intention must be high enough in comparison to other intentions. If this is not the case, then a fiat or decision to act upon the intention is required to launch the act (James, 1890; Moya, 1990; Wundt, 1902). Such a fiat can be conceived of as a second goal (or meta-goal) superimposed on the intention.

Another condition for the implementation of an intention is the feasibility of the act.[4] This condition encompasses two subfactors. First, there must be an opportunity to act. In order to implement the intention to pick a flower, there must be a flower. Gollwitzer (1990) argued that when an opportunity to engage in the act is absent, the likelihood to benefit from a future opportunity is increased when the person has specified in advance a cue that signals a suitable opportunity. For example, "next time I see a flower, I will pick it". Gollwitzer has introduced the term "implementation intention" to refer to the mental link between the representation of the cue and the representation of the act that is to follow.[5] When such an implementation intention is formed, the risk that opportunities to act go by unnoticed is strongly reduced. A second subfactor of feasibility is skill (Heider, 1958; Mele & Moser, 1994). A person can only be expected to intentionally pro- duce an act when he/she has the skill to perform that act. Acts that depend too much on luck, such as winning the lottery, cannot be performed intentionally.

To summarize, an act is intentional (under a certain description) when it is caused (in the right way) by the goal representation of that act (under that descrip-tion). Several conditions must be fulfilled in order for the act to come about. Some of these conditions must always be fulfilled (e.g., opportunity, skill); other condi-tions must only be fulfilled when still other conditions are not (e.g., a fiat is required when strength is too low, and an implementation intention is required when there is no current opportunity).

An unintentional act is an act that was not caused by an intention. An act can be unintentional for two reasons: there is no intention, there is only an act; or there is an intention and there is an act, but there is no causal connection between both ingredients.

We also wish to clarify the relation between the feature *intentional* and the feature *goal-dependent*. A goal-dependent act is an act for which a goal must be in place. This goal may be either the proximal goal to engage in the act, in which case the goal-dependent act is also intentional, or a more remote goal. Thus, intentional acts can be considered as a subclass of the goal-dependent acts. Acts often depend on the combination of a remote and a proximal goal. For example, Little Red Cap may have the proximal goal to walk in the woods and this act may be instrumental for her remote goal to arrive at grandmother's house. However, proximal and remote goals can sometimes occur in isolation. Little Red Cap may have the proximal goal to walk in the woods, as a goal "an sich". Another scenario is that the remote goal to be at grandmother's house directly triggers the act of walking toward the house, without the mediation of the proximal goal to walk. In this case the act is goal-dependent but unintentional.

A final note is about the nature of the representations that cause acts in the causal view. Some theorists call them goal representations, imparting them with special dynamic qualities that are not shared by other kinds of representations, such as accumulation of strength over time and persistence in the face of obstacles (Bargh & Barndollar, 1996). Others argue that these are purely cognitive struc-tures, and that the same representations are used both to perceive and to engage in an act (i.e., common coding hypothesis; Prinz, 1990).

Emergent Intentionality Opponents of the causal view have rejected the trivial idea that every intentional act must be caused by an intention, that is, a (goal) representation of that act. The gist of their argument is that a person may be directed at an act without possessing a representation of that act. Wakefield and Dreyfus (1991) distinguished between two types of intentionality: R-intentionality and G-intentionality. R-intentionality stands for representation-mediated inten-tionality; G-intentionality stands for gestalt intentionality. As examples of G-intentional acts they mention subsidiary acts involved in skilled activities such as driving a car and playing the piano. These scholars believe it to be unlikely that each of the subsidiary acts in a routine act are preceded by a representation of the subsidiary act. Yet, they believe there are nevertheless reasons to classify such subsidiary acts as intentional. One of those reasons is that subsidiary acts *feel* different from reflexes or Penfield motions (i.e., motions caused by electrode firings in the motor cortex; Penfield, 1975). Intentional acts are accompanied by the feeling that one is the causal agent of one's acts and that these acts are appropriate to the situation.

One could, however, argue that the feeling of self-agency that one experiences with subsidiary acts stems from the fact that the overall act was intentional in a representation-mediated sense and that this produced a general feeling of self-agency. In our view then, G-intentionality corresponds to what we have previously called goal-dependence. Also, the idea that subsidiary acts can be preceded by representations should not be rejected on a priori grounds. Opponents of the causal view seem to rely on a narrow meaning of the word representation, taking representations to be always conscious and conceptual in nature. However, when one accepts that goal representations may also be unconscious (Bargh, 1990) or non-conceptual (e.g., image-like), the idea that subsidiary acts can be preceded by goal representations seems more plausible. In the end, the question of whether subsidiary acts of routine acts are intentional (in a representation-mediated sense) or unintentional but goal-dependent is an empirical question that cannot be solved by clever examples.

Emergent Behavior   Another view regarding intentionality is inspired by the dynamic systems framework. According to this framework, much (if not all) of our behavior emerges from bottom-up activity that satisfies multiple constraints and there is no need for top-down intentions (e.g., Kelso, 1995; Vallacher & Nowak, 1999; see also Carver & Scheier, 2002). Many acts, even complex ones, are not produced by intentions (representations of these acts) but are the result of multiple interacting forces combined with the unspecific tendency operating within all living systems toward increased coherence. These researchers do not question so much the causal definition of intentionality, but rather that much behavior and processing "out there" actually meets the requirements of that definition.

A similar view is endorsed by proponents of the connectionist framework. Whereas dynamic systems models reject the existence (and hence the causal role) of representations altogether, connectionist models postulate the existence of sub-symbolic representations. Many connectionists argue that acts are not caused by intentions, which are symbolic representations, but rather by underlying subsymbolic representations. In a similar vein, Wegner (2003; Wegner & Wheatley, 1999) argues that intentions do not have causal power but that there are underlying processes that give rise to both the felt intention and the act. According to Wegner, the folk idea that our intentions cause our acts is nothing but an erroneous attribution.

The question of which level has causal powers is a much debated issue in the philosophical literature. According to the commonsense view, acts are caused by mental states such as intentions, whereas according to the reductionist view all causal powers are situated on the lowest level of analysis. We think that the position that one adopts in this debate is highly dependent on the way in which one frames the question.

Certain authors have framed it as a problem of *causation* (e.g., Green & Vervaeke, 1996). According to the dominant view of causation, causes and effects must be situated on the same level of analysis and the cause must precede the effect. Causes must also be INUS conditions (Mackie, 1974), and they should be proportional to their effects (Yablo, 1992). Intentions and acts meet these formal criteria and can therefore be considered as potential causes and effects. The subsymbolic representations in connectionist models also precede acts, but they are situated at a lower level of analysis than most acts, and they include details that are not proportional to most acts (Green & Vervaeke, 1996). Subsymbolic representations have therefore been considered to be less ideal candidate causes of acts.

Other theorists have framed the problem as a problem of *causal explanation*. The dominant view of causal explanation is the reductionist view, which argues that the ultimate causal explanation is situated on the lowest level (for an alternative, see Menzies, 2001). Connectionists argue that the causal explanations of acts are to be found on the lower, subsymbolic level. This view can be considered as a variant of the reductionist view, although most reductionists would not stop at the subsymbolic level but go further down the ladder to neurology and finally physics. A strong reductionist view can be found in the dynamic systems framework.

(Un)Controlled/(Un)Controllable

In the previous section, we have delineated the features *intentional* and *goal-dependent*. The current section deals with the feature *controlled* and its relation to the feature *intentional*. The concept "control" has three ingredients in common with the concept "intentional": a goal and causation resulting in an effect. For instance, Wegner and Bargh (1998) posited that, at the most basic level, to control something is to influence it in a certain direction rather than in a random manner. Dennett (1984) likewise argued that control is not causation alone, but rather desired causation: A controls B if A can drive B to be in a state that A wants B to be in. Put differently, A controls B if A has a goal about B and this goal is achieved (i.e., the state represented in the goal occurs). We can thus say that a person controls an act if the person has a goal about the act and the goal is achieved. An act is controlled when a person controls it and uncontrolled when a person does not control it. An act is controllable when it is possible for a person to control and uncontrollable when it is impossible for a person to control.

As Dennett (1984) pointed out, A can only drive B into a state that belongs to B's normal range of states. Examples of normal-range goals about acts are the goals to alter, stop, avoid, and engage in the act. The goal to engage in the act can be parsed into the goals to start, continue, and complete the act. Given the multitude of goals that persons can pursue about acts, it is best to always specify which goal one envisions when using the terms control, (un)controlled, and (un)controllable.

Given the definition that an act is intentional when it is caused by the goal to engage in the act, and the definition that an act is controlled when the person has a goal about the act and this goal is achieved, we must conclude that intentional acts are a subclass of controlled acts. An intentional act is controlled in the sense of the goal to engage in the act. Other subclasses of controlled acts are those that are controlled in the sense of the goals to change, stop, or avoid the act. Table 1.1 gives an overview of the definitions of the features *goal-dependent, intentional,* and *controlled*. As explained above, intentional acts are a subclass of goal-dependent and a subclass of controlled acts.

The type of control discussed here corresponds to what engineers have attributed to open-loop systems (see also Wegner & Bargh, 1998). In open-loop systems there is a criterion or goal, and an action directed at attaining that criterion. Control in such a system is a fact when the criterion is reached, irrespective of whether the system has feedback about whether the criterion is reached. This type of control is contrasted to control in closed-loop systems. In closed-loop systems, the result of the action is fed back into the system (so that the loop is closed) and it is tested in a comparison module whether the criterion is reached. The action either ceases, when the criterion is reached, or it is repeated until the criterion is reached (Carver & Scheier, 1999; Miller, Gallanter, & Pribram, 1960). Feedback (and a comparison module to match it to the criterion) is an essential ingredient of control in closed-loop systems.

According to Powers (1973), another central ingredient of control is disturbance: A controls B if A influences B in a desired direction, thereby counteracting the effect of a disturbing influence on B. For example, Little Red Cap controls her act of walking down the path when she manages to stay on the path despite attempts of the wolf to lead her astray. Keeping in mind that there are other, more complex types of control, we will focus here on the simplest type, which is control as can be found in open-loop systems and that consists of only three ingredients: a goal about an act (the cause), achievement of the goal (the effect), and the causal relation between the two elements.

An act is controlled when a goal pertaining to the act (to engage in, avoid, alter, or stop the act) is a necessary part within the sufficient set of conditions for the effect (occurrence, prevention, change, or interruption of the act). By opposition, when an act is uncontrolled, it may mean several things. First, it may mean that (a) a goal pertaining to the act is absent, in which case the effect may (a1) also be

TABLE 1.1   Definitions for the Features *Goal-dependent, Intentional,* and *Controlled*

Feature	Cause	Effect
Goal-dependent	Goal (remote=any goal/proximal = goal to engage in the act)	The act
Intentional	Goal to engage in the act	The act
Controlled	Goal about the act (stop/alter/avoid/engage in the act)	State represented in the goal (end/change/prevention/ occurrence of the act)

absent, or (a2) be present, but due to another cause. Second, it may mean that (b) a goal pertaining to the act is present, but (b1) the effect is absent, or (b2) the effect is present but it is not caused by the goal. In case (b1), the set of conditions including the goal is not sufficient for the effect; in case (b2), the sufficient set of conditions does not include the goal as a necessary part. In the next sections, we define the features *autonomous* and *"purely stimulus-driven"*.

Autonomous   The word autonomous (deriving from the Greek words *auto* = self + *nomos* = law) literally means self-governed, not controlled by outside forces. When used as a predicate of the word *person*, it means that the person determines his/her own fate, and not someone else. When used as a predicate of the word *act*, however, it means that nothing outside of the act controls the act. A completely autonomous act is an act that is uncontrolled in the sense of every possible goal. More precisely, an act is autonomous when it is (a) unintentional and (b) uncontrolled in the sense of counteracting goals. That is, (a) the set of conditions sufficient for the occurrence of the act does not include the goal to engage in the act as a necessary part, and (b) insertion of the goals to alter, stop, or avoid the act in the current set does not result in the change, interruption or avoidance of the act.

For the sake of completeness, we need to mention that the definitions of autonomous given by other authors are somewhat different from our own. For example, Bargh (1989, 1992) defined an autonomous process as a process that, once started, runs to completion without the need for conscious guidance or monitoring. This definition is different from our own in at least two respects. First, Bargh defined autonomy in terms of the redundance of *conscious* goals. This means that a process can still be termed autonomous when it is influenced by *unconscious* goals. In our definition of autonomous the term *goal* covers both conscious and unconscious goals. Second, in Bargh's definition, autonomy has to do only with the second part of the process, after the process has started. In his account, an autonomous process may begin intentionally or unintentionally, but after its start no further monitoring is required. Our definition of an autonomous process (or act) as one that is uncontrolled in the sense of every possible goal also includes the goal to start the process (or the act). The difference between both accounts is subtle. Whereas Bargh's definition suggests that a process that was intentionally started but not intentionally continued and completed is an entirely autonomous process, we suggest that it is a partially autonomous process (only the second part of the process is autonomous, i.e., not controlled by outside forces).

Bargh's (1992) definition of autonomous bears close resemblance to Logan's (Logan & Cowan, 1984, p. 296; Zbrodoff & Logan, 1986) definition of ballistic. Logan defined a ballistic process as one that cannot be inhibited once it begins and so must run to completion. Note, however, that Bargh's definition of autonomous speaks about the goals to *continue* and *complete*, whereas Logan's definition of ballistic speaks about the goal to *stop*. A process that does not require a goal for its continuation and completion is not always impossible to stop.

Purely Stimulus-driven   An act is purely stimulus-driven when it is caused by the mere presence of the triggering stimulus. By assigning the stimulus as the cause (i.e., INUS condition) of an act, we are not saying that there are no other necessary conditions in the sufficient set for the act. We take the usual background conditions (e.g., that the light is on and the person's eyes are open in case of the processing of a visual stimulus) for granted. What we are saying is that awareness of the input, attention to the input, goals, and the outcomes of other acts are not necessary conditions in the sufficient set of conditions for the act.

According to our definitions, there is no complete overlap between the features *purely stimulus-driven* and *unintentional*. Purely stimulus-driven acts count as a subclass of unintentional acts. Other subclasses of unintentional acts do not require an intention to occur but they do require other conditions such as other goals or awareness of the input, and hence they are not purely stimulus-driven.

(Un)Conscious   Several authors have emphasized that the features *conscious* (or aware) and *unconscious* (or unaware) are not unitary concepts. Two often-mentioned ingredients of consciousness are Intentional and phenomenal aspects.

The word Intentional is used here in the philosophical sense, which is different from intentionality in the ordinary sense (cf. former sections we capitalize the former but not the latter, following Searle's convention, 1983). The common core in both terms is "directedness" (deriving from the Latin verb *intendere*: to be directed at). In philosophy, Intentionality refers to a property of mental phenomena by which they are directed at or about some state of affairs outside of themselves (Brentano, 1874). For example, desiring, believing, perceiving, remembering, and intending are Intentional because they require an object. In ordinary language, intentionality derives from the mental phenomenon of intending or having an intention and is a property of actions (e.g., Wakefield & Dreyfus, 1991). In our view the essential difference between Intentional and intentional is not that the former relates to mental phenomena and the latter to actions or acts, for when the category of acts is extended to include mental acts or processes the distinction between both concepts does not vanish. What we do believe to be crucial is that with Intentionality it is the mental act itself that is directed at some state of affairs outside the mental act, whereas with intentionality it is a person who is directed at engaging in the act. Formally, directedness can be considered as a relationship and the source and terminus of this relationship are different with Intentionality and intentionality. With Intentionality, the source is the mental act and the terminus is a state of affairs outside the mental act, whereas with intentionality, the source is a person and the terminus is the act. Otherwise put, Intentionality speaks about a mental state or act, whereas intentionality speaks about the way in which an act is produced (or about the source of the act, i.e., the person).

The phenomenal aspect is also known under the names of immediate qualia (Tolman, 1932), the qualitative aspect (Natsoulas, 1981), or the "what it is like" aspect of awareness (Nagel, 1994). The difference between the Intentional and the phenomenal aspect of awareness can be illustrated by the difference between knowing that one is hurt versus feeling pain.

Block (1995) issued the distinction between two types of consciousness: phenomenal   consciousness   (P-consciousness)   and   access   consciousness

(A-consciousness). This distinction is partially founded on the distinction between the two aspects of consciousness discussed above: P-conscious states have a phenomenal content; and A-conscious states have a content that is accessible for use in reasoning and in rational control of behavior and/or verbal report. Contents are accessible by virtue of their representational or Intentional format, but they are actually accessed when attention is directed to them as well. Therefore, A-conscious content coincides with those aspects that are in the focus of attention. In Block's view, contents may be P-conscious without being A-conscious. This means that contents that are outside of the focus of attention and not A-conscious may nevertheless be P-conscious. For example, the noise of a pneumatic drill in the street or the ticking of a clock may be P-conscious all along, but not A-conscious unless attention is directed to it. Turning it round, contents may be A-conscious without being P-conscious. Block cited the hypothetical case of superblindsight to illustrate this. Patients suffering from "regular" blindsight report a lack of P-consciousness but are nevertheless able to make successful guesses about presented stimuli. Because these guesses are not considered rational, they are not classified as demonstrations of A-consciousness. In the hypothetical case of super-blindsight, however, it is conjectured that patients know (that is, rationally) what stimuli have been presented, not via visual P-conscious experience, but in much the same way as a thought that suddenly pops to mind. A-consciousness without P-consciousness is also imputed to the virtual case of a philosophical zombie. A zombie is a creature that is functionally equivalent to a human being but with one difference: all is dark inside (Chalmers, 1996), which means that there is no P-consciousness. Although both illustrations for A-consciousness without P-consciousness are non-empirical, Block (1995) took them as support for the idea that the two types of consciousness can be separated on a conceptual level. He did acknowledge, however, that they go together under normal circumstances, and he even conceded that they may interact. Attention can alter the content or flavor of experience (see also Hardcastle, 1997). For example, there is a phenomenal difference between contents that are in and those that are outside the focus of attention (as in figure and ground).

Much of the conceptual debate is centred on Block's (1995) assumption that the two types of consciousness are independent. A first alternative states that P-consciousness is a precondition for A-consciousness (e.g., Schacter, 1989). According to this position, information must be represented in phenomenal consciousness before it can be accessed for use in voluntary behavior. A second alternative, termed epiphenomenalism, holds the reverse: only those contents that enter the executive system, and hence are A-conscious, can become P-conscious. Such assimilation of P-consciousness to A-consciousness probably stems from the desire to measure P-consciousness, together with the fact that measurement is based on verbal report or behavior. These methods are more suitable to measure A-consciousness than P-consciousness. A third alternative, called the collapse hypothesis, states that the distinction between the two types of consciousness is artificial and that P- and A-consciousness are one and the same thing (e.g. Baars, 1995; Kobes, 1995; Morton, 1995).

Two additional types of consciousness that Block described are monitoring consciousness (M-consciousness) and self-consciousness (S-consciousness). To be M-conscious is to be conscious of the fact that one is P- or A-conscious, and to be S-conscious is to be conscious about oneself. Several authors have made a distinction between only two types of consciousness, called, for example, minimal and full consciousness (Wegner & Bargh, 1998) or Type 1 and Type 2 experience (O'Shaughnessy, 1991). The first type corresponds to some combination of A- and P-consciousness, and the second type corresponds to M-consciousness.

Apart from the fact that the terms conscious and unconscious have different ingredients or come in different varieties, both terms may also be used as a predicate of different things. They may pertain to (a) the stimulus input that evokes a process, (b) the output of a process, (c) the process itself, and (d) the consequences of the process, such as its influence on subsequent processes (see also Bargh, 1994). It is best to specify which of these elements one has in mind when using the terms conscious and unconscious. This is important because there are many otherwise unconscious processes that require a conscious input in order to operate (cf. class of postconscious and goal-dependent processes, Bargh, 1992; see also Bargh & Barndollar, 1996). Note that the consequences of a process do not strictly belong to the critical process, but rather to a subsequent processing unit.

Keeping in mind that processes can be described at different levels of analysis (cf. Marr, 1982), we should point out that the only level that seems in principle to be accessible to consciousness is the functional level. Most theorists would probably agree that everything below that level is structurally inaccessible. All that the functional level of process understanding requires is that the person is able to link an output to an input. For example, a person may be aware that a certain advertisement influenced his/her decision to buy a product, without being aware of the formal characteristics of this process or the neural circuits involved. Further, we need to be more precise about the notion of input. This notion conceals some kind of initial (perceptual) process operating on the raw stimulus input and it is the output of this process that is potentially accessible to consciousness, not the raw stimulus input. It is important to distinguish between potentially accessible and structurally inaccessible parts because it only makes sense to invest effort in the investigation of the conscious or unconscious nature of parts that are potentially accessible to consciousness.

(Non)Efficient   The concept efficient has been defined in relation to limited attentional capacity or processing resources. An efficient process is a process that uses only a minimal amount of this capacity. The amount of available capacity is depicted as a continuum and hence the feature *efficient* is easily regarded as a gradual feature. Because efficient processes demand only minimal attentional capacity, they are likely to remain unaffected when resources are scarce due to the high demand of other concurrent processes. Degree of capacity consumption is therefore often operationalized as dual task interference (e.g., Baddeley, 1986; Logan, 1978, 1979; but see Shiffrin & Schneider, 1977). In dual task studies, participants perform a primary task simultaneously with a secondary task, which is assumed to consume a certain amount of resources. The processes involved in the primary task are efficient when varying (and especially, augmenting) the amount of capacity used by the secondary task has no impact on performance of the primary task (e.g., Hermans, Crombez, & Eelen, 2000). Because it is impossible to determine whether a particular secondary task exhausts all processing resources, the processes involved in the primary task can never be shown to be totally independent of resources.

The use of dual task paradigms is founded on the single resource view (or single-capacity view) of attention and especially on a number of assumptions inherent to that view. One of these assumptions is that the resource requirements for the simultaneous execution of two processes equal the sum of the individual resource requirements for each process. Another assumption is that the total amount of available resources remains constant under different conditions of secondary task load (see Navon & Gopher, 1979, for a complete list of assumptions). To the extent that these assumptions can be challenged, however, the usefulness of the dual task method can be called into question. From the multiple resource perspective, which postulates that the cognitive system has more than one resource and that different tasks may tap from different resources, the dual task paradigm is only useful when both tasks call on the same processing resource (Navon & Gopher, 1979; Wickens, 1984).

In the wake of the capacity view of attention, attention has been conceptualized as a limited source of energy, much like a barrel filled with liquid or a tank of gaz. Efficiency has been defined as the ability of a process to do without (or to do with very little of) this limited energy. However, besides quantity, attention may also be said to have a direction, as is embodied in another metaphor, that of attention as a spotlight (Baars, 1998; LaBerge, 1983; Posner, Snyder, & Davidson, 1980; Wundt, 1897). Both quantity and direction are aspects of attention that go together. However, there may be processes that depend on the specific direction of attention but at the same time use only a small amount of attention. For example, Stroop interference effects have been shown to diminish when relevant and irrelevant dimensions are spatially separated (e.g., Kahneman & Henik, 1981). The amount of capacity used by the processes tapped in these Stroop experiments may have been so small that these processes still deserve the label efficient.

Attention may be directed at the process (the relation between input and output) or, alternatively, at the input on which the process operates. The feature *efficient* can thus be used as a predicate of the critical process or, alternatively, as a predicate of the initial perceptual process operating on the raw stimulus input.

Fast(slow)   The concept *fast* is also a gradual feature. This feature has sometimes been ignored in lists of automaticity features, but the speedup of task performance is taken as an important indicator of automaticity in search studies (Shiffrin & Schneider, 1977) and other skill development studies (Smith & Lerner, 1986). Although the feature *fast* can only be used as a predicate of a process, it is useful to distinguish between the duration of the process and the duration of the stimulus input on which the process operates (see later).

GRADUAL CONCEPTUALIZATION OF FEATURES

A first question that we set out to examine is whether features are gradual. Only when they are gradual does it make sense to choose a gradual approach. A gradual feature is a feature that can be present to a certain degree. We already pointed out that the features *efficient* and *fast* are gradual features. Although less immediately obvious, the feature *(un)conscious* and the goal-related features can also be conceptualized as gradual. A gradual conception of consciousness is a natural position for connectionist models that consider the transition from unconscious to conscious cognition to be a matter of strength (cf. Cleeremans & Jiménez, 2002). It is more problematic for computational models that depict conscious and unconscious cognition as two separate systems or routes. Empirical evidence is mixed: certain studies support a gradual transition from unconscious to conscious perception (Bar et al., 2001), whereas others support a sharp non-linear transition (Sergent & Dehaene, 2004).

Goal-related features can also be conceptualized as gradual. Indeed, the correspondence between a processing goal and the outcome that is actually obtained can be less than perfect. We should point out that this is only true in cases where a goal is present. The presence of a goal was assumed in the definition of the features *intentional* and *controlled*, as well as in one type of unintentional and one type of uncontrolled process, in which only the causal connection between the goal and the effect is missing. In cases where there is no goal (there is only an effect), the features *unintentional* and *uncontrolled* are not gradual.

In addition to a gradual approach to the *conceptualization* of features, we also favor a gradual approach to the *measurement* of features. We accept support in favor of automaticity features even if this support is not infallible evidence. However, we do argue that empirical support for features of automaticity should be related to the ingredients of the features. For example, arguments for the intentional nature of a process may be stronger or weaker, but they have to be related to the ingredients of this feature, that is, the concepts *goal* and *causation*.

DECOMPOSITIONAL APPROACH

A second question that we set out to examine is to what extent it is possible to draw a conceptual distinction between features. This is an important issue because the separate investigation of features is only worthwhile when features can be conceptually separated. In the previous parts, we analyzed the most important features of automaticity and isolated their ingredients. Overlap is inevitable when features are defined in such a way that they share central ingredients. Apart from conceptual overlap, there are other types of relations between features that have implications for research. A certain feature can be a necessary and/or sufficient condition for another feature. We will refer to this type of relation as a modal relation. Modal relations have led authors to logically infer the presence or absence of one feature on the basis of the presence or absence of another feature.

We first discuss the conceptual overlap between features. After that, we look at assumptions of modal relations.

Conceptual Overlap

Overlap among Goal-related Features (and Purely Stimulus-driven) In the section about the definition of features, we already pointed out that there is partial overlap among several sets of goal-related features. Intentional processes are a subclass of the goal-dependent processes and a subclass of the controlled processes. Unintentional processes and autonomous processes are both subclasses of uncontrolled processes. Purely stimulus-driven processes are a subclass of unintentional processes. (For a more extended description of the conceptual overlap among goal-related features, see Moors & De Houwer, 2006). On the other hand, we do not assume overlap among different types of controlled processes that are based on different types of goals.

The definitions of certain other researchers, however, seem to lead to somewhat different conclusions. The features *(un)intentional* and *(un)controlled* are often presented as non-overlapping, whereas the features *unintentional* and *purely stimulus-driven* are often regarded as completely overlapping. For example, in Bargh's (1994) account, the feature *intentional* has to do with being in control of the start of a process, whereas the feature *controllable* has to do with the ability to alter or stop a process once it is started. Both features are portrayed as involving different kinds of processing goals: the feature *intentional* has to do with the goal to start a process, whereas the feature *controllable* has to do with the goals to alter or stop a process. These goals differ with regard to the part in the time course of the process (first vs. second part) as well as with regard to their content (promoting vs. counteracting goals). At first glance there seems to be no overlap between the features *intentional* and *controllable* in Bargh's definitions. However, a closer look reveals that his definition of *intentional* makes reference to the word *control* ("the feature intentional has to do with being in control of the start of the process"; see above). When one feature is defined in terms of another, then overlap is a fact. Another point of difference is that in our definitions, the word "intentional", which is shorthand for "intentionally produced", is not restricted to the start of the process but covers the whole process from start to completion. We stated that the goal to engage in a process can be parsed into the goals to start, continue, and complete a process. It is not unthinkable that a person would have the goal to merely start the process, or merely complete it, but in these cases we would call the process an intentionally started or an intentionally completed process rather than an entirely intentional or intentionally produced one.

Some researchers treat the features *unintentional* and *purely stimulus-driven* as completely overlapping. This is because they assume that processes generate from a two-factor universe of possible causes inhabited by stimuli and intentions. We have argued to take into account other possible causes such as remote goals, outputs of other processes, consciousness, and attention. The next paragraph deals with conceptual overlap between the goal-related features and consciousness.

Overlap among Goal-related Features and the Feature Conscious

Goal-related features involve a causal relation between a goal (to engage in, alter, or stop a process) and an effect (a process, a change, or an interruption of a process). No mention was made of the requirement that this goal be conscious. If one accepts that goals can also be activated in an unconscious manner, there is no need to suppose overlap between goal-related features and consciousness (cf. Bargh, 1990; Bargh, Gollwitzer, Lee-Chai, Barndollar, & Trötschel, 2001; Chartrand & Bargh, 1996; see review by Moskowitz, Li, & Kirk, 2004). Despite this, the terms intentional and controlled are often used as shorthand for the notions "consciously intentional" and "consciously controlled". Some theorists even argue that consciousness is an ingredient of the features intentional and controlled (e.g., Oatley, 1993). These theorists are likely to infer a lack of control on the basis of a lack of consciousness.

Modal Relations

In addition to conceptual overlap, investigators have also assumed modal relations among features. When feature A is a necessary condition for feature B, then evidence that A is absent allows one to logically infer that B is absent as well. When feature A is a sufficient condition for B, then evidence that A is present allows for the logical inference that B is present as well. These relations have contributed to the clustering of features and hence to the persistence of the all-or-none view of automaticity.

Many investigators have formally abandoned the all-or-none view, and grant that the relations between goals, attention, and consciousness are quite complex. However, in discussions of empirical results regarding the diagnosis of automaticity, they often seem to rely on a very simple set of one-to-one relations between these elements. First, we discuss what has almost been considered the holy trinity of goals, attention, and consciousness (see Figure 1.1 for a schematic overview). After that, we discuss why it is problematic to use this simple set of relations to draw logical inferences about features.

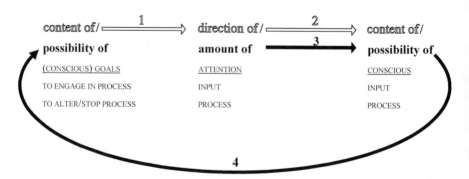

FIGURE 1.1   Simple set of interrelations between goals, attention, and consciousness.

Simple Set of Modal Relations

From goals to attention The relation between goals and attention is widely accepted. One scenario that connects goals to attention goes as follows. When a person has set the goal to engage in some process, this goal must still be implemented. To implement a goal, a suitable occasion is required, for example, in the form of an appropriate stimulus input. Attention may be conceived of as a tool that helps the organism to incorporate suitable input to launch the process. For instance, to implement the goal to evaluate a stimulus, there must at least be a stimulus in sight. If the stimulus is not in sight or not optimally so, the person may direct attention or zoom in on the stimulus (or on some aspect of the stimulus). In sum, goals determine where attention will be directed. To implement the goal to engage in a process, attention must be directed to an appropriate stimulus input; to implement the goal to alter/stop the process, attention must be directed to the process itself (Figure 1.1, Step 1).

From attention to consciousness Another close team is attention and consciousness. The common view is that the direction of attention determines the content of consciousness (Figure 1.1, Step 2). Whatever is in the focus of attention is conscious, everything else is unconscious (e.g., Baars, 1998; Merikle & Joordens, 1997; Posner, 1982, 1994; Shiffrin & Schneider, 1977; but see Baars, 1997).

Thus far, we stated that goals determine where attention will be directed (Step 1), and that the focus of attention, in turn, determines the content of consciousness (Step 2). By way of transitivity then, goals also determine the content of consciousness (Step 1 + Step 2).

Further, the *amount* of attention spent (to input or process) determines whether consciousness (of this input or process) will occur, or (for gradual models of consciousness) the amount or degree of consciousness that will occur (Step 3).

From consciousness to goals Many authors have suggested that consciousness is a necessary condition for the features *intentional* and *controlled* in the sense of alter/stop (Figure 1.1, Step 4). When stimulus input is conscious, it permits the setting and implementation of the goal to engage in the process. When the process itself is conscious, it permits the setting and implementation of the goals to alter or stop the process. This idea is truly pervasive (e.g., Bargh, 1992, 1994, 1999; Cleeremans & Jiménez, 2002; Dehaene & Naccache, 2001; Dienes & Perner, 1999, Uleman, 1989; Shallice, 1988). Let us reconsider Carver and Scheier's (2002) description of the evolution of a process. When an initially weak, emergent automatic process grows stronger due to repetition, it can be recognized by a conscious processor, who can use and manipulate it. With more top-down use, the process becomes so accurate that top-down control eventually becomes superfluous, and as a result the process drops out of consciousness (conform to James', 1890, parsimony principle that "consciousness deserts all processes when it can no longer be of use"). Both phases in the evolution of a process rest heavily on the assumption that it is awareness of the process that allows a person to control it. It is duly noted that the terms "intentional" and "controlled" are probably used here in the sense of "consciously intentional" and "consciously controlled" (see section on conceptual overlap; see also below).

Until now, we stated that the amount of attention (to input or process) determines the possibility of consciousness (of input or process) (Step 3), and that consciousness, in turn, determines the possibility of the setting and implementation of goals (to engage in or to alter/stop a process) (Step 4). By way of transitivity then, the amount of attention also determines the possibility of the setting and implementation of goals (Step 3 + Step 4). We can thus say that goals not only determine where attention will be *directed* (Step 1), but that the *amount* of attention available also determines whether information (input or process) will be detected (Step 3) and hence whether it can be used for the implementation of goals (to engage in or to alter/stop the process) (Step 4).

Problems with the Simple Set of Modal Relations   There are two problems that complicate the customary practice to generalize support from one feature to the next. The first problem is that the picture of interrelations is more complex than what is just described. The second problem is related to the gradual nature of the features. We discuss these two problems in turn.

Empirical research and theoretical analysis have extended the simple set of interrelations presented above and we describe a number of these additional relations below (see Figure 1.2 for a schematic overview).

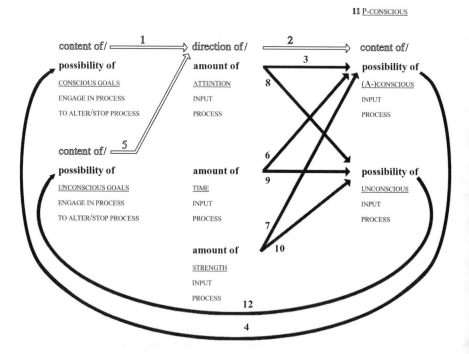

FIGURE 1.2   Extended set of interrelations between goals, attention, time, strength, and consciousness.

From goals to attention   Attention may not only be directed by conscious goals, but also by unconscious goals (Figure 1.2, Step 5). The distinction between an attention system guided by conscious goals and one guided by unconscious goals turns up in several theories (e.g., Baars, 1998; Luria, 1973; Posner & Rothbart, 1989; Shiffrin & Scheider, 1977; Yantis & Jonides, 1996).

There is considerable controversy about whether goals are necessary for attention orienting. Some authors have argued that goal relevance, particularly the discrepancy of a stimulus with a goal or *desired* state, is a necessary condition for attention orienting. Other authors have argued that attention orienting may also be elicited by novelty, or the discrepancy between the stimulus and an *expected* state (Gati & Ben-Shakar, 1990; Sokolov, 1963; but see Bernstein, 1969).

When attention orienting is driven by unconscious goals or by the mere novelty of the stimulus, there is no accompanying conscious experience of orienting or directing. It feels as if the stimulus grabs one's attention. This is reflected in use of the terms attention attraction, attentional grasp, orienting reflex (Sokolov, 1963), and "automatic" attention response (Shiffrin & Schneider, 1977). Of course, unless they are animate, stimuli cannot "do" something; they are simply there.

We should add that attention must not always be *directed* in order to be in a certain place. The attention spotlight may randomly travel around the visual field until it crosses goal-relevant or novel stimuli and it may then remain focused on these stimuli. Technically speaking, there is no *directing* of attention in this scenario, but there is nevertheless *allocation* of attention to a stimulus (Fox, Russo, Bowles, & Dutton, 2001).

From attention to consciousness   Several researchers argue that attention is not a sufficient condition for consciousness. The possibility or the degree of consciousness (of input or process) is not only determined by the amount of attention (to input or process) (Figure 1.2, Step 3), but also by other variables such as the amount of time or duration (of input or process) (Step 6), and the amount of strength (of input or process) (Step 7). When a stimulus is too weak or occurs too briefly so that activation of the corresponding nodes remains below a certain threshold, the stimulus may not be accessible to consciousness, despite adequate focusing of attention. This is illustrated by the fact that in subliminal perception research, stimuli are presented very briefly (in combination with masks) or in degraded form.

Certain authors argue that attention is not exclusive for consciousness. Some amount of attention, time, and strength may not only be required for conscious access (to input or process), but also for unconscious "access" (of input or process) (Steps 8–10). For example, Naccache, Blandin, and Dehaene (2002) observed that subliminal priming effects disappeared when attention was not focused on the time window in which the prime–target pair was presented. These observations are consistent with older studies in which subliminal priming effects disappeared when primes were not presented in the same position as the targets but rather in a "flanker" position (e.g., Inhoff, 1982). There also appear to be lower limits to the strength and presentation duration of stimuli that can lead to subliminal perception. We should note that attention, strength, and time are only a few of the many parameters that have been studied in subliminal perception research (for other parameters, see Verleger, Jaskowski, Aydemir, van der Lubbe, & Groen, 2004).

Most theorists assume that the *direction* of attention determines the content of consciousness: whatever is in the focus of attention is conscious; everything else is unconscious (e.g., Baars, 1988; Posner, 1982, 1994; Shiffrin & Schneider, 1977). Other theorists argue that attended information does not exhaust our conscious experience (e.g., Block, 1995; Hardcastle, 1997; Nelkin, 1993). Recall that Block (1995) coupled A-consciousness with attention, but saved P-consciousness as a form of consciousness that escapes attention (cf. his example of the pneumatic drill) (Step 11). Note that if P-consciousness is independent of the *direction* of attention, it should also be independent of the *amount* of attention. One could therefore say that attention is not even a necessary condition for consciousness.

From consciousness to goals   We think that the necessity of consciousness (of input and process) for the setting and implementation of the goals to engage in or to alter/stop a process (Figure 1.2, Step 4) may be true only when these goals are understood in the sense of *conscious* goals. Although it seems reasonable to assume that consciously intentional processes require a conscious input, this may not be true for unconsciously intentional processes. It is quite possible that unconsciously intentional processes can operate on unconscious input as well (Step 12). Similarly, in order to alter or change a process in a conscious way, it seems plausible that the person must be at least aware that the process is taking place. However, unconscious altering or stopping of a process may also be possible when processes are operating below the surface (e.g., Glaser & Banaji, 1999). In sum, the setting and implementation of unconscious goals (to engage in or alter/ stop a process) may not only be possible on the basis of conscious, but also on the basis of unconscious material (input or process).

The picture of interrelations is undoubtedly more complex than what we just sketched, but the main point is to show that the relations between features are not one-to-one relations and hence that arguments for the presence or absence of automaticity features based on logical inferences are likely to be flawed.

A second problem for the customary practice to generalize support from one feature to the next is posed by the gradual nature of the features. Let us consider the relations between the amount of attentional capacity, time, and strength on the one hand, and the possibility of consciousness on the other (Steps 3, 6, & 7). One should be able to conclude that awareness of a stimulus is prevented when attentional capacity, stimulus duration, and stimulus strength are too low. A major difficulty, however, is to determine exactly how much of these factors is needed to ensure awareness of the stimulus. This is further complicated by the fact that awareness of a stimulus can be realized with only a small amount of capacity and time (especially when an implementation intention is formed; cf. Gollwitzer, 1999). Thus, the process that uses conscious input may still count as efficient and fast. Another complication is the possibility of interdependence between these factors. For example, lack of time to incorporate a stimulus input may be compensated by increased attention to this stimulus or increased strength (salience) of the stimulus. Thus, it is dangerous to conclude on the basis of short presentation duration alone that some input was not consciously accessed (and therefore not processed in a consciously intentional way).

CONCLUSION

In the first part, we justified our choice for a feature-based approach to the definition and diagnosis of automaticity. In particular, we advocated a gradual and decompositional approach. Such an approach argues to examine each automaticity feature separately to determine the degree to which it is present. To see whether this gradual, decompositional approach can be carried through, we examined whether features are gradual and whether they can be conceptually and logically separated. Before we were able to answer these questions, we engaged in a conceptual analysis of the most important features: (un)intentional, goal-(in)dependent, (un)controlled, autonomous, purely stimulus-driven, (un)conscious, (non)efficient, and fast(slow). For each feature, we specified the minimal ingredients. In this way, different types could be distinguished for certain features. For example, we distinguished between two types of consciousness (A-consciousness vs. P-consciousness), each of which possess a different ingredient (Intentional vs. phenomenal aspect). We also distinguished between different types of control (open-loop vs. closed-loop; with vs. without disturbance; conscious vs. unconscious), each of which possess a different set of ingredients. We further specified what the features (or the ingredients of the features) can be a predicate of: the input, the output, the critical process (relation between input and output), or the initial perceptual process (which operates on the raw stimulus input and produces an output that is used by the critical process as an input).

This analysis led to the conclusion that features can to a large extent be defined in a nonoverlapping way. We could not avoid partial conceptual overlap between several goal-related features. On the other hand, because we argued for a separation of the different goals (engage in, alter, stop, avoid) that are involved in different types of controlled processes, we believe that our set of definitions is truly consistent with a decompositional approach. Other theorists have been less concerned with a rigorous conceptual separation of features, and assumptions of overlap seem to be the rule rather than the exception. In addition to conceptual overlap, many investigators assume modal relations among features, treating one feature as a necessary and/or sufficient condition for another feature. By drawing a more complex picture of interrelations, we showed that logically inferring the presence or absence of one feature on the basis of the presence or absence of another feature is not warranted. A decompositional approach is thus not only possible, but also desirable.

We also examined whether the features in our list can be conceptualized as gradual, and we concluded that this is indeed possible. The good news is that a gradual approach is justified. The bad news is that we have no objective criterion to draw a line between the automatic and the nonautomatic member in each feature pair: every process is efficient, uncontrolled, unconscious, and fast to some extent. The best solution that we can think of at present is to choose a subjective criterion to draw this line. In fact, most investigators are already doing this. When investigators say that a certain process is efficient, they implicitly rely on a subjective criterion to call the process efficient. We invite investigators to make explicit the subjective criteria they are using. This would greatly improve the communication about features. Examples of subjective criteria to call a process efficient are: "process A is more efficient than process B", "process A is more efficient than what is usually thought about the process", or "process A is more efficient than before practice". In fact then, our approach is not only a gradual but also a relative approach. The term "relative" involves more than the term "gradual": it involves a standard or criterion for comparison. Once a standard for comparison is specified, it becomes possible to draw a line between nonefficient and efficient processes (and between processes characterized by other feature pairs). The general term automatic may be kept as an umbrella term, as long as it is specified in what sense a process is automatic, that is, which features apply to the process and to what degree.

NOTES

1. Some authors have argued that connectionist models are no more grounded than their computational counterparts, and that they are prone to problems proper to any kind of correlational semantics (Christiansen & Chater, 1992).
2. Different meta-theoretical views exist about the relation between the computational and connectionist framework. According to a first view, both frameworks propose different metaphors of cognition that are incompatible. Eliminativists argue to replace the metaphor of symbol manipulation with the metaphor of pattern activation (e.g., Ramsey, Stich, & Garon, 1991; Smolensky, 1988). According to a second view, both frameworks pertain to a different level of analysis (as described by Anderson, 1987; Marr, 1982). Implementationalists have argued that connectionist models deal with a lower or more fine-grained level than computational models. In principle, processes described at different levels are not expected to make different predictions, and hence connectionist and computational models are not expected to compete with each other. However, there is disagreement about the level that has causal powers (Smolensky, 1995; see Green & Vervaeke, 1996), or about the level that should be of concern to psychologists (Anderson, 1987). Such disagreements rest on the assumption that the different levels that both frameworks occupy are more than just different descriptions of the same thing. Computational implementationalists argue that the higher level adds something extra which is missing at the lower level. For example, Fodor and Phylyshyn (1988) argue that the processes proposed by connectionist models are not in themselves sufficient to explain certain characteristics of human cognition. Connectionist implementationalists argue that the causal powers are situated on the lowest level. Still others propose genuinely hybrid models (e.g., Harnad, 1990).
3. The word goal can be understood in two senses. In the first sense, the word goal indicates a desired state in the future. This meaning is apparent in the phrase "to be directed toward a goal". One way in which a person can be directed at something is by forming a representation of it. In the second sense then, the word goal indicates a representation of the desired state, which, when activated, acts as an antecedent

cause that directs the organism toward that state. This meaning is apparent in the phrase "to be driven or caused by a goal".

4. In this context, we can point at the distinction commonly made in the motivation literature between goal setting (the phase in which a goal is chosen) and goal striving (the phase in which the goal is implemented) (Gollwitzer, 1990; Heckhausen, 1991). It should be clear that the present analysis only deals with goal striving. The feasibility factor that we discuss should thus not be confused with the feasibility factor mentioned in the literature on goal setting (cf. Gollwitzer, 1990).

5. This link is initially established in a deliberative manner, but once it is ꞏ̀ed in memory, the detection of the cue can trigger the act directly.

REFERENCES

Anderson, J. R. (1992). Automaticity and the ACT* theory. *American Journal of Psychology, 105*, 165–180.

Anderson, J. R. (1987). Methodologies for studying human knowledge. *Behavioral and Brain Sciences, 10*, 467–505.

Anderson, J. R. (1996). ACT: A simple theory of complex cognition. *American Psychologist, 51*, 355–365.

Baars, B. J. (1988). *A cognitive theory of consciousness.* Cambridge, UK: Cambridge University Press.

Baars, B. J. (1995). Evidence that phenomenal consciousness is the same as access consciousness. *Behavioral and Brain Sciences, 18*, 249.

Baars, B. J. (1997). Some essential differences between consciousness and attention, perception, and working memory. *Consciousness and Cognition 6*, 363–371.

Baars, B. J. (1998). Metaphors of consciousness and attention in the brain. *Trends in Neurosciences, 21*, 58–62.

Baddeley, A. (1986). *Working memory.* Oxford, UK: Clarendon Press.

Bar, M., Tootell, R. B., Schacter, D. L., Greve, D. N., Fischl, B., Mendola, J. D., Rosen, B. R., & Dale, A. M. (2001). Cortical mechanisms specific to explicit visual recognition. *Neuron, 29*, 529–535.

Bargh, J. A. (1989). Conditional automaticity: Varieties of automatic influence in social perception and cognition. In J. S. Uleman & J. A. Bargh (Eds.), *Unintended thought* (pp. 3–51). New York: Guilford.

Bargh, J. A. (1990). Auto-motives: Preconscious determinants of social interaction. In E. T. Higgins & R. M. Sorrentino (Eds.), *Handbook of motivation and cognition* (Vol. 2, pp. 93–130). New York: Guilford.

Bargh, J. A. (1992). The ecology of automaticity: Toward establishing the conditions needed to produce automatic processing effects. *American Journal of Psychology, 105*, 181–199.

Bargh, J. A. (1994). The four horsemen of automaticity: Awareness, intention, efficiency, and control in social cognition. In R. S. Wyer & T. K. Srull (Eds.), *Handbook of social cognition* (Vol. 1, pp. 1–40). Hillsdale, NJ: Erlbaum.

Bargh, J. A. (1996). Automaticity in social psychology. In E. T. Higgins & A. W. Kruglanski (Eds.), *Social psychology: Handbook of basic principles* (pp. 169–183). New York: Guilford.

Bargh, J. A. (1997). The automaticity of everyday life. In R. S. Wyer (Ed.), *Advances in social cognition* (Vol. 10, pp. 1–49). Mahwah, NJ: Erlbaum.

Bargh, J. A. (1999). The cognitive monster. The case against the controllability of automatic stereotype effects. In S. Chaiken & Y. Trope (Eds.), *Dual-process theories in social psychology* (pp. 361–382). New York: Guilford.

Bargh, J. A., & Barndollar, K. (1996). Automaticity in action: The unconscious as repository of chronic goals and motives. In P. M. Gollwitzer & J. A. Bargh (Eds.), *The psychology of action: Linking cognition and motivation to behavior* (pp. 457–481). New York: Guilford.

Bargh, J. A., & Chartrand, T. L. (2000). The mind in the middle: A practical guide to priming and automaticity research. In H. Reis & C. Judd (Eds.), *Handbook of research methods in social psychology* (pp. 253–285). New York: Cambridge University Press.

Bargh, J. A., Gollwitzer, P. M., Lee-Chai, A., Barndollar, K., & Trötschel, R. (2001). The automated will: Nonconscious activation and pursuit of behavioral goals. *Journal of Personality and Social Psychology*, *81*, 1014–1027.

Bartlett, F. C. (1932). *Remembering*. Cambridge, UK: Cambridge University Press.

Bernstein, A. (1969). To what does the orienting response respond? *Psychophysiology*, *6*, 338–350.

Block, N. (1995). On a confusion about a function of consciousness. *Behavioral and Brain Sciences*, *18*, 227–287.

Brand, M. (1989). Proximate causation of action. *Philosophical Perspectives*, *3*, 423–442.

Brentano, F. C. (1874). *Psychologie vom empirischen Standpunkt*, Leipzig: Duncke & Humblot.

Bruner, J. S. (1957). On perceptual readiness. *Psychological Review*, *64*, 123–152.

Bruner, J. S., & Goodman, C. C. (1947). Value and need as organizing factors in perception. *Journal of Abnormal Social Psychology*, *42*, 205–215.

Bryan, W. L., & Harter, L. (1899). Studies on the telegraphic language: The acquisition of a hierarchy of habits. *Psychological Review*, *6*, 345–378.

Carlson, R. A., & Lundy, D. H. (1992). Consistency and restructuring in cognitive procedural sequences. *Journal of Experimental Psychology: Learning, Memory, and Cognition*, *18*, 127–141.

Carver, C. S., & Scheier, M. F. (1999). Themes and issues in the self-regulation of behaviour. In R. S. Wyer (Ed.), *Advances in social cognition* (Vol. 12, pp. 1–105). Mahwah, NJ: Erlbaum.

Carver, C. S., & Scheier, M. F. (2002). Control processes and self-organization as complementary principles underlying behaviour. *Personality and Social Psychology Review*, *6*, 304–315.

Chalmers, D. J. (1996). *The conscious mind: In search of a fundamental theory*. New York: Oxford University Press.

Chartrand, T. L., & Bargh, J. A. (1996). Automatic activation of impression formation and memorization goals: Nonconscious goal priming reproduces effects of explicit task instructions. *Journal of Personality and Social Psychology*, *39*, 752–766.

Christiansen, M. H., & Chater, N. (1992). Connectionism, meaning and learning. *Connection Science*, *4*, 227–252.

Cleeremans, A. (1997). Principles for implicit learning. In D. Berry (Ed.) *How implicit is implicit learning?* (pp. 195–234). Oxford, UK: Oxford University Press.

Cleeremans, A. & Jiménez, L. (2002). Implicit learning and consciousness: A graded, dynamic perspective. In R. M. French & A. Cleeremans (Eds.), *Implicit learning and consciousness* (pp. 1–40). Hove, UK: Psychology Press.

Davidson, D. (1980): *Essays on actions and events*. Oxford, UK: Oxford University Press.

Dehaene, S., & Naccache, L. (2001). Towards a cognitive neuroscience of consciousness: basic evidence and a workspace framework. *Cognition, 79,* 1–37.

Dennett, D. C. (1984). *Elbow room: The varieties of free will worth wanting.* Cambridge, MA: MIT Press.

Dienes, Z., & Perner, J. (1999). A theory of implicit knowledge. *Behavioral and Brain Sciences, 22,* 735–808.

Erdelyi, M. H. (1992). Psychodynamics and the unconscious. *American Psychologist, 47,* 784–787.

Fazio, R. H. (2001). On the automatic activation of associated evaluations: An overview. *Cognition and Emotion, 15,* 115–141.

Fazio, R. H., Sanbonmatsu, D. M., Powell, M. C., & Kardes, F. R. (1986). On the automatic activation of attitudes. *Journal of Personality and Social Psychology, 50,* 229–238.

Fernandez-Duque D., & Johnson, M. L. (2002). Cause and effect theories of attention: The role of conceptual metaphors. *General Psychology, 6,* 153–165.

Fodor, J. (1983). *The modularity of mind.* Cambridge, MA: MIT Press.

Fodor, J. A., & Pylyshyn, Z. (1988). Connectionism and cognitive architecture: A critical analysis. *Cognition, 28,* 3–71.

Fox, E., Russo, R., Bowles, R., & Dutton, K. (2001). Do threatening stimuli draw or hold visual attention in subclinical anxiety? *Journal of Experimental Psychology: General, 130,* 681–700.

Francolini, C. M., & Egeth, H. (1980). On the automaticty of "automatic" activation: Evidence of selective seeing. *Perception and Psychophysics, 27,* 331–342.

Gati, I. & Ben-Shakar, G. (1990). Novelty and significance in orientation and habituation: A feature-matching approach. *Journal of Experimental Psychology: General, 119,* 251–263.

Gibson, E. J. (1969). *Principles of perceptual learning and development.* New York: Appleton-Century-Crofts.

Glaser, J., & Banaji, M. R. (1999). When fair is foul and foul is fair: Reverse priming in automatic evaluation. *Journal of Personality and Social Psychology, 77,* 669–687.

Gollwitzer, P. M. (1990). Action phases and mind-sets. In E. T. Higgins & R. M. Sorrentino (Eds.), *Handbook of motivation and cognition: Foundations of social behavior* (Vol. 2, pp. 53–92). New York: Guilford.

Gollwitzer, P. M. (1993). Goal achievement: The role of intentions. *European Review of Social Psychology, 4,* 141–185.

Gollwitzer, P. M. (1999). Implementation intentions: Strong effects of simple plans. *American Psychologist, 54,* 493–503.

Green, C. D. & Vervaeke, J. (1996). What kind of explanation, if any, is a connectionist net? In C. W. Tolman, F. Cherry, R. van Hezewijk, & I. Lubek (Eds.), *Problems of theoretical psychology* (pp. 201–210). North York, ON: Captus University Publications.

Hardcastle, V. G. (1997) Attention versus consciousness: A distinction with a difference. *Cognitive Studies: Bulletin of the Japanese Cognitive Science Society, 4,* 56–66.

Harnad, S. (1990). The Symbol Grounding Problem. *Physica D, 42,* 335–346.

Hasher, L., & Zacks, R. T. (1979). Automatic and effortful processes in memory. *Journal of Experimental Psychology: General, 108,* 356–388.

Heckhausen, H. (1991). Motivation and action (P. K. Leppman, Trans.). Berlin: Springer-Verlag. (Original work published 1990.)

Hermans, D., Crombez, G., & Eelen, P. (2000). Automatic attitude activation and efficiency: The fourth horseman of automaticity. *Psychologica Belgica, 40,* 3–22.

Inhoff, A. W. (1982). Parafoveal word perception: A further case against semantic preprocessing. *Journal of Experimental Psychology: Human Perception and Performance, 8,* 137–145.

James, W. (1890). *The principles of psychology.* New York: Holt, Rinehart & Winston.

Jastrow, J. (1906). *The subconscious.* Boston, MA: Houghton-Mifflin.

Johnston, W. A., & Dark, V. J. (1986). Selective attention. *Annual Review of Psychology, 37,* 43–75.

Kahneman, D. (1973). *Attention and effort.* Englewood Cliffs, NJ: Prentice-Hall.

Kahneman, D., & Chajczyk, D. (1983). Test of the automaticity of reading: Dilution of Stroop effects by color-irrelevant stimuli. *Journal of Experimental Psychology: Human Perception and Performance, 9,* 497–509.

Kahneman, D., & Henik, A. (1981). Perceptual organization and attention. In M. Kubovy & J. Pomerantz (Eds.), *Perceptual organization.* Hillsdale, NJ: Erlbaum.

Kahneman, D., & Treisman, A. (1984). Changing views of attention and automaticity. In R. Parasuraman & D. R. Davies (Eds.), Varieties of attention (pp. 29–61). Orlando, FL: Academic Press.

Kelso, J. A. S. (1995). *Dynamic patterns: The self-organization of brain and behavior.* Cambridge, MA: MIT Press.

Kobes, B. W. (1995). Access and what it is like. *Behavioral and Brain Sciences, 18,* 260.

Kramer, A. F., Strayer, D. L., & Buckley, J. (1990). Development and transfer of automatic processing. *Journal of Experimental Psychology: Human Perception and Performance, 16,* 505–522.

LaBerge, D. (1973). Attention and measurement of perceptual learning. *Memory & Cognition, 1,* 268–276.

LaBerge, D. (1983). Spatial extent of attention to letters and words. *Journal of Experimental Psychology: Human Perception and Performance, 9,* 371–379.

Logan, G. D. (1978). Attention in character classification tasks: Evidence for the automaticity of component stages. *Journal of Experimental Psychology: General, 107,* 32–63.

Logan, G. D. (1979). On the use of concurrent memory load to measure attention and automaticity. *Journal of Experimental Psychology: Human Perception and Performance, 5,* 189–207.

Logan, G. D. (1985). Skill and automaticity: Relations, implications, and future directions. *Canadian Journal of Psychology, 39,* 367–386.

Logan, G. D. (1988). Toward an instance theory of automatization. *Psychological Review, 95,* 492–527.

Logan, G. D. (1989). Automaticity and cognitive control. In J. S. Uleman & J. A. Bargh (Eds.), *Unintended thought* (pp. 52–74). New York: Guilford.

Logan, G. D. (1991). Automaticity and memory. In W. E. Hockley & S. Lewandowsky (Eds.), *Relating theory and data: Essays on human memory in honor of Bennet B. Murdock* (pp. 347–366). Hillsdale NJ: Erlbaum.

Logan, G. D. (1992). Attention and preattention in theories of automaticity. *American Journal of Psychology, 105,* 317–339.

Logan, G., & Cowan, W. B. (1984). On the ability to inhibit thought and action: A theory of an act of control. *Psychological Review, 91,* 295–327.

Luria, A. R. (1973). *The working Brain: An introduction to neuropsychology.* New York: Basic Books.

Mackie, J. L. (1974). *The cement of the universe: A study of causation*. Oxford, UK: Clarendon Press.

Mackie, J. L. (1975). Causes and conditionals. In E. Sosa (Ed.), *Causation and conditionals*. Oxford, UK: Oxford University Press.

Marr, D. (Ed.). (1982). *Vision: A computational investigation into the human representation and processing of visual information*. New York: Freeman.

Merikle, P. M., & Joordens, S. (1997). Parallels between perception without attention and perception without awareness. *Consciousness and Cognition, 6*, 219–236.

Mele, A. R. & Moser, P. K. (1994). Intentional action. *Noûs, 28*, 39–68.

Menzies, P. (2001). The causal efficacy of mental states. In J. M. Monnoyer (Ed.), *The Structure of the world: The renewal of metaphysics in the Australian School*. Paris: Vrin Publishers.

Miller, G. A., Galanter, E., & Pribram, K. (1960). *Plans and the structure of behavior*. New York: Holt.

Moors, A., & De Houwer, J. (2006). Automaticity: A theoretical and conceptual analysis. *Psychological Bulletin, 132*, 297–326.

Moors, A., De Houwer, J., & Eelen, P. (2004). Automatic stimulus–goal comparisons: Support from motivational affective priming studies. *Cognition and Emotion, 18*, 29–54.

Morton, A. (1995). Phenomenal and attentional consciousness may be inextricable. *Behavioral and Brain Sciences, 18*, 263–264.

Moskowitz, G. B. (2001). Preconscious control and compensatory cognition. In G. B. Moskowitz (Ed.), *Cognitive social psychology: The Princeton Symposium on the Legacy and Future of Social Cognition*. Hillsdale, NJ: Erlbaum.

Moskowitz, G. B., Li, P., & Kirk, E. R. (2004). The implicit volition model: On the preconscious regulation of temporarily adopted goals. In M. Zanna (Ed.), *Advances in experimental social psychology* (Vol. 34, pp. 317–414). San Diego, CA: Academic Press.

Moya, C. J. (1990). *The philosophy of action: An introduction*. Cambridge, UK: Polity Press.

Naccache, L., Blandin, E., & Dehaene, S. (2002). Unconscious masked priming depends on temporal attention. *Psychological Science, 13*, 416–424.

Nagel, T. (1994). What is it like to be a bat? *Philosophical Review, 83*, 434–450.

Natsoulas, T. (1981). Basic problems of consciousness. *Journal of Personality and Social Psychology, 41*, 132–178.

Navon, D., & Gopher, D. (1979). On the economy of the human processing system. *Psychological Review, 86*, 214–255.

Neisser, U. (1976). *Cognition and reality*. San Francisco: Freeman.

Nelkin, N. (1993). The connection between intentionality and consciousness. In M. Davies & G. W. Humphreys (Eds.), *Consciousness: Psychological and philosophical essays* (pp. 224–239). Oxford, UK: Blackwell.

Oatley, K. (1993). Freud's cognitive psychology of intention: The case of Dora. In M. Davies & G. W. Humphreys (Eds.), *Consciousness: Psychological and philosophical essays* (pp. 90–104). Oxford, UK: Blackwell.

O'Shaughnessy, B. (1991). Searle's theory of action. In E. Lepore & R. Van Gulick (Eds.), *John Searle and his critics*. Cambridge, MA: Blackwell.

Pashler, H. (1998). *The psychology of attention*. Cambridge, MA: MIT Press.

Penfield, W. (1975). *The mystery of the mind*. Princeton: Princeton University Press.

Posner, M. I. (1982). Cumulative development of attentional theory. *American Psychologist, 37*, 168–179.

Posner, M. I. (1994). Attention: The mechanism of consciousness. *Proceedings of the National Academy of Science, USA, 91*, 7398–7403.

Posner, M. I., & Rothbart, M. K. (1989). Intentional chapters on unintended thoughts. In J. S. Uleman & J. A. Bargh (Eds.), *Unintended thought* (pp. 450–469). New York: Guilford.

Posner, M. I., & Snyder, C. R. R., (1975a). Facilitation and inhibition in the processing of signals. In P. M. A. Rabbit & S. Dornic (Eds.), *Attention and Performance V* (pp. 669–682). New York: Academic Press.

Posner, M. I., & Snyder, C. R. R., (1975b). Attention and cognitive control. In R. L. Solso (Ed.), *Information processing and cognition: The Loyola symposium* (pp. 153–175). Hillsdale, NJ: Erlbaum.

Posner, M. I., Snyder, C. R. R., & Davidson, B. J. (1980). Attention and the detection of signals. *Journal of Experimental Psychology: General, 109*, 160–174.

Postman, L., Bruner, J. S., & McGinnies, E. (1948). Personal values as selective factors in perception. *Journal of Abnormal Social Psychology, 43*, 142–154.

Powers, W. T. (1973). *Behavior: The control of perception.* Hawthorne, NY: Aldine DeGruyter.

Prinz, W. (1990). A common coding approach to perception and action. In O. Neumann & W. Prinz (Eds.), *Relationships between perception and action* (pp. 167–201). Heidelberg: Springer-Verlag.

Pylyshyn, Z. W. (1984). *Computation and cognition: Toward a foundation for cognitive science.* Cambridge, MA: MIT Press.

Ramsey, W., Stich, S. P., & Garon, J. (1991). Connectionism, eliminativism, and the future of folk psychology. In W. Ramsey, S. P. Stich, & D. E. Rumelhart (Eds.), *Philosophy and connectionist theory* (pp. 199–228). Hillsdale, NJ: Lawrence Erlbaum.

Regan, J. E. (1981). Automaticity and learning: Effects of familiarity on naming letters. *Journal of Experimental Psychology: Human Perception and Performance, 7*, 180–195.

Rosenbloom, P. S., & Newell, A. (1986). The chunking of goal hierarchies: A generalized model of practice. In R. S. Michaliski, J. G. Carbonell, & T. M. Mitchell (Eds.), *Machine learning: An artificial intelligence approach* (Vol. 2, pp. 247–288). Los Altos, CA: Morgan Kaufmann.

Schacter, D. L. (1989). On the relation between memory and consciousness: Dissociable interactions and conscious experience. In H. L. Roediger & F. I. M. Craik (Eds.), *Varieties of memory and consciousness: Essays in honour of Endel Tulving* (pp. 355–389). Mahwah, NJ: Erlbaum.

Schneider, W., & Fisk, A. D. (1984). Automatic category search and its transfer. *Journal of Experimental Psychology: Learning, Memory, and Cognition, 10*, 1–15.

Searle, J. R. (1983). *Intentionality: An essay in the philosophy of mind.* Cambridge: Cambridge University Press.

Searle, J. R. (1992). *The Rediscovery of the Mind.* Cambridge, MA: MIT Press.

Sergent, C. & Dehaene, S. (2004). Is consciousness a gradual phenomenon? Evidence for an all-or-none bifurcation during the attentional blink. *Psychological Science, 15*, 720–728.

Shallice, T. (1988). Information-processing models of consciousness: Possibilities and problems. In A. J. Marcel & E. Bisiach (Eds.), *Consciousness in contemporary science* (pp. 305–333). Oxford, UK: Oxford University Press.

Shiffrin, R. M. (1988). Attention. In R. C. Atkinson, R. J. Hernstein, G. Lindzey, & R. D. Luce (Eds.), *Stevens' handbook of experimental psychology* (Vol. 2, pp. 739–811). New York: Wiley.

Shiffrin, R. M., & Schneider, W. (1977). Controlled and automatic human information processing: II. Perceptual learning, automatic attending and a general theory. *Psychological review*, *84*, 127–190.

Smith, E. R., & Lerner, M. (1986). Development of automatism of social judgements. *Journal of Personality and Social Psychology*, *50*, 246–259.

Smolensky, P. (1995). Constituent structure and explanation in an integrated connectionist/ symbolic architecture. In C. MacDonald & G. MacDonald (Eds.), *Connectionism: Debates on psychological explanation* (pp. 223–290). Oxford: Blackwell.

Sokolov, E. N. (1963). *Perception and the conditioned reflex*. New York: Macmillan.

Solomons, L. & Stein, G. (1896). Normal motor automatism. *Psychological Review*, *3*, 492–512.

Tolman, E. C. (1932). Concerning the sensation quality: A behavioristic account. *Psychological Review*, *29*, 140–145.

Treisman, A., Vieira, A., & Hayes, A. (1992). Automaticity and preattentive processing. *American Journal of Psychology*, *105*, 341–362.

Tzelgov, J., Henik, A., Sneg, R., & Baruch, B. (1996). Unintentional word reading via the phonological route: The Stroop effect with cross-script homophones. *Journal of Experimental Psychology: Learning, Memory, and Cognition*, *22*, 336–349.

Tzelgov, J., Yehene, V., Kotler, L., & Alon, A. (2000). Automatic comparisons of artificial digits never compared: Learning linear ordering relations. *Journal of Experimental Psychology: Learning, Memory, and Cognition*, *26*, 103–120.

Uleman, J. S. (1989). A framework for thinking intentionally about unintended thoughts. In J. S. Uleman & J. A. Bargh (Eds.), *Unintended thought* (pp. 425–449). New York: Guilford.

Uleman, J. S., & Moskowitz, G. B. (1994). Unintended effects of goals on unintended inferences. *Journal of Personality and Social Psychology*, *66*, 490–501.

Vallacher, R. R., & Nowak, A. (1999). The dynamics of self-regulation. In R. S. Wyer (Ed.), *Advances in social cognition* (Vol. 12, pp. 241–259). Mahwah, NJ: Erlbaum.

Vallacher, R. R., & Wegner, D. M. (1987). What do people think they're doing? Action identification and human behavior. *Psychological Review*, *94*, 3–15.

Verleger, R., Jaskowski, P., Aydemir, A., van der Lubbe, R. H. J., & Groen, M. (2004). *Journal of Experimental Psychology: General*, *133*, 494–515.

Wakefield, J. and Dreyfus, H. (1991). Intentionality and the Phenomenology of Action. In E. Lepore & R. Van Gulick (Eds.), *John Searle and his critics*. Cambridge, MA: Blackwell.

Wegner, D. M. (2003). The mind's best trick: How we experience conscious will. *Trends in Cognitive Sciences*, *7*, 65–69.

Wegner, D. M., & Bargh, J. A. (1998). Control and automaticity in social life. In D. Gilbert, S. T. Fiske, & G. Lindzey (Eds.), *Handbook of social psychology* (4th ed, Vol. 1, pp. 446–496). New York: McGraw-Hill.

Wegner, D. M., & Wheatley, T. (1999). Apparent mental causation: Sources of the experience of will. *American Psychologist*, *54*, 480–492.

Wickens, C. D. (1984). Processing resources in attention. In R. Parasuraman & R. Davies (Eds.), *Varieties of attention* (pp. 63–102). New York: Academic Press.

Wundt, W. (1897). *Outlines of psychology*. (C. H. Judd, Trans.). Leipzig: Wilhelm Engelmann. (Original work published 1896.)

Wundt, W. M. (1902). *Grundzüge der physiologischen Psychologie* (Vol. 1). Leipzig: Wilhelm Engelmann.

Yablo, S. (1992). Cause and essence. *Synthese*, *93*, 403–449.

Yantis, S., & Jonides, J. (1996). Attentional capture by abrupt onsets: new perceptual objects or visual masking? *Journal of Experimental Psychology: Human Perception and Performance, 22,* 1505–1513.

Zbrodoff, N. J., & Logan, G. D. (1986). On the autonomy of mental processes: A case study of arithmetic. *Journal of Experimental Psychology: General, 115,* 118–130.

2

Effects of Priming and Perception on Social Behavior and Goal Pursuit

AP DIJKSTERHUIS, TANYA L. CHARTRAND, and HENK AARTS

Let's say you pick up a rock and you throw it. And in midflight you give that rock consciousness and a rational mind. That little rock will think it has free will and will give you a highly rational account of why it has decided to take the route it's taking . . . (From *I Am Charlotte Simmons* (p. 283) by Tom Wolfe (2004), published by Jonathan Cape. Reprinted by permission of the Random House Group Ltd.)

*I*f the editor would have asked us to write about automaticity in social behavior 25 years ago, he would have met a blank stare. And we do not mean that we would have been puzzled because we were kids at the time, more interested in playing with Lego than in writing chapters. The whole concept of automatic or unconscious behavior would have struck anyone as odd at that time. Sure, we do not need consciousness to breathe or perhaps not even to brush our teeth, but automaticity in behavior that social psychologists are traditionally interested in? Automaticity in social interaction? Automatic goal pursuit? Of course not! We are conscious agents and automaticity was reserved for relatively unimportant routine actions only. It would have become a very short chapter indeed.

Needless to say, things have changed. The idea of the sovereign conscious agent determining our behavior received many blows over the years from social cognition (and other) researchers. We learned that impressions of people are influenced by contextual factors of which we are unaware (Bargh & Pietromonaco, 1982; Higgins, Rholes, & Jones, 1977; Srull & Wyer, 1979). Subsequently, we were confronted with the fact that social stereotypes are activated automatically (Devine, 1989; Macrae, Milne, & Bodenhausen, 1994). Only just recovered from that major setback, we had to accept that changes in social behavior and intellectual performance could be completely automatic (Bargh, Chen, & Burrows, 1996; Dijksterhuis & van Knippenberg, 1998). And finally, we had to accept the fact that even goal-directed behavior was largely under "unconscious control" (Aarts & Dijksterhuis, 2000a,b; Bargh, Gollwitzer, Lee Chai, Barndollar, & Trötschel, 2001; Chartrand & Bargh, 1996; Moskowitz, Li, & Kirk, 2004; Shah, 2003). In sum, the picture of a free willing social agent has been crumbling down, quickly and surely (Bargh, 1997, 2005; Bargh & Chartrand, 1999; Wegner, 2002; Wilson, 2002). If we wanted to write a short chapter, perhaps we should have asked the editor to assign us a chapter on conscious processes in social behavior.

Research on automaticity has often been met with resistance (Bargh & Chartrand, 1999; Dijksterhuis, Aarts, & Smith, 2005). In hindsight, we can conclude we have witnessed a scientific tug-of-war. All human behavior was neatly divided between two camps: one favoring automaticity, the other believing in an essential, decisive role of consciousness. An interesting intellectual debate ensued during which both camps strived for a share as big as realistically possible. That is, the discussion during these years centered around the question of what behavior is automatic and what behavior requires some sort of conscious decision. However, every few years people firmly believing in a decisive role of consciousness had to give in a few feet. Automaticity researchers would throw up yet another new priming experiment demonstrating some aspect of our functioning to be automatic, and others could do not much more than dislike it and give in ("Oh no! Goals too?"). After all these years, most people would agree that, in principle at least, almost anything can be done automatically. We can brush the sand off our clothes and move on.

Now what will we do with our clean, sandfree clothes? In this chapter, we will first argue that the question that dominated the field for a long time – what behavior requires a conscious decision and what behavior does not – is an odd question for various reasons. Both scientific evidence as well as recent (and not so recent) philosophical debates indicate that this question is already answered: Behavior does not originate with a conscious decision. Secondly, assuming that behavior is in principle of unconscious origin, we will present a descriptive representational model with which all unconscious behavior that has recently been documented can be categorized and at least partly understood. In this model, there is as yet no role for consciousness. The model will be introduced with the aid of three typical automaticity experiments. In our third (and long) section, we will review the findings from the domain of automaticity in behavior. This section will be divided into three sections: one on mimicry and imitation (the "mimicry route"); one on effects of category and trait activation on behavior (the "trait route"); and one on goal-related behavior (the "goal route"). In all three sections, we will discuss findings that shed light on the processes underlying these routes, as well as review recent findings pertaining to these routes. We end this section by a discussion on the differences between the trait route and the goal route. Finally, in our last section, we will briefly turn back to the role of consciousness. We assume that behavior does not start with a conscious decision, but there is no denying that we are often conscious of our behavior. The question is why? What self-regulatory function, if any, does consciousness have? For instance, if we want to achieve a difficult goal, does it help to be consciously aware of it from time to time?

WHERE ACTION STARTS

While writing a sentence, one consciously thinks about what words to use ("Shall I write 'what words to use' or perhaps 'which specific words to use' "). Or while walking to the fridge after the sudden realization that one is thirsty, one can think about what to have ("let's have some juice"). Such conscious thoughts are often predictive of actual behavior. We are often conscious of what we do or are about to do, and it feels like conscious thoughts, or conscious decisions, shape our actual behavior (see Wegner, 2002). The question, however, is when and where the preparation of behavior starts. If we end up having juice, is the moment we feel we consciously decide to have juice the actual starting point? Was that conscious thought the first step towards having juice, rather than say a glass of milk or a beer?

The answer is no. The unconscious preparation of even the simplest action starts before we are conscious of the action we are about to perform. Quite some time ago, Kornhuber and Deecke (1965) did experiments in which they asked their participants to perform a simple action, such as flexing a finger. At the same time, they measured the EEG to assess when the brain starts to prepare for the action. The outcome was that the first sign of unconscious preparation precedes an action by about 800 milliseconds. This really is quite a lot of time and it led Libet to wonder whether conscious awareness of the decision to act appears as long in advance as well. If it does, it would allow us to conclude that consciousness is indeed the starting point for the action. However, if conscious awareness of the decision to act precedes the action by much less than 800 milliseconds, we have a problem. We would have to conclude that the action does not start in consciousness. Indeed, Libet and colleagues (1983) showed exactly this. In their famous experiments, they replicated the Kornhuber and Deecke (1965) experiments while adding another measure: conscious awareness of the decision to act. It became clear that conscious decisions *follow* unconscious preparation and only precede the actual execution of the action by about 200 milliseconds. In other words, the unconscious makes the decision to act.

In many cases, the unconscious communicates its decision to consciousness, and this makes it feel as if consciousness has decided (see e.g., Norretranders, 1998; Wegner, 2002). However, it did not. Such "feelings of will" are illusory, and, as work by Wegner and his colleagues has shown, often result when conscious thought precedes corresponding behavior by a natural time interval. For instance, if I flex my finger about a second after I thought about doing so, it may feel as consciously willed behavior. However, if I flex my finger 30 seconds after I thought about doing so, it does not feel as consciously willed, as we do not tend to see a causal relation between thought and action (see, e.g., Wegner & Wheatley, 1999). Importantly, such effects do not speak to the actual cause of behavior as they are, as we argue, unconscious. They do show, however, when and why people so firmly believe in a decisive or causal role of consciousness.

To turn back to our example, the preparation of our decision to drink juice starts unconsciously. One could come up with a different example of course. What if we walk to the fridge in the absence of knowing exactly what we will find there? We open the fridge, our attention is drawn by the brightly colored carton of juice, and we consciously say to ourselves "Ah, I forgot I still had juice, let's have some". Is that not a conscious decision in the sense that it was the first step to the act of having juice? The answer is still no. First, becoming conscious of the juice is not the starting point of perceiving the juice. Perceiving juice starts with perceiving some shapes and colors, and various cognitive processes distill the meaningful information "juice" from this array of sensory information (see, e.g., Norretranders, 1998). In a way, one can say that consciousness does not "see" any juice until after the unconscious has "seen" it sometime earlier. Second, and more importantly, during this process of translating sensory information into meaningful perception, preconscious processes decide to what we pay attention (e.g., Bruner, 1957; Neisser, 1967). That is, unconscious cognitive processes work on the vast array of sensory information and at some point decide that it is likely that there is juice, milk, and beer in the refrigerator. And during this process the decision is made to focus attention on the juice rather than the milk or beer. This happens before what phenomenologically feels like a conscious decision to have juice. So, again, unconscious processes make the first decision.

One may argue that our reasoning as well as the findings of Libet and colleagues may not generalize across more complex or more important behavior. However, there is no a priori reason why it should not. Libet's findings emphasize the idea that conscious thought is always the result of unconscious processes, irrespective of how important the thoughts are. Say you set yourself the goal to become president of the United States at some point in the future. In the course of many years, you will often be consciously aware of this goal. Perhaps these moments of awareness serve an important regulatory function (see later this chapter), but the first moment you were aware of this goal was not the starting point. Apart from scientific evidence, there is also an appealing logical argument. These days, most of us assume that consciousness resides in the brain. This necessarily means that conscious awareness is a function of other (unconscious) processes in the brain, except if one maintains the belief of a true "ghost in the machine". It would be truly mystifying if behavior *would* start consciously. Norretranders (1998, p. 221) put it as such: ". . . unless consciousness just hovers freely in the air, it must be linked to processes in the brain, and they must necessarily start up before consciousness appears. It is not our consciousness that initiates, for only the conscious is conscious".

Finally, the idea that the unconscious is responsible for behavioral control becomes more and more inescapable in light of recent neuropsychological evidence. Bargh (2005) recently made the case that consciousness and behavioral (motor) systems are fundamentally dissociated in the brain and hence that the workings of the motor systems are inaccessible to consciousness (see also Prinz, 2003). Bargh (2005, p. 43) concludes that ". . . a dissociation between motoric behavior and conscious awareness is now emerging as a basic structural feature of the human brain". Not surprisingly, there is growing evidence for automatically controlled motor systems. Rizzolatti et al. (1996) locates this function in the (neo) cerebellum. With frequent experience of the same behavior(s), this brain area links perceptual input to low-level motor programs, whereas its output extends to the prefrontal cortex, our main planning area.

The fact that behavior starts unconsciously is important for our understanding of automaticity. It follows that we should treat the fact that behavior is unconscious as the default. This in turn means that there really are two kinds of behaviors. First, there are behaviors of which we are never consciously aware in that the entire process from initiation to completion is unconscious. Second, there are behaviors of which we do become aware (once or more often), somewhere between initiation and final completion. In other words, there is true unconscious behavior, and there is unconscious behavior that is mediated by instances of conscious awareness. In our view, this makes the next challenge for automaticity researchers to find out when we become aware of our behavior, and what (if any) function these instances of consciousness awareness serve. We will return to this challenge later in this chapter.

Three Representative Experiments on Automatic Behavior

For now, given that we may conclude that behavior is unconscious by default, we may ask ourselves what the necessary building blocks are for a model explaining the large amount of data on automatic behavior acquired during the past twenty years. The model will be aimed at covering automatic effects of our (social) environment on behavior. Such effects are often mediated by activation of cognitive constructs such as stereotypes or traits, or by motivational constructs such as goals. Automatic attitudinal effects on behavior will not be discussed in this chapter (see Chapter 5). The breadth of the domain will be illustrated by three (not so randomly selected) representative experiments. These experiments correspond to the later sections of our review. The first experiment demonstrates effects of mimicry. The second experiment demonstrates effects of stereotype activation on behavior, whereas the third describes automatic effects of goals on behavior.

Chartrand and Bargh (1999) investigated whether people would automatically mimic mundane and inconsequential actions such as foot shaking or nose rubbing. In their first experiment, a confederate worked on a task with participants and this confederate was instructed to either rub her nose or shake her foot while working on this task. During the few minutes during which the confederate and participants worked together, the behavior of the participants was surreptitiously videotaped. Their hypothesis, that participants would indeed mimic the behavior of the confederate, was confirmed. Under conditions where the confederate rubbed her nose participants engaged more in nose-rubbing than in foot-shaking, whereas the opposite was true when participants interacted with the confederate who shook her foot. As one may have expected, participants were completely unaware of their imitative behavior. Chartrand and Bargh (1999) replicated and extended their findings in further experiments.

Bargh, Chen, and Burrows (1996, Experiment 2) were the first to report effects of category activation on motor behavior. In their experiment, which is already a modern classic in experimental social psychology, half of the participants were primed with the category of the elderly whereas others were not. The participants were primed by exposing them to words related to the elderly (e.g., grey, bingo, walking stick, Florida) in the context of a scrambled sentence language task (see Srull & Wyer, 1979). In such a task, participants construct grammatically correct sentences out of a random ordering of words, as a purported test of language ability. Participants in the control condition completed the same task without exposure to the critical, elderly related, words. After participants finished the priming task, they were told that the experiment had finished. However, the time it took participants to walk from the experimental room to the nearest elevator was surreptitiously recorded. The data showed that participants primed with the elderly category walked significantly slower than control participants. People displayed behavior in line with the activated stereotype of the elderly. Elderly are associated with slowness, and activating this stereotype of the elderly indeed led to slowness among the participants.

Finally, Aarts and Dijksterhuis (2000a) investigated the dynamics of habitual behavior. They first asked Dutch undergraduate students how often they used their bicycle to reach various destinations (note that, especially in cities, bicycle use in Holland is about as common as car use in the US). Subsequently, participants were divided into habitual bicycle users (people who use their bike all the time) and non-habitual bicycle users (people who use their bike only occasionally or not at all). In the actual experiments, participants were given a certain goal implying a specific location, such as the goal to "attend a lecture". The locations that were implied (such as the university) could be reached by bicycle, but also by other means, such as by car or by various modes of public transport. Upon presenting habitual bicycle users with such goals, the concept of bicycle was automatically activated. Among non-habitual bicycle users, activating a relevant goal did not lead to activation of this concept. In other words, among habitual bicycle users there was a one-to-one relation between the goal and the means to reach that goal, implying that the decision about how to reach the goal is completely automatized.

In sum, people automatically mimic each other. Social categories and associated traits automatically lead to corresponding behavior, and even goal-directed behavior is at least partly automatized. Now, with these (and other) experiments in mind, what could a model explaining and categorizing behavior look like?

THE BUILDING BLOCKS OF A BEHAVIOR PRODUCER

In order to explain the experiments discussed above – or experiments on automaticity in social behavior in general – five key concepts are crucial: an input system, an output system, and three mediating concepts. First, to start the behavior machine in the first place we need input and this input is either caused by *perception* or by inner forces such as *thoughts*. An example of the first is the Bargh, Chen, and Burrows (1996) experiment in which reading words related to the elderly activates the stereotype and subsequent stereotype-congruent behavior. An example of the latter is when certain physiological processes indicating a state of thirst lead us to get up and walk to the fridge. In our chapter, we will focus largely on perception as input and not on thought, because the former is more interesting from a social perspective. At the output end of the descriptive model are *motor programs*. These motor programs are ultimately responsible for our behavioral output. They eventually make us leave the room to walk to the elevator.

Between the input and output modules, there are three key mediating elements. Effects of perception or thought on the activation of motor programs, and ultimately behavior, are usually mediated by either *traits* or *goals* and by *behavior representations*. These three concepts are central in the model and, except for very simple forms of mimicry, all social behavior is mediated by activation of at least one (but usually two) of these concepts. Because of the centrality of these concepts, a little more is said about how they are defined in the present context, and about how they are learned and represented.

Traits refer to general classes of behavior. A trait is an abstract term associated with many concrete behaviors representative of this trait. They are usually learned at a relatively young age (e.g., Bargh, 2005; Luria, 1961), often because others (such as parents) explicitly map a trait concept (e.g., polite) onto a concrete behavior (e.g., a child said "thank you" for the first time in a shop after being given a candy). Traits are regularly activated during social interaction (see later in this chapter) and activation of a trait results in activation of the associated behavior representations, the so-called perception–behavior link (Dijksterhuis & Bargh, 2001). For example, in the Bargh et al. experiment discussed earlier, participants activated traits associated with the category of elderly ("slow"), and these traits, in turn, activated the actual behavior (i.e., walking slowly down the corridor). Traits are associated with many different behaviors (Maass, Colombo, Colombo, & Sherman, 2001; Sherman, 1980), and although experimenters generally assess only one behavior in an experiment (such as walking down the hallway) it is likely that trait activation leads to multiple behavioral changes at the same time. The effects of the trait route are pervasive and presumably permeate social behavior continuously. Finally, traits, unlike goals, do not have inherent motivational properties (see Bargh et al., 2001) and behavior induced by trait-activation is unintentional. It is a passive process and merely the consequence of the way we are wired (see Dijksterhuis & Bargh, 2001).

In order to make our behavior purposeful over time we have *goals*. Goals are defined as positively valued behavioral endstates (Custers & Aarts, 2005a), whether it be getting a cool drink on a hot day or becoming president of the US. Many goals are learned in two steps. First, people (children) have to learn the effects of consequences of their behaviors. That is, they have to learn to represent behavioral endstates (Elsner & Hommel, 2001). Second, behavioral endstates can over time become associated with positive affect (Custers & Aarts, 2005a). Positive affect makes people *want* to achieve the associated endstate. In other words, it gives a behavioral endstate its motivational power. Unlike traits, goals contain a feedback mechanism in order to monitor progress towards goal achievement. This gives our behavior a certain degree of consistency over time. In addition, goals are represented in a hierarchy, in which higher goals are associated with lower order subgoals (see, e.g., Vallacher & Wegner, 1985).

The effects of both traits and goals on actual behavior are mediated by activation of *behavior representations*. In the Aarts and Dijksterhuis (2000a,b) experiments, participants who had adopted the goal to travel (e.g., to go to the supermarket or to the university) activated the means to achieve the goal: the behavior representation of cycling. Likewise, the Bargh et al. priming procedure led to activation of the trait "slow", but effects of activation of this trait on actual behavior are likely mediated by activation of a behavior representation (e.g., dawdle). Like traits, such behavior representations are learned, mostly during infancy, by explicitly mapping verbs onto concrete behaviors (Bargh, 2005; Luria, 1961). Behavior representations can develop strong associations with multiple traits and goals over time. For instance, the behavior to concentrate hard on an exam can be associated with the trait *intelligent* and with the goal *to achieve*.

The resulting model, then, can be depicted as in Figure 2.1. As can be seen, the paths in the model – all referring to different psychological processes – are numbered. In what follows, we discuss three different routes that can be distinguished in our model: the mimicry route (consisting of Paths 1, 2, and 7); the trait route (consisting of Paths 3, 4, and 7); and the goal route (consisting of Paths 5, 6, and 7). Evidence for the relation between behavior representations and the motor system or motor programs (Path 7) applies to all three routes but will be discussed in the section on the mimicry route.

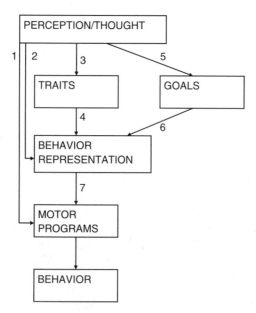

FIGURE 2.1   The building blocks of a behavior producer.

THE MIMICRY ROUTE

In what now follows, we review the mimicry route (Paths 1, 2, and 7). We start out by discussing the underlying processes by specifying the three paths in our model, followed by a brief review of the evidence of unconscious behavioral mimicry in three different domains: speech-related variables, facial expressions, and gestures and movements. In a third section, moderators of mimicry will be discussed. Finally, we end by presenting a functional perspective on mimicry and a discussion of the consequences of mimicry.

Path 1: From Perception to Motor Programs

After having read about the Chartrand and Bargh (1999) mimicry studies, it may have struck one as odd that perception can have a direct, unmediated effect on overt behavior in sophisticated species such as humans. One should note, though, that perception is no end in itself. We do not see things simply because we want to see them or because we want to understand them. Ultimately, we want to see things because it allows us to engage in appropriate behavior (Dijksterhuis & Bargh, 2001; Fiske, 1993; James, 1890; Milner & Goodale, 1995; Powers, 1973). As Milner and Goodale put it, "Natural selection operates on the level of overt behavior; it cares little about how well an animal 'sees' the world, but a great deal about how well the animal forages for food, avoid predators, finds mates, and moves efficiently from one place in the environment to another" (p. 11). Essentially, the function of perception is to activate behavior. Perception is our most prominent action control device.

The notion that perception is directly related to action without necessary mediation of processes such as conscious recognition or understanding is also supported by recent neuropsychological findings (Bargh, 2005). Research on patients with lesions in the parietal lobe (Goodale, Milner, Jakobsen, & Carey, 1991) demonstrates that people can show appropriate action towards an object (e.g., grasping a horizontally versus a vertically held book) without any conscious awareness of the objects itself. This has led various theorists to conclude that we have separate visual pathways for action (e.g., Decety & Grezes, 1999; Jeannerod, 2003) and for (conscious) recognition. That is, we have a dorsal visual pathway responsible for appropriate behavior that usually operates outside awareness and a ventral pathway that is responsible for recognizing and understanding an object. Importantly, the processes in the ventral stream are usually accessible to consciousness but are *not* related to the instigation of overt behavior.

The idea of an intimate linkage of perception and action dates back to well over a century ago (Carpenter, 1884; James, 1890; Lotze, 1852). William James observed that: "I sit at table after dinner and find myself from time to time taking nuts or raisins out of the dish and eat them. My dinner properly is over, and in the heat of the conversation I am hardly aware of what I do, but the perception of the fruit and fleeting notion that I may eat it seem fatally to bring the act about" (1890, p. 523). James used this as an example of "ideomotor action". He, and others (most notably Lotze, 1852), advanced the idea that the mere fleeting notion of an action is enough to bring about the action itself. Originally, the concept of ideomotor action was used to explain how thoughts (and not perception) could automatically elicit behavior. We have a "fleeting notion" of eating nuts and raisins and that in itself is enough to actually eat. However, in the writing of James (especially in the examples he used), it is apparent that thought and perception were often used interchangeably. The goal behind both perception and thought is to evoke overt behavior.

Later, Greenwald (1970, 1972) and Prinz (e.g., 1990, 2005) greatly advanced our understanding of ideomotor action and explicitly argued that perception and thought are under many circumstances functionally equivalent. As Prinz (2005) argues "If it is true that thinking of an act . . . has the power to prompt and instigate that act, this should be even more true in the case of perceiving that act, for instance as performed by someone else" (p. 143). And indeed, it does. What is crucial for eliciting a smile is the activation of the executing motor programs, and it does not matter whether it is brought about internally (by thought) or externally (by perception).

The evidence for mimicry by Chartrand and Bargh (1999) discussed earlier is an example of a direct effect of perception on motor programs. That is, behavior representations do not need to become active for perception to influence behavior because the perception automatically activates the motor programs themselves. The first empirical evidence that we know of that demonstrated our disposition to mimic what we perceive comes from Eidelberg (1929). Long before people had heard about motor programs, he showed that the mere perception of an act tends to result in the action itself. In his experiment, participants were instructed to point at their nose upon hearing the word "nose" and to point at a lamp upon hearing the word "lamp." The experimenter, who was clearly visible to the participants, also pointed at his or her nose or at the lamp upon hearing the corresponding instruction. At some point, the experimenter started to make "mistakes," in that he or she pointed at his or her nose upon hearing the word lamp and vice versa. As a result, participants started to make these same mistakes as well. They spontaneously mimicked the gestures made by the experimenter, despite the instruction to follow the verbal cues (i.e., the words "nose" and "lamp") and not the gestures of the experimenter. This work suggests that we are "wired" to spontaneously mimic. The mere perception of a gesture activated corresponding motor programs leading to the tendency to perform the gesture.

The most direct evidence, however, comes from research on "mirror neurons". At first, it was observed that the same neurons in the prefrontal cortex in a monkey brain "fire" both when a monkey perceives a gesture and when it performs a gesture (Gallese, Fadiga, Fogassi, & Rizzolatti, 1996; Rizzolatti, Fadiga, Fogassi, & Gallese, 1996). Later, findings among human participants were obtained using PET and fMRI that also show common brain regions for perception and execution of simple motor actions (e.g., Decety & Grezes, 1999; Fadiga, Fogassi, Pavesi, & Rizzolatti 1995; Iacoboni et al., 1999). The findings show a relation between perception and action that is as direct as it can possibly get: The same neurons (or at least neuronal regions) are responsible for perceiving an action and for executing that same action.

In sum, simple imitative motor movements can be brought about by a direct effect of perception on motor programs. As we shall see in the coming section, however, such effects can also be mediated by activation of behavior representations.

Path 2: From Perception to Behavior Representations

Effects of perception on behavior representations can be divided into two different processes. The first is the psychological process whereby perception of behavior leads to activation of the corresponding behavior representation and to imitative behavior itself. The process is reminiscent of the effects of perception on motor programs described above (and it is not always easy to disentangle the two different processes) except that here the effect of perception on motor behavior is mediated by activation of a behavior representation. The second class of processes contain instances whereby perception automatically activates associated opportunities to act (cf. the notion of affordances; Gibson, 1979; McArthur & Baron, 1983). The anecdote by William James cited earlier provides a good example. The mere perception of peanuts and raisins activates the behavior representation "eat" and leads to actual eating behavior.

The first process – that perceiving behavior leads to activation of the corresponding behavior representation in the perceiver – is very straightforward, and indeed almost trivial. It basically means that when we see someone run, we indeed activate the concept of running; or that if we see someone hit another person, we activate the representation of hitting. In the literature on attributions (e.g., Gilbert & Malone, 1995; Trope, 1986; Uleman, Newman, & Moskowitz, 1996; Winter & Uleman, 1984), activation of a behavior representation is seen as the first step in the attribution process. Before we assign traits or intentions to people, we first identify and categorize their behavior. However, it may be noted that the perception of the same behavior does not necessarily always lead to activation of the same behavior representation. How we construe and identify behavior is partly dependent on the ambiguity of the behavior and on various personal and contextual factors (e.g., Gilbert & Malone, 1995; Vallacher & Wegner, 1985).

One way in which perception activates behavior representations is when the perception of people or objects activates associated opportunities or affordances. Unlike the effect whereby perception activates corresponding action, these affordances are not innate but learned. However, the process of activating affordances is often completely automatized. Morever, we can often observe one-to-one relations between objects and activated behavior representations. Peanuts and raisins activate "eat," perception of a chair activates "sit," and the repeated perception of the bug that has been annoying one of us greatly while writing this activates "squash."

Of course, for social psychologists, instances where people (rather than physical objects) activate behavior representations are the most interesting. It is indeed known that the perception of (features of) people automatically activates typical response behaviors. Alley (1981) demonstrated that perceiving persons whose head shape and bodily features are babyish activates behavior representations such as "cuddle". Likewise, people with an elderly appearance evoke the response to protect (see McArthur & Baron, 1983, for an early review). Such responses can also be brought about by social category labels. Work by Jonas and Sassenberg (in press) demonstrate, for instance, that the label "doctor" automatically activates behavior representations such as "to consult" or "to heed advice", that the label "victim" activates "to help", and the label "star" activated "to adore" or "to admire".

Interestingly, recent evidence shows that the route from perception to behavior representations is bi-directional. Mussweiler (2006) demonstrated in a series of studies that when people were induced to engage in behavior stereotypical for a certain group, they later perceived a target person in terms of stereotypical characteristics of that group. For instance, people who were induced to walk slowly rated a target person higher on traits stereotypical of the elderly than people who walked in a normal pace.

In sum, perception activates behavior representations in two ways. First, perception of an action often leads to activation of the corresponding behavior representation (and, as an aside, vice versa), and therefore to imitative behavior. Second, perception of objects or people often activates affordances or typical response behaviors.

Path 7: From Behavior Representations to Motor Programs

The study of relation between behavior representations and motor programs can be dated back quite some time, if one is willing to equate the activation of "motor programs" with actual behavior (see Wegner, 2002 for an overview). As said earlier, already in the 19th century people were interested in ideomotor action, or the idea that merely thinking about an action is enough to engage in it. Jastrow and West (1892) used an "automatograph" in their experiments, a device with which subtle hand movements can be registered. They showed that merely thinking "left" or "to the left" leads participants to move their hand slightly to the left. Even imagining a picture on the left wall of the experimental room led participants to move their hand to the left. Later, these effects were replicated and extended by Tucker (1897) who demonstrated these direct effects of thought on action with a host of other paradigms. He for example also showed that imagining playing the piano led to subtle finger movements reminiscent of actual play. Jastrow and West concluded on the basis of their work that "thought is repressed action".

Jacobson (1932) did comparable experiments with more modern equipment and reached comparable conclusions. He asked people to imagine certain movements (such as bending an arm) and demonstrated that merely imagining bending an arm caused some muscle tension in the appropriate muscles. In other words, the (conscious) activation of a behavior representation does activate at least some components of the actual movements. Recently, Decety, Jeannerod, and colleagues (e.g., Decety, Jeannerod, Germain, & Pastene, 1991) demonstrated a host of other physiological consequences of merely thinking about a behavior. They had participants imagine activities such as weightlifting or running and showed that heart rate and respiration rate went up, as if people actually engaged in such activities.

Jeannerod (1994, 1997) demonstrated effects of activated behavior representations on motor programs. He compared people imagining an action with people engaging in these actions (again, such as weightlifting, rowing, or running) and showed that under both conditions the same motor areas became active. Some sport psychologists have also used the EMG to show that imagining an action and engaging in an action often have the same neurophysiological consequences (Hale, 1982; Paus, Petrides, Evans, & Meyer, 1993). This and other work led Jeannerod (1995) to conclude that "simulating a movement is the same as performing it, except that the execution is blocked" (p. 1421). Recent research went even further and demonstrated that merely hearing a verb or retrieving a verb from memory activates corresponding motor representations (Jeannerod, 1999; Perani et al., 1999; see also Grezes & Decety, 2001).

In sum, activation of a behavior representation (by thinking about it or hearing it) leads to activation of motor programs and to actual behavior. One may note that the work by Jeannerod shows that activated motor programs do not necessarily lead to overt behavior. Some inhibitory factors can still stop actual execution (see also Dijksterhuis & Bargh, 2001). However, it is beyond the scope of this chapter to discuss these inhibitors (see Jeannerod, 1997, for a discussion of the neurology of such inhibitors).

The Mimicry Route: The Effects Themselves

In our review of effects of unconscious mimicry, we differentiate mimicry in three different domains. We start with mimicry of speech patterns.

Speech Patterns   First, there is support for various types of imitation of speech-related variables. One phenomenon that has been studied is that of syntactic persistence, or the tendency to use certain syntax when that syntax is made cognitively available. For example, in an experiment by Levelt and Kelter (1982; see also Schenkein, 1980) an experimenter called various shops and asked either "What time does your shop close?" or "At what time does your shop close?". If the first form of the question was asked, the shopkeepers most often answered "Five o'clock", however, if the latter form of the questions was posed, the shopkeepers most often answered "At five o'clock". Syntactic structures appear to carry over from one sentence to another (see also Bock, 1986, 1989). Importantly, these effects have also been found for imitation of single words, clauses, and for the structural format of entire sentences (Levelt & Kelter, 1982; Schenkein, 1980). Additionally, Levelt and Kelter found that cognitive load did not increase speech imitation effects, which suggests that they are automatic in nature.

Neumann and Strack (2000) found that interaction partners tend to mimic the tone of each other's voice. In one study that was ostensibly about the reproduction of speech content, participants listened to a stranger read an audiotaped speech. While they were listening, participants were asked to repeat what they heard and were audiotaped themselves. Participants adopted the tone of voice of the person on the tape they heard. Thus, a sad tone of voice on the tape led to a sad tone of voice in the participant, and a happy voice elicited a happy voice in the participant.

It is important to note that participants did not see the person who delivered the speech, and did not know who the person was. This again speaks to the nonconscious nature of mimicry.

Facial Expressions   There is also abundant evidence that people imitate the facial expressions of other people (e.g., Dimberg, 1982; Vaughan & Lanzetta, 1980, Zajonc et al., 1982). As said before, yawning is an example of a very contagious facial expression that is familiar to us all. If someone around you starts to yawn, it is very common to feel the need to yawn as well. Another example of imitation of facial expressions comes from research conducted by Bavelas and colleagues (Bavelas, Black, Lemery, & Mullett, 1986, 1987). During their research studies participants witnessed a painful accident to a confederate which resulted in a wince. It was found that the participants imitated the expressions of the confederate, especially when the wince was more visible to the participant. The more visible the expression of the confederate was to the participant, the more the participant imitated the expression. In other words, the easier it was to perceive the expression, the greater the effect on their own behavior.

Research on couples has revealed similar results. Zajonc and colleagues (Zajonc, Adelmann, Murphy, & Niedenthal, 1987) reasoned that couples who have lived together for a period of time have experienced similar emotions at the same time. Since frequent facial expressions eventually lead to changes in facial lines, they predicted that partners should start to look more like one another the longer they are together. As predicted, the results of their studies showed that participants judged couples who had been married 25 years to resemble each other more than random pairs of people the same ages as the married couples and more than newly-wed couples. Although these findings were originally interpreted as evidence of shared emotional experience, they are also consistent with the hypothesis of a direct effect of perception on behavior. Frequent perception of a partner's expressions leads one to adopt those expressions repeatedly oneself which in turn leads to similarity in facial lines between the two partners.

Imitation of facial expressions is related to the study of emotional contagion (e.g., Hatfield, Cacioppo, & Rapson, 1994). Facial expressions affect emotions through a process of feedback elicited by facial muscles (Neumann & Strack, 2000; Strack, Martin, & Stepper, 1988). As a result, imitation of facial expressions leads to shared emotions. For example, seeing a happy face can lead to a happy expression on the perceiver, and the perceiver will in turn begin to feel happy as a consequence. Zajonc et al. (1987) found a strong relationship between shared facial expressions and shared emotions. They hypothesized that life partners who have grown to look like each other more would be happier together than those who have not, because their resemblance is due to a greater history of shared emotions, and shared emotions lead to a stronger bond between partners. A study supported this hypothesis, with a strong relationship between resemblance and self-reported happiness.

Behavior Matching   Nonconscious mimicry is not limited to speech and facial expressions. We also mimic others' postures, gestures, and mannerisms. Social scientists for many years simply assumed the automatic adoption of other's physical behaviors (e.g. Allport, 1968; Köhler, 1927). An early study conducted by Eidelberg (1929) provided suggestive evidence that behavioral matching was indeed a common occurrence. Participants were instructed to point to the object in the room when they heard the name of the object. The experimenter also pointed at the object but sometimes made "mistakes" and would point at a different object. These mistakes caused participants to make the same mistakes as well due to their spontaneous imitation of the gestures of the experimenter.

Bernieri (1988; see also Bernieri, Reznick, & Rosenthal, 1988) provided solid evidence for posture imitation. First, two participants (A and B) were asked to interact (interactions were videotaped). Later, the two participants A and B were asked to switch partners with another dyad, C and D, such that A interacted with C and B would interact with D. Subsequently, two videotapes were constructed on which the gestures and postures of participants A and B were displayed. One videotape showed the actual interaction between A and B. The other tape, using a splicing technique, appeared to show A and B together, but actually showed A when A was interacting with C, and B when B was interacting with D. Judges – who were unaware of which tape displayed the actual interaction between A and B, and which was the "fake" interaction – estimated the degree of posture similarity. The degree of matching was deemed greater on the first tape (the actual interaction) than on the second, providing evidence for posture matching.

A study by Chartrand and Bargh (1999) extended these effects. Their study focused on specific mannerisms rather than on basic posture mirroring. Specifically, participants interacted with two different confederates during two consecutive dyadic sessions. Each session involved the participant and the confederate taking turns describing some photographs. One confederate touched her face while the other shook her foot throughout their respective interactions with the participant. Facial expressions of the confederates also varied such that one confederate smiled at the participant while the other did not. Interactions were videotaped and coded for amount of face-touching and foot-shaking displayed by the participant.

Chartrand and Bargh found that participants were more likely to touch their own faces when they interacted with the face-touching confederate than when they interacted with the foot-shaking confederate, but were more likely to shake their own feet when they interacted with the foot-shaking confederate than when they interacted with the face-touching confederate. Moreover, mimicry was not limited to the conditions in which the confederate smiled and appeared friendly. Importantly, participants were oblivious to the confederates' subtle mannerisms during the interactions, and were all the more unaware of having mimicked these mannerisms themselves. Given that the interactions were designed to minimize any mediating motivational variables, the findings of this study support the notion that mimicry can occur as a direct result of the perception of that behavior. Thus, just like chameleons, people automatically change their own "colors" (i.e., behaviors) to blend in with their current environment.

Moderators of Nonconscious Mimicry

Several factors have recently been found to moderate nonconscious mimicry. The first of these moderators is based on the previously described findings that mimicry and rapport are related. The question arises, if mimicry serves to create liking and harmonious interactions between people, then is it possible that individuals nonconsciously mimic more when in situations in which they want to affiliate with another person? If so, this could be an example of a nonconscious process being used "strategically," to the advantage of the mimicker, in a functional and adaptive way (since we know that it does in fact lead to liking).

Goal to Affiliate

Directly activated goal to affiliate   Recent research has demonstrated that mimicking the behaviors of others is a natural response in situations where there is a desire to affiliate. For example, people who are given a conscious affiliation goal (i.e., "you will be interacting with this person as part of a cooperative task in which it is important to get along and work well together") or a nonconscious affiliation goal (i.e., subliminally primed with words related to affiliation – *affiliate, friend, together*) are more likely to mimic the behaviors of an interaction partner than people who do not have a goal to affiliate (Lakin & Chartrand, 2003). Situations where there is a conscious or nonconscious desire to affiliate activate the tendency to mimic the behaviors of interaction partners.

Lakin and Chartrand (2003) further examined a situation in which the desire to affiliate might be even stronger. They reasoned that a recent failure when trying to affiliate with another person might substantially increase the desire to affiliate with a different person. Participants were subliminally primed with an affiliation goal or not, and then were led to be successful or unsuccessful in their attempt to affiliate with a first confederate. The interaction of interest occurred with a second confederate, who shook her foot throughout her interaction with the participant. It was predicted that failing at an affiliation goal would increase subsequent affiliation goal-directed behaviors, including unintentional mimicry of the confederate's mannerisms. Results were as predicted. In the no goal condition, participants were equally likely to mimic the second confederate after succeeding or failing. However, in the affiliation goal condition, participants were much more likely to mimic the confederate if they had failed in their attempt to affiliate with the first confederate than if they had succeeded.

One might wonder whether the increased mimicry was actually helpful to participants in the failure condition who were trying to affiliate with the second confederate. The second confederate provided ratings of her interaction with each participant, and analysis of this information revealed that the most-liked participants were those who were primed with an affiliation goal and had failed in their first attempt to accomplish it. Thus, the results of this second study demonstrate that initially failing at an affiliation goal leads to increased efforts to affiliate with a new interaction partner. These efforts manifest themselves in greater mimicry of that person's mannerisms – which appears effective in increasing the liking of the mimicker.

Naturalistic triggers of an affiliation goal   In the Lakin and Chartrand (2003) studies, a goal to affiliate was directly activated in participants. But there are many naturalistic triggers of an affiliation goal. Recent evidence suggests that these situations can automatically lead to more mimicry as well.

Peers Cheng and Chartrand (2003, Study 1) assumed that college students would have a goal to affiliate with a fellow undergraduate student, whereas they would not be as motivated to affiliate with someone of a different age group – either a high school student or a graduate student. It was further hypothesized that high self-monitors would be more aware of differences in age and what that meant for them, and would therefore be more attuned to situations where they might gain a friend (the undergraduate) versus situations where they would not (high school or graduate student). Participants interacted with a female confederate, who was ostensibly a high school student, an undergraduate student, or a graduate student, who subtly touched her face throughout the interaction. The results supported the hypothesis: low self-monitors did not differentially mimic the confederate, yet high self-monitors mimicked the fellow undergraduate student more than they did either the high school student or the graduate student.

Powerful others Another type of social information that individuals might be attentive to is difference in relative power. In another study (Cheng & Chartrand, 2003, Study 2), participants were told that they were the "leader" or "worker" during an interaction with another participant (actually a confederate). It was predicted that high self-monitors would be more likely than low self-monitors to have an affiliation goal automatically activated when the situational cues indicated that it might be useful for them (i.e., when they were the worker and the other person had command over them). This was consistent with what was found: high self-monitors mimicked the confederate more when the confederate was their "leader" than when she was their "worker," whereas low self-monitors did not differentially mimic the confederate.

Feeling too different from others Another situation that might result in increased mimicry would be feeling too dissimilar from an important group. According to Brewer's Optimal Distinctiveness Theory (1991), people are in a continual quest to balance their need for *distinctiveness* (or seeing themselves as different from others) and their need for *assimilation* (or seeing themselves as the same as others). This leads to the prediction that individuals who currently feel too different from an important group (i.e., they are experiencing a heightened need for assimilation) should engage in behaviors that bring them closer to the group (i.e., mimicry). Pilialoha, Hall, and Chartrand (in prep.) tested this hypothesis by giving participants false feedback on a bogus "personality inventory" that suggested they had either a relatively rare or a relatively common personality profile (compared to other undergraduate students at the same institution). After they received the bogus feedback, they engaged in a task with a confederate who shook her foot throughout the interaction. As expected, participants who were made to feel too distinct by being placed in the rare category mimicked the confederate more than those who were made to feel the same as everyone else by being placed in the common category. Thus, participants mimicked more when they were in a situation where they felt too different from a peer group.

Ostracism Lakin, Chartrand, and Arkin (2006) expected that a recent social exclusion experience may be another factor that increases nonconscious behavioral mimicry. Because exclusion is such a negative experience, people should be motivated to engage in behaviors that will help them recover from this negative state. To the extent that behavioral mimicry satisfies this objective, people who are excluded from a social group should mimic the behaviors of a subsequent interaction partner more than people who are included in a social group.

Data from two studies support the argument that mimicry should increase after being socially excluded (Lakin & Chartrand, 2005; Lakin et al, 2006). In an initial study, they recruited participants for an experiment on visualization and description. Participants were told that they would be completing two unrelated experiments. The first involved playing an online ball-tossing game (Cyberball: Williams et al., 2000) with three other participants and trying to visualize the other players and the situation in which the game was being played. Participants were told that they would be completing a questionnaire following the mental visualization experience that would allow them to describe what they were visualizing and their experience while playing the game. With the exception of the three other players' initials (e.g., K.S.), participants had no information about their fellow players and did not expect to ever meet or interact with them. In reality, the other players were computer-controlled, and were programmed to either exclude or include participants while playing the ballgame.

Once the Cyberball game was completed, participants completed a photo description task with a new confederate. It was hypothesized that participants who were excluded would mimic the behaviors of the confederate more than participants who were included. This is exactly what happened. Controlling for the amount of foot-shaking that occurred during the baseline period, excluded participants mimicked the foot-shaking behavior of the confederate significantly more than participants who were included.

Given the relationship between mimicry and affiliation, the increase in mimicking tendencies seen after exclusion suggests that participants may be trying to recover from their exclusion experience by affiliating with their new interaction partner. It is therefore important to note that the mimicry behavior of the participants seemed to have the desired effect. When the confederate (who was blind to condition) was asked to evaluate her interactions with each participant, she reported that the interactions with excluded participants had gone more smoothly than the interactions with included participants.

A second experiment was conducted to explore whether the heightened affiliation need that results from exclusion can be addressed by mimicking the behaviors of *any* interaction partner (Lakin et al., 2006). That is, would mimicry of an interaction partner's behaviors still occur if the interaction partner did not share a salient characteristic with the excluding group? If increases in mimicry are only observed when an interaction partner shares a salient characteristic with the excluding group, then one could conclude that people may be able to "use" mimicry to re-establish themselves in groups from which they have been excluded.

In the first experiment, participants presumably thought that the confederate was someone with whom they may have been able to develop a positive relationship. They attempted to affiliate with a later interaction partner whom they thought could address that threatened need. But some people may be better able to address threatened belongingness needs than others. Mimicry should occur to a greater extent in a situation where the person who can be mimicked shares a salient characteristic with the person who was excluded *and* with members of the excluding group.

To explore this idea, female participants were recruited to participate in an experiment similar to the visualization and description one described earlier. In a female exclusion condition, unambiguous female name labels appeared next to the players' icons. In the male exclusion condition, unambiguous male name labels appeared next to the players' icons. Thus, participants were aware of the sex of the people who excluded them. Finally, during the photo description task, the sex of the confederate with whom participants interacted was manipulated. Results revealed that participants in the female exclusion condition mimicked the female confederate more than the male confederate, but there were no differences between mimicry of the female and male confederates in the male exclusion or control conditions. A planned contrast comparing the female exclusion/female confederate condition to all five of the other conditions was also significant.

In sum, ostracized individuals mimic more, but they especially mimic members of the group that excluded them in the first place, emphasizing the possibility that mimicry after exclusion is aimed at restoring bonds.

Other Moderators

Processing Style   One's style of information processing may be another moderator of mimicry. If one is in a context-dependent mind-set, she should perceive the environment more, and more mimicry should result. Van Baaren, Horgan, Chartrand, and Dijkmans (2004a) found that processing style modulates the extent to which an individual mimics others. To the degree that individuals are engaging in context-dependent processing, which involves perceiving objects and people as being integrated with the broader context, they will mimic more. If they are engaging in context-independent processing, however, which calls for perceiving objects and people as isolated and separate from the broader context, they will mimic less. This is exactly what van Baaren, Holland, Steenaert, and van Knippenberg (2003a) found. They further discovered that the relationship between processing style and nonconscious mimicry is bi-directional. In another study, those who were mimicked were more likely to later engage in context-dependent processing in a second, unrelated task.

Self-Construal   Yet another moderator of nonconscious mimicry is self-construal. Individuals at times have an independent, "Western" sense of self, and at other times have a more "Eastern" interdependent self-construal. Building on this research, van Baaren, Maddux, Chartrand, de Bouter, and van Knippenberg (2003b) primed participants with either independence, interdependence, or neither through a scrambled sentence task. Participants then engaged with a confederate who was playing with a pen. A hidden videocamera recorded the extent to which the participant mimicked the confederate. The researchers found that interdependence-primed participants mimicked more than independent-primed participants. In a follow-up study, they also found that individuals with chronically interdependent self-construals (in this study, Japanese immigrants) were also found to mimic more than those with a chronically independent self-construal (Caucasian participants). Again, the relationship was bi-directional, which was shown in a follow-up study in which participants who were mimicked were more likely to temporarily take on an interdependent self-construal.

Perspective Taking   Chartrand and Bargh (1999, Study 3) hypothesized that individual differences in empathy might influence the likelihood of mimicking the behavior of an interaction partner. Perspective-taking, or the ability to adopt and understand the perspective of others, is one component of empathy (Davis, 1983), and likely a characteristic that would have conferred an advantage on anyone who was trying to be accepted by a social group. Understanding the perspectives of others would make it easier to predict and control their behaviors, which would help the individual to have more control over their own inclusion in the group. Chartrand and Bargh (1999, Study 3) found that people who scored high on the perspective-taking subscale of Davis' (1983) empathy questionnaire were more likely than those who scored low to mimic the behavior of others. Thus, the ability to take the perspectives of others increases behavioral mimicry, suggesting that individuals who are able to affiliate with group members because of their ability to understand others also routinely utilize mimicry behavior.

Mood   One final moderator of nonconscious mimicry is mood state. Van Baaren, Fockenberg, Holland, Janssen, and van Knippenberg (in press). Building on the evidence that a positive mood leads people to rely more on automatic processes, whereas a negative mood leads to caution and to a reliance on more deliberate forms of action (see e.g., Schwarz & Clore, 1996), they hypothesized that people in a positive mood would mimic more than people in a negative mood. This is indeed what they found.

Mimicry as Social Glue

The importance of successful social interactions is certainly clear from an evolutionary perspective. Ages ago, individuals who "did their own thing" were not always able to survive and successfully reproduce (Buss & Kenrick, 1998; Johanson & Edgar, 1996). The complex environment of evolutionary adaptation was difficult to navigate, and individuals relied on their fellow humans to help with necessary survival activities (e.g., raising children, defending the home, finding food and shelter). Those who cooperated with others and maintained harmonious group relations were more likely to continue to be included in the group and were therefore at an evolutionary advantage (Caporael, 1997, 2000, 2001; de Waal, 1989; Lewin, 1993; Poirier & McKee, 1999). On the other hand, those who were ostracized from the group were less likely to survive.

Behaviors that allowed individuals to successfully maintain important group relationships would have eventually become widespread throughout the population (for a similar argument, see Cosmides & Tooby, 1992). Importantly, over time, these behaviors would have become automatized – that is, occur without conscious awareness or intention (Bargh, 1994). Automatic mimicry has been proposed to be one such behavior that fostered group relations (Lakin, Jefferis, Cheng, & Chartrand, 2003).

From an evolutionary perspective, it is easy to understand how mimicry (and a direct perception–behavior link in general) would have significant adaptive value for survival. The behavior of conspecifics tells us about our current environment, such as the presence of predators, prey, or potential mates. Our perceptions of others' behaviors should then be used to guide our own behavior. If we see others running away from a bear, we should also start running – automatically and without any conscious reflection (Chartrand, Maddux, & Lakin, 2005).

In fact, the *automaticity* of the mimicry process is crucial. In an emergency situation, one cannot afford the time to carefully consider why others are running before following suit. Indeed, our ability to perceive evolved not because we needed it to analyze and comprehend our world, but because we needed it to behave – to flee from predators, to capture prey, and to seek out potential mates (Dijksterhuis & Bargh, 2001; Milner & Goodale, 1995). Possessing a direct perception–behavior link was therefore critical to our survival as a species, and natural selection ensured that those of us who had automatic mimicking tendencies survived. Thus, it seems likely that we inherited this nonconscious mimicry from our ancestors; it may in essence be a by-product from an earlier time. Supporting this are the findings that mimicry is not limited to humans; lower animals have inherited a perception–behavior link as well (see Dijksterhuis & Bargh, 2001).

Although immediate mimicry may have been important to physical survival for the majority of human evolutionary history, it may have taken on a somewhat different role in the last couple of millennia. As our physical and ecological world has evolved, so has our social world. Although automatic mimicry may have been initially adaptive for physical survival, it may now serve to help us survive in our social world. Humans have a fundamental need to belong and to affiliate (Baumeister & Leary, 1995; Brewer, 1991); our constant motivation to get along with others and to gain social acceptance suggests that automatic mimicry is functional in modern, daily life. Thus, we argue that automatic mimicry has remained adaptive for humans, although its specific purpose might have shifted to one of bonding people together. In other words, automatic mimicry functions today as "social glue."

The Correlation between Mimicry and Rapport   Supporting these ideas of nonconscious mimicry as social glue is research on the relationship between rapport and liking on the one hand, and mimicry of postures and mannerisms on the other (Bernieri, 1988; Charney, 1966; Dabbs, 1969; La France, 1982;

La France & Broadbent, 1976; Maurer & Tindall, 1983; Scheflen, 1964). For instance, La France (1982) found that students tend to mimic their teachers' posture, and that the degree of posture mimicking was positively correlated with ratings of rapport between students and teacher. In another naturalistic setting, Maurer and Tindall (1983) found that counselors who mimicked their clients were liked more than counselors who did not mimic their clients.

In another stream of research, mother–child interactions, which are driven by close, loving, nurturing, and interdependent relationships, were found to be physically "in sync" with each other. In a demonstration of this, Bernieri (1988) recorded several different mother–child interactions with separate cameras. He created several different versions of the interactions, each with the mother on the right side of the screen and the child on the left. One version showed the true, real-time mother–child interaction, while other versions varied the mothers and children paired together, as well as the exact timing of the interactions. Participants could not indicate whether mothers were interacting with their own children or different children. However, participants rated mothers as more physically in sync with their own children than with other children.

Behavioral matching occurs even among strangers. Bernieri (1988) had dyads who did not know one another beforehand teach each other words and definitions for 10 minutes. An analysis of the videotapes of these interactions revealed that the couples whose movements were most in sync with each other also experienced the most rapport. Mimicry is not just correlated with more rapport; it is associated with more favorable evaluations on other dimensions as well. For instance, Dabbs (1969) found that participants rated confederates who mimicked them as having good ideas and as being well-informed. He also obtained evidence that "anti-mimicking", or doing the opposite of what someone else does, can have a detrimental effect on interactions. Confederates were liked less if their posture (e.g., slouching versus sitting erect) was opposite from the participants.

Consequences of Nonconscious Mimicry

Nonconscious mimicry is a curious phenomenon that turns us into "copy-cats" on a regular basis. Uncovering the moderators of mimicry helps us understand *why* we mimic and speaks to the functional nature of the effect; that we mimic more when it is to our advantage suggests that mimicry is an adaptive strategy nonconsciously used by individuals to get others to like them. But does the story of nonconscious mimicry end at the imitation of another's behavior? Research on the consequences of mimicry answers this question with a firm "no"; in fact, the downstream consequences of mimicry are not trivial. Our emotions, behavior, and self-regulatory capacity are all affected by our tendency to mimic others (and this may just be the beginning). Understanding these consequences is critical in our understanding of mimicry, and speaks powerfully to the importance of further exploration of this phenomenon.

Again, Rapport   In the previous section, we discussed research on the relation between rapport and mimicry. Chartrand and Bargh (1999, Study 2) showed that behavioral mimicry *creates* rapport. Chartrand and Bargh (1999, Study 2) examined the functionality of behavioral mimicry. Participants were engaged in a task with a confederate who either mimicked their mannerisms or had neutral, nondescript mannerisms. Compared to those who were not mimicked, participants who were mimicked later reported liking the confederate more and that the interaction had been more smooth and harmonious. These results suggest that behavioral mimicry actually increases liking between interaction partners, which is consistent with the argument that mimicking would be evolutionarily advantageous to the extent that it helps rapport develop between group members.

Prosocial Emotions   The first consequence of mimicry was described earlier in the Chartrand and Bargh (1999, Study 2) experiment in which confederates purposely mimicked the participant. Recall that participants who were mimicked liked the confederate more and thought the interaction went more smoothly than those who were not mimicked.

Ashton-James, van Baaren, Chartrand, and Decety (2006) found that prosocial emotions extend beyond the immediate dyadic interaction. After being mimicked by a confederate or not, participants were asked to engage in the Aron and Aron circle task which requires them to draw two circles to indicate how close they feel to other people in general. Greater overlap of the circles indicated greater perceived closeness. Participants who were mimicked created greater circle overlap than those who were not mimicked, suggesting that the positive emotions generated by mimicry extend beyond the dyad in which the mimicry occurs.

Prosocial Behaviors   It turns out that mimicry not only leads to prosocial emotions; it also leads to prosocial behavior. Van Baaren, Holland, Steenaert, and van Knippenberg (2003a) conducted a field experiment in which waitresses at a restaurant in the Netherlands were instructed to either mimic her patron's orders exactly, or to paraphrase the order. The amount of tips she received at the end of the night was the dependent measure and, as predicted, waitresses received more tips from patrons whom they mimicked than patrons whom they paraphrased. But this prosocial behavioral tendency extends beyond just tipping behavior. Van Baaren et al. (2003b) found that participants who were mimicked by an experimenter were more likely to help that experimenter pick up pens when she "accidentally" dropped them. Thus, being mimicked leads to more prosocial behavior towards the person doing the mimicking. Recall that prosocial emotions were found to extend beyond the mimicker to people in general. Is the same true for prosocial behaviors? Van Baaren et al. (2003b) found that the answer is yes; when participants were mimicked by an experimenter, they gave more money to charity than when they were not. Thus, the prosocial behaviors extended toward others, not just the person who mimicked you.

Persuasion   Another consequence of mimicry is persuasion; when an individual is mimicked by another person, that individual will be more persuaded by that person. Domains of persuasion thus far include important attitudes and product preferences.

Mimicry of Others as Route to Persuasion   In a preliminary study, Ferraro, Bettman, and Chartrand (2006) sought to test whether the mimicry of consumption behavior might influence subsequent preferences for the consumed product. That is, if an individual mimics the consumption of Product X without awareness, then might that lead to increased liking of Product X? If so, this would elucidate an important nonconscious source of preferences.

Participants first engaged in a task with a confederate who was casually eating one of two snacks that were in two separate bowls on a table in front of him: goldfish crackers or animal crackers. (There were two additional bowls filled with the same snacks in front of the participant.) During an ostensibly unrelated second study, participants completed a survey that asked how much they like various snacks (including animal and goldfish crackers).

Results revealed that participants with the goldfish-eating confederate ate more goldfish than animal crackers, and those with the animal cracker-eating confederate ate more animal than goldfish crackers. Importantly, participants were not aware that they had mimicked the confederate's eating behavior; the mimicry was nonconscious. Moreover, there were consequences of this mimicry for consumer preferences. That is, participants who mimicked the goldfish-eating confederate reported liking goldfish crackers more than animal crackers, and vice versa for those who mimicked the animal cracker confederate. Path analyses indicated that mimicry mediated the relationship between what the confederate ate and what the participant reported liking more. Thus, people's preferences can be partially determined by nonconscious mimicry of other people's consumption behaviors. Importantly, when asked why they like what they do, none of the participants mentioned the confederate in general, or their eating patterns or the mimicry thereof in particular. Instead, they attributed their preferences to pre-existing evaluations and/or attributes of the snacks.

Being Mimicked by Others as Route to Persuasion

Bailenson and Yee (2005) examined situations in which participants interacted with an embodied agent inside of an immersive virtual reality simulation. The realistic-looking agent (or "avatar") administered a verbal persuasive message 3 min in length. The avatar mimicked the participants in one condition, such that its head movements were an exact mimic of the subject's head movements at a four second delay. In the other condition, the avatar's head movements mimicked a different participant's head movements. Results demonstrated that (a) participants rarely detected their own gestures when those gestures were utilized by the agents, and (b) participants were more persuaded by the agent, liked the agent more, and actually looked at the agent more in the mimic condition than in the non-mimicked (i.e., recorded) condition.

Tanner, Chartrand, and van Baaren (2006) tested whether these persuasion effects would extend to real people doing the mimicking and product preferences as the domain of persuasion. Participants were introduced to an ostensibly "new product" that was supposedly in the final testing stages and would be put on the market shortly. In reality, the product was Gatorade Ice (which has a generic sports-drink taste and no color). It was in a pitcher that was kept at room temperature in order to maintain "ideal testing parameters". A confederate asked the participants various questions about the drinks they like, whether they often drink sports drinks, whether they knew various facts about sports drinks (e.g., electrolyte restoration), what drinks they preferred, and so on. During these questions, the confederate was either mimicking the posture, gestures, and mannerisms of the participant or was engaging in "anti-mimicry" – doing globally different behaviors (e.g., if the participant slouched, the confederate sat up straight in the chair; if the participant crossed his legs, the confederate uncrossed his).

After being asked the questions, participants were asked by the confederate to taste as much of the new product as they would like. They were also asked to give their opinion of the product on a survey. Results indicated that participants who were mimicked by the confederate during the presentation of the product drank more of it and stated they would be more likely to buy it than those who were not mimicked. Thus, preference effects were found on both a self-report measure and a behavioral (drinking the product) measure. Importantly, it was never clear to participants whether the confederate cared one way or the other about the product; he was not a salesman overtly trying to influence them, he was merely a "facilitator". Thus, the positive feelings generated by mimicry (Chartrand & Bargh, 1999) transferred to the product at hand, even though that product was not endorsed by the mimicker.

Tanner et al. (2006) conducted a follow-up study to test whether the role of the confederate influences the effects found on preference. Specifically, what if the confederate is invested in the product? Based on previous research, individuals should not be aware of the mimicry itself, but should be aware of the positive feelings generated by that mimicry (Chartrand & Bargh, 1999, Experiment 2). Yet when asked to express opinions about the salesperson and product, individuals would not attribute those positive feelings to the salesman, so instead they would be attributed or "funneled" toward the product. Counterintuitively, this would lead to greater liking for the product in the salesperson/mimicry condition. The study was the same as the first one, except that the confederate introduced himself in one of two ways: he was either a disinterested third party collecting data on the product, or he was working for the company and earned more money if the product succeeded. He then mimicked or anti-mimicked the participants, and their opinions toward the product were measured (i.e., how much they tasted the product, how much they liked the product, if they thought the product would succeed, how likely they were to buy the product).

Replicating the first study, Tanner et al. (2006) found that participants in the disinterested confederate condition who were mimicked liked the product more than those who were anti-mimicked. As predicted, this boost in liking for the product among mimicked participants was even stronger for those in the salesman condition. Unlike in previous research (Chartrand & Bargh, 1999), participants in the mimicry condition did not report liking the salesman more, suggesting that the positivity generated by the mimicry that would normally affect perceptions of the mimicker was entirely transferred to the product.

Self-Regulation   Finkel et al. (in press) were the first to uncover effects of mimicry on subsequent self-regulation. In this study, participants were mimicked or not by a confederate while engaging in a photo description task. This was intended as a subtle manipulation of social coordination; being mimicked would lead to less effortful, more efficient interaction, relative to not being mimicked. After the photo description task, participants engaged in a game of Operation, which is a commercial board game for children that involves removing up to 12 fake plastic body parts (e.g., heart, adam's apple) from a cartoon patient using a tweezer-like device. Each of the 12 fake body parts rested in a shallow pit surrounded by metal edges. Whenever the participant inadvertently touched the tweezers against the metal edges, the game emitted a loud buzzing noise and the cartoon patient's nose glowed red. The experimenter explained that the participant's tasks were to remove each of the plastic body parts in a smooth movement in which the tweezers did not touch the metal edges, and to do so as quickly as possible.

Given that almost all adults are capable of eventually removing all the pieces if they have sufficient motivation and concentration to do so, our central measure of self-regulation was *removal failures*, or the number of pieces participants failed to remove. We also examined the effect of the mimicry manipulation on *removal efficiency*, or the ratio of the number of pieces successfully removed divided by the total number of removal attempts the participant made. Participants who were mimicked by the confederate in the earlier task had significantly fewer removal failures and greater removal efficiency than those who were not mimicked. This study provides the first evidence that mimicry has consequences for self-regulation.

In sum, evidence for the mimicry route is abundant. We mimic various speech-related variables, facial expressions and as well as postures and gestures. Various moderators and consequences of mimicry have been uncovered in recent years.

THE TRAIT ROUTE

In what now follows, we review the research on the "trait route" (Paths 3, 4, and 7 of model). In this area of research, it is firmly established that social perception automatically affects behavior through the activation of traits, either directly or via activation of other constructs such as social categories. The vast majority of the research has been conducted in the past ten years, following the seminal paper by Bargh, Chen, and Burrows (1996) on the perception–behavior link. However, it should be noted that the effect of trait activation on overt behavior had been suggested before, although in earlier work the relative automaticity of the effects of traits on behavior was not clear (Carver, Ganellen, Froming, & Chambers, 1983; Herr, 1986). In retrospect, one may conclude that the effects on behavior described in these latter papers have not received the attention they deserved.

The review consists of three subsections. First, we discuss the process underlying the effects of the trait route in which we distinguish between the different paths in the model. We begin with the relation between perception and traits (Path 3), followed by the relation between traits and behavior representations (Path 4). Second, the effects of category or trait activation on behavior documented in the literature will be listed and discussed. In the third subsection, known moderators of the effects will be reviewed. We will first discuss contrast effects on behavior followed by a discussion on various moderators that have to do with self-relevance of the primed construct and with activation of the self-concept.

Path 3: From Perception to Traits

There are multiple ways in which social perception can lead to the activation of trait constructs, but two processes stand out in that they are widely documented and presumably heavily permeate daily life.

First, people generate trait inferences on the basis of the behaviors of others. Such inferences (e.g., aggressive, smart) are themselves not literally perceived, but are constructed upon the perception of behavior observed in the environment. These inferences are made spontaneously – that is, unintentionally and immediately – upon perception of the observable behavior (e.g., Gilbert, 1989; Uleman, Newman, & Moskowitz, 1996; Winter & Uleman, 1984). If we learn that "John drove 90 miles an hour on the highway", we automatically translate this concrete behavior into a personality trait. Without being aware of it, we draw the conclusion that John is a rather reckless person. We make trait inferences spontaneously, unconsciously and presumably very frequently, and as such they are an integral part of everyday social perception (Higgins, 1989; Higgins & Bargh, 1987).

Second, traits can be activated through activation of social categories. Social perceivers go beyond the information present in the environment through the activation of social categories and stereotypes. These social categories are activated on the basis of easily detectable identifying features of social groups, such as gender or racial features (Brewer, 1988; Fiske & Neuberg, 1990). Stereotypes are integrated collections of trait concepts purportedly descriptive of the social group in question. Unlike trait inferences, however, stereotypes are concepts that do not have a one-to-one correspondence with events being perceived.

Upon seeing a person, we not only automatically categorize that person as a member of his or her group based on these characteristics, but we usually also activate the stereotypical traits associated with that group (Bargh, 1999; Devine, 1989; Greenwald & Banaji, 1995; Lepore & Brown, 1997). Merely seeing an African-American face (even subliminally) is sufficient to cause the activation of the stereotype of African-Americans in randomly selected White US college students (Bargh, Chen, & Burrows, 1996; Chen & Bargh, 1997). Stereotype activation, like trait inferences, occurs as a natural and automatic part of the process of everyday social perception.

It seems a logical assumption that, for social categories to indeed lead to trait activation, it is necessary that they are indeed associated. If a person, for whatever reason, does not associate the category elderly with the trait slow (as people generally do, as in the Bargh, Chen, and Burrows experiment), activation of the category elderly should not lead to slowness for this person. Dijksterhuis, Aarts, Bargh, and van Knippenberg (2000; see also Brown, Croizet, Bohner, Fournet, & Payne, 2003) tested and confirmed this assumption. They first established how strongly experimental participants associated the category *elderly* with the trait *forgetfulness*. Later they activated the category *elderly* and measured memory performance among their participants. As expected, activation of the stereotype of the elderly led to forgetfulness, but only among participants who indeed associated elderly with forgetfulness in the first place. That is, only participants who indeed activated the trait *forgetfulness* after being primed with the category *elderly* displayed actual forgetfulness. Hence, the effects of social category activation on behavior were mediated by activation of traits.

It may be possible for social category activation to affect behavior directly by activation of behavioral representation. That is, category activation may elicit behavioral changes while bypassing trait activation. Kawakami, Young, and Dovidio (2002) activated the social category of elderly among their participants and showed that this slowed down participants on a reaction time task. They also obtained evidence for activation of the trait slow, but they did not find evidence for mediation of trait activation on actual behavior. Hence, Kawakami et al. (2002) concluded that social categories can directly activate behavior, without mediation by activated traits. Although it should be noted that it is hazardous to use mediation analyses to show that something does *not* mediate, their general conclusion that social categories can directly activate behavior may well hold. Especially occupational stereotypes are often strongly associated with prototypical behavior. For example, a nurse may well activate "tidying the bed" without first activating the traits "caring" or "tidy".

Somewhat less important from an ecological perspective but nevertheless interesting ways to activate traits through perception were described by a number of others. Macrae et al. (1998) demonstrated that priming participants with the Formula One world champion Michael Schumacher led to the activation of speed. In the work by Aarts and Dijksterhuis (2002) participants were either primed with animals associated with speed (cheetah, antilope) or with slow animals (snail, turtle) and they also showed participants' behavior to become faster, or slower, respectively. Recently, Nelson and Norton (2005) showed that activation of the representations of superheroes increased people's degree of helpfulness.

To recapitulate, traits can be activated in multiple ways, presumably the most important ways being through spontaneous trait inferences upon perceiving behavior and through automatic stereotype activation.

Path 4: From Traits to Behavior Representations

The relation between traits and behavior representations is bi-directional. Before, evidence was discussed demonstrating that observing behavior leads to the spontaneous inference of underlying traits (e.g., Uleman, Newman, & Moskowitz, 1996; Winter & Uleman, 1984). In such a case, behavior representations activate traits. The fact that we often do "translate" concrete behavior into trait constructs is important, as impressions of others in terms of trait constructs are much more useful than impressions of others consisting of mere behavioral instances (e.g.,

Gilbert & Malone, 1995; Kunda, 1999). In concrete terms, the knowledge that Gavin "had a fun night out with friends" is much less predictive for his future behavior than the more general knowledge that Gavin is "extraverted and out-going". It is no wonder then, that our impressions of others are indeed centered around trait constructs, rather than around concrete behavior representations. Park (1986) asked college students enrolling in a small seminar to describe their impressions of each other and found that traits accounted for 65% of the information people listed. Concrete behavioral descriptions accounted for a mere 23%.

However, the question is whether traits activate behavior representations rather than vice versa. Experiments from the "person memory" domain indeed suggest that this happens. In a typical experiment, participants read a number (between 15 and 40 or so) of behavioral descriptions about a hypothetical person. In some studies, these descriptions all imply one of two or three underlying traits (e.g., intelligent and extraverted). Evidence shows that people organize their impressions around these underlying trait constructs (Dijksterhuis & van Knippenberg, 1996; Hamilton, Driscoll, & Worth, 1989; Hamilton, Katz, & Leirer, 1980). That is, in memory the "intelligent" behaviors are lumped together in one cluster, whereas the "extraverted" ones are grouped together in a different cluster. Such clustering becomes apparent during free recall, when participants are asked to retrieve as many of the earlier encoded behavioral descriptions as possible. During recall the trait constructs are activated first, and these traits subsequently guide retrieval by activating the behaviors that are representative of that trait.

Cued-recall paradigms that are often used to investigate spontaneous trait inferences that are based on the same logic (e.g., Winter & Uleman, 1984). Here, participants read a number of trait-implying sentences. Later, they are asked to recall these sentences either without any cues, or with the underlying traits given as a retrieval cue. Generally, participants show superior recall when they have been given these retrieval cues, demonstrating that the behavior descriptions were encoded in terms of traits in the first place. For the present purposes, the retrieval process is important. The reason why behavior descriptions are easier to recall when the underlying trait is given as a cue is that the trait cue activated the behavior representation.

The Trait Route: The Effects Themselves

In reviewing the documented effects, a distinction will be made between three areas of behavior: motor behavior, interpersonal behavior, and mental perform-ance. In this section, only assimilative effects of primed constructs will be reviewed.

Effects of Category or Trait Activation on Motor Behavior   The
Bargh, Chen, and Burrows (1996) experiment in which priming the category eld-erly led to changes in walking speed is the most well-known example of effects of category activation on motor behavior. The effect has been replicated by Hull, Slone, Meteyer, and Matthews (2001), who used the same social category and the same dependent variable. Spears, Gordijn, Dijksterhuis, and Stapel (2004) primed

the category of business people among their participants and showed that it made people walk (and generally behave) faster. Macrae et al. (1998) primed people with Formula 1 World Champion Michael Schumacher and showed that people started to read faster. Finally, Aarts and Dijksterhuis (2002) made participants walk faster or slower by activating the representation of animals associated with speed (cheetah, gazelle) or slowness (turtle, snail).

Apart from the speed with which people walked, activated categories have also been shown to affect reaction times in a lexical decision task. Dijksterhuis, Spears, and Lepinasse (2001) had some participants form an impression of a group of elderly people on the basis of pictures and some verbal information, whereas other participants formed an impression of young people. In a later lexical decision task, participants who activated the category *elderly* reacted more slowly compared to control participants. Mean differences in reaction times between experimental and control participants averaged about 70 milliseconds – an effect of considerable magnitude. Kawakami, Young, and Dovidio (2002) and Schubert and Häfner (2003) also demonstrated effects of the activation of the elderly categories on reaction times.

Banfield, Pendry, Mewse, and Edwards (2003) recently presented interesting new findings that shed some more light on how category activation may affect motor behavior. They primed some participants with the category of the elderly and had participants grasp an object (an egg). They carefully analyzed the action sequence of participants and distinguished between various actual ballistic movements (e.g., movement of the arm, movement of the fingers while grasping) and the pauses between the various stages of the action sequence. Interestingly, they found that category activation did not change the speed of the actions themselves. Instead, people primed with the elderly became slower only because they paused longer between actions. Banfield et al. (2003) conclude that motor preparation, rather than motor action itself, was affected by the prime. They conclude that their findings are fully in line with neuropsychological findings. Simple visuomotor actions are dorsally driven and do not need much attentional input, making it unlikely that these actions are sensitive to activation of perceptual representations such as social categories. Motor preparation, on the other hand, is at least partly the result of prefrontal control and of the integration of various perceptual processes. This, in turn, makes it more likely that such preparation processes can be affected by activated constructs such as social categories or traits.

Effects of Category or Trait Activation on Interpersonal Behavior

Demonstrations of effects of category or trait activation on overt behavior are already numerous. Negative effects (e.g., participants being made more hostile) as well as positive effects (e.g., participants being made more helpful or cooperative) have been obtained, both as a result of category activation and of trait activation.

Carver and colleagues (Carver, Ganellen, Froming, & Chambers, 1983) can be argued to have been the first to show effects of trait priming on overt behavior. They asked participants to complete a scrambled sentence task (see e.g., Srull & Wyer, 1979) in which words or phrases related to hostility were hidden (e.g., "hits he her them"). In the experimental condition, 80% of the content of the scrambled sentence task pertained to hostility, whereas in the neutral priming condition a mere 20% did. In a second, unrelated part of the experiment, participants had to fulfill the role of a teacher in a learning experiment based on the famous work by Milgram (1963). Participants asked the "learner" (a confederate separated from the participant by a wooden partition) 34 questions, of which the confederate answered 20 incorrectly. Participants were requested to administer an electric shock to the learner upon every incorrect answer. Importantly however, the participants could determine the level of each shock. As predicted by the experimenters, participants primed with hostility gave shocks of higher intensity than control participants.

Bargh, Chen, and Burrows (1996, Experiment 3) demonstrated effects of activation of the African-American stereotype on participants' aggression. In their experiment, participants were seated in front of a computer and performed a laborious task. While engaging in this task, some participants were subliminally primed with photographs of male African-American faces whereas others were subliminally presented with male Caucasian faces. After participants had been performing the boring task for quite a while, the computer program beeped and displayed an error message stating "F11 error: Failure saving data." Subsequently, the (non-Black) experimenter pressed a button upon which the message "You must start the program over again" appeared. The participants were videotaped and the dependent variable was the level of hostility participants displayed upon hearing that they had to start all over again. As expected, both the experimenter (who was blind to conditions) as well as several independent coders rated the reaction of the participants primed with the stereotype of African-Americans as more hostile than the reaction of the participants primed with Caucasian faces. This finding was replicated and extended to the domain of self-fulfilling prophecy effects by Chen and Bargh (1997).

Recently, Anderson and colleagues (Anderson, Carnagey, & Eubanks, 2003) investigated the idea that merely processing aggressive words can elicit aggressive behavior with more ecologically appealing stimuli. In various experiments, they had participants listen to music with aggressive lyrics. Indeed, after listening to aggressive lyrics, participants felt more aggressive. Importantly, this effect held across different songs and song types.

Bargh, Chen, and Burrows (1996, Experiment 1) presented their participants with a scrambled sentence task. In one condition the scrambled sentences contained words related to rudeness (e.g., aggressively, bold, rude), whereas in a second condition the scrambled sentences contained words pertaining to politeness (e.g., respect, patiently, polite). In a third (control) condition, the scrambled sentence task did not contain words related to either rudeness or politeness. The experimenter left the room after the participants had been given the instruction necessary to complete the scrambled sentence task. Participants were requested to meet the experimenter in a different office upon finishing the task. When participants approached the experimenter, the experimenter was talking to a confederate. Of interest to the experimenters was the proportion of participants who interrupted the conversation within a time frame of ten minutes. As expected, participants who were primed with rudeness were more likely to interrupt (63%)

than were control participants (38%), whereas participants primed with politeness were least likely to interrupt (17%). These findings were recently replicated and extended by Krolak-Schwerdt (2003), who primed participants with the traits extraverted or introverted and found corresponding behavioral effects.

In experiments reported by Macrae and Johnson (1998), consequences of activation of the trait "helpful" were investigated. In their experiments, half of the participants were primed with the concept of helpfulness through the use of a scrambled sentence task, whereas the remaining participants were not primed. Upon finishing the task, the experimenter picked up her possessions from a desk (books, a paper, a bag, pens) and asked the participants to follow her to another experimenter. As she approached the door, she "accidently" dropped some of the items she was carrying. As expected, participants primed with helpfulness picked up more items from the floor (i.e., behaved in a more helpful way) than did control participants. Walther, Muller, & Schott (2001) recently showed effects on helpfulness with a more indirect priming procedure. Rather than priming the concept of helpfulness itself, they used a scrambled sentence task to prime altruism (or egoism) and demonstrated more (or less) helpfulness among participants.

Recently, Nelson and Norton (2005) made an interesting contribution. They primed participants with the category "superhero" in various experiments. It was demonstrated that priming this category led participants to be more helpful. In an ecologically appealing setting, Nelson and Norton showed that participants showed more commitment to future volunteer work. Finally, they were the first to truly show long-term effects of primes on behavior. Increased willingness to do volunteer work after activating the category superhero was still reported three months (!) after the priming episode.

A number of researchers have shown that activated traits or categories can lead to more or less cooperation in paradigms such as the Prisoner's Dilemma Game (PDG). Hertel and Fiedler (1998) were probably the first to show increased cooperation in a social dilemma after priming cooperation (although Neuberg, 1988, reports data that can be interpreted as behavior priming effects). Comparable effects were later obtained by a number of other researchers (Bargh, Gollwitzer, Lee-Chai, Barndollar, & Trötschel, 2001; Kay & Ross, 2003; Utz, Ouwerkerk, & van Lange, 2004). Others have obtained evidence of more or less cooperation with the use of other primes. Smeesters and colleagues (Smeesters, Warlop, van Avermaet, Corneille, & Yzerbyt, 2003) generally obtained changes in cooperation after primes related to might or morality, whereas Brown and colleagues (Brown, Croizet, Bohner, Fournet, & Payne, 2003) found decreased cooperation among highly prejudiced individuals after priming participants with the category African-Americans. Finally, Hertel and Kerr (2003) demonstrated that priming loyalty and equality affected choices in a mimimal group paradigm (MGP). Participants primed with loyalty showed strong ingroup bias, whereas ingroup bias was attenuated among participants primed with equality.

Although the data on the relation between priming and cooperation or competition are abundant now, the effects are not that stable between different laboratories. The experiments by Kay and Ross (2003) can be seen as an example of relatively straightforward findings. Some participants received a scrambled sentence task in which they were primed with cooperation; others received a scrambled sentence task in which they were primed with competition. Indeed, later behavior in a PDG showed corresponding effects: People primed with cooperation became more cooperative, whereas people primed with competition became more competitive. However, matters are not always that simple. Oftentimes, the effects of the primes are moderated by individual differences in social value orientation. For instance, Utz et al. (2004) only found effects of priming among dispositionally competitive individuals. Smeesters and colleagues (2003) generally found effects in the direction they predicted (i.e., morality primes increased cooperation, might primes reduced it) except for effects of morality primes on dispositionally competitive individuals: Among these people morality primes reduced rather than increased competition.

Another interesting question is whether cooperation and competition primes affect behavior directly, or whether the effects are mediated by the impression of the interaction partner or construal of the situation. In other words, does a cooperation prime lead to more cooperation directly, or does a cooperation prime lead to the expectation of more cooperation among the partner, and hence to more cooperation among the participant? This is also not clear yet. Kay and Ross (2003) found evidence for both. They showed that primes affected behavior directly, but that situational construal can strengthen the effects. Brown and colleagues (2003) did not find evidence for mediation by impression, whereas Neuberg (1988) strongly suggests such mediation. Finally, Smeesters et al. (2003) carefully conclude that primes may change the expectation of the partners' behavior and that these changed expectations guide subsequent behavior in a mix-motive dilemma. However, the evidence they present supporting their position is rather meager. For now, the most plausible conclusion seems to be that effects of cooperation or competition primes on actual behavior can be both direct and mediated by expectations or construals and that both processes can be at work at the same time in an additive fashion.

Epley and Gilovich (1999) primed participants with stimuli related to either conformity or to non-conformity. A third group of participants was not primed. Later, participants were asked to evaluate various aspects of the experiment in the presence of a number of confederates, who expressed their favorable evaluations before participants were given the opportunity to give their opinions. As predicted, participants primed with conformity evaluated the experiment more positively (i.e., they conformed more) than no-prime controls and than participants who were primed with non-conformity. Participants primed with non-conformity, however, did not conform less than no-prime controls. There are various explanations for this asymmetric finding (see Epley & Gilovich, 1999; see also Dijksterhuis & Bargh, 2001); in our view the most likely is that the social pressure to conform in the experimental situation was fairly strong, leaving less room for the non-conformity prime to be effective.

Pendry and Carrick (2001) replicated and extended the effects obtained by Epley and Gilovich (1999). They investigated conformity in an adaptation of the well-known conformity paradigm developed by Asch (1951) and had pretested several social categories on their perceived tendency to conform. Punks were seen as nonconformists, whereas accountants were conceived of as conformists. Indeed, participants who had looked at a photograph of a punk for a while demonstrated less conformity later in the experiment than participants who had looked at the photograph of the accountant.

Effects of Category or Trait Activation on Mental Performance

Like priming effects on interpersonal behavior, priming effects on mental performance have been documented extensively. Both category activation as well as trait activation have been shown to be able to improve as well as deteriorate performance in several intellectual domains.

Dijksterhuis and van Knippenberg (1998) improved people's intellectual performance by activation of both social categories as well as traits. In their first experiment, they requested some of their participants to think about college professors and to write down everything that came to mind regarding the typical attributes of professors, whereas others were not given this task. In an ostensibly unrelated second phase, participants were asked to answer 42 general knowledge questions that were taken from the game "Trivial Pursuit" (such as "What is the capital of Bangladesh?" a. Dhaka, b. Bangkok, c. Hanoi, d. Delhi). In line with the prevailing stereotype of professors as being intelligent, primed participants answered more questions correctly than did no-prime control participants. In their set of studies, it was also shown that the magnitude of the change in intellectual performance was a linear function of the strength of the priming manipulation. Participants primed for longer durations outperformed participants primed for shorter durations, who in turn outperformed participants who were not primed. In other experiments, it was shown that participants could also be led to perform worse on a general knowledge task by having them think previously about soccer-hooligans, a social group that is associated with stupidity. Finally, it was shown that performance on the general knowledge task could be changed by priming traits (intelligent or dumb) rather than social categories.

The effects obtained by Dijksterhuis and van Knippenberg (1998) have been replicated and extended a number of times by now (Dijksterhuis & van Knippenberg, 2000; Dijksterhuis, Spears et al., 1998; Haddock, Macrae, & Fleck, 2002; Hull, Slone, Meteyer, & Matthews, 2001; LeBoeuf & Estes, 2004; Schubert & Häfner, 2003). In addition to soccer-hooligans, the categories supermodels (Dijksterhuis, Spears et al., 1998; Haddock, Macrae, & Fleck, 2002) and "tramps" (Schubert & Häfner, 2003) also have the honor to be able to temporarily reduce intellectual performance. Hull and colleagues (2001) obtained their effects on intellectual performance after priming participants with "success". Finally, changes in intellectual performance have not only been shown with general knowledge questionnaires. For instance, Haddock, Macrae, and Fleck (2002) obtained positive effects of priming the category of professors on the proficiency with which participants acquired and understood new knowledge.

Various researchers have demonstrated that social category priming can affect calculus or math performance. Wheeler, Jarvis, and Petty (2001) primed their participants with the stereotype of African-Americans, after which these participants performed worse on a math test compared to control participants. Shih and colleagues (Shih, Ambady, Richeson, Fujita, & Gray, 2002) showed that priming participants with the category Asian-Americans, a group associated with very good math performance, indeed improved math performance. However, in their experiments the prime needed to be rather blatant, as a more subtle subliminal priming procedure yielded no effects.

It has also been shown that activation of the stereotype of the elderly affects memory performance among undergraduate participants (Dijksterhuis, Aarts, Bargh, & van Knippenberg, 2000; Dijksterhuis, Bargh, & Miedema, 2000; but see Levy, 1996). In an experiment conducted by Dijksterhuis, Bargh, and Miedema (2000) participants were seated behind a desk on which 15 objects were placed (a book, a pencil, a bag, etc.). Some participants were asked to answer questions about elderly people ("How often do you meet elderly people?", "Do you think elderly people are conservative?"); others were asked to answer questions about college students. After answering questions for three minutes, participants were placed in a different experimental room and asked to recall as many objects present in the previous room as possible. As expected, participants primed with the elderly stereotype recalled fewer objects than other participants. The deteriorating effects of activation of the elderly stereotype on memory have been replicated and extended by Dijksterhuis, Aarts, Bargh, and van Knippenberg (2000) who used subliminal priming procedures and different memory paradigms.

Recently, Förster, Friedman, Butterbach, and Sassenberg (2006) enhanced participants' creativity by priming. They first established that people perceive deviancy and creativity to be semantically associated. In later experiments, they indeed found that primes related to deviancy enhanced creativity. In one experiment, they primed participants with either a punk or an engineer. Participants were asked to work on creative insight problems and on analytical reasoning problems. As expected, participants primed with a punk solved more creative insight problems (and more analytic reasoning problems) than participants primed with an engineer.

Dijksterhuis and van Knippenberg (2000) demonstrated behavioral effects of activation of the stereotype of politicians. In pilot testing, they had established that politicians are associated with longwindedness. People generally think that politicians talk a lot without saying much. In an experiment, Dijksterhuis and van Knippenberg activated the stereotype of politicians with the use of a scrambled sentence procedure for half of their participants. Subsequently, participants were asked to write an essay in which they argued against the French nuclear testing program in the Pacific (this experiment was carried out in 1996). As expected, participants primed with politician-related stimuli wrote essays that were considerably longer than did control participants.

Finally, recent research shows that stereotype activation can lead to converging attitudes (Kawakami, Dovidio, & Dijksterhuis, 2003). In the experiments by Kawakami and colleagues, half of the participants were primed with the stereotype of the elderly. In different experiments, different priming methods were used, ranging from bold, conscious manipulations to subtle subliminal manipulations. In a second, ostensibly unrelated task, participants were asked to what extent they agreed with attitude statements such as "There is too much sex and nudity on TV these days" and "More people should go to church these days". Based on the prevailing stereotype of elderly as being somewhat conservative, it was predicted that primed participants would indeed become more conservative in their attitudes. The results showed that this was indeed the case. Participants primed with the elderly were suddenly worried about the amount of sex on TV and about the decreasing number of churchgoers in the Netherlands, relative to control participants who were not primed. In a conceptual replication, Kawakami and colleagues (2003) also showed that activation of the social category skinhead led to more racist attitudes.

Moderators

One may wonder, after reading about the myriad of findings listed above, whether category or trait activation always leads to corresponding behavior. The answer is, it does not. Various moderators have been identified that change or inhibit effects of category or trait activation on behavior. In what follows, we discuss the most important moderators. We begin by discussing assimilation versus contrast effects. In a second section, we elaborate on various moderators that have in common that they are in one way or another related to the self, or in which activation of the self-concept plays a role.

Assimilation versus Contrast   In the experiments described above, behavior always *assimilated towards* the implications of the activated category or trait. Activation of the category of elderly makes one slow (Bargh, Chen, & Burrows, 1996), whereas activation of the category of professors or the trait intelligent makes you smart (Dijksterhuis & van Knippenberg, 1998). These effects are reminiscent of classic experiments on effects of trait or category activation on social judgment (Higgins, Rholes, & Jones, 1977; Srull & Wyer, 1979). In this work it was demonstrated that activated traits affected participants' judgment of a stimulus person. For instance, merely activating the trait "hostile" led people to form an impression of an ambiguous stimulus person as more hostile. However, a few years after such assimilation effects on judgments were documented for the first time, social judgment researchers also started to show the opposite: contrast effects (e.g., Herr, 1986; Herr, Sherman, & Fazio, 1983; see also Wyer & Srull, 1989). For example, Herr (1986) showed that priming participants with the hostile exemplar "Hitler" did lead participants to judge a stimulus person to be less hostile, rather than more.

Dijksterhuis, Spears, and colleagues (Dijksterhuis, Spears et al., 1998) asked the question whether the same could be true for behavior. Based on earlier work showing that category or trait activation usually leads to assimilation in judgments whereas activation of exemplars usually leads to contrast (Stapel, Koomen, & van der Pligt, 1996, 1997; see also Wyer & Srull, 1989), Dijksterhuis, Spears, and colleagues assessed behavioral effects of exemplar activation in addition to category activation. In their first experiment, they either primed participants with categories or with exemplars. The categories as well as the exemplars could designate intelligence or a relative lack thereof. Concretely, participants were either primed with college professors, with supermodels, or with the specific exemplars Albert Einstein or Claudia Schiffer. After the priming procedure, participants answered a number of trivia questions. Not surprisingly in light of earlier work (Dijksterhuis & van Knippenberg, 1998) participants primed with professors out-performed those primed with supermodels. More importantly however, priming exemplars lead to behavioral contrast. Participants primed with Albert Einstein performed worse on the general knowledge questions than participants primed with Claudia Schiffer. In further studies, these effects of behavioral contrast effects were also demonstrated in the paradigm first used by Bargh, Chen, and Burrows (1996). Whereas they had shown that priming the elderly stereotype led participants to walk slower, Dijksterhuis, Spears, and colleagues (1998) showed that priming an elderly exemplar (the 88-year old Dutch Queen Mother) prompted participants to walk faster.

In later work, the finding that the activation of exemplars leads to contrast in behavior was replicated a number of times (Dijksterhuis, Spears, & Lepinasse, 2001; Haddock, Macrae, & Fleck, 2002; Nelson & Norton, 2005; Stapel & Suls, 2004; but see Macrae et al., 1998). Haddock and colleagues demonstrated, in line with Dijksterhuis et al. (1998), that activation of exemplars associated with stupid-ity makes people actually smarter, whereas activating exemplars associated with intelligence makes people more stupid. Nelson and Norton (2005) tested their ideas in a different domain. They repeatedly show that whereas the activation of the category "superhero" led people to become more helpful, activation of the exemplar "Superman" actually led to less helpfulness among participants.

Dijksterhuis, Spears, and Lepinasse (2001) extended their own initial work on behavioral assimilation and behavioral contrast to actual impression formation processes. The fact that exemplars lead to contrast whereas traits and also categor-ies lead to assimilation led to the more general assumption that concrete stimuli lead to contrast whereas more abstract stimuli lead to assimilation. From the impression formation literature it has been known that person perceivers usually form rather abstract, stereotypical impressions of people, whereas on some occa-sions they form more concrete, individuated impressions (see e.g., Bodenhausen, Macrae, & Sherman, 1999; Brewer, 1988; Fiske & Neuberg, 1990). Dijksterhuis, Spears, and Lepinasse (2001) applied this knowledge to the domain of behavioral contrast. In various experiments, they asked participants to form impressions of an elderly person or of elderly people, while manipulating various moderators that are known to affect the stereotypicality of impressions people form. In one experiment, for instance, it was demonstrated that whereas an impression of a single elderly person under normal circumstances led to contrast, an impression made under conditions of cognitive load (known to lead to more categorically-driven (i.e., stereotypical) impressions [Bodenhausen & Lichtenstein, 1987; Dijk-sterhuis & van Knippenberg, 1995; Macrae, Hewstone, & Griffiths, 1993]) led to assimilation. Based on multiple experiments, the conclusion could indeed be drawn that more stereotypical impressions led to behavioral assimilation, whereas individuated impressions led to behavioral contrast.

What causes contrast?   On the basis of the findings just discussed, one may draw the conclusion that activation of categories or traits always leads to assimilation in behavior, whereas activation of exemplars always leads to contrast in behavior. A number of findings, however, demonstrate this not to be true. It is fruitful to discuss these findings against the background of theoretical models aimed at explaining assimilation and contrast effects in social judgments. This way, we can perhaps not only determine when to expect behavioral contrast, but also why. Let us briefly look at two models that were advanced recently.

Dijksterhuis, Spears, and colleagues (1998) based their hypotheses on work by Stapel, Koomen, and colleagues (Stapel & Koomen, 2001; Stapel, Koomen, & van der Pligt, 1996, 1997). Their "Interpretation/Comparison Model" (ICM) explains assimilation and contrast effects in social judgments as the result of the presence or absence of a *comparison process*. If a primed stimulus (such as a category, trait, or exemplar) is used to interpret aspects of the person (or other stimulus) to be judged, assimilation ensues. In other words, when the trait "hostile" is activated and we are then confronted with a person who behaves in an ambiguously hostile way, we use the trait to interpret the ambiguous behavior. We interpret the behavior as more hostile, and assimilation ensues. However, on other occasions primed stimuli are used as comparison standards, and if this happens, a contrast effect is obtained. For example, if we are primed with the extremely hostile exemplar Adolf Hitler and are then confronted with an ambiguously hostile person, we start to compare ("Well, compared to Hitler he isn't that hostile") and we judge the person to be less hostile – a contrast effect.

Important in the ICM are the factors that render comparisons more or less likely. Quite a number of these factors have been identified, and we will only briefly mention the two factors we deem most relevant for the present purposes (i.e., to explain contrast in behavior). First, the "concreteness" or distinctness of the prime is important. The more concrete or distinct a primed representation is, the higher the probability is that a comparison ensues. For this reason, the probability that rather broad and vague stimuli such as categories or traits lead to comparisons is low (and hence, they usually lead to assimilation), whereas the likelihood that a distinct exemplar elicits a comparison is high (and hence, they usually lead to contrast). Second, the potential relevance of a stimulus for a comparison is very important. Simply stated, people are more likely to compare themselves to another person than to a monkey, a tree, or a frozen Margarita. Comparison relevance predicts whether we compare or not (and hence, whether we get contrast or not) and can be affected by different variables, probably the most prominent one being category membership: Comparisons within categories are more likely than comparisons between categories (Manis, Biernat, & Nelson, 1991).

Mussweiler (2003) also cites the experiments conducted by Dijksterhuis, Spears, and colleagues (1998) as supporting his "Selective Accessibility Model" (SAM). In this model, both assimilation and contrast are assumed to be the result of a comparison process. In fact, underlying Mussweiler's theorizing is the idea that judgments are by definition relative and always the result of some sort of comparative process. The *nature of the comparison*, however, is crucial for determining whether assimilation and contrast will ensue. If a certain stimulus is primed, people assess the relative similarity of the prime and the to-be-judged target. This assessment is relatively quick and holistic and the outcome determines the nature of the resulting comparison. If the prime and target are judged to be relatively similar, a similarity testing process follows, leading knowledge supporting the hypothesis that target and prime are similar to become more accessible. Such a process results in assimilation in judgment. Conversely, when prime and target are judged to be relatively dissimilar, a dissimilarity testing process follows, leading knowledge supporting the hypothesis that target and prime are dissimilar to become more accessible. This process, in turn, results in contrast in judgment.

Now can these models, developed to explain effects on judgments, be used to explain effects of activated representation on behavior? When it comes to judgments, the relation between the prime and the to-be-judged target is crucial, whereas with behavior, we have to translate this to the relation between the prime and to-be-behaving target: the self. Dijksterhuis, Spears, and colleagues (1998) did an experiment to investigate whether the contrast effects on behavior they had obtained could indeed be attributed to a comparison between the primed exemplar (in this case Einstein) and the self. Are people more stupid after being primed with Einstein because they engage in a comparison between Einstein and themselves? They indeed obtained evidence that a comparison between the primed exemplar and the self is crucial for contrast to occur. It was shown that priming professors only led to heightened accessibility of the construct of intelligence whereas priming Einstein led to the formation of an association between the self-concept and the construct of stupidity. In other words, after priming Einstein – but not after priming professors – participants draw the conclusion "I am stupid", reflecting the comparison they made between Einstein and themselves. These findings support the ICM, but they are certainly not inconsistent with the SAM.

Whereas both models make the same predictions regarding assimilation and contrast in the majority of cases, there are differences. As argued before, the ICM regards comparison relevance as a crucial determinant. We are more likely to compare things that are in some way relevant to each other. In such cases, the ICM would predict contrast. Generally, things that are more relevant are also more similar, leading to the hypothesis that primed representations that are more similar to the self should render contrast more likely. Conversely, things that are relatively similar should, according to the SAM, result in similarity testing. And this, in turn, should lead to assimilation. In other words, activating knowledge that is relatively similar to the self should lead to contrast according to the ICM, and to assimilation according to the SAM.

Both Aarts and Dijksterhuis (2002) and LeBoeuf and Estes (2004) tested the role of comparison relevance in the behavioral domain. Aarts and Dijksterhuis (2002) primed participants with either slow (snail, turtle) or fast (cheetah, antelope) animals. In addition, they manipulated the perceived comparability or comparison relevance of the animals. In one condition, they emphasized the similarities between humans and other animals, whereas in a second condition they emphasized the differences between humans and animals. Later, participants were asked to pick up a questionnaire in a different experimental room. Unbeknown to the participants, the time it took the participants to collect this questionnaire was measured. Participants who were led to believe humans and other animals are comparable showed behavioral contrast (that is, participants primed with fast animals became slow and people primed with slow animals became fast), whereas participants who were led to believe humans and animals to be completely different showed assimilation. These findings are clearly consistent with the ICM and inconsistent with the hypothesis one could derive from the SAM.

Recently, LeBoeuf and Estes (2004) extended these ideas. In various experiments they primed participants with the category college professors or the exemplar Einstein (as in Dijksterhuis & van Knippenberg 1998; Dijksterhuis et al., 1998) while additionally manipulating comparison relevance. They asked some participants to think about the prime (either Einstein or professors) in terms of how similar they were to them, whereas others were asked to think about dissimilarities. Participants' performance on trivia tests showed that participants primed with professors under similarity conditions showed behavioral contrast, whereas participants primed with Einstein under dissimilarity conditions showed behavior assimilation. In a later study they again primed participants either with college professors or with Einstein. In addition, they asked participants to list aspects of the prime (more or less replicating Dijksterhuis et al., 1998), whereas others were asked to engage in similarity or dissimilarity comparisons again. The results showed that merely listing attributes yielded results comparable to those of Dijksterhuis et al. (1998): The category professors led to assimilation whereas the exemplar Einstein led to contrast. More importantly, in the similarity and dissimilarity conditions they replicated their own results: Similarity led to contrast, whereas dissimilarity led to assimilation. In sum, the results of LeBoeuf and Estes, like those of Aarts and Dijksterhuis, are consistent with the ICM and inconsistent with the SAM.

It should be noted though, that although the above results make clear that the SAM cannot easily be extended to the behavioral domain, this does not mean that dissimilarity and similarity testing do not have effects on behavior. If similarity and dissimilarity focus are explicitly manipulated, as Haddock and colleagues (2002) did, the results on behavior can follow predictions made by the SAM. Haddock and colleagues asked participants to look at a number of pictures of supermodels. Some participants were asked to focus on similarities among them, according to Mussweiler (2001) a manipulation that fosters similarity testing in general (so also between a prime and the self). As expected, these participants started to perform better in a Trivia test. The reverse was true for people who focused on dissimilarities among the models. However, these results can also support the ICM if one is willing to assume that similarity focus led to a more categorical or stereotypical impression of the models, whereas dissimilarity testing merely led to an impression of the models as a few distinct exemplars. In that sense, the results by Haddock et al. (2002) map on to those by Dijksterhuis, Spears, and Lepinasse (2001) discussed before.

Suggestive evidence for the importance of comparison relevance was also obtained by Macrae and colleagues (1998). They found that priming the exemplar Michael Schumacher did not lead to contrast effects in behavior (as, again, exemplars usually do) but to assimilation: it made people count faster. It is probably the case that Schumacher made the construct of speed accessible, thereby causing assimilation, while the comparison was not relevant enough for the task to cause contrast. It could be that a comparison with Schumacher does not lead to the conclusion "I am slow," but that it leads to the narrower conclusion "I am a slow driver." Given that the task was a counting task that had nothing to do with driving, the comparison was not relevant enough to cause contrast. Again, this finding does seem to support the ICM.

Recently, Stapel and Suls (2004) reported a number of experiments on contrast effects in judgments and behavior, and concluded that the SAM may primarily have explanatory power in the domain of judgments when people make explicit comparisons, whereas the ICM seems to be superior in explaining effects of implicit comparisons. According to this conclusion, it is no wonder that the ICM is better suited to explain contrast effects of behavior primes. After all, primed stereotypes and exemplars hardly ever lead to explicit comparisons with the self. Instead, in the vast majority of cases these comparisons are made spontaneously and merely implicitly.

Finally, both Schubert and Häfner (2003) as well as Spears, Gordijn, Dijksterhuis, and Stapel (2004) provide additional evidence for the importance of comparison processes in causing contrast. Both groups of researchers wondered why the activation of "outgroup" categories almost always resulted in behavioral assimilation. Why would undergraduate students (i.e., participants in almost all social psychological experiments) adopt the behavior of elderly, professors, or supermodels? After all, research from the domain of intergroup relations often shows that people try to differentiate themselves from outgroups (e.g., Brewer, 1991; Tajfel & Turner, 1979). Both Schubert and Häfner (2003) as well as Spears and colleagues (2004) showed that outgroup priming can evoke behavioral contrast rather than behavior assimilation when comparisons between the self and the outgroup are elicited. This can be done, for instance, by explicitly creating an intergroup comparison (Schubert and Häfner, 2003), or by priming words related to such a comparison, such as "us–them" (Spears et al., 2004), or by merely making one's own ingroup identity (Spears et al., 2004) or self-concept (Schubert & Häfner, 2003) salient.

The Role of the Self

The experiment by Schubert and Häfner (2003) in which they primed the self-concept brings us to a second set of moderators of behavioral priming effects. In recent years, various researchers have tested the potential moderating effects of self-related phenomena. In this section, these effects will be summarized. The research will be divided into two groups. The first group of studies describes the role of the *self-relevance* of the prime. The second group pertains to work where the self is *activated* during the behavior priming process.

Self-Relevance   In the work reviewed above, the experimental participants were primed with categories to which they did not belong. The categories, in other words, were never self-relevant. What happens when categories are self-relevant? In other words, what happens when the category elderly is primed among elderly participants themselves?

There is no a priori reason why activated categories should not affect behavior among people for whom the category is self-relevant, and indeed it does. We know that activation of the category of the elderly slows down both young people (Bargh, Chen, & Burrows, 1996) and old people (Hausdorff, Levy, & Wei, 1999), whereas the same prime can also lead to worse memory performance among both young people (Dijksterhuis, Aarts, Bargh & van Knippenberg, 2000) and old people (Levy, 1996). In addition, Shih, Pittinsky, and Ambady (1999) showed that activation of the category of Asian-Americans (associated with superior math skills) led to improved math performance among Asian-American women, whereas activation of the female stereotype (associated with poor math abilities) among these same participants led to poor math performance.

Importantly however, there are reasons why the effects on behavior may well be *stronger* for self-relevant categories than for non self-relevant categories. First, it is possible that the same priming episodes lead to stronger activation levels when the priming is self-relevant, because people are more sensitive to self-relevant stimuli (e.g., Levy, 1996; Shih, Ambady, Richeson, Fujita, & Gray, 2002). Evidence for this increased sensitivity comes from people who have studied effects of category activation of the elderly on memory performance. Levy (1996) primed the category among both elderly and young participants. However, an interesting potential moderator was tested. In one set of conditions the category was activated with the use of negative terms related to the elderly (e.g., senile), whereas in another set of conditions the category was activated with the use of positive terms (e.g., experienced). The findings showed that activation of the category in a negative light deteriorated memory performance, whereas activation of the positive category improved it. However, this was only true for old participants. Young participants showed no effects. This research shows that primes that lead to effects among people for whom the prime is self-relevant can be too subtle to lead to effects among people for whom the prime was not self-relevant. Comparable findings were also reported by Hess, Auman, Colcombe, and Rahhal (2003) and by Hess, Hinson, and Stratham (2004).

Shih and colleagues (Shih, Ambady, Richeson, Fujita, & Gray, 2002) made self-relevance of the prime the focus of their research. They activated the Asian-American category among both Asian-Americans and non Asian-Americans in either a blatant way or a subtle (subliminal) way. Their results showed that both blatant and subtle self-relevant category activation could affect behavior, whereas non self-relevant category activation only activated behavior when the activation was blatant. This should not be taken as evidence that subliminal priming only works for self-relevant categories (as others have shown otherwise), but it does support the general claim that people are more sensitive to self-relevant primes, and hence that effects of self-relevant primes on behavior are sometimes bigger and easier to obtain.

A second way in which self-relevant categories can exacerbate effects on behavior is through stereotype threat (e.g., Steele, 1997; Steele & Aronson, 1995;

Steele, Spencer, & Aronson, 2002). Stereotype threat can occur when a negative self-relevant (and task-relevant) stereotype is activated. Under such circumstances, performance can be disrupted, for instance because people may become aware that they run the risk of confirming the stereotype. Such feelings can cause anxiety and thereby deteriorate performance. It has been shown, for instance, that Blacks perform worse than Whites on standardized tests when the category of Blacks is activated, but not when the category is not activated. It is beyond the scope of this article to elaborately discuss stereotype threat, but it may be noted that stereotype threat differs from behavior priming effects in various ways. First, for effects of threat to occur, it is necessary that a category is self-relevant and the behavior important. Second, effects of threat are mediated by a disruptive state resulting from the fear to confirm a stereotype. This subsumes that for threat to occur, people should at least temporarily be consciously aware of the negative stereotype. In our view (see also Dijksterhuis & Bargh, 2001) effects of behavior priming and stereotype threat can be at work simultaneously and have additive effects.

Self-Activation   In the experiment by Schubert and Häfner (2003) discussed earlier, self-concept activation changed an assimilation effect into a contrast effect, presumably by eliciting a comparison between the self and the prime. Is it true that self-concept activation renders a contrast effect more likely? Perhaps it is, but unfortunately the current state of affairs is that the relation between self-concept activation and behavior priming is unclear and the results are inconsistent.

Dijksterhuis and colleagues (Dijksterhuis, Bargh, & Miedema, 2000; Dijksterhuis & van Knippenberg, 2000) investigated the potential moderating role of self-focus. Their analysis was based on the literature on action control (Norman & Shallice, 1986; Shallice, 1988) and on a vast body of research on self-focus. The literature on action control demonstrates that sometimes multiple action tendencies are active. Under these circumstances, these various action tendencies strive for mental dominance. The one that eventually gains dominance inhibits the other action tendencies and guides overt behavior. Increased self-focus, or increased self-concept activation, is known to activate action tendencies (Carver & Scheier, 1981; Duval & Wicklund, 1972; Gibbons, 1990). Self-focus makes norms, behavioral standards, and important goals more salient and more accessible. This means that under conditions of self-focus, effects of perception on behavior may be overruled. After all, as the literature on action control suggests, activated norms or goals can inhibit other action tendencies, such as primed constructs. This hypothesis was tested and confirmed in various experiments. Participants were seated in front of a mirror (a manipulation known to enhance self-focus; see Duval & Wicklund, 1972) or not while they were primed with a social category. In various studies it was shown that participants not seated in front of a mirror showed normal behavior priming effects, whereas participants with increased self-focus showed no behavioral priming effects.

Shortly after Dijksterhuis and colleagues published their findings, Hull and colleagues (Hull, Slone, Meteyer, & Matthews, 2002) basically published the opposite effects. They assessed differences in people's self-consciousness prior to priming them with traits or categories, and obtained evidence for their hypothesis that only people high in self-consciousness show behavior priming effects. They found this moderating effect a number of times with the use of different primes and different behaviors.

Wheeler, Jarvis, and Petty (2001) obtained results that are to some extent comparable to those of Hull and colleagues (2002). They primed their participants with the stereotype of African-Americans, after which these participants performed worse on a math test compared to control participants. The participants were all non African-Americans, but Wheeler et al. (2001) reported an interesting moderator. Their priming procedure consisted of the instruction to write about a day in the life of a certain individual (either a person with a typical African-American name or with a typical Caucasian American name). Some participants wrote their short stories in the first person (thereby adopting the perspective of the target and activating the self-concept), while others wrote their stories in the third person. The participants who activated their self-concept showed stronger priming effects than participants who wrote in the third person.

In sum, Schubert and Häfner (2003) showed that self-concept activation leads to contrast, whereas Hull et al. (2002) and Wheeler et al. (2001) demonstrated that self-concept activation is associated with larger (assimilative) behavior priming effects. Finally, Dijksterhuis and van Knippenberg (2000) showed that self-concept activation inhibits behavioral priming effects. Of course, the manipulations used in the various experiments differ, and it is very well possible that the results can be reconciled by additional research. For now however, the relation between the self and behavior priming is unclear. To put it bluntly, it is a bit of a mess.

Wheeler, DeMarree, and Petty (2005) shed some more light on the relation between self and behavior priming with their recently proposed "active self-concept account" of behavior priming effects. They argue that primes exert effects on behavior to the extent that they become part of a working self-concept. That is, if we prime people with the category of professors, various traits associated with professors not only become active, but they are also seen as belonging to the self. The more people feel these traits are part of the self-concept, the stronger the effects on behavior. This is an interesting idea that can indeed provide a deeper understanding of the findings by Hull and colleagues (2002) and Wheeler and colleagues (2001), demonstrating that self-concept activation results in larger behavior priming effects. On the other hand, a model involving an active role of the self-concept may have difficulties explaining the finding that even very negative primes have been shown to lead to behavioral assimilation. Assuming a role of the self in behavior priming also subsumes some sort of motivational or "critical" element, in the form of something that decides which primes can be made part of the self-concept and which primes cannot. Given that activating categories such as racists, hooligans, and tramps have been shown to affect behavior, the conclusion should be that there likely is no such critical gatekeeper. Alternatively, merely assuming that the self is a sponge, simply absorbing all primes, renders the whole idea of the self as a mediator rather superfluous, in our view.

To summarize, evidence for the trait route is abundant. Activated categories and traits affect overt behavior and presumably permeate daily behavior continuously. Usually these effects are assimilative, however, sometimes behavioral contrast ensues. Finally, various self-related phenomena can inhibit or exacerbate behavioral priming effects.

THE GOAL ROUTE

In what now follows, we review the goal route (Paths 5, 6, and 7). We first give a brief account on the conceptualization of goals and the underlying processes that allow human beings to act on and strive for goals automatically, followed by a brief review of the evidence of automatic goal pursuit. We confine this review to studies that explicitly address and examine the influence of mere perception or priming on goal-directed, motivational activity. Finally, findings from recent studies will be discussed that shed light on the nature of the cognitive processes supporting automatic goal pursuit.

Automatic Goal Pursuit

Central to the idea of automatic goal pursuit (the goal route in Figure 2.1, Paths 5, 6, and 7) is the assumption that goals are mentally represented as desired states pertaining to behaviors (e.g., consuming fruit, performing well, socializing) or outcomes (e.g., owning money, being proud; see summaries by Carver & Scheier, 1998; Gollwitzer & Moskowitz, 1996). Furthermore, goals are assumed to be part of knowledge structures including the context, the goal itself, and actions as well as means (i.e., behavioral representations) that may aid goal pursuit (Aarts & Dijksterhuis, 2000a,b; Bargh & Gollwitzer, 1994; Kruglanski, Shah, Fishbach, Friedman, Chun, & Sleeth-Keppler, 2002). For example, the goal of consuming fruit may be related to eating a banana while having lunch in the University cafeteria. Or, a visit to an exclusive restaurant may be connected to interacting with good friends and the desire to socialize and go out. Thus, people can rely on contextual as well as behavioral information in order to set, adopt, and implement goals.

Conceptualizing goals as representations of desired states suggests the operation of two informational features (Aarts, Custers, & Holland, in press; Custers & Aarts, in press): a cognitive one and an affective-motivational one. The cognitive feature provides the knowledge of the state that is desired and, referred to as standard or reference value, is the point at which perception and cognition are directed to attaining and monitoring progress towards the goal (Carver & Scheier, 1981; Miller, Galanter, & Pribram, 1960; Powers, 1973; Schank & Abelson, 1977). The affective-motivational feature signals the individual that the state has incentive value, and is desired and worth pursuing (Peak, 1955; Pervin, 1989; Young, 1961). Perception of goal-related stimuli, then, affects goal-relevant cognitive as well as motivational processes.

Theory and research emphasizing the role of conscious awareness in goal-directed behavior have taught us a lot about people's explicit experiences and thoughts accompanying their goal pursuits. We have learned that goal-setting is characterized by a conscious reflection process, and that goal adoption (i.e., the implementation and striving of goal-directed action) is associated with conscious intent (e.g., Bandura, 1986; Deci & Ryan, 1985; Gollwitzer, 1990; Locke & Latham, 1990; Oettingen & Gollwitzer, 2001). However, this research does tell us little about the possible unconscious processes that initiate and guide people's goal pursuits, that is, whether the mere perception of goal-related stimuli affects the goals we set, adopt, or implement. Accordingly, in our review of research that bears on the perception–goal–behavior route, we organize previous research into knowledge priming effects on three processes that are commonly distinguished in research on goal-directed behavior. The first is goal-setting and refers to the process by which perceptual processes lead to the formation of goals. The second process is goal adoption. This process describes how perception of our social environment leads to the activation of goals. Both goal-setting and goal adoption can be classified as effects of perception on goals (Path 5 in the model). Finally, goal implementation refers to the link between goals and behavior representations (Path 6). Whereas the scientific study on automatic goal-directed behavior mainly has focused on priming effects on goal adoption and goal implementation, recently researchers have began to explore the effects of priming on goal-setting. We turn to this latter issue first.

Path 5: From Perception to Goals: Goal-setting

Goal-setting commonly refers to the process leading to an explicit statement or description of the goals one wants to achieve. Goal-setting emerges when a person needs to disambiguate a given goal situation, or otherwise is triggered to reflect on and describe one's desires and goals before or after action performance. Given that conscious awareness usually accompanies goal-setting tasks, the intriguing question is whether and how goal-setting may be guided by the mere perception of information related to the goal state. That is, do our explicitly stated goals and wants allow for influential processes that occur outside of conscious awareness?

We know that the perception of social categories, such as stereotypes and exemplars, colors people's explicit social judgments without their awareness of the source or the influence on their judgments (e.g., Dijksterhuis et al., 2005; Higgins, 1996). These effects occur because the activated knowledge is applicable to the judgmental task at hand. In a similar vein, priming effects on goal-setting arise from facilitated access to representations of goal-relevant information in memory (e.g., Aarts, Dijksterhuis, & De Vries, 2001; Moskowitz, 2002; Strahan, Spencer, & Zanna, 2002). For instance, research on thirst and drinking by Aarts and co-workers (2001) illustrates how the accessibility of drinking-related information emanating from the feeling of thirst can guide assessment of drinking goals. In a task allegedly designed to assess mouth-detection skills, some of their participants were made to feel thirsty, whereas others were not. Results revealed that participants who were made thirsty responded faster to drinking-related items in a lexical decision task, and performed better on an incidental recall task of drinking-related items, relative to no-thirst control participants. This enhanced accessibility of goal-relevant material, then, may guide the assessment of one's goals and plans. That is, the priming of goal-related information renders the goal representation more likely to adjust explicit expectations and wants, given the appropriate goal context ("Can I get you something?"). This nonconscious accessibility effect on explicit goal assessment can occur in several ways.

Priming may affect goal-setting directly. Such direct influence materializes when people have to describe the goals they aim to attain in a concrete situation or certain point in time. For instance, Custers and Aarts (2006) used a parafoveal priming method to enhance the accessibility of the goal of looking well-groomed outside of participants' conscious awareness. Next, they asked their participants to list five attributes that would describe how they wanted to look physically. The priming effects were tested on a goal-setting index that reflected both primacy and frequency of nominating the goal (see also Higgins et al., 1982). Results showed that subliminal priming of the goal led to stronger goal-setting: Compared to a no-prime control condition, participants in the prime condition described their desire of personal physical appearance more in terms of looking well-groomed.

In another recent study, Holland, Hendriks, and Aarts (2005) examined whether the mere perception of odor is capable of directly guiding action plans. They exposed participants to the scent of all-purpose cleaner without participants' conscious awareness of the presence of the scent. Because the scent of all-purpose cleaner was assumed to enhance the accessibility of the concept of cleaning, Holland et al. hypothesized that this behavior concept would be more likely to be used in describing one's future home activities. Thus as a measure of goal-setting, participants were asked to list five activities that they wanted to do during the rest of the day. As it turned out, in the scent condition participants were more likely to include cleaning in their plans than participants in the control condition. These findings suggest that accessible goal representations are readily used when people retrieve attributes and plans to shape and arrive at a goal statement.

Wegner's (2002; see also Wegner & Wheatley, 1999) theory of apparent mental causation provides another different possibility of how priming effects on goal-setting occur. Normally, the thoughts people have prior to action and result-ing desired effect are experienced as goal intentions, and are felt to cause the behavioral event. People are not always aware of the causes of their actions, and therefore heavily rely on effect information to arrive at a sense of goal-setting ("Did I want to cause that?"). However, because one cannot directly observe causal connections between one's own actions and resulting effects, the assess-ment of goal-setting is an inference and not something directly observable. For example, when one pushes a button and a coke comes out of a machine, one can only infer that the coke was the result of the action and desire to get it (even though one can never be sure whether the coke came out by itself). According to Wegner (2002), in such cases the mind is a system that produces appearances for its owner, which may lead to *apparent mental causation*: the experience we have of wanting to cause events that arises whenever our thoughts are inferred to cause these events. Thus, the mere priming of the representation of action effects enhances the feeling that one wanted to cause the effect when it actually occurs.

In a recent test of this idea, Aarts, Custers, and Wegner (2005) designed an experimental set-up in which participants and the computer independently moved a rapidly moving square on a computer display. Participants had to press a key, thereby stopping the movement. However, the participant or the computer could have caused the square to stop on the observed position, and accordingly the stopped position of the square could be conceived of as the potential effect resulting from participants' action of pressing the stop key. The location of this position was primed or not just before participants stopped the movement. Because the stopped position was determined by the computer, actual control over causing the stops was absent. Results showed that subliminal priming of the position enhanced feeling of wanting and causing the square to stop. Subsequent experimentation demonstrated that this process of authorship ascription does not require intentional thinking in order to occur, thus bolstering the idea that goal-setting can merely follow from a belief-like mental state. In other words, a person may feel that she behaved in a specific goal-directed way because she thought about the goal or outcome just before it occurred (see also Aarts, in press).

To recap, priming or the mere perception of goal-related stimuli can influence explicit goal-setting measures in several ways. Accessible goal representations guide the construal of the situation pertinent to goal-setting, and are used (prior or after action performance) to arrive at goal-setting assessment. These effects are nonconscious, in the sense that people are not aware of the fact that the primed goal information guides their goal-setting responses. Accessible goal information, then, seems to enter consciousness because this information is applicable to the goal-setting task at hand.

It is important to note that priming does not always affect measures of goal-setting. For example, in a recent set of studies we assessed goal priming effects on explicit measures of goal-wanting as to strongly positive, desirable goals, such as the goal of socializing or seeking casual sex among heterosexual male students, and did not observe differences between primed and no-primed control participants on goal-setting (Aarts, Custers, & Holland, in press; Aarts et al., 2004). These findings suggest that priming may not guide explicit goal-setting when people already have a strong and clear goal in their mind and do not need to disambiguate their desire for the goal (cf., Kay, Wheeler, Bargh, & Ross, 2004). In addition, if the goal is chronically accessible (e.g., due to frequent goal activation and pursuit), priming is less likely to affect goal-setting when retrieving attributes or plans to describe one's goals. For instance, Custers and Aarts (2006) showed that priming the goal of looking well-groomed only caused non-chronic participants to refer to this goal attribute to describe their desire of physical appearance, whereas those chronic on this goal listed it irrespective of priming. In short, when a goal preexists as a desired state and can be easily accessed in the individual's mind, conscious goal-setting seems to be a redundant step in the process of goal pursuit. In principle, such goals can operate outside of conscious awareness. Accordingly, priming the representation of these goals may directly lead to goal adoption.

Path 5: From Perception to Goals: Goal Adoption

Goal adoption occurs if a person implements and strives for the goals assigned or suggested by other people. People automatically adopt a goal to the extent that the goal signifies an instant positive, desired state or incentive to themselves in the situation at hand (Aarts, Dijksterhuis, & Dik, in press). Once the desired goal is activated, people will recruit resources in order to enact and work for the goal, to select means and procedures to attain the goal, to keep the goal mentally alive until it is attained, or to shield it from interfering goals (Brehm & Self, 1989; Geen, 1995; Hyland, 1988; Lewin, 1951). Thus, a goal that is primed in the course of perceiving goal-relevant stimuli should automatically direct as well as energize activity that is instrumental in attaining the goal.

One of the first empirical demonstrations of this notion comes from Chartrand and Bargh's (1996) research program on goal priming effects on information processing. In one of their studies, they subliminally primed their participants either with an impression formation goal or not by parafoveally exposing them to words such as "impression", "judgment". Next, they explored whether the nonconsciously activated goal led to more on-line judgments than to memory-based judgments. Several other studies have shown that explicit instructions to form an impression of a specific target cause individuals to form evaluative judgments as soon as information is provided about the target (hence, the term "on-line"). In other words, this research shows that people readily adopt impression formation goals they receive from other persons (e.g., the experimenter). When a subsequent judgment of the target is required, they rely on the now available judgment that is formed on-line, but otherwise consult memory of the information of the target to arrive at the judgment (e.g., Custers & Aarts, 2003; Lichtenstein and Srull, 1987; McConnell, Leibold, & Sherman, 1997; for a discussion on this topic, see Hastie & Park, 1986). Chartrand and Bargh showed that goal priming indeed led to more on-line rather than memory-based judgments, suggesting that participants automatically implemented the mental activity instrumental in attaining the impression formation goal.

Further research established that (conceptual) priming of goals via exposure to words that are closely related to them exerts an unconscious influence on overt action. For example, Bargh and colleagues (2001) unobtrusively exposed participants to words such as "strive" and "succeed" to prime the achievement goal (a goal that is held by most students), and then gave them the opportunity to perform well (finding as many words as possible in an anagram puzzle task). Results indicated that participants primed with the achievement goal outperformed those who were not primed with the goal. Bargh et al. (2001) also demonstrated that such goal priming leads to qualities associated with motivational states or "goal-directedness", such as persistence and increased effort in working for the goal. These, and other recent experimental demonstrations (e.g., Hassin, 2005; Lakin & Chartrand, 2003; Oikawa, 2004; Shah, Friedman, & Kruglanski, 2002; Sheeran, Aarts, et al., 2005), indicate that the mere activation of a goal representation suffices to motivate people to work on the primed goal without conscious thought and intent.

The work alluded to above shows that goal adoption can be automatically put in place if the representation of the goal is *directly* primed. Recently, researchers have started to identify the specific aspects in the social environment that provide information of others' goals. Thinking about others in terms of their goals allows an understanding of their intentions, and to anticipate how, when, and where these others may act on the basis of these intentions (e.g., Heider, 1958; Meltzoff, 1995). Furthermore, perceiving other people's goals may have important implications for one's own behavior. For instance, it has been argued that humans and great apes can use others' goals to represent, organize, and guide their own courses of goal-directed actions (Byrne & Russon, 1998; Tomasello, Kruger, & Ratner, 1993). Specifically, an appreciation of the goals motivating other people's movements allows one to entertain similar goals and to try to attain them oneself. Knowing the goals of others, then, is not only important for a direct understanding of the intentions of people we interact with, but also for the successful pursuit of one's own needs, desires, and goals. From this perspective, three social sources of automatic goal adoption have been studied: when goals are inferred from the behavior of others; when goals are activated in the presence of important others; and when goals are triggered by social stereotypes.

Goal Adoption and the Perception of Other People's Behavior As social beings, humans attribute goals to other agents' behaviors. Although goal attribution is traditionally treated as a deliberative and reflective process (e.g., McClure, 2002), there is research to suggest that people automatically – that is, without conscious intent – infer the goals they perceive in others' behavior while reading text (for an overview, see Aarts, Dijksterhuis, & Dik, in press). Studies on text comprehension have shown that people automatically draw goal inferences when they encounter scripted behavioral information (Hassin, Aarts, & Ferguson, 2005; Long & Golding, 1993; Poynor & Morris, 2003). For instance, in a test of their Automatic Causal Inference (ACI) model, Hassin et al. (2005) exposed participants to sentences that described a behavior performed to attain a specific goal (e.g., "the student is cycling to the campus as fast as he can" implies the goal of attending a lecture), or a similar behavior that does not imply this goal (e.g., "the student is cycling away from the campus as fast as he can"). The emergence of goal inferences was assessed by measuring enhanced mental accessibility of the goal representation in a lexical decision task after each sentence was read. Results showed that goal-implying sentences did enhance the accessibility of the goal representation, indicating that goals were inferred. Of importance, these causal inferences occurred without conscious intent; participants did not require explicit instructions and were unaware of their intentions to make them. These findings provide strong evidence for the notion that people automatically infer other people's goals from descriptions of behaviors.

An interesting implication of the automatic goal inference effect established by Hassin and colleagues is that people may also be able to automatically adopt and thus strive for the goals they infer from or perceive in others' goal-directed actions. Evidence for such automatic goal adoption comes from a recent study conducted by Aarts et al. (2004). Aarts and colleagues reasoned that goals inferred from another person's actions may be readily adopted when these goals represent a positive, desired state for the perceiver (cf. Heider, 1958), thus leading to what they termed *goal contagion*. To investigate this, in one of their studies they employed a text reading paradigm to briefly expose students to a short script implying the goal of earning money or not. After reading the goal-implying scenario, participants were told that they could participate in a lottery in which they could win money, but only if there was enough time left. They were then given a mouse-click (filler) task, and the question was whether participants would speed up their performance (as a mean) to make sure that they could participate in the goal-relevant task. Results showed that participants who were exposed to the behavior implying the goal of earning money were indeed faster than those in the control condition. These behavioral changes occurred without the students' conscious intent, and were more pronounced when their desire to earn money was relatively strong at the moment of participating in the experiment. These findings were replicated in another experiment testing automatic goal-adoption effects after exposing heterosexual male students to a written scenario implying the goal of seeking casual sex.

The research discussed above suggests that the human system is well-tuned towards adopting goals they infer during reading text about a specific pattern of actions performed by a person. Inspired by Heider and Simmel's (1944) seminal work on causality and social perception, in a recent set of studies we explored whether this goal contagion effect also pertains to the mere perception of animated movements of objects (Dik & Aarts, 2005). In particular, we tested the basic idea that effort is an important characteristic of motivational goal-directed behavior (e.g., Bindra, 1974; Geen, 1995; Toates, 1986; Wright, 1996), and is therefore naturally used as a perceptual cue to identify the goals driven by the observed movement. In our experiments, we exposed participants to a specifically designed movie featuring animated movements of a ball that implied the goal of helping. The amount of behavioral effort in pursuing the implied goal was experimentally manipulated by varying the number of different movements the ball initiated in trying to attain the goal. Results showed that an increase in perceived amount of effort led to stronger automatic inferences of the implied goal, as was established by enhanced accessibility of the goal representation in a word completion and lexical decision task. Furthermore, perceiving more effort made participants more strongly pursue the inferred goal of helping. These findings indicate that an increase in perceived amount of effort in goal pursuits leads to stronger goal inferences and facilitates the occurrence of automatic goal adoption. Moreover, the findings suggest that the mere perception of an agent's movements may cause the perceiver to access and pursue the very same goal implied by the movements.

Goal Adoption and the Perception of Significant Others   Goals may also be automatically adopted from significant others. Research has shown that goals and resultant actions are activated when people are exposed to the names of friends, parents, and spouses (Fitzsimons & Bargh, 2003; Shah, 2003). For example, Fitzsimons and Bargh (2003) hypothesized that people readily take on the goals they share with others on the basis of the interpersonal interactions they have with them. Hence, priming the names of these others leads to the automatic adoption of the goals associated with them Accordingly, capitalizing on the notion that the goal of helping is part of, and strongly associated with interpersonal

interactions with good friends, Fitzsimons and Bargh found that participants who were merely instructed to think of a good friend (compared to a control group) more often participated in a subsequent task as a possible means to help. These automatic goal-adoption effects were replicated for different relationships and different interpersonal goals, such as child–mother relations and the goal of achievement, and were moderated by the degree to which participants possessed the goal under investigation themselves.

In a slightly different version of automatic goal adoption upon exposure to important others, Shah (2003) examined the priming effects of the names of significant others from the perspective of an inner audience function. In much of our social relationships with significant others we want to please, and to be accepted by them and pursuing the goals they have for us may be a means to this end. Because interpersonal relationships may become well-established, the mere presence of close others can lead to the automatic adoption of the goals we associate with them. To demonstrate this idea, Shah (2003) gave participants an anagram task. However, before participants took the task they were asked to list the name of a significant other who would want them to perform well on the task and who does not want them to possess this goal attribute. Next, participants were subliminally primed with the name of one of the nominated persons during a lexical decision task assessing the accessibility of the task goal. They then filled out questions about commitment to this goal and finally performed the anagram task (the names of the others were primed again before each anagram trial). The type of prime influenced the anagram task performance: Participants primed with the "do your best on the task" name performed better. However, this pattern of results only showed up for those who felt close to the person they listed at the beginning of the study. In other words, persons who are really close to us may implicitly force us to adopt the goals and standpoints they have for us. If they like us to be good at a task, we perform better on the task, and if they do not like us to be good, we simply leave out an additional effort to perform on the task.

Goal Adoption and the Perception of Social Groups

There are two lines of research showing that features of social groups are capable of automatically activating goals and subsequent goal-directed activity relevant to the situation at hand. One such research program comes from Moskowitz and colleagues' work on chronic egalitarian motives (that is, an enduring and strong motivation to treat all people equal) and social stereotyping (Moskowitz, Gollwitzer, Wasel, & Schaal, 1999; Moskowitz, Salomon, & Taylor, 2000). In one set of studies, Moskowitz and co-workers (1999) exposed their participants to a prime (a photograph of a male vs. female) that was then followed by an attribute (a personal trait) that participants were asked to pronounce. Nonchronics showed clear evidence for stereotype use – response latencies to stereotypical female traits were faster after female (vs. male) primes. Chronic egalitarians, however, did not show this stereotyping effect, even when the stimulus onset asynchrony was too short to allow for conscious control. Importantly, Moskowitz et al. further showed that people who have a chronic egalitarian goal towards women are well aware of the cultural stereotypes of women, suggesting that the control in stereotyping upon exposure to the stereotyped group does not result from differences in associations between the category *women* and stereotypes. In another line of experimentation Moskowitz and colleagues (2000) established similar effects with the African-American stereotype. More specifically, in this work they suggest that for chronic egalitarians black primes automatically activate their egalitarian goal that, in turn, controls the stereotype – resulting in what they term "preconscious control".

In another line of research, Aarts and colleagues (Aarts, Chartrand, et al., 2005) tested and confirmed the hypothesis that activation of a social category causes individuals to pursue the goals that are stereotypically associated with these categories (see also Bargh et al., 2001; Wheeler & Petty, 2001; for proposing a potential goal-directed behavior priming effect as a result of stereotype activation). Aarts et al. (2005) subliminally primed participants with social groups (e.g., nurses) that are strongly stereotyped in terms of the goal of helping. Upon finishing the study, participants were asked to provide feedback on an earlier performed computer-skill task that was allegedly designed by a fellow student. At this point participants could either decide to leave the lab as quickly as possible or to stay a little longer and give feedback to attain the desired state of helping. The question was whether helping-goal-primed participants took this opportunity to accomplish the goal of helping. As expected, the results showed that participants who were primed with nurses helped more than those in the no-prime control group. These effects were affected by goal strength, in the sense that they were more pronounced when the associated goal more strongly pre-existed as a desired state in the perceivers' mind. A second experiment replicated and extended these findings by showing similar effects for a different group associated with a different goal (the goal to make money pursued by stockbrokers).

Goal Adoption and the Perception of Objects   Finally, Fitzsimons, Chartrand, and Fitzsimons (2006) showed that objects can prime goals if these objects are strongly associated with certain characteristics. For instance, they primed some participants with dogs and others with cats. They then read scenarios about the behavior of a good friend. After having read these scenarios, it was assessed how loyal participants were with respect to the transgressions of their friend. As expected, people primed with dogs – strongly associated with loyalty displayed more loyalty than participants primed with cats. In another experiment, they showed that people primed with Mac computers showed more creativity in a subsequent task than people primed with IBM computers.

Conclusions   We observed that individuals are capable of automatically adopting the goals they perceive in other agent's concrete movements, significant others, and social groups. The range of potential social stimuli that promote goal contagion by triggering the individual to entertain the goals of others and to try to attain them is rather broad, and even includes anthropomorphized nonhuman stimuli for which one establishes some sort of social bonding, such as pets, robots, and computers (Fitzsimons, Chartrand, and Fitzsimons, 2006; Mitchell, Thompson, & Miles, 1997). Of importance, there is evidence suggesting that perceivers do not always automatically take on the goal of others. What may matter is whether the goal prevails already as a desired state in the perceivers' mind and how closely they feel attached to those other people. Under these conditions, perceivers access the appropriate behavior representations and implement the necessary courses of actions relevant to the goal in question in a fairly automatic way. In the next section, we will briefly discuss research that has directly addressed the mechanisms that render the automatic implementation of goal-related behavior possible.

Path 6: From Goals to Behavior Representations: Goal Implementation

In order for goal activation to have the desired effects, behavior representations need to be activated that represent appropriate means to attain the goal. Under some circumstances, this is very straightforward, such as when there is only one behavior that can satisfy the goal. Here, a goal also has a unique, one-to-one relation with a behavior, not because the behavior is habitual, but simply because there is only one way to attain the goal. Kruglanski et al. (2002) provide a good example. A mother could teach her child that the way to produce water is to turn the faucet, and this will establish an immediate link between goal and behavior representation.

However, usually there is no one-to-one relation between goals and behaviors. Specifically, three different processes have been described that are relevant for our understanding of the relationship between goals and behavior and the way in which goal priming leads to overt behavior.[1]

The Role of Habits   One of the most common views on automatic goal pursuit deals with habit formation processes (e.g., Aarts & Dijksterhuis, 2000a; Bargh, 1990; Moskowitz, Li, & Kirk, 2004). Specifically, for goal implementation to become automatized one needs to practice the selection and execution of the means in the goal-relevant situation. According to current models of goal-directed behavior, goals are associated with different actions or means (Aarts, Verplanken, & Van Knippenberg, 1998; Kruglanski et al., 2002; Markman & Brendl, 2000; Wyer & Srull, 1986). In an extensive research program, Kruglanski et al. demonstrated how the accessibility of means upon goal priming depends on the structure of the goal–mean network. In one of their studies, for example, they established a kind of "fan-effect" (Anderson, 1983), meaning that when the number of means associated with a goal increases, priming of the goal leads to less enhanced accessibility of each of the means. Or in other words, the way in which goals and means are interconnected determines the accessibility and selection of means by the principle of spreading of activation.

Given this multiple-option context, goal pursuit can be conceived of as originating in a decision process that requires the most appropriate mean to be selected in order to attain the goal in the situation at hand. Or, in other words, the desired behavior representations should be accessed in order to guide the motor system. Idiosyncratically learned goal–mean links in memory gain strength by extensive direct practice. These links emanate from the selection process in which an action is regularly selected and performed that is perceived to be most proper in obtaining a goal (e.g., taking the bicycle instead of bus to go to the university). As a consequence, priming these goals automatically activates behavior representation and resultant action according to an "if–then" rule, enabling the goal-directed behavior to occur directly and independent of conscious intentions (e.g., Aarts et al., 1998; Bargh, 1990; Ouellette & Wood, 1998).

Aarts and Dijksterhuis (2000a,b), in the work alluded to earlier, directly tested the habitual goal–mean idea underlying automatic goal pursuit in the realm of travel behavior. In one set of studies, they employed a response latency paradigm to demonstrate that habitual bicycle users respond faster to the mean "bicycle" after priming of the goal of traveling to a certain destination. For example, habitual and nonhabitual bikers were unobtrusively primed with the goal to travel to the university or not. In a subsequent reaction time task, they measured the accessibility of the concept of bicycle. Results showed that the travel goal facilitated access to the concept of bicycle, but only for those persons that regularly use the bicycle for this trip, suggesting that cycling was automatically activated by the goal to travel to the university for those persons.

Sheeran, Aarts, et al. (2005) recently established that this habitual goal–mean activation process also pertains to health behavior. They showed that, in comparison to nonhabitual drinkers, habitual drinkers were more likely to access the mental representation of drinking and were more inclined to actually drink alcohol after priming of the goal of socializing. These effects were obtained without participants' awareness of the priming of the goal. These findings further illustrate the important point that automatic goal pursuit can be based on the dominant goal-directed response in the situation at hand.

Not all goals are habitual in the sense of being preceded by extensive practice of selecting the same means to reach the same goals in the same situations. Yet, even when goals are not habitual, people may be able to automatically access behavior representations and execute actions in a goal-relevant situation. We briefly discuss two ways in which this may occur.

The Power of Opportunities One way in which nonhabitual goals may be automatically translated into behaviors pertains to the role of opportunities in triggering associated goal-directed action. For instance, work on prospective memory suggests that goal pursuit makes effective use of cues that are appropriate for goal attainment. According to McDaniel, Robinson-Riegler, and Einstein (1998), for example, the enactment of pending goals is supported by the medial-temporal/hippocampal module – a reflexive associative memory system – as described by Moscovitch (1994). This module supports the retrieval of a goal-directed action when a target event is perceived by automatically producing interactions between the event and memory traces previously associated with the event. Only if there is sufficient interaction between the target event and the memory trace of the goal-directed action will the action be accessed: rapidly, obligatorily, and with few attentional resources (see also Van den Berg, Aarts, Midden, & Verplanken, 2004b). In this way, goal-directed actions can be efficiently executed in relatively new situations and task conditions.

The role of opportunities has also been explored in the realm of automatic goal pursuit research (Shah & Kruglanski, 2003). For example, Shah and Kruglanski activated participants with a task goal (solving a high number of anagrams), and provided an opportunity to achieve the task goal. Next, participants were either primed or not with the opportunity and subsequently took the anagram task. Results showed that opportunity-primed participants performed better on the task than no-primed participants. These data suggest that a given (new) task goal and the accompanying motivational action instrumental for the new task are automatically facilitated when the relevant opportunity is perceived. These findings further indicate that cognitive links between situations, goals, means, and opportunities can be established by the act of planning or even just thinking about these aspects, and that such links may directly become operational in a similar way to those formed by habits (Aarts & Dijksterhuis, 2000b; Aarts, Dijksterhuis, & Midden, 1999; Gollwitzer, 1993; 1999; Holland, Aarts, & Langendam, in press).

Conforming to Behavioral Norms   There is research to suggest that situational norms interact with automatic goal pursuit in a different way than idiosyncratically learned habits (Aarts & Dijksterhuis, 2003; Aarts, Dijkterhuis, & Custers, 2003; Cialdini, Reno, and Kallgren, 1990). Situational norms are socially shared beliefs representing links between specific situations and normative behaviors. We all know, for example, that one has be quiet as much as possible when entering a library or that one does not litter (too much) in classrooms. Such norms are also known as customs or conventions that are the product of socialization and cultural construal (Camic, 1986; Durkheim, 1893), and do not require much direct practice to become well-established (Sperber, 1990). Direct practice may be essential to learn how to execute the behavioral part (e.g., lower one's voice to be quiet) of norms, but not to associate normative behavior to a given goal situation. These associations can easily establish by indirect experiences (Lieberman, 2000). Situational norms thus are able to directly become active in a goal-directed situation without much direct experience with that situation (cf. Cohen, 1997).

Aarts and Dijksterhuis (2003) investigated normative behavior in the context of automatic goal pursuit in specific environments. In their experiments, participants were briefly exposed to a picture of an environment (e.g., a library which was strongly associated with the norm of behaving silently). Some participants were activated with the goal to visit the displayed environment, whereas others only looked at the picture. The dependent variables consisted of a measure of accessibility of behavior representations related to the norm under investigation (response latencies to words, such as quiet assessed in a lexical decision task) and actual behavior (voice intensity assessed in a pronunciation task). The results indicated that exposure to the environment automatically enhanced the accessibility of behavior representation and decreased the loudness of the voice. However, these accessibility effects were moderated by the activation of the goal to visit the environment.

These findings fit into the general notion that environments are capable of priming normative behaviors when the environment is of immediate behavioral relevance (Barker, 1968; Leff, 1978). According to this view, for instance, there would be little point in reducing the volume of one's voice when one passes (and sees) a library on one's way to the cafeteria, because this normative behavior is not relevant to one's current goal. In taking this functional view on social behavior one step further, Aarts and Dijksterhuis (2003) posited that the goal to visit a (socially relevant) environment causes individuals to activate (albeit implicitly) thoughts about how one should behave in the environment, thereby triggering the normative behavior associated with the environment automatically. In other words, when participants have the goal to visit a library their tendency to conform to norms renders the representations of behaving silently more accessible and thus causes them to perform their goal-directed behavior in a quiet way. Indeed, follow-up research demonstrated that the accessibility effects reported above are moderated by conformity tendencies: Automatic access to representations of normative behavior emerged when conformity tendencies were active.

In short, priming the goal to visit particular environments or to engage in specific situations is capable of automatically enhancing the accessibility of and actual adjustment to the behavioral norm associated with the environments or situations. In fact, this automatic activation of normative behavior in the context of goal pursuit in environments can be classified as an instance of unintended goal-dependent automaticity (Bargh, 1989) – unintended in the sense that it occurs as a result of the instigation of another goal.

The Nature of the Cognitive Processes Supporting Automatic Goal Pursuit

Earlier we showed that goal-directed behavior is characterized by motivational activity: People work harder, try alternatives, and exhibit actions in new settings that are instrumental to attain a goal, even if the goal is no longer in short-term memory. Such goal-directed behavior is assumed to be supported by cognitive processes that render effective goal attainment more likely to ensue (Carver & Scheier, 1998; Curtis & D'Esposito, 2003; Miller et al., 1960; Powers, 1973). In particular, goal pursuit is accompanied by a mental system that allow us to keep the goal in mind, shield it from other interfering thought and goals, select proper actions, and monitor when and how the goal-directed action can be implemented. We already discussed the evidence supporting the suggestion that the selection and implementation of goal-directed behaviors can occur automatically and often outside of conscious awareness. Below we will briefly discuss recent advances into the inquiry of the cognitive processes that serve this achievement of goals.

Persistent Activation   Recent investigations into goal-directed cognition provide clues as to the dynamic status of goal-related material in memory upon the instigation of a goal (Anderson, 1983; Goschke & Kuhl, 1993; Marsh, Hicks, & Bink, 1998; Maylor, Darby, & Della Sala, 2000). Specifically, it is demonstrated that a task goal causes persistent activation of the goal representation in memory – in comparison to the mere activation of semantic knowledge, which shows a rapid decay of activation in memory over very short periods of time, usually within a couple of seconds (Forster, Booker, Schacter, & Davis, 1990; Higgins, Bargh, & Lombardi, 1985; Mckone, 1995; Wyer & Srull, 1986). For instance, Goschke and Kuhl (1993) instructed participants to either execute a certain behavior (e.g., arranging a dinner table) or to merely observe the behavior at a later moment in the experimental session. Before this event occurred, they measured the accessibility of items related to the goal in a recognition task. They showed that a few minutes after the goal was given, the goal items were more accessible in memory in the execution instruction group compared to the observation instruction group. This effect has been replicated with different paradigms and goals, and demonstrated to be moderated by the expectance and value of the task goal (Forster, Liberman, & Higgins, 2005).

It should be noted that these experiments rely on explicit task instructions. Accordingly, one could argue that the persistent activation effects emerge because participants strategically rehearse and update the goal in order to keep it in mind. However, in follow-up studies, Goschke and Kuhl (1993) demonstrated that the effects also occur when participants were mentally taxed, suggesting that active goals have a special status in memory. This idea has led to what they called the *intention superiority effect*.

Although the Prospective Memory research discussed above shows that explicitly activated goals do not need rehearsal to sustain accessible, recent studies in the domain of automatic goal pursuit reveal similar effects. Aarts, Custers and Holland (in press) examined how the mental accessibility of a goal after a short interval changes as a function of subliminally priming the goal. In one of their studies, participants were either primed with the goal to socialize or not, and 1 minute later were tested for accessibility of the goal in a lexical decision task. Results showed that the representation of the goal of socializing stayed accessible when participants were primed to attain the goal. However, this is not the whole story. Their experiment had a twist. Some of their participants were primed with the goal in temporal proximity to the activation of negative affect, assuming that this would render the goal less desired or appealing. Aarts et al. showed that the goal-state indeed lost its motivational power as a result of a reduction in the incentive value, and that the activation level readily dropped to baseline. These findings indicate that a goal representation remains accessible when the primed goal operates as an incentive, and that these goal activation effects disappear quickly when the desire for the goal is reduced and one becomes demotivated to pursue it. From a functional point of view, the observation that the accessibility of a less desired goal is nullified makes perfect sense. The goal no longer represents an incentive, and hence one does not need to keep that particular goal at a heightened level of activation in order to increase the probability of acting on it when encountering goal-relevant opportunities (e.g., asking a friend to meet up later in the bar).

Apart from goal priming effects on mental accessibility, a couple of studies also examined persistent goal activation effects on behavioral level. For instance, based on the theory of dynamics of action (Atkinson & Birch, 1970), Bargh and colleagues (2001) suggested that goal-directed action tendencies remain active (rather than decrease) in strength over time until the goal is attained. To test this, they primed participants with the achievement goal via exposure to words related to the concept and asked them to solve anagrams immediately or after a 5 minute filler task. They established goal priming effects on actual performance directly after the priming event, and these effects even increased over a period of five minutes (Bargh et al., 2001; Experiment 3). In a recent program of research, Aarts et al. (2004) replicated and extended this persistent goal activation on behavior in the realm of goal contagion and seeking casual sex.

In short, studies on persistent activation effects suggest that nonconsciously triggered goals remain accessible and responsible for goal-directed action until the goal loses its incentive value or is overruled by other competing thoughts and goals.

Inhibition of Competing Goal Information   In reality, people are rarely free of concerns and environmental triggers that may distract them from ongoing goal pursuits. This acknowledgment has led to empirical work scrutinizing the mental processes promoting humans to stay tuned and keep on track of their current goals. For instance, research on Prospective Memory suggests that the representation of a goal is immediately inhibited upon attaining the goal (Förster et al., 2005; Marsh et al., 1998). This inhibition of attained goals is assumed to decrease the probability of interference of that goal when moving to another (competing) goal, and accordingly smoothes goal pursuit.

Work on mental accessibility as a source of interference during information processing suggests that items that show enhanced accessibility upon the selection of another competing item are temporarily inhibited to effectively guide the selection process in comparison to items that are not or less accessible (e.g., Anderson, 2003; Danner, Aarts, Bender, & De Vries, 2005; Dempster & Brainerd, 1995; Norman & Shallice, 1986). Following this rationale, Shah and colleagues (2002) show that the activation of a given goal inhibits the representation of alternative accessible goals that compete for attentional resources.

In one of their studies they asked their participants to nominate behavioral goals they perceived as important to attain in life (e.g., studying, going out). Next, participants were given a verification task, requiring them to indicate as fast as possible whether a target represented a personal attribute or not. Among these targets were one of the nominated goal (e.g., going out), and this goal was preceded by very short flashes (50 ms) of another goal (e.g., studying) they listed before. Thus, the rationale here is if the goal of going out is accessible (e.g., due to previous exposure), then this goal should interfere with the subsequent instigation of the goal of studying. As a consequence, the goal of going out is automatically inhibited (that is, lower accessibility than baseline). This is exactly what Shah et al. observed (cf., the earlier discussed work by Moskowitz et al., 1999, on stereotype control effect upon the activation of egalitarian goals). Further experimentation showed that these automatic inhibition (or what they called "goal-shielding") effects are positively related to goal achievement, but that the interference resulting from a primed competing goal may draw resources away from the focal goal (Shah & Kruglanski, 2002). This latter finding raises the suggestion that the automatic process of goal-shielding consumes some sort of mental resources. In fact, it seems almost necessary that they do, unless one assumes that some mental processes do not require resources at all.

Discrepancy Detection

People often engage in goal-directed behavior to reduce the discrepancy between their actual state and the desired goal-state. However, in many cases this is only half the story. Once a desired state has been established, people often have to compare their desired state with the actual state, and react to arising discrepancies with that state in order to maintain it. Although most theories on goal pursuit recognize and emphasize that discrepancy-detection and reduction plays an essential role in attaining and maintaining desired states (e.g., Carver & Scheier, 1998; Lewin, 1936; Miller et al., 1960, Powers, 1973), they rarely make reference to the issue of whether this process can occur automatically and requires conscious awareness of the goal that is pursued (Moskowitz, Li, & Kirk, 2004).

Research on automatic goal pursuit has opened the possibility that discrepancy detection and reduction can emerge in an automatic way. Importantly, because this process depends on information about both the actual and the desired state, goal discrepancies can arise in two fundamentally different ways. First a desired state or goal can be set or adopted that is discrepant with the actual state, creating a tension that motivates people to attain it. Second, a discrepancy can arise when an actual state that first matched a desired state is forced away from that state, motivating people to restore their desired state.

Evidence that speaks to automaticity of the first type of discrepancy process has been discussed before under Path 5. Specifically, we reviewed research that demonstrates that rendering a goal-state more accessible is enough to trigger the comparison process and motivate goal-directed behavior in the same way as consciously setting or adopting a desired state does. Aarts and colleagues (2004; Experiment 1), for example, primed participants with the goal to make money by having them read a story describing another person's behavior that implied that goal. They found that compared to control participants, primed participants worked harder on a mouse-click task if this would allow them to engage in another task in which they could make money, thereby actively reducing the discrepancy between their actual state and the goal-state. Thus, increasing the accessibility of a goal-state can create a discrepancy and motivate people to attain that state.

Evidence supporting the suggestion that discrepancy detection and reduction can arise automatically when an actual state deviates from a desired state, thereby motivating people to restore their desired state, comes from recent work by Custers and Aarts (2006). In their study, chronic and nonchronic participants as to the goal of "looking well-groomed" took a probe-recognition task, measuring accessibility of instrumental actions upon perception of goal-discrepant situations – a paradigm that has been successfully used to assess the automatic emergence of concept accessibility effects during text comprehension (e.g., McKoon and Ratcliff, 1986). Thus, participants who engage in this task read a sentence (e.g., having dirty shoes) after which they are immediately presented with words (e.g., polishing) for recognition. Before presenting the sentences, they were either subliminally primed with the goal of "looking well-groomed" or not. Automatic discrepancy detection and reduction are assumed to occur if the goal-discrepant situations render the instrumental action more accessible (in this case, longer times as the enhanced accessibility of the actions interferes with indicating that it was not in the sentence). The results showed that chronicity and priming interacted in the accessibility effects of the instrumental means. In particular, they found that (1) perceived actual states that are discrepant with a desired state automatically facilitate access to representations of actions that are instrumental in maintaining or restoring the goal state, and (2) that such automatic discrepancy reduction requires the goal representation to be either temporally or chronically accessible.

In sum, several lines of research suggest that automatic goal pursuit is blessed with dynamic mental processes that promote effective goal pursuit. Furthermore, these processes seem to run fast and below the threshold of consciousness.

TRAIT PRIMING VERSUS GOAL PRIMING

After reading the summaries of recent research on trait priming, category priming, and goal priming, one may wonder how the trait route and the goal route can be distinguished. When do we prime traits, and when do we prime goals? If we prime helpfulness, or cooperation, are we merely priming a trait, or are we priming a goal? Indeed, these processes of trait priming and goal priming are not always easy to distinguish. In the literature, the processes are sometimes used interchangeably, such as when people use "ideomotor" theory (an old idea describing how thoughts or percepts cause overt behavior, see earlier this chapter) as well as the "automotive" model (a recent model posited by Bargh and Gollwitzer [1994] to explain automaticity in goal pursuit) to describe the same priming effect.

The fogginess, however, is caused by our priming methodology, and there is no reason to assume that it is based on any ambiguity in real-life processes. In real life matters are relatively straightforward. The trait route, as argued before, causes nonmotivational overt behavior (usually) in line with our environment. It makes us automatically adjust our behavior. We become a bit more slow in a "slow" social environment (e.g., amidst senior citizens), whereas we become a little more "smart" in an intelligent (amidst college professors) environment. The goal route, however, is entirely different. It causes a myriad of motivated behaviors that are to some extent consistent over time. Whereas our immediate social environment continuously changes behavior through the trait route, its effects on goals are different. Goals, like traits, can be activated by our immediate social environment, however other goals remain active for a long time, "surviving" many different immediate environments.

The two routes clearly "behave" in different ways (see Dijksterhuis & Smith, 2005). The trait route does not instigate "new" social behavior. Instead, it adjusts ongoing behavior. In the Bargh, Chen, and Burrows (1996) experiment, people did not walk to the elevator because of the prime. Instead, they walked to the elevator because the experimenter had told them the experiment was over and they only walked *more slowly* because of the prime. Likewise, in the Dijksterhuis and Van

Knippenberg (1998) experiments participants did not answer trivia questions because of the prime. Rather, they answered trivia questions because the experimenter asked them to, whereas they answered them *better* because of the prime. The trait route, in other words, changes the parameters of ongoing behavior, whereas it does not lead to truly new behavior.[2] The goal route, of course, does more than that. The goal route may change the parameters of behavior (e.g., people may walk faster when they are in a hurry to catch a bus), but it is also responsible for truly new behavior (although it needs to be said that not that much recent goal-priming research has actually shown this yet).

However, whereas goals and traits are clearly different modes that can be distinguished in the real world, in the psychological laboratory things are far from straightforward. In quite a number of experiments reviewed here (about half of them), participants were primed with a semantic construct in order to activate a trait or a goal. In such cases, it is not always clear when trait or when goals were primed. Trait-priming and goal-priming can be distinguished ad hoc, as Bargh et al. (2001) and Aarts et al. (2004) did when they observed persistence after priming achievement. Task persistence is a sign of motivational activity, which means that a goal was primed. But can these processes be distinguished other than in such an ad hoc way? As said, the problem arises because of the priming methodology. In most cases, researchers prime semantic constructs (e.g., helpful) that can both designate a trait ("this man is helpful") as well as a goal ("this women wants to help right now"). Now, what happens when such a construct is primed? How do we activate a trait? How do we activate a goal? And can both be active simultaneously?

In our view, when one primes helpful (or creative, or cooperative, etc., but let us just stick to the helpfulness example) through the presentation of a number of words related to helpfulness, one activates the semantic trait construct. It is hard to envisage how such a priming procedure could not lead to the activation of the corresponding trait construct. If one is willing to assume this is true, it follows that we always prime a trait when we prime a semantic construct that can potentially designate a trait (such as helpful, cooperative, competitive, stupid, aggressive, intelligent, slow, creative, polite, rude, hostile, neat, etc.). This, in turn, means that we should always find behavioral effects of the trait route after priming such constructs, except when somehow the effects on trait activation on behavior are blocked (see earlier under moderators of the trait route) and provided, of course, there are opportunities to engage in trait-corresponding behavior (e.g., there has to be an opportunity to be helpful).

But when do these primes also lead to goal activation? If we define goals as positively valenced behavior or as a behavior endstate, priming helpfulness can lead to goal activation if some conditions are met (Custers & Aarts, 2005b). First, as with trait priming, there have to be opportunities to indeed engage in helpful behavior. Second, positive affect has to be activated. This can either be brought about by the behavior itself (helping) when this is evaluated positively by the perceiver, or by clearly positively valenced endstates (if I help him, he'll like me more) that are constructed. The factors that may affect whether theses conditions are met have been discussed before under Path 5 (goal-setting) and will not be further elaborated upon.

The conclusion, however, is that the trait route and the goal route may operate simultaneously. Priming helpfulness may, provided there are opportunities, lead to helpfulness via the trait route. In addition, if other conditions are also met, the goal to help can become active. Since both goals and traits increase the activation level of relevant behavior representations, it is highly likely that the processes are additive. Helpful behavior fed by the trait route and the goal route should be more intense (and prolonged) so that helpful behavior only fed by the trait route, such as conceptualization, can easily be tested (Custers & Aarts, 2005b). If we use a construct that some people associate with positive affect, whereas others do not or to a lesser extent (competition is perhaps an option), the former group should become more competitive than the latter group after priming, because the former has the trait and the goal activated, whereas the latter group only has the trait activated. Furthermore, the behavior of the former should, because it has a motivational component, be more persistent and more resistant to change by other interventions (such as other primes).

SO WHEN DO WE BECOME CONSCIOUS? AND WHY?

No one yet has provided a convincing answer to the question of why we have consciousness, and neither will we. Understanding why we have consciousness and how consciousness works is one of the great barriers – if not the greatest barrier – for scientists still to cross. Especially what some have called "the hard question" (Chalmers, 1996; Gray, 2004) is puzzling. The hard question deals with how physical processes in our brain (really, some chemical processes and a bit of electricity working on brain tissue) can cause conscious experience. No one knows and no one will know for quite a while.

Within the confines of our model, however, we can ask a more specific and much less taxing question. We have described our model and the three routes to social behavior. Furthermore, it has been shown that all these routes can – from start to end – run without any conscious awareness. On the other hand, there is no denying that we sometimes are consciously aware of our behavior ("I'm going to get a cup of coffee now") or of our goals ("I want coffee"). One way to shed light on why we may sometimes be consciously aware of our behavior or of our goals is to first ask the question whether there are any regularities as to when we are consciously aware. Is this merely random, or are there moments during the mimicry route, the trait route, or the goal route that we are more often aware of than others. In terms of the model (Figure 2.1), does consciousness shine its light on some paths or boxes more often than on others?

First, it is more fruitful to look at the boxes than at the paths. The paths describe processes rather than constructs and, as researchers have observed long ago (e.g., Watt, 1905), such processes are not accessible to conscious awareness. For instance, if you are asked "What's the capital of the UK", you are consciously aware of the question, and within a second or so also of the answer. However, how your memory search took place and how it came up with "London" is a part of the process that is introspectively blank. Likewise, upon the perception of an

African-American, we automatically activate the category and the associated stereotypical traits (e.g., Bargh, 1994; Devine, 1989). During this process, one is usually unaware of the category and the traits (the boxes) but occasionally one is. It is far from impossible. However, one is never aware of how a category activates associated stereotypical traits. So boxes it is, rather than paths.

To start at the top, we are usually consciously aware of part of what we perceive. We can perceive a lot at the same time, and usually some part of what reaches our senses reaches consciousness. In terms of our model however, the fact that we are conscious of some of our percepts is not a very illuminating observation. First of all, we remain unaware of most of what reaches our senses (Dijksterhuis, Aarts & Smith, 2005; Norretranders, 1998; Wilson, 2002). That is, conscious perception is only a small part of perception as a whole. Furthermore, we do not seem to be consciously aware of those percepts that immediately affect our behavior more often than of those that do not affect behavior. We are rarely aware of social categories, or of facial expressions, for instance. One could even make the opposite case. Many have remarked that "perceiving is for doing" but this applies more to general (unconscious and conscious) perception and much less so to conscious perception per se. Conscious perception can easily be detached from behavioral consequences, such as when one consciously enjoys the view from the top of a skyscraper without any changes in behavior at all. Also, if we are becoming aware of a stimulus that can affect behavior, we often do so after we have already acted upon it. You first pull back your hand, and only then become aware of the pain caused by the hot pan. In sum, unconscious perception is for doing, but conscious perception often is not.

Let us first focus on the trait and mimicry routes for now and leave goals for later. We can observe that we are rarely aware of traits or of behavior representations. We can be ("Gee, that's a smart question she just asked"!), but usually we are not. In addition, we are also unaware of motor system activity. As argued earlier in this chapter, there is more and more evidence that consciousness and behavioral motor systems are dissociated in the brain (Bargh, 2005; Goodale & Milner, 2005). It is still possible that conscious awareness of some aspects of motor control is helpful in indeed achieving motor control (e.g., Blakemore, Wolpert, & Frith, 2002), but most of the recent evidence suggests that the motor system does not need conscious awareness to do its job properly. A nice demonstration of how the motor system adjusts to changes without any conscious awareness was given by Goodale (1994; see Blakemore, Wolpert, & Frith, 2002, for other examples). In the experiment reported by Goodale, participants were requested to point at a visual target. During participants' saccades, the target was sometimes displaced a little. As it turned out, participants automatically adjusted the position of their moving, while obviously being oblivious to the changed position of the target.

Finally, what about goals? Here, the seeming paradox between recent data and our own experiences is most apparent. We can achieve goals without ever becoming aware of them, whereas it is obvious we are often aware of our goals. Perhaps, here is our future agenda. When, during the goal route from goal-setting to goal achievement, do we become aware of our goals, and why? As to when, a reasonable hypothesis can be raised.

Perhaps we become aware of our goals when progress towards achieving them is problematic, for instance because the environment poses enormous hurdles or because one has two conflicting goals. We know we ruminate about unfulfilled goals, and awareness of the moment goal progress goes astray can be observed for major life goals as well as for very simple behavior. Upon receiving a rejection letter one becomes aware of the very salient goal to apply (and get) tenure next year. Upon reaching in vain for a cup of coffee someone has just secretly misplaced, one becomes aware of the goal to have a sip of coffee. Progress towards goal achievement is monitored, and it is highly likely that this monitoring process is related to conscious experience when severely obstructed.

This hypothesis is in line with the act of consciousness as creating global access to many different unconscious modules (e.g., Baars, 2002) and even to act as some kind of referee to decide between the priority of modules (e.g., Morsella, 2005). The conscious access hypothesis maintains that "consciousness might help to mobilize and integrate brain functions that are otherwise separate and independent" (Baars, 2002, p. 47). Troublesome progress towards goal achievement could, in principle at least, benefit from such a function. One module observes that goal progress is problematic and in order to achieve progress it calls other modules for help. However, in order to access mobilize other modules, it needs conscious awareness as a mediator.

This reasoning is obviously speculative. But assuming that we can indeed show empirically that people become aware of goals when they are frustrated and that conscious awareness of goals changes goal achievement, have we shown that consciousness does indeed serve a function in causing behavior? Can we save consciousness as something that is actually useful by showing that? Unfortunately, we do not (see Searle, 1983; Wegner, 2002). We will still not know whether consciousness indeed causes something, or whether it is merely a correlate (i.e., a by-product) of some unconscious process that really did the job.

NOTES

1. Other than psychological processes, there are also relevant principles guiding the goal–behavior links such as equifinality and multifinality. For more on such principles, see Kruglanski et al. (2002).
2. Of course, if one defines a finger movement as a new behavior, the trait route can instigate new behavior. However, we mean socially relevant behavior here.

ACKNOWLEDGMENTS

The writing of this chapter was supported by NWO grants (Vernieuwingsimpuls 016-025-030 and VIDI-grant 452-02-047).

REFERENCES

Aarts, H. (in press). Unconscious authorship ascription: The effects of success and effect specific information priming on experienced authorship. *Journal of Experimenta. Social Psychology.*

Aarts, H., Chartrand, T. L., Custers, R., Danner, U., Dik, G., & Jefferis, V. (2005). Socia stereotypes and automatic goal pursuit. *Social Cognition, 23,* 464–489.

Aarts, H., Custers, R., & Holland, R. W. (in press). On the cessation of nonconscious goa pursuit: When goals and negative affect are co-activated. *Journal of Personality ana Social Psychology.*

Aarts, H., Custers, R., & Wegner, D. M. (2005). On the inference of personal authorship Enhancing experienced agency by priming effect information. *Consciousness ana Cognition, 14,* 439–458.

Aarts, H., & Dijksterhuis, A. (2000a). The automatic activation of goal-directed behaviour. The case of travel habit. *Journal of Environmental Psychology, 20,* 75–82.

Aarts, H., & Dijksterhuis, A. (2000b). Habits as knowledge structures: Automaticity in goal-directed behavior. *Journal of Personality and Social Psychology, 78,* 53–63.

Aarts, H., & Dijksterhuis, A. (2002). Comparability is in the eye of the beholder: Contrast and assimilation effects of primed animal exemplars on person judgments. *British Journal of Social Psychology, 41,* 123–138.

Aarts, H., & Dijksterhuis, A. (2003). The silence of the library: Environment, situational norm, and social behavior. *Journal of Personality and Social Psychology, 84,* 18–28.

Aarts, H., Dijksterhuis, A., & Custers, R. (2003). Automatic normative behavior in environments: The moderating role of conformity in activating situational norms. *Social Cognition, 21,* 447–464.

Aarts, H., Dijksterhuis, A., & De Vries, P. (2001). On the psychology of drinking: Being thirsty and perceptually ready. *British Journal of Psychology, 92,* 631.

Aarts, H., Dijksterhuis, A., & Dik, G. (in press). Goal contagion: Inferring goals from other's actions – and what it leads to. In J. Y. Shah & W. L. Gardner (Eds.), *Handbook of motivation science.* New York: Guilford.

Aarts, H., Dijksterhuis, A. P., & Midden, C. (1999). To plan or not to plan? Goal achievement of interrupting the performance of mundane behaviors. *European Journal of Social Psychology, 29,* 971–979.

Aarts, H., Gollwitzer, P. M., & Hassin, R. R. (2004). Goal contagion: Perceiving is for pursuing. *Journal of Personality and Social Psychology, 87,* 23–37.

Aarts, H., Verplanken, B., & van Knippenberg, A. (1998). Predicting behavior from actions in the past: Repeated decision making or a matter of habit? *Journal of Applied Social Psychology, 28,* 1355–1374.

Alley, T. R. (1981). *Caregiving and the perception of maturational status.* Unpublished doctoral dissertation, University of Connecticut.

Allport, G. W. (1968). The historical background of modern social psychology. In G. Lindzey & E. Aronson (Eds.), *Handbook of social psychology* (2nd ed., Vol. 1, pp. 1–80). Reading, MA: Addison-Wesley.

Anderson, C. A., Carnagey, N. L., & Eubanks, J. (2003). Exposure to violent media: The effects of songs with violent lyrics on aggressive thoughts and feelings. *Journal of Personality and Social Psychology, 84,* 960–971.

Anderson, J. R. (1983). *On the architecture of cognition.* Cambridge, MA: Harvard University Press.

Anderson, M. C. (2003). Rethinking interference theory: Executive control and the mechanisms of forgetting. *Journal of Memory and Language, 49,* 415–445.

Asch, S. E. (1951). Effects of group pressure upon the modification and distortion of judgments. In H. Guetzkow (Ed.), *Groups, leadership, and men.* Pittsburgh, PA: Carnegie Press.

Ashton-James, C., van Baaren, R., Chartrand, T. L., & Decety, J. (2006). Understanding the positive social consequences of nonconscious imitation: The mediating role of self-construal. Manuscript submitted for publication, Duke University.

Atkinson, J. W., & Birch, D. (1970). *A dynamic theory of action.* New York: Wiley.

Baars, B. J. (2002). The conscious access hypothesis: Origins and recent evidence. *Trends in Cognitive Sciences, 6,* 47–52.

Bailenson, J. N., & Yee, N. (2005). Digital chameleons: Automatic assimilation of nonverbal gestures in immersive virtual environments. *Psychological Science, 16,* 814–819.

Bandura, A. (1986). *Social foundations of thought and action: A social cognitive theory.* Englewood Cliffs, NJ: Prentice-Hall.

Banfield, J. F., Pendry, L. F., Mewse, A. J., & Edwards, M. G. (2003). The effects of an elderly stereotype prime on reaching and grasping actions. *Social Cognition, 21,* 299–319.

Bargh, J. A. (1989). Conditional automaticity: Varieties of automatic influence in social perception and cognition. In J. S. Uleman & J. A. Bargh (Eds.), *Unintended thought* (pp. 3–51). New York: Guilford Press.

Bargh, J. A. (1990). Auto-motives: Preconscious determinants of social interaction. In E. T. Higgins & R. M. Sorrentino (Eds.), *Handbook of motivation and cognition* (Vol. 2, pp. 93–132). New York: Guilford.

Bargh, J. A. (1994). The four horsemen of automaticity: Awareness, efficiency, intention and control in social cognition. In R. S. Wyer & T. K. Srull (Eds.), *Handbook of social cognition* (2nd ed., pp. 1–40). Hillsdale, NJ: Erlbaum.

Bargh, J. A. (1997). The automaticity of everyday life. In R. S. Wyer (Ed.), *The automaticity of everyday life: Advances in social cognition* (Vol. 10, pp. 1–61). Mahwah, NJ: Erlbaum.

Bargh, J. A. (1999). The cognitive monster. In S. Chaiken & Y. Trope (Eds.), *Dual process theories in social psychology* (pp. 361–382). New York: Guilford Press.

Bargh, J. A. (2005). Bypassing the will: Towards demystifying the nonconscious control of social behavior. In R. R. Hassin, J. S. Uleman, & J. A. Bargh (Eds.), *The new unconscious* (pp. 37–60). New York: Oxford University Press.

Bargh, J. A., Chaiken, S., Raymond, P., & Hymes, C. (1996). The automatic evaluation effect: Unconditional automatic attitude activation with a pronunciation task. *Journal of Experimental Social Psychology, 32,* 104–128.

Bargh, J. A., & Chartrand, T. L. (1999). The unbearable automaticity of being. *American Psychologist, 54,* 462–479.

Bargh, J. A., Chen, M., & Burrows, L. (1996). Automaticity of social behavior: Direct effects of trait construct and stereotype activation on action. *Journal of Personality and Social Psychology, 71,* 230–244.

Bargh, J. A., & Gollwitzer, P. M. (1994). Environmental control of goal-directed action: Automatic and strategic contingencies between situations and behavior. *Nebraska Symposium on Motivation, 41,* 71–124.

Bargh, J. A., Gollwitzer, P. M., Lee-Chai, A. Y., Barndollar, K., & Trotschel, R. (2001). Bypassing the will: Automatic and controlled self-regulation. *Journal of Personality and Social Psychology, 81,* 1014–1027.

Bargh, J. A., & Pietromonaco, P. (1982). Automatic information processing and social perception: The influence of trait information presented outside of conscious awareness on impression formation. *Journal of Personality and Social Psychology, 43,* 437–449.

Barker, R. G. (1968). *Ecological psychology: Concepts and methods for studying the environment of human behavior.* Stanford, CA: Stanford University Press.

Baumeister, R. F., & Leary, M. R. (1995). The need to belong: Desire for interpersonal attachments as a fundamental human motivation, *Psychological Bulletin, 117,* 497–529.

Bavelas, J. B., Black, A., Lemery, C. R., & Mullett, J. (1986). "I show how you feel": Motor mimicry as a communicative act. *Journal of Personality and Social Psychology, 50,* 322–329.

Bavelas, J. B., Black, A., Lemery, C. R., & Mullett, J. (1987). Motor mimicry as primitive empathy. In N. Eisenberg & J. Strayer (Eds.), *Empathy and its development* (pp. 317–338). Cambridge: Cambridge University Press.

Bernieri, F. J. (1988). Coordinated movement and rapport in teacher–student interactions. *Journal of Nonverbal Behavior, 12*(2), 120–138.

Bernieri, F., Reznick, J. S., & Rosenthal, R. (1988). Synchrony, pseudo synchrony, and dissynchrony: Measuring the entrainment process in mother-infant interactions. *Journal of Personality and Social Psychology, 54,* 243–253.

Bindra, D. (1974). A motivational view of learning, performance, and behavior modification. *Psychological Review, 81,* 199–213.

Blakemore, S., Wolpert, D. M., & Frith, C. (2002). Abnormalities in the awareness of action. *Trends in Cognitive Sciences, 6,* 237–242.

Bodenhausen, G. V., & Lichtenstein, M. (1987). Social stereotypes and information processing strategies: The impact of task complexity. *Journal of Personality and Social Psychology, 52,* 871–880.

Bodenhausen, G. V., Macrae, C. N., & Sherman, J. W. (1999). On the dialectics of discrimination: Dual processes in social stereotyping. In S. Chaiken & Y. Trope (Eds.) *Dual process theories in social psychology* (pp. 271–292). New York; Guilford Press.

Bock, J. K. (1986). Syntactic persistence in sentence production. *Cognitive Psychology, 18,* 355–387.

Bock, J. K. (1989). Closed-class immanence in sentence production. *Cognition, 31,* 163–186.

Brehm, J. W., & Self, E. A. (1989). The intensity of motivation. *Annual Review of Psychology, 40,* 109–131.

Brewer, M. B. (1988). A dual process model of impression formation. In R. S, Wyer, Jr., and T. K. Srull (Eds.), *Advances in social cognition* (Vol. 1, pp. 1–36). Hillsdale, NJ: Erlbaum.

Brewer, M. B. (1991). The social self: On being the same and different at the same time. *Personality and Social Psychology Bulletin, 17,* 475–482.

Brown, R., Croizet, J.C., Bohner, G., Fournet, M., & Payne, A. (2003). Automatic category activation and social behavior: The moderating role of prejudiced beliefs. *Social Cognition, 21,* 167–193.

Bruner, J. S. (1957). On perceptual readiness. *Psychological Review, 64,* 123–152.

Buss, D. M., & Kenrick, D. T. (1998). Evolutionary social psychology. In D. T. Gilbert, S. T. Fiske & G. Lindzey (Eds.), *The handbook of social psychology* (4th ed., pp. 982–1026). New York: Oxford University Press.

Byrne, R. W., & Russon, A. E. (1998). Learning by imitation: A hierarchical approach. *Brain and Behavioral Sciences, 21,* 667–684.

Camic, C. (1986). The matter of habit. *American Journal of Sociology, 91,* 1039–1087.

Caporael, L. R. (1997). The evolution of truly social cognition: The core configurations model. *Personality and Social Psychology Bulletin, 1,* 276–298.

Caporael, L. R. (2000). Evolutionary psychology: Toward a unifying theory and a hybrid science. *Annual Review of Psychology*, 52, 607–628.

Caporael, L. R. (2001). Parts and wholes: The evolutionary importance of groups. In C. Sedikides & M. B. Brewer (Eds.), *Individual self, relational self, collective self* (pp. 241–258). Philadelphia, PA: Psychology Press.

Carpenter, W. B. (1884). *Principles of mental physiology*. New York: Appleton.

Carver, C. S., Ganellen, R. J., Froming, W. J., & Chambers, W. (1983). Modeling: An analysis in terms of category accessibility. *Journal of Experimental Social Psychology*, 19, 403–421.

Carver, C. S., & Scheier, M. F. (1981). *Attention and self-regulation: A control theory approach to human behaviors*. New York: Springer.

Carver, C., & Scheier, M. F. (1998). *On the self-regulation of behavior*. New York: Cambridge University Press.

Chalmers, D. J. (1996). *The conscious mind*. New York: Oxford University Press.

Charney, E. J. (1966). Psychosomatic manifestations of rapport in psychotherapy. *Psychosomatic Medicine*, 28, 305–315.

Chartrand, T. L., & Bargh, J. A. (1996). Automatic activation of impression formation and memorization goals: Nonconscious goal priming reproduces effects of explicit task instructions. *Journal of Personality and Social Psychology*, 71, 464–478.

Chartrand, T. L., & Bargh, J. A. (1999). The chameleon effect: The perception–behavior link and social interaction. *Journal of Personality and Social Psychology*, 76, 893–910.

Chartrand, T. L., Maddux, W. W., & Lakin, J. L. (2005). Beyond the perception–behavior link: The ubiquitous utility and motivational moderators of nonconscious mimicry. In R.R. Hassin, J. S. Uleman, & J. A. Bargh (Eds.), *The new unconsciouss* (pp. 334–361). New York: Oxford University Press.

Chen, M., & Bargh, J. A. (1997). Nonconscious behavioral confirmation processes: The self-fulfilling consequences of automatic stereotype activation. *Journal of Experimental Social Psychology*, 33, 541–560.

Cheng, C. M., & Chartrand, T. L. (2003). Self-monitoring without awareness: Using mimicry as a nonconscious affiliation strategy. *Journal of Personality and Social Psychology*, 85, 1170–1179.

Cialdini, R. B., Reno, R. R., & Kallgren, C. A. (1990). A focus theory of normative conduct – recycling the concept of norms to reduce littering in public places. *Journal of Personality and Social Psychology*, 58, 1015–1026.

Cohen, D. (1997). Ifs and thens in cultural psychology. In R. S. Wyer, Jr. (Ed.), *Advances in social cognition* (Vol. 10, pp. 121–131). Mahwah, NJ: Erlbaum.

Cosmides, L., & Tooby, J. (1992). Cognitive adaptations for social exchange. In J. H. Barkow, L. Cosmides & J. Tooby (Eds.), *The adapted mind: Evolutionary psychology and the generation of culture* (pp. 163–228). New York: Oxford University Press.

Curtis, C. E., & D'Esposito, M. (2003). Persistent activity in the prefrontal cortex during working memory. *Trends in Cognitive Sciences*, 7, 415–423.

Custers, R., & Aarts, H. (2003). On the role of processing goals in evaluative judgments of environments: Effects of memory–judgment relations. *Journal of Environmental Psychology*, 23, 289–299.

Custers, R., & Aarts, H. (2006). Goal-discrepant situations prime goal-directed actions if goals are temporarily of chronically accessible. Manuscript submitted for publication.

Custers, R., & Aarts, H. (2005a). Positive affect as implicit motivator: On the nonconscious operation of behavioral goals. *Journal of Personality and Social Psychology, 89,* 129–142.

Custers, R., & Aarts, H. (2005b). Beyond accessibility: The role of affect and goal-discrepancies in implicit processes of motivation and goal-pursuit. *European Review of Social Psychology, 16,* 257–300.

Custers, R., & Aarts, H. (in press). In search of the nonconscious sources of goal-pursuit: Accessibility and positive valence of the goal state. *Journal of Experimental Social Psychology.*

Dabbs, J. M. (1969). Similarity of gestures and interpersonal influence. Paper presented at the *77th Annual Convention of the American Psychological Association,* Washington, DC.

Danner, U. N., Aarts, H., Bender, M., & De Vries, N. K. (2005). The regulatory merits of inhibiting alternatives in the selection of means for goals. Manuscript under review.

Davis, M. H. (1983). Measuring individual differences in empathy: Evidence for a multidimensional approach. *Journal of Personality and Social Psychology, 44,* 113–126.

Decety, J., & Grezes, J. (1999). Neural mechanisms subserving the perception of human actions. *Trends in Cognitive Sciences, 3,* 172–178.

Decety, J., Jeannerod, M., Germain, M., & Pastene, J. (1991). Vegetative response during imagined movement is proportional to mental effort. *Behavioral Brain Research, 42,* 1–5.

Deci, E. L., & Ryan, R. M. (1985). *Intrinsic motivation and self-determination in human behavior.* New York: Plenum.

Dempster, F. N., & Brainerd, C. J. (1995). *Interference and inhibition in cognition.* New York: Academic Press.

Devine, P. G. (1989). Stereotypes and prejudice: Their automatic and controlled components. *Journal of Personality and Social Psychology, 56,* 5–18.

de Waal, F. (1989). *Peacemaking among primates.* Cambridge, MA: Harvard University Press.

Dijksterhuis, A., Aarts, H., Bargh, J. A., & van Knippenberg, A. (2000). On the relation between associative strength and automatic behavior. *Journal of Experimental Social Psychology, 36*(5), 531–544.

Dijksterhuis, A., Aarts, H., & Smith, P. K. (2005). The power of the subliminal: On subliminal persuasion and other potential applications. In R. R. Hassin, J. S. Uleman & J. A. Bargh (Eds.), *The new unconscious* (pp. 77–106). New York: Oxford University Press.

Dijksterhuis, A., & Bargh, J. A. (2001). The perception–behavior expressway: Automatic effects of social perception on social behavior. In M. P. Zanna (Ed.), *Advances in experimental social psychology* (Vol. 33, pp. 1–40). San Diego, CA: Academic Press.

Dijksterhuis, A., Bargh, J. A., & Miedema, J. (2000). Of men and mackerels: Attention, subjective experience, and automatic social behavior. In H. Bless & J. P. Forgas (Eds.), *The message within: The role of subjective experience in social cognition and behavior* (pp. 37–51). Philadelphia: Psychological Press.

Dijksterhuis, A., & Smith, P. K. (2005). What do we do unconsciously? And how? *Journal of Consumer Psychology, 15,* 225–229.

Dijksterhuis, A., Spears, R., & Lepinasse, V. (2001). Reflecting and deflecting stereotypes: Assimilation and contrast in impression formation and automatic behavior. *Journal of Experimental Social Psychology, 37,* 286–299.

Dijksterhuis, A., Spears, R., Postmes, T., Stapel, D., Koomen, W., van Knippenberg, A., et al. (1998). Seeing one thing and doing another: Contrast effects in automatic behavior. *Journal of Personality and Social Psychology, 75,* 862–871.

Dijksterhuis, A., & van Knippenberg, A. (1995). Memory for stereotype-consistent and stereotype-inconsistent information as a function of processing pace. *European Journal of Social Psychology*, 25, 689–694.

Dijksterhuis, A., & van Knippenberg, A. (1996). The knife that cuts both ways: Facilitated and inhibited access to traits as a result of stereotype activation. *Journal of Experimental Social Psychology*, 32, 271–288.

Dijksterhuis, A., & van Knippenberg, A. (1998). The relation between perception and behavior, or how to win a game of Trivial Pursuit. *Journal of Personality and Social Psychology*, 74, 865–877.

Dijksterhuis, A., & van Knippenberg, A. (2000). Behavioral indecision: Effects of self-focus on automatic behavior. *Social Cognition*, 18(1), 55–74.

Dik, G., & Aarts, H. (2005). Behavioral Cues to Others' Motivation and goal-pursuits: The perception of effort facilitates goal inference and contagion. Manuscript under review.

Dimberg, U. (1982). Facial reactions to facial expressions. *Psychophysiology*, 19, 643–647.

Durkheim, E. (1893) 1933/1964. *The division of labor in society*. Translated by George Simpson. New York: Free Press.

Duval, S., & Wicklund, R. A. (1972). *A theory of objective self-awareness*. New York: Academic Press.

Eidelberg, L. (1929). Experimenteller Beitrag zum Mechanismus der Imitationsbewegung. *Jahresbücher für Psychiatrie und Neurologie*, 46, 170–173.

Elsner, B., & Hommel, B. (2001). Effect anticipation and action control. *Journal of Experimental Psychology: Human Perception and Performance*, 27, 229–240.

Epley, N., & Gilovich, T. (1999). Just going along: Nonconscious priming and conformity to social pressure. *Journal of Personality and Social Psychology*, 35, 578–589.

Fadiga, L., Fogassi, L., Pavesi, G., & Rizzolatti, G. (1995). Motor facilitation during action observation: A magnetic stimulation study. *Journal of Neurophysiology*, 73, 2608–2611.

Ferraro, R., Bettman, J. R., & Chartrand, T. L. (2006). I see, I do, I like: The consequences of behavioral mimicry for consumer preferences. Manuscript submitted for publication, Duke University.

Finkel, E. J., Campbell, W. K., Brunell, A. B., Dalton, A. N., Scarbeck, S. J., & Chartrand, T. L. (in press). High maintenance interaction: Inefficient social coordination impairs self-regulation. *Journal of Personality and Social Psychology*.

Fiske, S. T. (1993). Controlling other people: The impact of power on stereotyping. *American Psychologist*, 48, 621–628.

Fiske, S. T., & Neuberg, S. E. (1990). A continuum of impression formation from category-based to individuating processes: Influences of information and motivation on attention and interpretation. In M. Zanna (Ed.), *Advances in experimental social psychology* (Vol. 23, pp. 1–74). San Diego, CA: Academic Press.

Fitzsimons, G. M., & Bargh, J. A. (2003). Thinking of you: Nonconscious pursuit of interpersonal goals associated with relationship partners. *Journal of Personality & Social Psychology*, 84(1), 148–163.

Fitzsimons, G. M., Chartrand, T. L., & Fitzsimons, G. J. (2006). Automatic effects of brand exposure on behavior. Manuscript submitted for publication, Duke University.

Förster, J., Friedman, R. S., Butterbach, E. B., & Sassenberg, K. (2006). Automatic effects of deviancy cues on creative cognition. *European Journal of Social Psychology* (in press).

Förster, J., Liberman, N., & Higgins, E. T. (2005). Accessibility from active and fulfilled goals. *Journal of Experimental Social Psychology*, 41, 220–239.

Forster, K. I., Booker, J., Schacter, D. L., & Davis, C. (1990). Masked repetition priming: Lexical activation or novel memory trace? *Bulletin of the Psychonomic Society, 28,* 341–345.

Gallese, V., Fadiga, L., Fogassi, L., & Rizzolatti, G. (1996). Action recognition in the premotor cortex. *Brain, 119,* 593–609.

Geen, R., G. (1995). *Human motivation: A social psychological approach.* Belmont, CA: Wadsworth.

Gibbons, F. X. (1990). Self-attention and behavior. A review and theoretical update. In M. P. Zanna (Ed.), *Advances in experimental social psychology* (Vol. 23, pp. 249–303). San Diego, CA: Academic Press.

Gibson, J. J. (1979). *The ecological approach to visual perception.* Boston: Houghton-Mifflin.

Gilbert, D. T. (1989). Thinking lightly about others: Automatic components of the social inference process. In J. S. Uleman & J. A. Bargh (Eds.), *Unintended thought* (pp. 189–211). New York: Guilford Press.

Gilbert, D. T., & Malone, P. S. (1995). The correspondence bias. *Psychological Bulletin, 117,* 21–38.

Goodale, M. A. (1994). The nature and limits of orientation and pattern processing visuomotor control in a visual form agnosic. *Journal of Cognitive Neuroscience, 6,* 46–56.

Goodale, M. A., & Milner, A. D. (2005). *Sight unseen: An exploration of conscious and unconscious vision.* Oxford: Oxford University Press.

Goodale, M. A., Milner, A. D., Jakobson, L. S., & Carey, D. P. (1991). Perceiving the world and grasping it: A neurological dissociation. *Nature, 349,* 154–156.

Gollwitzer, P. M. (1990). Action phases and mind-sets. In E. T. Higgins & R. M. Sorrentino (Eds.), *Handbook of motivation and cognition* (pp. 53–92). New York: Guilford Press.

Gollwitzer, P. M. (1993). Goal achievement: The role of intentions. In W. Stroebe & M. Hewstone (Eds.), *European review of social psychology* (Vol. 4, pp. 141–185). London: Wiley.

Gollwitzer, P. M. (1999). Implementation intentions: Strong effects of simple plans. *American Psychologist, 54,* 493–503.

Gollwitzer, P. M., & Moskowitz, G. B. (1996). Goal effects on thought and behavior. In E. T. Higgins & A. W. Kruglanski (Eds.), *Social psychology: Handbook of basic principles* (pp. 361–399). New York: Guilford Press.

Goschke, T., & Kuhl, J. (1993). Representation of intentions: Persisting activation in memory. *Journal of Experimental Psychology: Learning, Memory, and Cognition, 19,* 1211–1226.

Gray, J. (2004). *Consciousness: Creeping up the hard problem.* Oxford: Oxford University Press.

Greenwald, A. G. (1970). Sensory feedback mechanisms in performance control: With special reference to the ideomotor mechanism. *Psychological Review, 77,* 73–99.

Greenwald, A. G. (1972). On doing two things at once: Time sharing as a function of ideomotor compatibility. *Journal of Experimental Psychology, 94,* 52–57.

Greenwald, A. G., & Banaji, M. R. (1995). Implicit social cognition: Attitudes, self-esteem, and stereotypes. *Psychological Review, 102*(1), 4–27.

Grezes, J., & Decety, J. (2001). Functional anatomy of execution, mental simulation, observation, and verb generation of actions: A meta-analysis. *Human Brain Mapping, 12,* 1–19.

Haddock, G., Macrae, C. N., & Fleck, S. (2002). Syrian science and smart supermodels: On the when and how of perception–behavior effects. *Social Cognition, 20,* 461–481.

Hale, B. D. (1982). The effects of internal and external imagery on muscular and ocular concomitants. *Journal of Sport Psychology, 4,* 379–387.

Hamilton, D. L., Driscoll, D. M., & Worth, L. T. (1989). Cognitive organization of impressions: Effects of incongruency in complex representations. *Journal of Personality and Social Psychology, 57,* 925–937.

Hamilton, D. L., Katz, L. B., & Leirer, V. O. (1980). Cognitive representation of personality impression: Organizational processes in first impression formation. *Journal of Personality and Social Psychology, 39,* 1050–1063.

Hassin, R. R. (2005). Non-conscious control and implicit working memory. In R. R. Hassin, J. S. Uleman & J. A. Bargh (Eds.), *The new unconscious* (pp. 196–224). New York: Oxford University Press.

Hassin, R. R., Aarts, H., & Ferguson, M. J. (2005). Automatic goal inferences. *Journal of Experimental Social Psychology, 41,* 129–140.

Hastie, R., & Park, B. (1986). The relationship between memory and judgment depends on whether the judgment task is memory-based or on-line. *Psychological Review, 93,* 258–268.

Hatfield, E., Cacioppo, J., & Rapson, R. L. (1994). *Emotional contagion.* Cambridge: Cambridge University Press.

Hausdorff, J. M., Levy, B. R., & Wei, J. Y. (1999). The power of ageism on physical function of older persons: Reversibility of age-related gait changes. *Journal of the American Geriatrics Society, 47,* 1346–1349.

Heider, F. (1958). *The psychology of interpersonal relations.* New York: Wiley.

Heider, F., & Simmel, M. (1944). An experimental study of apparent behavior. *American Journal of Psychology, 57,* 243–259.

Herr, P. M. (1986). Consequences of priming: Judgment and behavior. *Journal of Personality and Social Psychology, 51,* 1106–1115.

Herr, P. M., Sherman, S. J., & Fazio, R. H. (1983). On the consequences of priming: Assimilation and contrast effects. *Journal of Experimental Social Psychology, 19,* 323–340.

Hertel, G., & Fiedler, K. (1998). Fair and dependent versus egoistic and free: Effects of semantic and evaluative priming on the "ring measure of social values". *European Journal of Social Psychology, 28,* 49–70.

Hertel, G., & Kerr, N. L., (2003). Priming in-group favoritism: The impact of normative scripts in the minimal group paradigm. *Journal of Experimental Social Psychology, 37,* 316–324.

Hess, T. M., Auman, C., Colcombe, S. J., & Rahhal, T. A. (2003). The impact of stereotype threat on age differences in memory performance. *Journals of Gerontology Series B – Psychological Sciences and Social Sciences, 58,* 3–11.

Hess, T. M., Hinson, J. T., & Stratham, J. A. (2004). Explicit and implicit stereotype activation effects on memory: Do age and awareness moderate the impact of priming? *Psychology and Aging, 19,* 495–505.

Higgins, E. T. (1989). Knowledge accessibility and activation: Subjectivity and suffering from unconscious sources. In J. S. Uleman & J. A. Bargh (Eds.), *Unintended thought* (pp. 75–123). New York: Guilford Press.

Higgins, E. T. (1996). Knowledge activation: Accessibility, applicability, and salience. In E. T. Higgins, & A. W. Kruglanski (Eds.), *Social psychology: Handbook of basic principles* (pp. 133–168). New York: Guilford.

Higgins, E. T. & Bargh, J. A. (1987). Social cognition and social perception. In M. R. Rosenzweig & L. W. Porter (Eds.), *Annual review of psychology* (Vol. 38, pp. 369–425). Palo Alto, CA: Annual Reviews.

Higgins, E. T., Bargh, J. A., & Lombardi, W. (1985). The nature of priming effects on categorization. *Journal of Experimental Psychology: Learning, Memory and Cognition, 11*, 59–69.

Higgins, E. T., King, G. A., & Mavin, G. H. (1982). Individual construct accessibility and subjective impressions and recall. *Journal of Personality and Social Psychology, 43*, 35–47.

Higgins, E. T., Rholes, W. S., & Jones, C. R. (1977). Category accessibility and impression formation. *Journal of Experimental Social Psychology, 13*, 141–154.

Holland, R. W., Aarts, H., & Langendam, R. (in press). Breaking and creating habits on the working Floor: A field-experiment on the power of implementation intentions. *Journal of Experimental Social Psychology*.

Holland, R. W., Hendriks, M., & Aarts (2005). Smells like clean spirit: Nonconscious effects of scent on cognition and behavior. *Psychological Science, 16*, 689–693.

Hull, J. G., Slone, L. B., Meteyer, K. B., & Matthews, A. R. (2002). The nonconsciousness of self-consciousness. *Journal of Personality and Social Psychology, 83*(2), 406–424.

Hyland, M. E. (1988). Motivational control-theory – an integrative framework. *Journal of Personality and Social Psychology, 55*, 642–651.

Iacoboni, M., Woods, R. P., Brass, M., Bekkering, H., Mazziotta, J. C., & Rizzolatti, G. (1999). Cortical mechanisms of human imitation. *Science, 286*, 2526–2528.

Jacobson, E. (1932). The electrophysiology of mental activities. *American Journal of Psychology, 44*, 677–694

James, W. (1890). *Principles of psychology*. New York: Holt.

Jastrow, J. & West, J. (1892). A study of involuntary movements. *American Journal of Psychology, 4*, 398–407.

Jeannerod, M. (1994). The representing brain: Neural correlates of motor intention and imagery. *Behavioral and Brain Sciences, 17*, 187–245.

Jeannerod, M. (1995). Mental imagery in the motor cortex. *Neuropsychologia, 33*, 1419–1432.

Jeannerod, M. (1997). *The cognitive neuroscience of action*. Oxford: Blackwell.

Jeannerod, M. (1999). To act or not to act: Perspectives on the representation of actions. *Quarterly Journal of Experimental Psychology, 52A*, 1–29.

Jeannerod, M. (2003). Consciousness of action and self-consciousness: A cognitive neuroscience approach. In J. Roessler & N. Eilan (Eds.), *Agency and self-awareness: Issues in philosophy and psychology*. New York: Oxford University Press.

Johanson, D., & Edgar, B. (1996). *From Lucy to language*. New York: Simon & Schuster Editions.

Jonas, K., & Sassenberg, K. (in press). Knowing what to do: automatic response activation from social categories. *Journal of Personality and Social Psychology*.

Kawakami, K., Dovidio, J. F., & Dijksterhuis, A. (2003). Effects of social category priming on personal attitudes. *Psychological Science, 14*, 315–319.

Kawakami, K., Young, H., & Dovidio, J. F. (2002). Automatic stereotyping: Category, trait, and behavioral activations. *Personality and Social Psychology Bulletin, 28*(1), 3–15.

Kay, A. C., & Ross, L. (2003). The perceptual push: The interplay of implicit cues and explicit situational construals on behavioral intentions in the Prisoner's Dilemma. *Journal of Experimental Social Psychology, 39*, 634–643.

Kay, A. C., Wheeler, S. C., Bargh, J. A., & Ross, L. (2004). Material priming: The influence of mundane physical objects on situational construal and competitive behavioral choice. *Organizational Behavior and Human Decision Processes, 95*, 83–96.

Köhler, W. (1927). *The mentality of apes* (2nd ed.). New York: Harcourt.

Kornhuber, H. H., & Deecke, L. (1965). Hirnpotentialanderungen bei Wilkurbewegungen und passiv Bewegungen des Menschen: Berietschaftpotential und reafferente Potentiale. *Pflugers Archiv fur Gesamte Psychologie, 284,* 1–17.

Krolak-Schwerdt, S. (2003). The cognition–behavior link: Effects of activated trait categories on social behavior. *Zeitschrift fur Sozialpsychologie, 34,* 79–90.

Kruglanski, A. W., Shah, J. Y., Fishbach, A., Friedman, R., Chun, W. Y., & Sleeth-Keppler, D. (2002). A theory of goal-systems. In M. P. Zanna (Ed.), *Advances in Experimental Social Psychology* (Vol. 34, pp. 331–378). New York: Academic Press.

Kunda, Z. (1999). *Social cognition.* Cambridge: MIT Press.

La France, M. (1982). Posture mirroring and rapport. In M. Davis (Ed.), *Interaction rhythms: Periodicity in communicative behavior* (pp. 279–298). New York: Human Sciences Press.

La France, M., & Broadbent, M. (1976). Group rapport: Posture sharing as a nonverbal indicator. *Group and Organizational Studies, 1,* 328–333.

Lakin, J. L., & Chartrand, T. L. (2003). Using nonconscious behavioral mimicry to create affiliation and rapport. *Psychological Science, 14*(4), 334–339.

Lakin, J. L., & Chartrand, T. L. (2005). Exclusion and nonconscious behavioral mimicry. In J. P. Forgas, K. D. Williams & W. von Hippel (Eds.), *The social outcast: Ostracism, social exclusion, rejection, and bullying.* New York: Psychology Press.

Lakin, J. L., Chartrand, T. L., & Arkin, R. (2006). I am too just like you: The effects of ostracism on nonconscious mimicry. Manuscript submitted for publication, Drew University.

Lakin, J. L., Jefferis, V. E., Cheng, C. M., & Chartrand, T. L. (2003). The chameleon effect as social glue: Evidence for the evolutionary significance of nonconscious mimicry. *Journal of Nonverbal Behavior, 27,* 145–162.

LeBoeuf, R. A., & Estes, Z. (2004). "Fortunately, I'm no Einstein": Comparison relevance as a determinant of behavioral assimilation and contrast. *Social Cognition, 22,* 607–636.

Leff, H. L. (1978). *Experience, environment, and human potential.* New York: Oxford University Press.

Lepore, L., & Brown, R. (1997). Category and stereotype activation: Is prejudice inevitable? *Journal of Personality and Social Psychology, 72,* 275–287.

Levelt, W. J. M., & Kelter, S. (1982). Surface form and memory in question answering. *Cognitive Psychology, 14,* 78–106.

Levy, B. (1996). Improving memory in old age through implicit self-stereotyping. *Journal of Personality and Social Psychology, 71,* 1092–1107.

Lewin, K. (1936). *Principles of topological psychology.* New York: McGraw-Hill.

Lewin, K. (1951). *Field theory in social science.* Chicago: University of Chicago Press.

Lewin, K. (1993). *Human evolution: An illustrated introduction* (3rd ed.). Boston: Blackwell Scientific Publications.

Libet, B., Gleason, C. A., Wright, E. W., & Pearl, D. K. (1983). Time of conscious intention to act in relation to onset of cerebral activity (readiness-potential): The unconscious initiation of a freely voluntary act. *Brain, 106,* 623–642.

Lichtenstein, M., & Srull, T. K. (1987). Processing objects as a determinant of the relationship between recall and judgment. *Journal of Experimental Social Psychology, 23,* 93–118.

Lieberman, M. D. (2000). Intuition: A social cognitive neuroscience approach. *Psychological Bulletin, 126,* 109–137.

Locke, E. A., & Latham, G. P. (1990). *A theory of goal setting and task performance.* Englewood Cliffs, NJ: Prentice-Hall.

Long, D. L., & Golding, J. M. (1993). Superordinate goal inferences: Are they automatically generated during comprehension? *Discourse Processes, 16,* 55–73.

Lotze, R. H. (1852). *Medicinische Psychologie oder Physiologie der Seele. (Medical psychology or the physiology of the soul).* Leipzig: Weidmannshe Buchhandlung.

Luria, A. R. (1961). *The role of speech in the regulation of normal and abnormal behavior.* New York: Macmillan.

Maass, A., Colombo, A., Colombo, A., & Sherman, S. J. (2001). Inferring traits from behaviors versus behaviors from traits: The induction–deduction asymmetry. *Journal of Personality and Social Psychology, 81,* 391–404.

Macrae, C. N., Bodenhausen, G. V., Milne, A. B., Castelli, L., Schloerscheidt, A. M., & Greco, S. (1998). On activating exemplars. *Journal of Experimental Social Psychology, 34,* 330–354.

Macrae, C. N., Hewstone, M., & Griffiths, R. J. (1993). Processing load and memory for stereotype-based information. *European Journal of Social Psychology, 23,* 77–87.

Macrae, C. N., & Johnston, L. (1998). Help, I need somebody: Automatic action and inaction. *Social Cognition, 16,* 400–417.

Macrae, C. N., Milne, A. B., & Bodenhausen, G. V. (1994). Stereotypes as energy-saving devices: A peek inside the cognitive toolbox. *Journal of Personality and Social Psychology, 66,* 37–47.

Manis, M., Biernat, M., & Nelson, T. F. (1991). Comparison and expectancy processes in human judgment. *Journal of Personality and Social Psychology, 61,* 203–211.

Markman, A. B., & Brendl, C. M. (2000). The influence of goals on value and choice. *Psychology of Learning and Motivation: Advances in Research and Theory, 39,* 97–128.

Marsh, R. L., Hicks, J. L., & Bink, M. L. (1998). Activation of completed, uncompleted and partially completed intentions. *Journal of Experimental Psychology: Learning, Memory, and Cognition, 24,* 350–361.

Maurer, R. E., & Tindall, J. H. (1983). Effect of postural congruence on client's perception of counselor empathy. *Journal of Counseling Psychology, 30,* 158–163.

Maylor, E. A., Darby, R. J., & Sala Della, S. (2000). Retrieval of performed versus to-be-performed tasks: A naturalistic study of the intention-superiority effect in normal aging and dementia. *Applied Cognitive Psychology, 14,* S83–S98.

McArthur, L. Z., & Baron, R. M. (1983). Toward an ecological theory of social perception. *Psychological Review, 90,* 215–238.

McClure, J. (2002). Goal-based explanations of actions and outcomes. *European Review of Social Psychology, 12,* 201–235.

McConnell, A. R., Leibold, J. M., & Sherman, S. J. (1997). Within-target illusory correlations and the formation of context-dependent attitudes. *Journal of Personality and Social Psychology, 73,* 675–686.

McDaniel, M. A., Robinson-Riegler, B., & Einstein, G. O. (1998). Prospective remembering: Perceptually driven or conceptually driven processes? *Memory & Cognition, 26,* 121–134.

Mckone, E. (1995). Short-term implicit memory for words and nonwords. *Journal of Experimental Psychology: Learning, Memory and Cognition, 21,* 1108–1126.

McKoon, G., & Ratcliff, R. (1986). Inferences about predictable events. *Journal of Experimental Psychology: Learning, Memory, and Cognition, 12,* 82–91.

Meltzoff, A. N. (1995). Understanding the intentions of others – reenactment of intended acts by 18-month-old children. *Developmental Psychology, 31,* 838–850.

Milgram, S. (1963). Behavioral study of obedience. *Journal of Abnormal and Social Psychology, 67,* 371–378.

Miller, G. A., Galanter, E., & Pribram, K. H. (1960). *Plans and the structure of behavior.* Oxford, England: Holt.

Milner, A. D., & Goodale, M. A. (1995). *The visual brain in action.* Oxford: Oxford University Press.

Mitchell, R. W., Thompson, N. S., & Miles, H. (1997). *Anthropomorphism, anecdotes, and animals.* Albany, NY: State University of New York Press.

Morsella, E. (2005). The function of phenomenal states: Supramodular interaction theory. *Psychological Review, 112*, 1000–1021.

Moscovitch, M. (1994). Memory and working with memory: Evaluation of a component process model and comparisons with other models. In E. Tulving & D. L. Schacter (Eds.), *Memory systems* (pp. 269–310). Cambridge, MA: MIT Press.

Moskowitz, G. B. (2002). Preconscious effects of temporary goals on attention. *Journal of Experimental Social Psychology, 38*, 397–404.

Moskowitz, G. B., Gollwitzer, P. M., Wasel, W., & Schaal, B. (1999). Preconscious control of stereotype activation through chronic egalitarian goals. *Journal of Personality and Social Psychology, 77*, 167–184.

Moskowitz, G. B., Li, P., & Kirk, E. R. (2004). The implicit volition model: On the preconscious regulation of temporarily adopted goals. In M. P. Zanna (Ed.), *Advances in experimental social psychology* (Vol. 36, pp. 317–404). New York: Academic Press.

Moskowitz, G. B., Salomon, A. R., & Taylor, C. M. (2000). Implicit control of stereotype activation through the preconscious operation of egalitarian goals. *Social Cognition, 18*, 151–177.

Mussweiler, T. (2001). Focus of comparison as a determinant of assimilation versus contrast in social comparison. *Personality and Social Psychology Bulletin, 27*, 38–47.

Mussweiler, T. (2003). Comparison processes in social judgment: Mechanisms and consequences. *Psychological Review, 110*(3), 472–489.

Mussweiler, T. (2006). Doing is for thinking: Stereotype activation by stereotypic movements. *Psychological Science, 17*, 17–21.

Neisser, U. (1967). *Cognitive psychology.* New York: Appleton-Century Cofts.

Nelson, L. D., & Norton, M. I. (2005). From student to superhero: Situational primes shape future helping. *Journal of Experimental Social Psychology, 41*, 423–430.

Neuberg, S. L. (1988). Behavioral implications of information presented outside of conscious awareness: The effect of subliminal presentation of trait information on behavior in the Prisoner's dilemma game. *Social Cognition, 6*, 207–230.

Neumann, R., & Strack, F. (2000). "Mood contagion": The automatic transfer of mood between persons. *Journal of Personality and Social Psychology, 79*(2), 211–223.

Norman, D. A., & Shallice, T. (1986). Attention to action: Willed and automatic control of behavior. In R. J. Davidson, G. E. Schwartz & D. Shapiro (Eds.), *Consciousness and self-regulation: Advances in research and theory* (Vol. 4, pp. 1–18). New York: Plenum.

Norretranders, T. (1998). *The user illusion.* New York: Viking.

Oettingen, G., & Gollwitzer, P. M. (2001). Goal setting and goal striving. In A. Tesser & N. Schwartz (Eds.), *Blackwell handbook of social psychology: Intraindividual processes.* Oxford: Blackwell.

Oikawa, M. (2004). Moderation of automatic achievement goals by conscious monitoring. *Psychological Reports, 95*, 975–980.

Ouellette, J. A., & Wood, W. (1998). Habit and intention in everyday life: The multiple processes by which past behavior predicts future behavior. *Psychological Bulletin, 124*, 54–74.

Park, B. (1986). A method for studying the development of impressions of real people. *Journal of Personality and Social Psychology, 51*, 907–917.

Paus, T., Petrides, M., Evans, A. C., & Meyer, E. (1993). Role of human anterior cingulate cortex in the control of oculomotor, manual and speech responses: A positron emission tomography study. *Journal of Neurophysiology, 70*, 453–469.

Peak, H. (1955). Attitude and motivation. In M. R. Jones (Ed.), *Nebraska symposium on motivation: 1955* (pp. 149–189). Lincoln, NE: University of Nebraska Press.

Pendry, L. & Carrick, R. (2001). Doing what the mob do: Priming effects on conformity. *European Journal of Social Psychology, 31*, 83–92.

Perani, D., Cappa, S. F., Schnur, T., Tettamanti, M., Collina, S., Rosa, M. M., & Fazio, F. (1999). The neural correlates of verb and noun processing. A PET study. *Brain, 122*, 2337–2344.

Pervin, L. A. (1989). Goal concepts: Themes, issues, and questions. In L. A. Pervin (Ed.), *Goal concepts in personality and social psychology* (pp. 473–479). Hillsdale, NJ: Erlbaum.

Pilialoha, B., Hall, C., & Chartrand, T. L. (manuscript in preparation). *Social chameleons: Effects of social identity motives on nonconscious mimicry.*

Poirier, F. E., & McKee, J. K. (1999). *Understanding human evolution* (4th ed.). Upper Saddle River, NJ: Prentice Hall.

Powers, W. T. (1973). Feedback: Beyond behaviorism. *Science, 179*, 351–356.

Poynor, D. V., & Morris, R. K. (2003). Inferred goals in narratives: Evidence from self-paced reading, recall, and eye movements. *Journal of Experimental Psychology – Learning Memory and Cognition, 29*, 3–9.

Prinz, W. (1990). A common coding approach to perception and action. In O. Neumann & W. Prinz (Eds.), *Relationships between perception and action* (pp. 167–201). Berlin: Springer-Verlag.

Prinz, W. (2003). How do we know about our own actions? In S. Maasen, W. Prinz, & G. Roth (Eds.), *Voluntary action: Brains, minds, and sociality* (pp. 21–33). New York: Oxford University Press.

Prinz, W. (2005). An ideomotor approach to imitation. In S. Hurley & N. Chater (Eds.), *Perspectives on imitation: From mirror neurons to memes* (pp. 141–156). Cambridge, MA: MIT Press.

Rizzolatti, G., Fadiga, L., Gallese, V., & Fogassi, L. (1996). Premotor cortex and the recognition of motor actions. *Cognitive Brain Research, 3*, 131–141.

Schank, R. C., & Abelson, R. P. (1977). *Scripts, plans, goals and understanding: An inquiry into human knowledge structures.* Hillsdale, NJ: Erlbaum.

Scheflen, A. E. (1964). The significance of posture in communication systems. *Psychiatry, 27*, 316–331.

Schenkein, J. (1980). A taxonomy of repeating action sequences in natural conversation. In B. Butterworth, *Language production, Vol 1, Speech and talk*. New York: Academic Press.

Schubert, T. W., & Häfner, M. (2003). Contrast from social stereotypes in automatic behavior. *Journal of Experimental Social Psychology, 39*, 577–584.

Schwarz, N., & Clore, G. (1996). Feelings and phenomenal experiences. In E. T. Higgins & A. W. Kruglanski (Eds.), *Social psychology: Handbook of basic principles* (pp. 433–465). New York: Guilford.

Searle, J. R. (1983). *Intentionality: An essay on the philosophy of mind.* New York: Cambridge University Press.

Shah, J. Y. (2003). The motivational looking glass: How significant others implicitly affect goal appraisals. *Journal of Personality & Social Psychology, 85*(3), 424–439.

Shah, J. Y., Friedman, R., & Kruglanski, A. W. (2002). Forgetting all else: On the antecedents and consequences of goal shielding. *Journal of Personality and Social Psychology, 83,* 1261–1280.

Shah, J. Y., & Kruglanski, A. W. (2002). Priming against your will: How accessible alternatives affect goal pursuit. *Journal of Experimental Social Psychology, 38,* 368–383.

Shah, J. Y., & Kruglanski, A. W. (2003). When opportunity knocks: Bottom-up priming of goals by means and its effects on self-regulation. *Journal of Personality and Social Psychology, 84,* 1109–1122.

Shallice, T. (1988). *From neuroscience to mental structure.* New York: Cambridge University Press.

Sheeran, P., Aarts, H., Custers, R., Webb, T. L. Cooke, R., & Rivis, A. (2005). The goal-dependent automaticity of drinking habits. *British Journal of Social Psychology, 44,* 1–18.

Sherman, S. J. (1980). On the self-erasing nature of errors of prediction. *Journal of Personality and Social Psychology, 39,* 211–221.

Shih, M., Ambady, N., Richeson, J. A., Fujita, K., & Gray, H. (2002). Stereotype performance boosts: The impact of self-relevance and the manner of stereotype-activation. *Journal of Personality and Social Psychology, 83,* 638–647.

Shih, M., Pittinsky, T. L., & Ambady, N. (1999). Stereotype susceptibility: Identity salience and shifts in quantitive performance. *Psychological Science, 10,* 80–83.

Smeesters, D., Warlop, L., van Avermaet, E., Corneille, O., & Yzerbyt, V. (2003). Do not prime hawks with doves: The interplay of construct activation and consistency of social value orientation on cooperative behavior. *Journal of Personality and Social Psychology, 84,* 972–987.

Spears, R., Gordijn, E., Dijksterhuis, A., & Stapel, D. A. (2004). Reaction in action: Intergroup contrast in automatic behavior. *Personality and Social Psychology Bulletin, 30,* 605–616.

Sperber, D. (1990). The epidemiology of beliefs. In C. Fraser, & G. Gaskell (Eds.), *The social psychological study of widespread beliefs* (pp. 25–44). New York: Clarendon Press/Oxford University Press.

Srull, T. K., & Wyer, R. S., Jr. (1979). The role of category accessibility in the interpretation of information about persons: Some determinants and implications. *Journal of Personality and Social Psychology, 37,* 1660–1672.

Stapel, D., & Koomen, W. (2001). I, we, and the effects of others on me: How self-construal level moderates social comparison effects. *Journal of Personality and Social Psychology, 80,* 766–781.

Stapel, D. A., Koomen, W., & van der Pligt, J. (1996). The referents of traits inferences: The impact of trait concepts versus actor-trait links on subsequent judgments. *Journal of Personality and Social Psychology, 70,* 437–450.

Stapel, D. A., Koomen, W., & van der Pligt, J. (1997). Categories of category accessibility: The impact of trait versus exemplar priming on person judgments. *Journal of Experimental Social Psychology, 33,* 44–76.

Stapel, D. A., & Suls, J. (2004). Method matters: Effects of explicit versus implicit social comparisons on activation, behavior, and self-views. *Journal of Personality and Social Psychology, 87,* 860–875.

Steele, C. M. (1997). A threat in the air: How stereotypes shape intellectual identity and performance. *American Psychologist, 52,* 613–629.

Steele, C. M., & Aronson, J. (1995). Stereotype threat and the intellectual test performance of African Americans. *Journal of Personality and Social Psychology, 69,* 797–811.

Steele, C. M., Spencer S. J., & Aronson, J. (2002). Contending with group image: The psychology of stereotype and social identity threat. In M. P. Zanna (Ed.), *Advances in experimental social psychology* (Vol. 34, pp. 379–440). New York: Academic Press.

Strack, F., Martin, L. L., & Stepper, S. (1988). Inhibiting and facilitating conditions of the human smile: A nonobtrusive test of the facial feedback hypothesis. *Journal of Personality and Social Psychology, 54,* 768–777.

Strahan, E. J., Spencer, S. J., & Zanna, M. P. (2002). Subliminal priming and persuasion: Striking while the iron is hot. *Journal of Experimental Social Psychology, 38,* 556–568.

Tajfel, H., & Turner, J. C. (1979). An integrative theory of intergroup conflict. In W. G. Austin & S. Worchel (Eds.), *The social psychology of intergroup relations* (pp. 33–47). Monterey, CA: Brooks/Cole.

Tanner, R., & Chartrand, T. L., & van Baaren, R. (2006). Strategic mimicry in action: The effect of being mimicked by salesperson on consumer preference for brands. Manuscript submitted for publication, Duke University.

Toates, F. (1986). *Motivational systems.* Cambridge, UK: Cambridge University Press.

Tomasello, M., Kruger, A. C., & Ratner, H. H. (1993). Cultural Learning. *Behavioral and Brain Sciences, 16,* 495–511.

Trope, Y. (1986). Identification and inferential processes in dispositional attribution. *Psychological Review, 93,* 239–257.

Tucker, M. A. (1897). Comparative observations on the involuntary movements of adults and children. *American Journal of Psychology, 8,* 394–404.

Uleman, J., Newman, L. S., & Moskowitz, G. B. (1996). People as flexible interpreters: Evidence and issues from spontaneous trait inference. In M. Zanna (Ed.), *Advances in experimental social psychology* (Vol. 28, pp. 179–211). San Diego, CA: Academic Press.

Utz, S., Ouwerkerk, J. W., & van Lange, P. A. M. (2004). What is smart in a social dilemma? Differential effects of priming competence on cooperation. *European Journal of Social Psychology, 34,* 317–332.

Vallacher, R. R., & Wegner, D. M. (1985). *A theory of action identification.* Hillsdale, NJ: Erlbaum.

van Baaren, R. B., Fockenberg, D. A., Holland, R. W., Janssen, L., & van Knippenberg, A. (in press). The moody chameleon: The effect of mood on non-conscious mimicry. *Social Cognition.*

van Baaren, R. B., Holland, R. W., Steenaert, B., & van Knippenberg, A. (2003a). Mimicry for money: Behavioral consequences of imitation. *Journal of Experimental Social Psychology, 39,* 393–398.

van Baaren, R. B., Horgan, T. G., Chartrand, T. L., & Dijkmans, M. (2004a). The forest, the trees and the chameleon: Context-dependency and mimicry. *Journal of Personality and Social Psychology, 86,* 453–459.

van Baaren, R. B., Maddux, W. W., Chartrand, T. L., de Bouter, C., & van Knippenberg, A. (2003b). It takes two to mimic: Behavioral consequences of self-construals. *Journal of Personality and Social Psychology, 84*(5), 1093–1102.

Van den Berg, S., Aarts, H., Midden, C., & Verplanken, B. (2004b). The role of executive processes in prospective memory tasks. *European Journal of Cognitive Psychology, 16,* 511–533.

Vaughan, K. B., & Lanzetta, J. T. (1980). Vicarious instigation and conditioning of facial expressive and autonomic responses to a model's expressive display of pain. *Journal of Personality and Social Psychology, 38,* 909–923.

Walther, E., Muller, D., & Schott, O. (2001). Automatic social behavior: How does priming of egoism and altruism influence helping behavior? *Zeitschrift fur Experimentelle Psychologie, 48,* 248–257.

Watt, H. J. (1905). Experimentelle beitrage zur einer theorie des denkens. *Archiv für geschichte der Psychologie, 4,* 289–436.

Wegner, D. M. (2002). *The illusion of conscious will.* Cambridge, MA: MIT Press.

Wegner, D. M., & Wheatley, T. (1999). Why it feels as if we're doing things: Sources of the experience of will. *American Psychologist, 54,* 480–492.

Wheeler, S. C., DeMarree, K. G., & Petty, R. E. (2005). The roles of the self in priming-to-behavior effects. In A. Tesser, J.V. Wood, & D. A. Stapel (Eds.), *On building, defending and regulating the self* (pp. 245–271). New York: Psychology Press.

Wheeler, S. C., Jarvis, W. B. G., & Petty, R. E. (2001). Think unto others: The self-destructive impact of negative racial stereotypes. *Journal of Experimental Social Psychology, 37*(2), 173–180.

Wheeler, S. C., & Petty, R. E. (2001). The effects of stereotype activation on behavior: A review of possible mechanisms. *Psychological Bulletin, 127*(6), 797–826.

Williams, K. D., Cheung, C. K. T., et al. (2000). Cyberostracism: Effects of being ignored over the Internet. *Journal of Personality and Social Psychology, 79,* 748–762.

Wilson, T. D. (2002). *Strangers to ourselves.* Cambridge, MA: Harvard University Press.

Winter, L., & Uleman, J. (1984). When are social judgments made? Evidence for the spontaneousness of trait inferences. *Journal of Personality and Social Psychology, 47,* 237–252.

Wolfe, T. (2004). *I am Charlotte Simmons.* London: Jonathan Cape.

Wright, R. A. (1996). Brehm's theory of motivation as a model of effort and cardiovascular response. In J. A. Bargh & P. M. Gollwitzer (Eds.), *The psychology of action: Linking cognition and motivation to behavior* (pp. 424–453). New York, US: Guilford Press.

Wyer, R. S., & Srull, T. K. (1986). Human cognition in its social context. *Psychological Review, 93,* 322–359.

Wyer, R. S., & Srull, T. K. (1989). *Memory and cognition in its social context.* Hillsdale, NJ: Erlbaum.

Young, P. T. (1961). *Motivation and emotion.* New York: John Wiley.

Zajonc, R. B., Adelmann, K. A., Murphy, S. T., & Niedenthal, P. M. (1987). Convergence in the physical appearance of spouses. *Motivation and Emotion, 11,* 335–346.

Zajonc, R. B., Pietromonaco, P., & Bargh, J. A. (1982). Independence and interaction of affect and cognition. In M. S. Clark & S. T. Fiske (Eds.), *Affect and cognition: The seventeenth annual Carnegie symposium on cognition* (pp. 211–227). Hillsdale, NJ: Lawrence Erlbaum.

3

Automaticity in Close Relationships

SERENA CHEN, GRÀINNE M. FITZSIMONS, and
SUSAN M. ANDERSEN

C lose relationships are the subject of countless films, novels, songs, self-help
books, and philosophical reflections – not to mention ordinary, everyday
conversation and thought. They can be the source of joy, love, and security, as well as of pain, anxiety, and sorrow. They capture our attention and interest,
and demand time, energy, and resources. Put simply, close relationships are a core
element of daily interpersonal life. People devote deliberate thought to their close
relationships, and often take great care in choosing their words and deeds in them.
Yet at the same time, mounting theory and evidence indicate that many if not most
relationship processes and phenomena occur rather automatically.

The past two decades have witnessed an explosion of social-psychological
theory and research on automaticity, as well as the development of new empirical
techniques to measure automatic processes (Hassin, Uleman, & Bargh, 2005;
Uleman & Bargh, 1989). It is thus unsurprising that notions of automaticity have
increasingly appeared in the close relationships literature. The study of automaticity in this literature is part of a broader trend towards bridging the fields of
social cognition and close relationships. The result has been the birth of a new field
– relationship cognition – which focuses explicitly on social-cognitive structures
and processes underlying relationship phenomena (Reis & Downey, 1999).

In this chapter, we present a broad sampling of theory and evidence on
automaticity in close relationships. We begin by offering a definition of close
relationships, and then briefly lay out some basic definitions and assumptions
regarding automaticity. From there, we describe a diverse group of distinctly
social-cognitive approaches to close relationships, a group that has produced some
of the most direct evidence for automaticity in the close relationships domain. We
conclude with a discussion of common themes underlying much of this evidence –
namely, the perpetuation of prior relationship experiences and their re-emergence
in present-day encounters.

DEFINITIONS

Defining Close Relationships

The formation and maintenance of close relationships are likely manifestations of the fundamental human need for belonging and connection (Baumeister & Leary, 1995; see also Andersen, Reznik, & Chen, 1997). We define close relationships in terms of the self in relation to significant others, and assume that each relationship with a significant other is mentally represented in this form. Specifically, the cognitive structure of each relationship is comprised of knowledge about the relevant significant other and self-knowledge reflecting who one is in the context of one's relationship with the other. Such self- and significant-other knowledge structures are bound in memory by linkages that embody the typical patterns of self–other interaction. Although each relationship is unique in some manner (e.g., Hinkley & Andersen, 1996), we recognize that generalized relationship structures exist alongside relationship-specific ones (e.g., Klohnen, Weller, Luo, & Choe, 2005; Ogilvie & Ashmore, 1991; Pierce & Lydon, 2001). Numerous approaches to close relationships assume that significant-other representations are distinct in memory from self representations, and yet also assume, as we do, that these representations are linked in memory. Evidence supports both of these assumptions, even though exact models of representation may vary (e.g., Andersen & Chen, 2002; Aron, Aron, Tudor, & Nelson, 1991; Baldwin, 1992).

As cognitive structures, close relationships can be activated and used, thereby exerting assimilative influences on cognition, affect, motivation, and behavior. For example, an activated relationship structure may lead people to expect to be treated by others as relationship partners have previously treated them. In terms of affect and motivation, we assume that people are emotionally and motivationally invested in their significant others and relationships (Andersen & Chen, 2002; Bowlby, 1969; James, 1890; Sullivan, 1953). Thus, the activation of any given relationship structure should and does shape a variety of affective, motivational, and self-regulatory processes. As a final example, when a relationship structure is activated, people may enact behaviors that reflect previous patterns of relating.

We conceptualize the activation of relationship structures in terms of social-cognitive principles of knowledge accessibility (Higgins, 1989, 1996). The higher the accessibility level of any given knowledge structure, the more likely it will be activated. Accessibility arises from either or both temporary and chronic sources (Bargh, Bond, Lombardi, & Tota, 1986). The temporary activation of a relationship structure occurs by virtue of a recent event in the environment (e.g., being reminded of a significant other) that momentarily increases the structure's accessibility. In addition, to the extent that relationship structures have been frequently activated in the past, they are chronically accessible – they have a chronic readiness to be activated even in the absence of temporary accessibility (Andersen, Glassman, Chen, & Cole, 1995; Baldwin, Keelan, Fehr, Enns, & Koh-Rangarajoo, 1996). Importantly, regardless of its temporary or chronic nature, the activation of relationship structures often occurs automatically, as will be seen in the evidence we review.

Defining Automaticity

Although notions of automaticity are as old as the discipline of psychology itself (James, 1890), modern-day roots of the study of automaticity were not planted until the 1970s in the realm of cognitive psychology (Schneider & Shiffrin, 1977), and it was nearly another decade before social psychologists began to tackle automatic processes in earnest (Bargh, 1989; Uleman & Bargh, 1989). In the decades since, automatic or implicit processes have been studied in an impressively broad range of domains, among them attitudes, stereotyping, self-esteem, motivation, and behavior (e.g., Bargh, 1990, 1994; Devine, 1989; Fazio, Sanbonmatsu, Powell, & Kardes, 1986; Greenwald & Banaji, 1995; Wilson & Brekke, 1994; for more recent reviews, see Andersen, Moskowitz, Blair, & Nosek, in press; Bargh, 2005; Moors & De Houwer, 2006; Wegner & Bargh, 1998).

Early definitions of automaticity imposed strict, all-or-none criteria for a process to be deemed automatic. Current views of automaticity, though, recognize that a process need not be categorized as exclusively automatic or not automatic; instead, a process is considered to be automatic if it meets at least one of four basic criteria. These criteria are the perceiver's lack of awareness, the perceiver's absence of intention, the efficiency of the process (i.e., its minimal use of cognitive resources), and the perceiver's lack of control (Bargh, 1989, 1994). Thus, a process may be considered automatic in varying senses and to varying degrees, depending on the particular criteria it meets.

All automatic processes are conditional in some respect; that is, their occurrence depends on the presence of certain conditions, however minimal (Bargh, 1989). For instance, some automatic processes simply require the presence of a triggering stimulus, whereas others require that perceivers are aware of the stimulus. Still others may require a conscious intention for their instigation. Three very broad varieties of conditional automaticity have been delineated (Bargh, 1989, 1994). Preconscious automatic processes occur under the most minimal of conditions, requiring only that perceivers "notice the presence of the triggering stimulus in the environment" (Bargh, 1994, p. 4). Put another way, these processes occur immediately upon registering the stimulus, and they are completed before perceivers grasp, if they ever do, that such a process has occurred. Of course, people are usually conscious of the end-product(s) of these processes, while remaining unaware of the processes themselves.

Preconscious automatic processes include the activation and use of knowledge structures that occur upon perceivers' subliminal exposure to relevant triggering cues, or that occur by virtue of the chronic accessibility of the knowledge structures. Such processes typically meet all four automaticity criteria. For example, in the case of chronically accessible knowledge structures, perceivers typically do not consciously intend, nor are they aware of, the activation of these highly accessible structures and the consequent meaning they impart. Moreover, the activation and use of such structures typically occur efficiently and uncontrollably.

Postconscious automatic processes are similar to preconscious ones except that they require some form of recent, conscious processing (Bargh, 1994), such as the processing initiated by many social-cognitive priming manipulations. For example, perceivers may engage in a priming task that requires them to unscramble strings of words to form grammatical sentences. In doing so, they end up consciously processing semantic associates of a given knowledge structure that have been embedded in the word strings. This conscious processing results in the temporary activation of the knowledge structure and, in turn, responses that are colored by this structure. Thus, whereas chronic accessibility effects are presumed to be preconscious in nature, requiring no conscious involvement at all, temporary accessibility effects are postconscious insofar as they result from the "residual activation of conscious processing" (Bargh, 1994, p. 5). Importantly, although they are instigated by conscious processing, postconscious automatic processes themselves typically occur efficiently and in the absence of intention, awareness, and control.

Finally, goal-dependent automatic processes are those that occur by virtue of a conscious goal or intent (Bargh, 1994), such as the conscious goal to form an impression of a target person. A perceiver with such a goal may, for instance, judge the target person along well-learned, stereotypical attribute dimensions automatically. An empirical test of such automaticity might entail the use of a dual-task paradigm wherein perceivers are required to engage in two tasks at once. To the extent that perceivers are able to respond to one of the tasks without any interference from the other, it is assumed that the processes involved in the former require minimal cognitive resources, one of the criteria of automaticity (e.g., Bargh & Tota, 1988). To illustrate, a perceiver with a conscious, impression formation goal may make stereotypical judgments of a target person as quickly while engaging in a competing task as when not engaging in such a task, implying that his or her judgments were rendered automatically. Thus, although conscious intention is initially involved in goal-dependent automaticity, once the goal or intent is triggered, subsequent processes may nonetheless meet one or more of the other three automaticity criteria.

Evidence for many of the above varieties of automaticity can be found in the close relationships literature. Although seldom are the criteria of automaticity spelled out theoretically or explicitly measured, evidence for automatic processes in the domain of close relationships is mounting rapidly. The lack of precision in definitions and in operational specificity in the study of automaticity in close relationships is not unique to this literature. Notions of automaticity have become so common, and the assumption that a process that meets any of the criteria of automaticity can be deemed automatic so widely accepted, that providing unequivocal evidence for automaticity per se is becoming increasingly less mandatory. Nonetheless, in the pages that follow, we offer a sampling of theory and evidence for automatic processes and phenomena in the realm of close relationships and try to specify throughout the particular bases on which automaticity can be reasonably assumed.

SOCIAL-COGNITIVE APPROACHES TO CLOSE RELATIONSHIPS

Fittingly, evidence for automaticity in the close relationships literature comes from theoretical approaches that are fundamentally social-cognitive in nature. In this section, we lay out the key assumptions of a diverse group of these approaches, before describing evidence for the automaticity of a variety of specific relationship processes and phenomena. We also describe the social-cognitive methods that research in a given area typically uses. In so doing, we point out the variety or varieties of automaticity that are usually demonstrated and on which this can be assumed. Although evidence for automaticity can be found elsewhere in the literature, we focus primarily on the following theoretical frameworks and processes because their social-cognitive underpinnings are especially well-defined and elaborated.

Transference and the Relational Self

Transference refers to the phenomenon whereby aspects of relationships experienced in the past resurface in the present (Freud, 1958; Sullivan, 1953). The social-cognitive model of transference (Andersen & Glassman, 1996) maintains that the phenomenon occurs by virtue of the activation and use of a mental representation of a significant other. Significant-other representations contain many forms of "cold" and "hot" information, such as the personality attributes of significant others, evaluations of them, goals pursued with them, and the emotions one experiences with them. When a significant-other representation is activated in an encounter with a new person, the perceiver interprets and responds to the person in ways derived from the representation. For example, the perceiver infers that the new person possesses attributes that characterize his or her significant other, and responds toward the person as he or she typically does toward the significant other (Andersen & Cole, 1990; Chen, Andersen, & Hinkley, 1999).

The social-cognitive model of transference has recently been elaborated into a theory of the relational self – that is, the self in relation to significant others (Andersen & Chen, 2002). This theory assumes that each significant-other representation is linked in memory to knowledge reflecting the relational self – the particular self one is in the context of the significant other. Linkages between a significant-other representation and the relational self embody the typical patterns of relating between self and other. The theory maintains that activation of a significant-other representation spreads across these linkages to associated relational-self knowledge. This activates the relevant relational self and self-other relational patterns. In short, when transference occurs, people become in part the self they are with the relevant significant other, only with newly encountered others. For example, they see themselves in terms of the qualities that characterize their relational self and shift how they evaluate themselves to reflect their sense of self-worth when with the relevant significant other (Hinkley & Andersen, 1996).

Research indicates that the activation and use of significant-other representations – that is, the triggering of transference – often occurs automatically.

Specifically, studies have shown that significant-other representations are chronically accessible (Andersen et al., 1995; Chen et al., 1999).[1] The use of a significant-other representation solely on the basis of such chronic accessibility reflects a preconscious automatic process, one that occurs efficiently and uncontrollably, and without the perceiver intending or registering that it has.

Evidence for the preconscious automatic activation of significant-other representations and transference can also be found in research in which participants were subliminally presented with descriptors about a new person that were derived from descriptors they themselves had generated in a pretest session to describe a significant other (Glassman & Andersen, 1999). These descriptors served as cues for the activation of the corresponding significant-other representation. Entirely unaware of the subliminal triggering cues, participants did not intend, were not aware of, invested no effort in, and could not control the resulting activation and use of their significant-other representation.

While the social-cognitive model of transference presumes that the automatic activation of significant-other representations is often preconscious, most research on transference has focused on documenting a more goal-dependent form of automatic activation. Specifically, in the typical transference paradigm, participants are exposed supraliminally to descriptors about a new person that are derived from descriptors that they had generated earlier about a significant other. During this exposure, they are given the conscious goal to remember the descriptors (e.g., Andersen & Cole, 1990). Although transference is elicited using such minimalist instructions, participants are often also given the conscious goal of forming an impression of the new person in anticipation of an interaction with him or her (e.g., Andersen, Reznik, & Manzella, 1996). Giving participants the conscious goal to process the significant-other-derived descriptors instigates the consequent activation of the relevant significant-other representation. This goal-dependent activation is nonetheless automatic in that it occurs relatively efficiently, uncontrollably, and in the absence of participants' awareness. The influence of such activation on participants' subsequent responses is similarly automatic, although participants can and do consciously report on the end-products of this activation, such as how much they like or dislike the new person and their expectations about the new person's acceptance or rejection of them.

Relational Schemas

The relational schema approach views close relationships in terms of cognitive structures comprised of three components: schemas of the self and significant other, and an interpersonal script (Baldwin, 1992, 1997). In this approach, the interpersonal script is primary. Interpersonal scripts embody learned, generalized patterns of self–other interaction that typically cut across specific relationships. These interaction patterns are conceptualized in terms of if–then contingencies, which involve expectations about how significant others respond to the self (e.g., "If I seek support, then my spouse will provide it"). Over time, people derive rules of self-inference from such interpersonal expectations. For example, repeated experience with the if–then contingency "If I make a mistake, then others will criticize and reject me" may give rise to the self-inference rule "If I make a mistake, then I am unworthy" (Baldwin, 1997, p. 329). Relational schemas are assumed to be activated by virtue of their chronic or temporary accessibility or both. When a relational schema is activated, the if–then contingencies and self-inference rules that are stored as part of it are elicited, leading the perceiver to anticipate previously-experienced responses from others and to evaluate the self accordingly.

Using a variety of social-cognitive techniques, research has shown that the activation of relational schemas is often provoked automatically. Because the three components of relational schemas are associated in memory, the temporary or chronic activation of any one of them is thought to elicit the activation of the relational schema as a whole (Baldwin, 1992). One of the most commonly used techniques to temporarily activate a relational schema has been a visualization exercise in which participants are asked to think about and visualize interacting with a significant other (e.g., Baldwin & Holmes, 1987). Afterward, participants are asked to engage in a variety of ostensibly unrelated tasks designed to assess the effects of activating the relevant relational schema. In such studies, the activation and subsequent effects of the relational schema can be seen as postconsciously automatic, given that the visualization exercise requires conscious processing, yet the actual activation of the relational schema and its consequences generally occur effortlessly, uncontrollably, and without much in the way of participants' conscious awareness or intent.

Research using lexical decision tasks provides another form of evidence for automaticity in the activation and use of relational schemas. To illustrate, in one set of studies participants engaged in a lexical decision task, which required them to make word/nonword judgments for a series of target stimuli, each preceded by a prime. Some of the prime and target stimuli reflected, respectively, "ifs" and "thens" of the if–then expectations that characterize relational schemas involving contingently accepting significant others (e.g., "If I succeed, then I will be accepted" and "If I fail, then I will be rejected") (Baldwin & Sinclair, 1996; see also Baldwin, Baccus, & Fitzsimons, 2004). Prior to this task, participants visualized either a contingently or noncontingently significant other, which presumably resulted in the postconscious automatic activation of the relevant relational schema. As a result, participants responded more quickly to prime–target pairs reflecting contingent acceptance after visualizing a contingently-accepting significant other versus a noncontingently-accepting other.

The logic of the use of lexical decision tasks to document automaticity is that respondents are unaware that their response latencies are being assessed, and thus do not intentionally respond more quickly to some prime–target pairs over others. Moreover, respondents are consciously doing a different task (i.e., making word/nonword judgments about a set of letter strings), rather than explicitly thinking about the meaning of or relation between the prime and target stimuli. Finally, quicker response latencies in this kind of lexical decision task usually indicate the use of minimal cognitive resources, another criterion of automaticity.

Evidence for the preconscious automatic activation of relational schemas also exists. For example, research has used the subliminal presentation of the face of a significant other to activate the relational schema associated with this person (Baldwin, Carrell, & Lopez, 1990). Other work has relied on the chronic accessibility of relational schemas to document the preconscious effects of these schemas. For example, in the research on expectations of contingent acceptance, a response-latency pattern like the one seen among participants who had visualized a contingently-accepting significant other, thereby temporarily activating the associated relational schema, was seen among low self-esteem individuals – individuals who presumably possess chronically accessible relational schemas containing contingent-acceptance expectations (Baldwin & Sinclair, 1996). As with any chronically accessible knowledge structure, chronic relational schemas lead perceivers to register and interpret stimuli in schema-colored ways that are treated as objective reflections of reality.

Inclusion of Other in the Self

Also fundamentally social-cognitive in nature, the inclusion-of-other-in-self (IOS) model conceptualizes close relationships as involving the incorporation of aspects of relationship partners (e.g., their personality characteristics and perspectives) into the self-concept (Aron et al., 1991). Thus, rather than proposing linkages between the self and significant others, as do the two approaches we just described, the IOS model views close relationships in terms of the merging of representations of the self and others.

Evidence for automaticity in research on the IOS approach lies in studies that have made use of unobtrusive, implicit measures to document close others' inclusion in the self. For example, one study relied on Lord's (1980) finding that object words imagined in relation to the self (i.e., imagining the self interacting with the objects) are encoded and thus remembered less well than words imagined in relation to others (Aron et al., 1991). If significant others are included in the self, then the memory decrement people typically show for objects imagined in relation to the self should likewise hold for objects imagined in relation to significant others. This should occur because the other's perspective is taken as one's own; that is, people imagine the significant other interacting with the objects from the same perspective as when they imagine themselves doing so. In line with such reasoning, participants showed worse memory for words imagined in relation to both themselves and their mothers, relative to words imagined in relation to an acquaintance – presumably without any awareness or intent to do so. This memory-based effect can be presumed automatic in a preconscious sense in that people usually do not consciously register the actual process of inclusion, much less the effects of this inclusion on subsequent processes such as memory.

Evidence for the automaticity of the inclusion of others in the self has most often come from research using response latencies to measure the inclusion of close others' personality attributes (e.g., Aron et al., 1991). In this work, participants rate whether or not a list of traits describe themselves and then a close other. Later, they rate the self-descriptiveness of the same traits again, this time on a computer which records their response latencies. If close others' attributes are included in the self, it should take longer to judge the descriptiveness of traits that are descriptive of the self but not of the other, as well as vice versa, than to judge traits that do not differentiate the self and other. In line with this, faster response latencies are observed in judging traits previously endorsed for both the self and the other (or for neither) as compared with traits that differentiate the self from other. Attesting to the automatic nature of this effect, participants are neither aware that their response latencies are being assessed, nor aware of their differential response tendencies for traits that are shared versus not shared with their close others. Put another way, participants experience their self judgments as simple judgments of fact, rather than as reflecting inclusion.

On a cognitive level, the inclusion of others in the self is represented in the form of overlap between self and other representations, whereas on a phenomenological level such inclusion is experienced as a sense of "we-ness" (Aron et al., 1991). The concept of "we-ness" can also be seen in research conducted in the framework of interdependence theory (Agnew, Van Lange, Rusbult, & Langston, 1998; for a review, see Rusbult & Van Lange, 1996). This work tested the hypothesis that relationship commitment involves a state of cognitive interdependence, defined as possessing an "other-inclusive cognitive representation of the self-in-relationship" (p. 942). Cognitive interdependence was assessed in part in terms of participants' spontaneous use of plural pronouns (e.g., we, us). Just as people are probably not usually aware of, nor do they consciously intend, the consequences of others' inclusion in the self, they are presumably often unaware of and do not intend the consequences of cognitive interdependence, such as heightened plural pronoun use. Supporting the hypothesis that relationship commitment involves cognitive interdependence, commitment was associated with greater plural pronoun use. Though it is not always clear who one is referring to when using the pronoun "we" (e.g., Brewer & Gardner, 1996), such indices can be revealing about the relational perspective one is (or is not) adopting.

Relational-Interdependent Self-Construal

Similar to the view of close relationships put forth by the IOS model, the relational-interdependent self-construal construct (Cross, Bacon, & Morris, 2000) refers to a view of the self into which relationships have been incorporated. For individuals who hold such a self-construal, "representations of important relationships and roles share the self-space with abstract traits, abilities, and preferences" (Cross et al., 2000, p. 791). In short, these individuals define and evaluate themselves in terms of their close relationships. Research has treated the relational-interdependent self-construal as an individual difference construct. Of greatest relevance to the present chapter, individual differences in this construct have been linked to automatic, information-processing tendencies. Specifically, individuals who hold a relational-interdependent self-construal chronically process information in ways that support the maintenance of their close relationships.

Although individual differences in this self-construal are assessed via a conscious, self-report measure – the Relational-Interdependent Self-Construal (RISC) scale (Cross et al., 2000) – researchers have used unobtrusive, implicit measures to document the preconscious nature of the processing tendencies associated with holding a highly relational-interdependent self-view. For example, one study showed that high scores on the RISC scale were associated with the tendency to selectively attend to and thus better remember relationship-related information about others in a surprise recall task (Cross, Morris, & Gore, 2002). Participants were not only unaware that their memory was to be assessed, but presumably also unaware of, and did not intend, the selectivity of their attention and subsequent memory.

Attachment Working Models

Attachment theory is a highly influential theoretical model in the study of close relationships (Bowlby, 1969). Since the late 1980s (following the classic work of Hazan & Shaver, 1987), research on attachment theory has increasingly focused on how attachment processes manifest themselves in adult romantic relationships. Internal working models of the self and others are core constructs in this literature (Collins & Read, 1994; Griffin & Bartholomew, 1994; Pietromonaco & Barrett, 2000). According to attachment theorists, working models are developed in the course of early interactions with attachment figures and reflect the individual's experiences in these interactions. In broad strokes, relationships with responsive and caring attachment figures foster secure models, a view of the self as competent and worthy of love, and a view of others as available and responsive. By contrast, relationships with attachment figures who are inconsistently or not at all responsive give rise to insecure models, such as a conception of the self as incompetent and unworthy of love, and of others as unavailable and unresponsive.

A core attachment-theoretical assumption is that early working models are stored in memory and serve as templates for later relationships. Although early attachment theorists did not use the language of modern-day social cognition, they essentially assumed that working models exert their life-long influences by means of their activation and subsequent assimilative influences in attachment-relevant situations (e.g., Bowlby, 1969). They further assumed that working models of the self and others are complementary and thus that they are activated and exert their effects in tandem.

Contemporary research has shown that attachment working models can be activated on a chronic or temporary basis, and that such activation can occur automatically. In much of this research, working models have been treated as an individual difference, as assessed via self-report (e.g., Bartholomew, 1990; Hazan & Shaver, 1987). The assumption is that individual differences in attachment correspond to distinct chronically accessible working models. In support of this, there is now an extensive body of evidence showing that self-reported attachment styles (i.e., chronic working models) are associated with a variety of cognitive, affective, motivational, and behavioral responses.

As is the case for any chronically accessible construct, the activation of chronic working models of attachment is presumed to be preconscious. This assumption is best substantiated by research in which self-report measures of attachment models are administered in a session different from the one in which the effects of these models (i.e., evidence of their activation) are assessed. In such research, working models are activated and exert their effects solely based on their chronic accessibility, rather than also based on temporary activation arising from having just completed self-report measures of attachment (which are often quite explicit about what is being assessed). Of course, research in which participants complete these measures just prior to engaging in tasks designed to assess the effects of their working models may still provide evidence for automaticity, although it is probably safer to deem these effects postconscious. However, to warrant even this characterization, it is critical that participants are not aware of any relation between their self-reported attachment style and their subsequent responses.

In this vein, especially compelling evidence for the pre- or postconscious automatic effects of attachment working models can be found in research in which these effects have been assessed using unobtrusive measures. In such studies, even if attachment models are assessed immediately prior to the unobtrusive measures – and thus temporarily activated – one can safely assume that participants are unaware of the relation between their working models and the subsequent measures, thereby meeting a core criterion of automaticity. For example, research has used unobtrusive response latencies to assess the unique self-evaluative tendencies associated with distinct attachment working models (Mikulincer, 1995).

With growing evidence that most people have more than one set of attachment working models stored in memory (e.g., Baldwin et al., 1996; Overall, Fletcher, & Friesen, 2003), researchers are increasingly focused on documenting the temporary activation of these models. To do so, they have utilized various social-cognitive techniques, among them the subliminal presentation of attachment-relevant stimuli (e.g., Mikulincer, Hirschberger, Nachmias, & Gillath, 2001). Because participants do not consciously notice such subliminal stimuli, the resulting activation and effects of their working models are automatic in a preconscious sense. Finally, the temporary and postconscious automatic activation of attachment working models has also been demonstrated – for example, in research using the visualization exercise developed by relational-schema researchers (e.g., Mikulincer & Arad, 1999).

Rejection Sensitivity

Drawing in part on attachment-theoretical assumptions about the long-term consequences of early relationship experiences, rejection sensitivity theorists argue that early exposure to rejection results in rejection sensitivity, a cognitive-affective processing disposition to "anxiously expect, readily perceive, and overreact to" rejection (Downey & Feldman, 1996). Although theorizing on rejection sensitivity has generally not included assumptions about any particular cognitive structure – such as a representation, schema, or working model – the cognitive-affective processing tendencies that define rejection sensitivity are learned and thus presumably stored in memory. Substantial research has shown that in situations where rejection is possible, these processing tendencies are activated among high rejection-sensitive individuals, leading them to perceive, interpret, and behave in ways that confirm their anxious expectations of rejection.

To date, rejection sensitivity has been conceptualized as an individual difference construct, assessed via self-report using the Rejection Sensitivity Questionnaire (RSQ; Downey & Feldman, 1996), a measure tapping respondents' expectations of rejection, along with their anxiety about rejection. Although the assessment of rejection sensitivity involves conscious processing, the processing tendencies of high rejection-sensitive individuals are assumed to be chronic. Such individuals are chronically inclined to perceive more rejection than may actually exist, and to view such rejection as a reflection of reality – without registering the influence of their past rejection experiences on their processing tendencies. Thus, the effects of these processing tendencies reflect forms of preconscious automaticity.

In support of this, most research on rejection sensitivity has assessed individual differences in the construct several weeks or months prior to assessing the effects of the processing disposition. For example, a prospective study showed that rejection sensitivity assessed at Time 1 predicted a greater inclination to attribute a romantic partner's insensitive behavior to hurtful intentions at Time 2, several months later (Downey & Feldman, 1996). In this research, it was very unlikely that participants were aware of the relation between their (conscious) Time 1 responses to the RSQ and their Time 2 responses. Thus, although such research has not tended to address automaticity explicitly, it is fairly safe to assume that responses assessed well after individual differences in rejection sensitivity were assessed can be attributed to chronic differences in the tendency for high versus low rejection-sensitive individuals to perceive and interpret events in terms of rejection. Rooted in such chronic differences, these effects are preconscious, although clearly the assessment instruments used at Times 1 and 2 were consciously processed and completed.

Further evidence for the automatic influence of rejection sensitivity has been obtained in research using response latencies to tap the processing proclivities of high rejection-sensitive women (Ayduk, Downey, Testa, Yen, & Shoda, 1999). It was hypothesized that the tendency for these women to respond to rejection with hostility (as shown elsewhere; see Downey & Feldman, 1996) reflects the existence of an automatic mental association between rejection and hostility. Using a sequential-priming pronunciation task with rejection-related prime words and hostility-related target words, this research showed that high relative to low rejection-sensitive women were quicker to pronounce hostility-related target words that were preceded by rejection primes. As these response-latency patterns occurred without participants' awareness or intention, and required minimal cognitive resources, they provide clear evidence for the automatic nature of the effects of rejection sensitivity. In sequential-priming tasks such as the one used in this research, when the priming stimuli are presented supraliminally, their semantic meaning is processed consciously, implying that the automaticity demonstrated by such tasks is postconscious.

Other Approaches

Of course, other influential approaches to close relationships exist. Several of them focus on delineating the specific, relational patterns and norms that characterize different relationship categories or types, including types of close relationships. For example, in research on communal and exchange relationships, close relationships are akin to communal relationships, wherein members give benefits in response to each other's need without any specific expectation of receiving benefits in return (Clark & Mills, 1979; Clark, Mills, & Powell, 1986). In relational models theory, which proposes four basic models of relationships, close relationships fit the communal sharing category, which involves relationships wherein members treat one another as equivalent and emphasize what is common rather than distinct among members (Fiske, 1991, 1992). These examples, as well as other approaches (e.g., Bugental, 2000), presuppose the importance of close relationships, and have been deeply informative about such relationships. However, because notions of automaticity have been less central or less well-developed in these approaches, and these approaches go beyond close relationships, we include evidence from them only where especially relevant.

PROCESSES AND PHENOMENA

We now turn to evidence for the automaticity of a wide variety of specific relationship processes and phenomena. In particular, we describe evidence for the automatic nature of relationship-relevant information processing, affective responses and evaluation, acceptance and rejection expectations, self-definition and self-evaluation, motivation and self-regulation, and interpersonal behavior. Most of the research we review was provoked by one of the approaches above or from a closely related perspective. Throughout, our aim was to provide a few particularly illustrative examples of automaticity in each of the above processes and phenomena.

Automatic Information Processing

Encoding refers to the process by which perceivers register an external stimulus. Temporarily or chronically accessible knowledge structures influence whether and how a stimulus is encoded. More specifically, in most cases a structure is activated and leads perceivers to attend to and interpret stimuli in an assimilative manner. This assimilative influence often occurs automatically, with little awareness, effort, intention, and control. On a phenomenological level, perceivers simply register their conception of external stimuli as reality rather than as a product of an activated knowledge structure.

There is ample evidence for automatic encoding effects in research emerging from several of the social-cognitive approaches described above. Namely, the transference, relational schema, and attachment theories all assume that close relationships are mentally represented in the form of some kind of a cognitive structure, and that when relationship structures are temporarily or chronically activated, subsequently-encountered stimuli are especially likely to be encoded in terms of these structures. The activation of these structures is often automatic and, accordingly, so too is the assimilative influence of these structures on encoding.

In terms of the individual difference approaches we described, automatic encoding effects are assumed to be among the array of automatic, information-processing tendencies associated with construing the self in relational terms and with being high in rejection sensitivity. By definition, individuals with a relational-interdependent self-construal are attentive to and likely to interpret stimuli in terms of their relationship implications (Cross et al., 2002). Along similar lines, high rejection-sensitive individuals are attuned to rejection-relevant stimuli in the environment and prone to encoding stimuli in terms of rejection (Downey & Feldman, 1996).

Beyond encoding, a basic assumption about any knowledge structure is that, when activated, it may be used to "go beyond the information given" (Bruner, 1957) about a stimulus. That is, perceivers draw upon their stored knowledge to make inferences about new stimuli. To the extent that the activation of the knowledge structure itself is automatic, so too are the inferences that follow. To illustrate, research on stereotyping has shown that stereotype activation leads to automatic stereotype-based inferences about subsequently-encountered targets even among people who hold nonprejudiced, egalitarian beliefs (e.g., Devine, 1989). Analogously, in the close relationships domain, research on transference provides especially straightforward evidence for automatic inferences based on an activated relationship structure. Specifically, this work has repeatedly shown that the preconscious or goal-dependent activation of a significant-other representation in an encounter with a new person leads perceivers to infer that the new person possesses attributes of the relevant significant other more than is actually the case (Andersen & Cole, 1990; for reviews, see Andersen, Reznik, & Glassman, 2005; Chen & Andersen, 1999).

Also in the realm of inferences, researchers have shown that chronic working models of attachment influence how people process information to form inferences about others. For instance, research has shown that individuals with chronic, secure models engage in more information search, show less preference for cognitive closure, and fall less prey to the primacy effect than those with insecure models (Mikulincer, 1997). Other research has shown that temporarily or chronically activated secure models are associated with greater cognitive openness to expectancy-incongruent information about a relationship partner (i.e., greater change in perceptions of the partner after exposure to such information; Mikulincer & Arad, 1999). In each case, it was unlikely that participants had any awareness of the activation and subsequent information-processing influences of their attachment models. That is, there was no temporary priming because attachment models were assessed in a session prior to the one in which their processing tendencies were assessed, or the relation between participants' attachment models and the processing measures was disguised. Thus, one can safely presume that the activation and effects of attachment working models shown in this research were automatic.

Evidence for automatic memory effects also exists. For example, in the study just described, both temporary and chronic working models of secure attachment were associated with not only greater openness to expectancy-incongruent information, but also better memory for this information (Mikulincer & Arad, 1999). This memory effect was primarily seen when the information was positively valenced, suggesting that information that is consistent with the overall positive valence of secure working models of others is more likely to be processed in a manner that leads it to be retained. Another example is the research we described earlier showing that people with a highly relational-interdependent self-construal selectively attend to and thus have better memory for relationship-related information about others (Cross et al., 2002).

Research has also shown that holding a highly relational-interdependent self-construal is associated with an automatic tendency to use relationships as a tool to organize memory about others (Cross et al., 2002). Specifically, one study showed that higher scores on the Relational-Interdependent Self-Construal scale were associated with an implicit tendency to cluster memory for information items about a set of married couples according to the marital relationship. In other words, information items about married individuals were more likely to be recalled together than information about non-married individuals.

This work on the relational-interdependent self-construal drew partly from conceptualizations of relationships in terms of general types or categories, such as communal and exchange relationships (Clark & Mills, 1979). Work on communal and exchange relationships has generally not addressed notions of automaticity. One exception to this, though, is research showing the automatic activation of different goals – namely, other-focused versus self-focused goals – among communal- versus exchange-oriented individuals, respectively, when nonconsciously primed with the concept of power (Chen, Lee-Chai, & Bargh, 2001). Such automatic goal effects reflect the distinct power–goal associations of individuals with different relationship orientations. Other researchers have conceptualized relationships, including communal and exchange ones, as basic categories that people use to organize social stimuli (Fiske, 1992; Sedikides, Olsen, & Reis, 1993). For example, research on relational models theory (Fiske, 1991, 1992), noted earlier, has shown that people are more likely to confuse people (e.g., calling someone by someone else's name) with whom they share the same kind of relationship among the four basic relational models, implying that these four models are used as bases for categorization (Fiske, Haslam, & Fiske, 1991).

In other research, participants who were asked to recall and list the name of every person with whom they had interacted in the prior month showed clustering based on the four relational models; that is, participants tended to recall people with whom they share the same kind of relationship consecutively (Fiske, 1995). Although people may consciously think about their relationships in terms of the four relational models, it is argued that the use of these models as a basis for categorizing the social world often occurs automatically, efficiently, and without awareness or intention (Fiske & Haslam, 1996; Haslam & Fiske, 1992). Indeed, both confusions and clustering in recall can be seen as unobtrusive, implicit measures of categorization.

Automatic Affect and Evaluation

We now turn to evidence for automatic affect and evaluation. Although the vast majority of research has focused on the assessment of global, positive and negative affect and evaluation, we also describe some evidence for the automatic elicitation of discrete emotions.

A key assumption of the transference approach is that significant-other representations include affect-laden material that reflects the emotions and evaluations people associate with their significant others (Andersen & Glassman, 1996). Thus, the activation of a significant-other representation should automatically elicit this affect and evaluation. Indeed, numerous studies have shown that participants evaluated an anticipated interaction partner more favorably when the partner activated a representation of a positively rather than negatively evaluated significant other (e.g., Andersen & Baum, 1994; Andersen et al., 1996; Berk & Andersen, 2000). This was not observed when the partner was characterized by a yoked participant's descriptors about a positive or negative significant other. While the evaluation measures used in this research were self-report, the processes that underlie these evaluation effects – namely, the activation and use of a significant-other representation – are known to be automatic, as described earlier.

Further evidence for the automatic affective consequences of an activated significant-other representation can also be found outside of the transference realm. In one set of studies, for example, participants were subliminally exposed to the names and faces of either significant others or of themselves and then asked them to evaluate neutral, Chinese ideographs (Banse, 1999). The hypothesis was that more positive evaluation should be automatically elicited upon the activation of representations of significant others compared to the self because people tend to idealize their significant others (Murray, Holmes, & Griffin, 1996), and self representations contain more negative information. As predicted, participants evaluated the ideographs more positively in response to significant-other priming than to priming of their own name and face.

To capture the automatic affective consequences of the activation of a significant-other representation more directly in the transference paradigm, researchers have unobtrusively assessed participants' facial affect during exposure to descriptors about an upcoming interaction partner (Andersen et al., 1996). These descriptors were derived from ones participants had generated earlier to describe a positively or negatively evaluated significant other and thus, as usual, served as activation cues for the relevant representation. As predicted, participants expressed more pleasant affect in their facial expressions when their representation of a positive compared to negative significant other was activated. This pattern of representation-consistent affect was not seen in a control, no-transference condition in which the descriptors were derived from a yoked participant's descriptors about a positive or negative significant other (for related evidence, see Berenson & Andersen, in press).

In a different study, participants were likewise exposed to descriptors about an upcoming interaction partner who resembled the participants' own or a yoked participant's positively evaluated significant other, while the interpersonal role of the anticipated partner vis-à-vis the participant was manipulated (Baum & Andersen, 1999). That is, the partner's role (expert or novice) was either congruent or incongruent with the role typically occupied by the participant's significant other (who was an authority figure). Presumably, role incongruence is unpleasant because it signals that goals typically pursued with the significant other are unlikely to be satisfied. Indeed, activating participants' own significant-other representation in the context of role incongruence (vs. congruence) led to an increase in dysphoric mood. No such difference emerged when transference was not evoked (i.e., when the partner was characterized with a yoked participant's significant-other descriptors). As in most research on transference, the activation of a significant-other representation in the transference condition involved a goal-dependent form of automaticity, implying a conscious, instigating goal, and yet the presumed spread of activation to the interpersonal role of the significant other and the goals associated with this role was nonetheless automatic. That is, it is likely that the interaction between the activation of a significant-other representation and role congruence versus incongruence, even though occurring more downstream in the processing sequence, nonetheless occurred without participants' intention or awareness.

Also in the transference domain, research focused on emotional responding has evoked transference among participants with an ideal or ought self-discrepancy (Higgins, 1987) from the standpoint of a parent (Reznik & Andersen, 2005). When the descriptors about an upcoming interaction partner resembled the relevant parent and thus activated the representation of this parent, the ideal or ought self-discrepancy from this parent's standpoint was also activated. As a result, ideal- and ought-discrepant participants exhibited the affective responses predicted by self-discrepancy theory; ideal-discrepant participants reported increases in depressive mood, whereas ought-discrepant participants showed increases in hostility and decreases in calm. Once again, these affective states occurred in the context of transference, which was evoked by the goal-dependent, automatic activation of a significant-other representation. Thus, the consequent spread of activation from the parental representation to the relevant standard and self-discrepancy can be presumed automatic (Andersen et al., 2005).

Research on relational schemas has also produced evidence for automatic affective responses. For example, just after reading a short passage describing a sexually permissive situation, Roman Catholic women were shown subliminal images of Pope John Paul II with a disapproving expression, which were intended to activate relational schemas representing disapproval from a significant other (Baldwin et al., 1990). As a result, these women reported higher levels of negative affect (i.e., anxiety and tension) relative to a control group. Although these women were aware of the affective end-products of the subliminal activation of their Pope relational schema, the activation itself can be presumed automatic in a preconscious sense.

In a different set of studies, female participants underwent a conditioning procedure whereby particular stimuli (e.g., computer tones) were repeatedly paired with acceptance- or rejection-related thoughts (Baldwin & Main, 2001). Later, the conditioned stimuli were presented as cues for the activation of relational schemas reflecting acceptance or rejection while female participants had a stressful interaction with a male confederate. Participants high in public self-consciousness were affected by the cued activation of relational schemas; relative to a control group, they reported greater anxiety-related affect when rejection versus acceptance condition stimuli were presented during the interaction. Once more, although these participants consciously reported on their affect, they presumably were not aware of, and did not consciously intend, the activation of the relational schemas that produced this affect.

Affect and emotion have long been central to attachment theory (Bowlby, 1969), and investigations of the automaticity of attachment-related affect are growing in number. A particularly good example is research on secure base schemas, which can be characterized as relational schemas comprised of positive beliefs about the self and significant other, linked via an interpersonal script designating positive expectations about the availability and responsiveness of the other in times of stress (Mikulincer et al., 2001). It was hypothesized that given the positive connotations of their components, secure base schemas should be a source of positive affect, implying that when a secure base schema is activated, positive affect should automatically ensue. To test this, secure base schemas were activated by subliminally exposing participants to pictures connoting security (e.g., a mother holding her baby). Participants were then asked to evaluate various kinds of neutral stimuli. Across several studies, participants exhibited more positive affective reactions to the neutral stimuli after a secure base schema had been subliminally primed as compared to after a neutral prime or no priming. Moreover, the link between activated secure base schemas and positive affect held under both neutral and stressful conditions, whereas priming positively toned, but attachment-unrelated schemas only produced automatic positive affect under neutral conditions.

In terms of attachment-related evaluations, recent research has adapted the Implicit Association Test (IAT; Greenwald, McGhee, & Schwartz, 1998) to assess attachment differences in the nature of automatic evaluations elicited upon thinking about a significant other (Zayas & Shoda, 2005). Among various findings, this work showed that higher levels of secure attachment at both the general and specific level were associated with more automatic positive evaluations of relationship partners in a version of the IAT using the name of the relationship partner as one basis for categorization (e.g., John vs. not John).

Automatic Expectations of Acceptance or Rejection

Among the most basic and fundamentally relational of perceivers' beliefs and perceptions about their significant others are expectations about a significant other's acceptance or rejection of the self. Research on several of the social-cognitive approaches reviewed earlier suggests that such expectations are often elicited automatically.

The transference approach assumes that expectations about a significant other's acceptance or rejection are stored in memory as part of the linkages binding significant-other representations to knowledge reflecting the relevant relational self (Andersen & Chen, 2002). Research has shown that when a perceiver's significant-other representation is activated in a goal-dependent, automatic fashion in an encounter with a new person, activation spreads across these linkages, thereby eliciting stored acceptance/rejection expectations (Andersen et al., 1996). As a result, the perceiver comes to expect the new person to accept or reject him or her just as the significant other typically does (see also Berenson & Andersen, in press).

As described earlier, interpersonal expectations lie at the heart of the interpersonal scripts that define relational schemas (Baldwin, 1992). These expectations take the form of "if–then" contingencies that designate specific responses to the self (e.g., "If I seek help, my significant other provides it"), or more global, accepting or rejecting responses (e.g., "If I succeed, my significant other accepts me"). The relational schema approach assumes that the activation of a relational schema elicits automatic, schema-consistent expectations about others. For example, the study described earlier in which participants were quicker to respond to prime–target pairings that reflected expectations of contingent acceptance after a relational schema involving a contingently-accepting (vs. noncontingently accepting) significant other shows that such expectations are automatically activated (Baldwin & Sinclair, 1996).

Attachment working models of others are also comprised in large part with expectations regarding the responsiveness of significant others (Bowlby, 1969; Hazan & Shaver, 1987). Research adopting a relational schema approach has documented the automatic nature of such attachment-related expectations. This research hypothesized that chronic attachment working models are associated with distinct, if–then expectations about others (Baldwin, Fehr, Keedian, Seidel, & Thomson, 1993). Specifically, secure participants possess relational schemas with if–then expectations designating positive responses from significant others, whereas insecure participants possess ones with negative interpersonal expectations. In this research, a lexical decision task was used to show that participants with chronic, secure working models were able to identify positive outcome words (e.g., support) quicker after presentation of an interpersonal context prime (e.g., "If I depend on my partner, then my partner will . . ."), whereas participants with insecure models were faster to identify negative outcome words (e.g., leave).

As a final example, research on rejection sensitivity has produced wide-ranging evidence for the automatic elicitation of rejection expectations. Indeed, the very definition of rejection sensitivity involves the automatic tendency to expect and perceive rejection from others, as already noted (Downey & Feldman, 1996). To illustrate, research has found that individual differences in rejection sensitivity were positively associated with the tendency to overestimate a relationship partner's dissatisfaction and lack of commitment to the relationship. In another study, participants were confronted with an ambiguously rejecting situation – that is, they were not told why an upcoming interaction partner who was given information about them suddenly declined to participate in the interaction. Under such circumstances, rejection sensitivity predicted a higher likelihood of interpreting the situation in terms of rejection (Downey & Feldman, 1996). Such differential expectations of rejection as a function of individual differences in rejection sensitivity were not found in a condition in which participants were explicitly told that the interaction would not take place for reasons unrelated to them.

Automatic Bases of Self-Definition and Self-Evaluation

The basic notion that close relationships influence the self is nearly as old as the discipline of psychology itself (James, 1890). Newer is research that speaks to the automatic bases of this influence. Nearly all of the social-cognitive approaches we reviewed at the outset of this chapter offer relevant evidence.

According to the transference approach, by virtue of linkages between significant-other representations and relational-self knowledge, when a significant-other representation is activated, activation spreads to the relevant relational self. As a result, the working self-concept is infused in part with this relational-self knowledge, leading the self to be defined and evaluated in part as this relational self typically is (Andersen & Chen, 2002). Once activation of the significant-other representation occurs, the spread of this activation to the self should occur automatically. In research testing these ideas, participants were presented with descriptors about an upcoming interaction partner derived from descriptors that they (or a yoked participant) had generated in a pretest session to describe a positive or negative significant other (Hinkley & Andersen, 1996; see also Reznik & Andersen, 2004, cited in Andersen et al., 2005). As usual, the descriptors derived from one of the participants' own significant others should automatically elicit transference.

Immediately after presentation of the descriptors, participants were asked to describe themselves by generating a list of descriptors, after which they evaluated each of the self-descriptors they listed. The results showed that participants in the transference condition spontaneously described and evaluated themselves in a manner consistent with how they had described and evaluated the relevant relational self (i.e., the self with this significant other) at pretest. They became more the self they are with their significant other and shifts in their sense of self-worth occurred accordingly (i.e., reflected the valence of the relationship). Such self-definitional and self-evaluative effects were not seen in the yoked, no-transference condition.

As indicated, the relational schema approach argues that people derive rules of self-inference from repeated exposure to if–then contingencies that specify others' reactions to the self (Baldwin, 1992, 1997). Thus, when activated, relational schemas can be influential sources of self-evaluation. Particularly compelling evidence for the automaticity of the self-evaluative consequences of activated relational schemas can be found in research using subliminal priming techniques. For example, graduate-student participants were subliminally exposed to the disapproving face of their advisor (Baldwin et al., 1990). As a result, they evaluated their research ideas more negatively, presumably due to the preconscious activation of if–then contingencies linking the advisor's disapproval to negative self-evaluation.

A different study had participants engage in the visualization exercise to temporarily activate a relational schema involving either a contingently or non-contingently accepting significant other (Baldwin & Holmes, 1987). Afterward, participants who failed at a task evaluated themselves in a manner consistent with how they assumed they would be evaluated in the activated relationship; namely, participants in the contingently-accepting other condition evaluated themselves more negatively than those in the non-contingent condition.

Turning to the attachment-theoretical approach, attachment working models of the self are, by definition, comprised of positive or negative conceptions of the self. A large body of research has documented associations between attachment styles (i.e., chronic working models) and the positivity or negativity of self-views (Griffin & Bartholomew, 1994; Hazan & Shaver, 1987). Among all of this work, research using implicit measures to assess positivity or negativity in the self provides the most compelling evidence for the automatic nature of the self-evaluations that comprise working models of the self. In such work, participants are not even aware that their self-evaluations are being assessed, rendering it safe to conclude that these self-evaluations are not the product of conscious intention.

For example, the Stroop color-naming task has been used to assess the positivity and negativity of the self-views of participants with secure, anxious-ambivalent, or dismissing attachment styles (Mikulincer, 1995). In this task, participants named the printed color of positive and negative trait words that either were or were not self-relevant, as determined on the basis of ratings participants made in a pretest session. Self-descriptive traits should yield longer color-naming latencies because the trait's high accessibility interferes with the color-naming process. The results showed that secure individuals possess balanced views of themselves, with naming latencies slower for both positive and negative self-relevant traits compared to irrelevant ones. In contrast, anxious-ambivalent individuals were slowest to name the color of negative, self-relevant traits, while dismissing individuals were slowest for positive, self-relevant traits.

Further evidence for the automaticity of attachment working models of the self comes from research on security-based self-representations, which refer to aspects of the self developed in the context of security-enhancing interactions with attachment figures (Mikulincer & Shaver, 2004). Such representations should be indirectly activated when the attachment system is activated. Supporting this, research has found that when the attachment system was activated via a threat induction, participants who scored low in attachment anxiety (i.e., with chronic secure working models) described themselves using attributes that they had used earlier to characterize their security-based self-representations. Thus, the threat induction heightened the accessibility of attributes that these participants associate with these representations, shifting their self-definitions accordingly.

Research on the relational-interdependent self-construal construct also provides evidence for the automaticity of self-related perceptions. For example, one set of studies examined perceptions of self–other similarity as a function of individual differences on the Relational-Interdependent Self-Construal scale. It was hypothesized that high-RISC individuals, who define themselves in terms of their close relationships, should be especially motivated to see similarities between their own and close others' self-definitions, as similarities imply relationship closeness and harmony (Cross et al., 2002). To test this, the researchers used unobtrusive measures of perceived self-other similarity, measures that made it unlikely that participants were aware that their similarity perceptions were being assessed or that these perceptions were consciously intended. In one study, for example, participants rated a series of traits in terms of whether each described themselves, a close friend, or college students, unaware that their ratings would later be compared across targets. As expected, RISC scores were positively associated with correlations between self and friend ratings, but not between self and college student ratings.

Finally, research on the inclusion-of-other-in-self (IOS) approach has documented the automatic nature of incorporated aspects of close others in the self-concept by using unobtrusive measures (e.g., response latencies) to assess the self-concept (Aron et al., 1991), as noted. This research suggests that oftentimes people may not be aware of, nor consciously intend, the self-concept consequences of being in a close relationship. Other research suggests that the actual process of including others in the self may occur automatically. For example, one study showed that participants' reports of falling in love predicted greater change and diversity in their open-ended self-descriptions (Aron, Paris, & Aron, 1995). A different study found that befriending members of racial outgroups was linked to greater change and diversity in self-descriptions (Wright, McLaughlin-Volpe, & Brody, 2004). In both cases the effect of forming a new relationship on the self-concept was a process that may have occurred with little conscious awareness, intention, and effort on the part of participants. Of course, it is important to acknowledge that because specific evidence regarding which of these criteria were and were not met is lacking, we cannot definitively conclude that these self-concept effects were indeed automatic, nor can we know for sure what variety of automaticity they entailed.

Automatic Self-Regulation

Beyond cognitive and affective components of close relationships, motivational constructs like goals and needs also play an essential role in interpersonal life, and recent research suggests that associated self-regulatory processes also occur automatically. In this section, we review evidence for automatic self-regulatory processes pertaining to the activation and pursuit of the goals people associate with their significant others. Specifically, we address people's efforts to protect themselves and their relationships in the face of threat, as well as other forms of activated motives and self-regulatory strategies.

Automatic Goal Activation and Pursuit In the past decade, a number of studies have found evidence for the notion that goals are mentally represented and, as such, can be automatically activated by situational cues. Furthermore, people have been shown to pursue activated goals with little awareness, intention, effort, and control – that is, they automatically regulate their behavior in ways designed to fulfill active goals (e.g., Bargh, 1990; Bargh, Gollwitzer, Lee-Chai, Barndollar, & Trötschel, 2001).

In relationship contexts, research on transference has provided strong evidence for automatic goal activation. According to the transference approach, the goals people typically pursue in the context of their relationship with a significant other become part of the relational dynamics between the self and other and thus are stored in memory in the linkages that bind the relevant significant-other representation to the relevant relational self (Andersen & Chen, 2002). Thus, when a perceiver's significant-other representation is activated in an encounter with a new person, the goals associated with this other are accordingly activated. As a result, the perceiver pursues the goals typically sought with the significant other, only with the new person.

A fundamental need people have in relation to significant others is that of connection and belonging. Research has shown that the activation of a positive rather than a negative significant-other representation led participants to report a desire to approach (and not to avoid) an upcoming interaction partner (Andersen et al., 1996; Berk & Andersen, 2000). Just as they typically seek to approach the relevant significant other – to be close and disclosing, and to maintain the relationship – they pursue this with the partner, a phenomenon evoked by the automatic activation of a significant-other representation, though assessed via self-report. Moreover, this is distinguishable from evaluation. That is, people who have been harmed by a significant other but still love this other, as in the case of abuse by a parent, will recoil from the motive to disclose in a relevant transference (Berenson & Andersen, in press).

Building on findings from both the transference and relational schema approaches, recent research has examined the effects of automatically activating a significant-other representation on goal pursuit outside of the transference context. Specifically, several studies have shown that just thinking about a significant other (or being subliminally exposed to this person's name) automatically activates relationship goals. Individuals primed with a significant other behaved in line with goals that they previously reported associating with the other (Fitzsimons & Bargh, 2003). For example, participants who had the goal to please their mother and who were primed with their mother later achieved higher performance on a verbal achievement task, without exhibiting any conscious awareness of this or intent to do so.

Similarly, activating a significant-other representation has been shown to guide self-regulation through the activation of the significant other's goals for the self (Moretti & Higgins, 1999; Shah, 2003a). Significant others, once represented mentally, can in a sense "watch us from the back of our minds," as internal audiences, evoking goals and standards that guide individuals' behavior in line with the significant other's desires (Andersen & Chen, 2002; Baldwin & Holmes, 1987; Moretti & Higgins, 1999; Shah, 2003a). Ideal and ought discrepancies from the standpoint of a significant other are theorized to embody the goals or standards that the significant other holds for the self, and as such can guide the self's behavior (Moretti & Higgins, 1999). Indeed, in a transference context, ideal-discrepant participants exhibited promotion-oriented self-regulatory strategies, whereas ought-discrepant participants showed evidence of prevention-oriented strategies (Reznik & Andersen, 2005).

Likewise, further evidence for the automatic influence of significant others' goals for the self has been shown outside of the transference context. In one set of studies, for example, participants who were subliminally primed with the names of their significant other reported being more committed to their significant other's goals, and behaved more in accordance with the other's goals (Shah, 2003a). Furthermore, using response-latency measures, this research provided strong evidence for the automatic link between goal constructs and significant-other representations; for example, participants who felt their father cared about their academic achievement responded more quickly to the achievement-related target words that were immediately preceded with father-related prime words. A related set of studies showed that participants' appraisals of the difficulty of attaining a goal were colored by their beliefs about the significant other's expectations about their goal attainment (Shah, 2003b).

Finally, recent research on attachment has shown the automatic activation of attachment-related goals (Gillath, Mikulincer, Fitzsimons, Shaver, Schachner, & Bargh, in press). One study showed that subliminally priming the name of an attachment figure increased pursuit of proximity-enhancing goals. That is, they self-disclosed more and more quickly to a new person. In another study, subliminally exposing participants to the name of a significant other affected the accessibility of goal words related to secure, anxious, or avoidant attachment, depending on the attachment relationship. Participants who scored high on attachment avoidance and low on attachment anxiety took longer to identify secure goal words in a lexical decision task after being primed with a secure relationship, perhaps because such a relationship elicited conflictual feelings or resistance in such individuals (Gillath et al., in press).

Automatic Self- and Relationship-Protection Thus, people can regulate their interpersonal behavior to fit overarching goals linked with an activated significant-other representation without need for conscious involvement in the activation process. Two motivations of great importance in relationships are self-protection (when the self is threatened) and relationship-protection (when the relationship is threatened). We now turn to a variety of evidence suggesting that these motives and their self-regulatory functions may be evoked and function automatically.

Research on transference has provided clear evidence for automatic self- and relationship-protective motives. For example, when the representation of a negative significant other was activated, leading participants to negatively evaluate the relational-self qualities associated with the negative other that arose in their working self-concepts, participants responded by enhancing the positivity of their evaluations of their nonrelational-self attributes (Hinkley & Andersen, 1996; Reznik & Andersen, 2004). Presumably, this response reflected an attempt to protect the self in the face of the threat delivered by the influx of negative, relational-self attributes into the working self-concept. Although this research used self-report measures, the effect itself may nonetheless occur automatically (Andersen et al., 2005).

In terms of relationship-protective motives, research on transference has relied on a different methodology. Specifically, research has shown that when exposed to negative features of a positive significant other in transference, participants tend to respond with expressions of pronounced positive affect – in their facial expressions. Because these facial expressions arise virtually immediately, they presumably transform the negative valence into a positive one relatively automatically. Such a response presumably reflects an effort to protect the positivity of the image of the significant other and of the relationship in the face of the threatening, negative information (Andersen et al., 1996; for a related effect, see Berenson & Andersen, in press).

The motivation to protect the self from interpersonal threat is also at the core of rejection sensitivity, and has been theorized to guide behavior in an automatic fashion. People high in rejection sensitivity are susceptible to a wide range of negative interpersonal outcomes that are related to self-protective mechanisms. For example, their anxiety about being rejected by others causes them to behave more aggressively (Downey, Feldman, & Ayduk, 2000) and experience less satisfying relationships (Downey & Feldman, 1996). Although no research has directly examined people's awareness of these effects, it seems unlikely that people high in rejection sensitivity are aware of the influence of defensive, self-protective motives on their relationships.

Interestingly, the extent to which people are generally "good self-regulators" has been found to moderate the negative effects of rejection sensitivity on interpersonal outcomes (Ayduk et al., 2000). Rejection-sensitive people who can control their attention to delay immediate gratification do not suffer the same interpersonal ills. The extent to which people high in rejection sensitivity have automatized these self-control behaviors is as yet undetermined. It is conceivable that with enough practice and experience, people high in rejection sensitivity could learn to automatically inhibit the negative thoughts and habitual responses that follow from rejection, perhaps based on extensive practice of delay of gratification over time. However, it is also conceivable that this type of self-control process may require conscious attention and control to overcome the automatic, self-defensive response (also see Yovetich & Rusbult, 1994).

In related research, more direct evidence exists for the role of automatic self-protective motivations in response to interpersonal threat. According to the dependency regulation model, when people feel secure, they exhibit relationship-protective responses, viewing their partners more positively and seeking increased closeness (Murray, Holmes, & Griffin, 2000; Murray, Holmes, Griffin, Bellavia, & Rose, 2001). When people feel rejected, however, they engage in self-protective strategies, decreasing their attachment to their partner and increasing self-reliance. Recent research has tested a longstanding assumption in this model (see Murray, Rose, Griffin, & Bellavia, 2003) – namely, that these self- and relationship-protecting mechanisms occur outside of consciousness (DeHart, Pelham, & Murray, 2004). Two studies used "the name letter effect" (Nuttin, 1985) to examine participants' evaluations of their romantic partners. The name letter effect refers to people's preference for letters found in their own name, thought to reflect people's implicit self-evaluations. Extending this reasoning to evaluations of others, DeHart and colleagues reasoned that people's preference for letters found in the names of their romantic partners could be seen as implicit evaluations of their romantic partners. For people with low self-esteem, implicit evaluations of their partners (i.e., their preference for letters from their partners' names) were contingent on the current success of their relationship. By contrast, people with high self-esteem had positive implicit evaluations of their partners even when things were not going well in their relationship. These findings provide initial evidence that people can automatically self-regulate to fulfill higher-order self-protective and relationship-protective needs, in line with the highly practiced and frequently pursued motivational responses to threat.

Automatic responses to interpersonal threat can also play a role in parent–child relationships. Parents who perceive themselves as relatively low in power relative to their child have been shown to have chronically accessible constructs related to dominance and power (Bugental, Lyon, Krantz, & Cortez, 1997). These parents feel threatened by their lack of power in the relationship, and as such they respond by overactivating thoughts of power and control. With sufficient cognitive capacity, these power-threatened parents can regulate these thoughts and feelings, and can present themselves as being in control. However, under conditions of cognitive load, the threat of loss of power leads immediately to dominance ideations and corresponding cognitions and behaviors. This mix of automatic threat and defensive overcompensation may result in a negative parenting style and lead to problems within the parent–child relationship.

Similarly, threat can automatically elicit different affective, motivational, and behavioral responses from people who vary in attachment anxiety and avoidance (Mikulincer, Gillath, & Shaver, 2002). Mikulincer (1998) delineated self-regulatory strategies that characterize people who are chronically high versus low in attachment anxiety and avoidance. People high in anxiety are theorized to use strategies that hyperactivate the attachment motivational system, leading them to pursue security and closeness. People chronically high in avoidance are theorized to use strategies that deactivate the attachment motivational system, leading them to pursue self-protective strategies such as self-reliance and emotional distance. For example, they encode less information about attachment experiences as they occur (Fraley, Garner, & Shaver, 2000), and suppress thoughts of potentially threatening interpersonal outcomes (Fraley & Shaver, 1997). Both of these low-level self-regulation strategies help those chronically high in avoidance to avoid feeling attachment-related distress and inhibit motivations to seek comfort from attachment figures, and presumably do so in an automatic fashion.

Further evidence has accumulated that supports the role of self-regulatory strategies in adult attachment relationships. For example, individuals chronically high in attachment anxiety overestimate their similarity to attachment figures (Mikulincer, Orbach, & Iavnieli, 1998), and hold a negative view of themselves (Mikulincer, 1998). By contrast, individuals chronically high in attachment avoidance underestimate their similarity to attachment figures and hold an unusually positive view of themselves. These tendencies were found to be exacerbated under conditions of negative affect and distress, and were related to desires to win others' approval (for those chronically high in anxiety) and to validate a sense of self-reliance (for those chronically high in avoidance), thus emphasizing the motivational nature of these self-perceptual differences. Given that these effects stem from chronically accessible constructs, they are likely to function at a preconscious level of automaticity, requiring no conscious triggering.

A core component of Bowlby's (1969) original attachment theory and more recent adult attachment theories (e.g., Hazan & Shaver, 1987) has been that the attachment motivational system performs the majority of its functions outside of conscious awareness or control. That is, patterns set in childhood are thought to be habitual and automatized early on, allowing attachment working models to shape behavior. The working models themselves are thought to be stored representations of past interactions, and exert their influence on behavior at a "preconscious" level (Bowlby, 1980). Thus, the self-regulatory strategies reported above – such as suppressing negative thoughts or underestimating similarity to attachment figures – are theorized to function automatically. That most of the findings reflected the effects of chronic attachment working models supports these assumptions. However, more direct support can be found in recent research using a variety of social-cognitive techniques to measure the workings of the attachment motivational system.

For example, Mikulincer et al. (2002) found that people respond to threat by activating mental representations of attachment figures automatically – that is, with little or no effort, awareness, and intention. In some studies, threat is subliminally presented, providing some empirical evidence for the supposition that chronic attachment differences likely manifest themselves as a form of preconscious automaticity. Automatically bringing to mind thoughts of attachment figures presumably provides feelings of comfort and reduces negative affect. Attachment anxiety causes a hyperactivation of this strategy, with attachment figure representations becoming elicited more readily, while avoidance lessens the accessibility of those representations. Thus, automatic self-regulatory strategies depend on past relationship experiences and dynamics; that is, people pursue the goals and strategies that they have relied upon in the past to provide them with security, regardless of whether those are the most appropriate strategies for the current interpersonal environment.

Automatic Effects on Interpersonal Behavior

Finally, among the most provocative advances in the automaticity domain over the past decade is research on the automatic social behavior (Bargh, 2005; Dijksterhaus, & Bargh, 2001). In this section, we describe evidence for automatic interpersonal behavior in close relationships.

Research on transference suggests that when a significant-other representation is activated in an encounter with a new person, along with the beliefs and expectations stored as part of this representation, it automatically instigates a behavioral confirmation cycle. In one such study, for example, each participant (the perceiver) was exposed to descriptors about another participant (the target) with whom he or she then had an audiotaped conversation (Berk & Andersen, 2000). The descriptors bore no actual relation to the target, but instead were derived from descriptors that the participant or a yoked participant had generated in a pretest session to characterize a positive or negative significant other. As usual, the descriptors derived from participants' own significant-other descriptors elicited transference – that is, the activation of the corresponding significant-other representation.

Most important, the pleasantness of affect in participants' audiotaped, conversational behavior was coded by independent judges and the results offered evidence for behavioral confirmation in transference. That is, the target ended up expressing more pleasant affect when he or she resembled the perceiver's positive rather than negative significant other; no such effect was seen in the yoked, no-transference conditions. Presumably, the affect stored as part of perceivers' representations of positive and negative significant others, respectively, was activated in transference, in turn coloring perceivers' behavior and ultimately leading targets to respond in kind. As usual, the activation of a significant-other representation in the transference condition was automatic in a postconscious sense. Accordingly, perceivers in this condition were unaware of, and did not consciously intend to produce, the behavioral effects that ensued.

Behavioral confirmation also lies at the heart of the Michelangelo phenomenon (Drigotas, Rusbult, Wieselquist, & Whitton, 1999). In this phenomenon, a close partner perceives the self in ideal terms (i.e., partner perceptual affirmation) and then acts on his or her perceptions of the self's ideal (i.e., partner behavioral affirmation), leading the self to confirm the ideal. Thus, just as Michelangelo sculpted ideal forms from blocks of stone, relationship partners help sculpt each other's ideal forms by acting toward each other in ways that affirm these ideals. Across several studies, evidence for the Michelangelo phenomenon was found among both dating and married couples (Drigotas et al., 1999). Moreover, this research showed that the phenomenon has positive effects on couple well-being (e.g., intimacy). Although this work relied on conscious, self-report measures, the researchers argued that, in the course of the actual, day-to-day behavioral dynamics of relationships, the processes that underlie the Michelangelo phenomenon may involve either deliberate, conscious processes or automatic ones. Regarding the latter possibility, it seems quite likely, for example, that perceptions of a relationship partner in terms of that partner's ideals may over time become preconscious; relationship partners come to register these perceptions as objective reflections of reality.

Research on rejection sensitivity has also documented a form of behavioral confirmation between romantic partners (Downey, Freitas, Michaelis, & Khouri, 1998). This research has examined how the anxious rejection expectations of high rejection-sensitive individuals manifest in their behavior and ultimately lead their partners to respond in ways that confirm rejection expectations. Specifically, romantic partners were videotaped while discussing an unresolved relationship issue. Negative behaviors (e.g., making a demeaning comment about one's partner) during the discussion were then coded by independent judges. High rejection-sensitive women exhibited more negative behavior than low rejection-sensitive women, and the partners of the former group accordingly reported a greater increase in pre- to post-discussion anger. Mediational analyses showed that high rejection-sensitive women's negative behavior accounted for a significant portion of the variance of the effect of women's rejection sensitivity on the increase in their partners' anger.

Because rejection sensitivity involves the automatic tendency to expect more rejection than warranted, such automatic expectations are thought to be what trigger the behavioral cycle that results in a self-fulfilling prophecy for high rejection-sensitive individuals. Hence, the above findings can be taken as evidence that the anxious rejection expectations that define rejection sensitivity elicit automatic, expectancy-consistent behavior. Indeed, research indicates that self-fulfilling prophecy effects need not result from consciously held beliefs and expectations (e.g., Chen & Bargh, 1997). In addition, that the behavioral data described above were obtained from coders' ratings of videotapes of the *spontaneous* behaviors of romantic partners during a conflict discussion – partners who were aware that they were being videotaped but unaware of what was being coded – strongly suggests the automatic nature of rejection-sensitivity effects on behavior.

Observations of spontaneous, dyadic behaviors of relationship partners also serve as an evidentiary basis for automatic, attachment-related behaviors. Research assessing such behaviors suggests that chronic attachment working models automatically give rise to behavioral tendencies reflecting the beliefs, assumptions, and concerns comprising these models. For example, the spontaneous support-seeking and support-giving behaviors of members of heterosexual dating couples were unobtrusively recorded after the woman was placed in a stressful situation (Simpson, Rholes, & Nelligan, 1992). The results showed that women with chronic, secure working models of attachment sought more support the more anxious they felt, whereas women with avoidant working models did the opposite. Secure men offered more support the more their partners exhibited anxiety, whereas greater anxiety in their partners was linked to less support among avoidant men. Presumably, participants automatically perceived and interpreted the experimental situation through the lenses of their chronic attachment working models, which then gave rise to the distinct behavioral tendencies they exhibited.

Still clearer evidence for preconscious automatic effects of attachment working models on behavior can be found in research using subliminal priming techniques to assess the link between attachment security and compassion and altruism (Mikulincer, Shaver, Gillath, & Nitzberg, 2005). For example, one study showed that subliminal activation of attachment-security representations not only led participants to report higher compassion, but also led them to actually agree to do aversive tasks on behalf of an alleged other participant. Finally, the research described earlier on the automatic activation of attachment-related goals (Gillath et al., in press) offers another example of automatic, attachment-related behavior effects. Recall that this work showed that subliminal priming of the name of an attachment figure led participants to self-disclose more and quicker relative to various control conditions.

INTEGRATION AND BROADER CONSIDERATIONS: THE PERPETUATION OF THE PAST INTO THE PRESENT

We have described evidence for various forms of automaticity across a wide range of relationship processes and phenomena. In the spirit of integration, we now draw closer attention to a recurring theme in much of this work – namely, assumptions and tendencies learned in past or in current relationships with significant others are often perpetuated and re-created in present-day encounters with new others. It is no coincidence that evidence for automaticity in close relationships comes from research conducted in the framework of social-cognitive approaches. Such approaches share the core assumption that aspects of prior relationships are mentally represented in some form and thus, when activated, can exert automatic, assimilative influences. In line with such approaches, we suggest that tendencies learned in prior relationships "live on" in relational structures in the mind. This allows them to exert continuing, automatic influences within and beyond these relationships themselves, and even if these relationships end.

Despite differences in the exact assumptions and methods underlying research across different areas, as well as in the particular varieties of automaticity demonstrated, a feature common to all automatic processes is that precisely because they occur in the absence of individuals' awareness, intent, and control, and/or with little expenditure of cognitive resources, they are readily perpetuated. That is, they are strengthened with repetition and practice (even if subtle variations occur each time), rendering them more likely over time to find their way into present-day interpersonal encounters. In short, automaticity may lie at the heart of the perpetuation and re-emergence of previously-experienced relationship processes and phenomena.

The notion that relationships from the past are often perpetuated and re-created is central to nearly all of the social-cognitive approaches we reviewed. For example, transference refers to the very phenomenon whereby assumptions and tendencies from prior relationships with significant others re-surface in relations with new others, and research has shown that this occurs by virtue of the activation of significant-other representations and associated relational selves. Attachment working models of the self and others are the basis for the assumption that early experiences with attachment figures shape individuals throughout the life span. Interestingly, recent work suggests that transference may constitute a primary mechanism by which attachment working models exert their influence over time (Andersen, Bartz, Berenson, & Kezckemethy, 2006; Brumbaugh & Fraley, 2006). The relational schemas model suggests that expectations about new others' responses to the self are derived largely from the activation of past if–then dynamics stored in relational schemas. Rejection-sensitive individuals' automatic tendencies to expect, perceive, and overreact to rejection cues only serve to re-create prior rejection experiences, thus cementing these existing tendencies.

Though less obvious, notions of perpetuation and re-creation can also be found in IOS research examining how a significant other's befriending of an outgroup member can influence the nature of the self. In particular, when a significant other befriends an outgroup member and thus incorporates this outgroup member into his or her self-concept, the fact that a perceiver has included the significant other into the self therefore leads the perceiver to also incorporate the significant other's favorable evaluations of the outgroup (Wright, Aron, McLaughlin-Volpe, & Ropp, 1997). In other words, the outgroup member can be seen as included in the perceiver's self because the significant other, who is already included in the self, has included the outgroup member. This lays the foundation for the perceiver to befriend an outgroup member himself or herself, thus perpetuating, in some sense, the significant other's friendship.

In the relational-interdependent self-construal approach, the automatic, information-processing tendencies of individuals who hold such a self-construal appear to maintain the very relationships in which their self-construal is grounded. For example, research has shown that holding a relational-interdependent self-construal is associated with perceiving a relatively new relationship partner as viewing the relationship positively (Cross & Gore, 2003). Research has also shown that after a brief interaction with a high relationally-interdependent individual, participants were more likely to rate their interaction partners as responsive and self-disclosing than those who interacted with a low relationally-interdependent partner (Cross et al., 2000). Moreover, the former group rated their relationship with their partner more positively. Thus, highly relationally-interdependent individuals perceive and behave in ways that help perpetuate the very relationships that define them.

At this point, a reader may be left with the impression that much of what happens in close relationships does so automatically: Automaticity underlies how people think and feel about their significant others and themselves, whether people expect to be accepted or rejected, how they regulate themselves as they strive to attain goals associated with significant others or to protect themselves and their relationships, and, finally, how they behave toward others. Moreover, we have emphasized that this wide range of automatic processes and phenomena is likely to be maintained over time, repeatedly re-surfacing in new interpersonal encounters.

Nonetheless, we would strongly argue against the conclusion that relationship processes and phenomena are *always* automatic. People spend a great deal of time thinking about the people they love, as well as people they are bound to but may be ambivalent about or even loathe. People wish, plan, dream, scheme, rejoice, mourn, worry, approach, and avoid in the context of their relationships. Much of this occurs fully consciously and with deliberation. In fact, we assume that when made aware of most of the automatic processes we have described, and if armed with adequate time and cognitive resources, as well as enough motivation to bother, people should theoretically be able to exert enough control over these processes to circumvent and override them. This assumption is consistent with theorizing and data suggesting that people are concerned with biases or the "contamination" of their responses, even though their lay theories about what contaminates their responses are often inaccurate (Wilson & Brekke, 1994). This work highlights the fact that even when not unaware of the cues that provoked an automatic response, one may still experience the response as undesired – or to use a clinical term, as "ego-dystonic." In this case, the consequences of automatic processes are unwelcome.

But if circumventing or overriding the biases brought on by past relationship experiences is possible, why are relationship patterns so notoriously difficult to change? Indeed, it might be surmised that because people's emotional and motivational outcomes hinge so crucially on the nature of their close relationships, they would be especially likely to have awareness and to summon the resources and motivation necessary to exert control over relationship dynamics that they want to alter or end. However, within existing relationships, we suggest that the level of interdependence one experiences with significant others, the very fact that one's own outcomes depend on the other, can drain cognitive resources and make it ever more likely that automatic processes will hold sway. And, in the course of day-to-day encounters with new others (who are potential relationship partners), it is often not feasible or practical to carefully deliberate about who one is dealing with and how one ought to respond. Finally, people's inherent cognitive capacity limits conspire to make such encounters especially likely to be processed in terms of prior relationships. In short, it may be that time, resources, and motivation are seldom in great supply in the course of daily social life.

On a different note, not all relationships are maladaptive or problematic, and hence people may be motivated to leave well enough alone. And, even when relationships are painful and aversive, sometimes "the devil you know" may be easier to face than "the devil you don't." That is, people may place a premium on predictability and doing what they know, even if it means ending up with the same suboptimal or even harmful relationship patterns and outcomes they have experienced in the past. Thus, the familiarity of the relevant interpretations, affective responses, expectations, motives, self-regulatory efforts, and the like enables the recent or faraway past to perpetuate and re-emerge in the present.

Considering the interplay of automaticity and control in close relationships raises many intriguing issues and questions for future research to investigate. In the broader social cognition literature, researchers have shown that when perceivers are made aware of the potential influence of, for example, an activated trait construct on their judgments, contrast effects may occur (e.g., Herr, Sherman, & Fazio, 1983). That is, perceivers' judgments may contrast away from rather than assimilate toward the trait construct. Can and do analogous contrast effects occur when the activated construct is a relationship structure, such as a significant-other representation, relational schema, or attachment working model? Are more or distinct kinds of conscious processes required because the self is implicated in relationships and because of the generally higher emotional and motivational stakes involved? Of course, when people become aware of the potential automatic influence of their prior relationship tendencies on their present-day social encounters, the preferred or optimal response may not always be to literally contrast away from these tendencies, but rather it may be best to simply short-circuit and replace them with entirely different responses. Indeed, people may not know how much to contrast or correct for the influence of past relationships (e.g., Strack & Hannover, 1996).

Beyond being aware and having appropriate correction strategies, people clearly need to have motivation and cognitive resources if they are to override the automatic influences of past relationships. But how likely is it that such strategic attempts will succeed? If people can override such automatic influences from the past in their present-day interpersonal lives, what are the underlying processes involved? Is it the activation per se of existing relationship structures that is short-circuited or is it merely their use? Do new relationship experiences replace the content of existing relationship structures? Clearly, we are posing many more questions than we can currently answer. The general point is that with such ample and growing evidence for automaticity in close relationships, it seems the time has come to search for answers to how and when control can be exerted over the broad constellation of relationship processes and phenomena that unfold automatically.

We began this chapter by noting the deep fascination people have with the close others in their lives, and this fascination is reflected in the vibrant and growing literature on close relationships within social and personality psychology. As this literature expands still further, it will be of great value to understand more about the precise nature of the mental representations involved in relationship processes, as well as to ask questions about automaticity increasingly carefully and systematically. Doing so will build our knowledge about when automaticity is likely to occur and when it is not, and about the conditions that are likely to facilitate mindful, deliberative processing in relationships, given that there are times when this would be valuable (and even life-saving) to the individual and/or to the relationship. Put simply, it remains the case that relatively little is known about how people's attempts to become aware of and in some sense to consciously shape their own relational lives may in fact bear fruit. Perhaps this is simply too much to ask and these questions are too big to conquer. Or perhaps such revelations are just around the next few corners in this growing science.

NOTE

1. Although our focus is on the automatic nature of the activation of significant-other representations in the context of transference, related research has found various forms of evidence for automaticity in the content and structure of significant-other representations. For example, early research on significant-other representations found that people are quicker to retrieve features that characterize their significant others relative to various control targets in a free-retrieval description task (Andersen & Cole, 1990). Such results suggest the chronic accessibility of stored knowledge about significant others. More recent research has found evidence for automaticity in the structure of the "psychological-state theories" that people store as part of their significant-other representations. These theories reflect people's beliefs and inferences about the psychological states that give rise to their significant others' responses (Chen, 2003; see also Shoda & Mischel, 1993). In this research, participants were quicker to retrieve and generate the psychological states that explain the responses of their significant others relative to several control targets. This offers clues as to other ways in which significant-other representations may be associated with relatively automatic processing.

REFERENCES

Agnew, C. R., Van Lange, P. A. M., Rusbult, C. E., & Langston, C. A. (1998). Cognitive interdependence: Commitment and the mental representation of close relationships. *Journal of Personality and Social Psychology, 74*(4), 939–954.

Andersen, S. M., Bartz, J., Berenson, K. R., & Keczkemethy, C. (2006) Triggering the attachment system in transference: Evoking specific emotions through implicitly activating a parental representation. Unpublished manuscript, New York University.

Andersen, S. M., & Baum, A. B. (1994). Transference in interpersonal relations: Inferences and affect based on significant-other representations. *Journal of Personality*, *62*, 4, 460–497.

Andersen, S. M., & Chen, S. (2002). The relational self: An interpersonal social-cognitive theory. *Psychological Review*, *109*, 619–645.

Andersen, S. M., & Cole, S. W. (1990). "Do I know you?": The role of significant others in general social perception. *Journal of Personality and Social Psychology*, *59*, 384–399.

Andersen, S. M., & Glassman, N. S. (1996). Responding to significant others when they are not there: Effects on interpersonal inference, motivation, and affect. In R. M. Sorrentino & E. T. Higgins (Eds.), *Handbook of motivation and cognition* (Vol. 3, pp. 262–321). New York: Guilford.

Andersen, S. M., Glassman, N. S., Chen, S., & Cole, S. W. (1995). Transference in social perception: The role of chronic accessibility in significant-other representations. *Journal of Personality and Social Psychology*, *69*, 41–57.

Andersen, S. M., Moskowitz, D. B., Blair, I. V., & Nosek, B. A. (in press). Automatic thought. In E. T. Higgins & A. W. Kruglanski (Eds.), *Social psychology: Handbook of basic principles* (2nd ed.). New York: Guilford Press.

Andersen, S. M., Reznik, I., & Chen, S. (1997). Self in relation to others: Cognitive and motivational underpinnings. In J. G. Snodgrass & R. L. Thompson (Eds.), *The self across psychology: Self-recognition, self-awareness, and the self-concept* (pp. 233–275). New York: New York Academy of Science.

Andersen, S. M., Reznik, I., & Glassman, N. S. (2005). The unconscious relational self. In R. Hassin, J. S. Uleman, & J. A. Bargh (Eds.), *The new unconscious* (pp. 421–481). New York: Oxford University Press.

Andersen, S. M., Reznik, I., & Manzella, L. M. (1996). Eliciting transient affect, motivation, and expectancies in transference: Significant-other representations and the self in social relations. *Journal of Personality and Social Psychology*, *71*, 1108–1129.

Aron, A., Aron, E. N., Tudor, M., & Nelson, G. (1991). Close relationships as including other in the self. *Journal of Personality and Social Psychology*, *60*, 241–253.

Aron, A., Paris, M., & Aron, E. N. (1995). Falling in love: Prospective studies of self-concept change. *Journal of Personality and Social Psychology*, *69*, 1102–1112.

Ayduk, O., Downey, G., Testa, A., Yen, Y., & Shoda, Y. (1999). Does rejection elicit hostility in rejection sensitive women? *Social Cognition*, *17*(2), 245–271.

Ayduk, O., Mendoza-Denton, R., Mischel, W., Downey, G., Peake, P. K., & Rodriguez, M. (2000). Regulating the interpersonal self: Strategic self-regulation for coping with rejection sensitivity. *Journal of Personality and Social Psychology*, *79*, 776–792.

Baldwin, M. W. (1992). Relational schemas and the processing of information. *Psychological Bulletin*, *112*, 461–484.

Baldwin, M. W. (1997). Relational schemas as a source of if-then self-inference procedures. *Review of General Psychology*, *1*, 326–335.

Baldwin, M. W., Baccus, J. R., & Fitzsimons, G. M. (2004). Self-esteem and the dual processing of interpersonal contingencies. *Self and Identity*, *3*, 81–93.

Baldwin, M. W., Carrell, S. E., & Lopez, D. F. (1990). Priming relationship schemas: My advisor and the Pope are watching me from the back of my mind. *Journal of Experimental Social Psychology*, *26*, 435–454.

Baldwin, M. W., Fehr, B., Keedian, E., Seidel, M., & Thompson, D. W. (1993). An exploration of the relational schemata underlying attachment styles: Self-report and lexical decision approaches. *Personality and Social Psychology Bulletin, 19*, 746–754.

Baldwin, M. W., & Holmes, J. G. (1987). Salient private audiences and awareness of self. *Journal of Personality and Social Psychology, 52*, 1087–1098.

Baldwin, M. W., Keelan, J. P. R., Fehr, B., Enns, V., & Koh-Rangarajoo, E. (1996). Social-cognitive conceptualization of attachment working models: Availability and accessibility effects. *Journal of Personality and Social Psychology, 71*, 94–109.

Baldwin, M. W., & Main, K. J. (2001). Social anxiety and the cued activation of relational knowledge. *Personality & Social Psychology Bulletin, 27*, 1637–1647.

Baldwin, M. W., & Sinclair, L. (1996). Self-esteem and "if . . . then" contingencies of interpersonal acceptance. *Journal of Personality and Social Psychology, 71*, 1130–1141.

Banse, R. (1999). Automatic evaluation of self and significant others: Affective priming in close relationships. *Journal of Social and Personal Relationships, 16*, 803–821.

Bargh, J. A. (1989). Conditional automaticity: Varieties of automatic influence in social perception and cognition. In J. S. Uleman & J. A. Bargh (Eds.), *Unintended thought* (pp. 3–51). New York: Guilford.

Bargh, J. A. (1990). Auto-motives: Preconscious determinants of social interaction. In E. T. Higgins & R. M. Sorrentino (Eds.) *Handbook of motivation and cognition: Foundations of social behavior* (Vol. 2, pp. 93–130). New York: Guilford Press.

Bargh, J. A. (1994). The four horsemen of automaticity: Awareness, intention, efficiency, and control in social cognition. In R. S. Wyer & T. K. Srull (Eds.), *Handbook of social cognition* (2nd ed., pp. 1–40). Hillsdale, NJ: Erlbaum.

Bargh, J. A. (2005). Bypassing the will: Towards demystifying behavioral priming effects. In R. Hassin, J. Uleman & J. Bargh (Eds.), *The new unconscious* (pp. 37–60). New York: Oxford University Press.

Bargh, J. A., Bond, R. N., Lombardi, W. J., & Tota, M. E. (1986). The additive nature of chronic and temporary sources of construct accessibility. *Journal of Personality and Social Psychology, 50*, 869–878.

Bargh, J. A., Gollwitzer, P. M., Lee-Chai, A., Barndollar, K., & Trötschel, R. (2001). The automated will: Nonconscious activation and pursuit of behavioral goals. *Journal of Personality and Social Psychology, 81*, 1014–1027.

Bargh, J. A., & Tota, M. E. (1988). Context-dependent automatic processing in depression: Accessibility of negative constructs with regard to self but not others. *Journal of Personality and Social Psychology, 54*, 925–939.

Bartholomew, K. (1990). Avoidance of intimacy: An attachment perspective. *Journal of Personal and Social Relationships, 7*, 147–178.

Baum, A. & Andersen, S. M. (1999). Interpersonal roles in transference: Transient mood states under the condition of significant-other activation. *Social Cognition, 17*, 161–185.

Baumeister, R. F., & Leary, M. R. (1995). The need to belong: Desire for interpersonal attachments as a fundamental human motivation. *Psychological Bulletin, 117*, 497–529.

Berenson, K. R., & Andersen, S. M. (in press). Childhood physical and emotional abuse by a parent: Transference effects in adult interpersonal relationships. *Personality and Social Psychology Bulletin*.

Berk, M. S., & Andersen, S. M. (2000). The impact of past relationships on interpersonal behavior: Behavioral confirmation in the social-cognitive process of transference. *Journal of Personality and Social Psychology, 79*, 546–562.

Bowlby, J. (1969). *Attachment and loss: Vol. 1. Attachment.* New York: Basic Books.

Bowlby, J. (1980). *Attachment and loss, Vol. 3: Loss, sadness and depression.* New York: Basic Books.

Brewer, M. B., & Gardner, W. (1996). Who is this "we?" Levels of collective identity and self representations. *Journal of Personality and Social Psychology, 71*, 83–93.

Brumbaugh, C. C., & Fraley, R. C. (2006). Transference and attachment: How do attachment patterns get carried forward from one relationship to the next? *Personality and Social Psychology Bulletin, 32*, 552–560.

Bruner, J. S. (1957). Going beyond the information given. In H. E. Gruber, K. R. Hammond, & R. Jessor (Eds.), *Contemporary approaches to cognition* (pp. 41–60). Cambridge, MA: Harvard University Press.

Bugental, D. B. (2000). Acquisition of the algorithms of social life: A domain-based approach. *Psychological Bulletin, 126*, 187–219.

Bugental, D. B., Lyon, J. E., Krantz, J., & Cortez, V. (1997). Who's the boss? Differential accessibility of dominance ideation in parent–child relationships. *Journal of Personality and Social Psychology, 79*, 1297–1309.

Chen, S. (2003). Psychological-state theories about significant others: Implications for the content and structure of significant-other representations. *Personality & Social Psychology Bulletin, 29*, 1285–1302.

Chen, S., & Andersen, S. M. (1999). Relationships from the past in the present: Significant-other representations and transference in interpersonal life. In M. P. Zanna (Ed.), *Advances in Experimental Social Psychology* (Vol. 31, pp. 123–190). San Diego, CA: Academic Press.

Chen, S., Andersen, S. M., & Hinkley, K. (1999). Triggering transference: Examining the role of applicability and use of significant-other representations in social perception. *Social Cognition, 17*, 332–365.

Chen, S., Lee-Chai, A. Y., & Bargh, J. A. (2001). Relationship orientation as a moderator of the effects of social power. *Journal of Personality and Social Psychology, 80*, 173–187.

Chen, M., & Bargh, J. A. (1997). Nonconscious behavioral confirmation processes: The self-fulfilling consequences of automatic stereotype activation. *Journal of Experimental Social Psychology, 33*, 541–560.

Clark, M. S., & Mills, J. (1979). Interpersonal attraction in exchange and communal relationships. *Journal of Personality and Social Psychology, 37*, 12–24.

Clark, M. S., Mills, J., & Powell, M. C. (1986). Keeping track of needs in communal and exchange relationships. *Journal of Personality and Social Psychology, 51*(2), 333–338.

Collins, N. L., & Read, S. J. (1994). Cognitive representations of attachment: The structure and function of working models. In K. Bartholomew & D. Perlman (Eds.), *Attachment processes in adulthood* (Vol. 5, pp. 53–90). Philadelphia, PA: Jessica Kingsley.

Cross, S. E., Bacon, P. L., & Morris, M. L. (2000). The relational-interdependent self-construal and relationships. *Journal of Personality and Social Psychology, 78*, 791–808.

Cross, S. E., & Gore, J. S. (2003). Cultural Models of the self. In M. R. Leary & J. P. Tangney (Eds.), *Handbook of self and identity* (pp. 536–564): New York: Guilford Press.

Cross, S. E., Morris, M. L., & Gore, J. S. (2002). Thinking about oneself and others: The relational-interdependent self-construal and social cognition. *Journal of Personality and Social Psychology, 82*, 399–418.

DeHart, T., Pelham, B., & Murray, S. (2004). Implicit dependency regulation: Self esteem, relationship closeness, and implicit evaluations of close others. *Social Cognition,* *22*(1), 126–146.

Devine, P. G. (1989). Stereotypes and prejudice: Their automatic and controlled components. *Journal of Personality and Social Psychology, 56,* 5–18.

Dijksterhaus, A., & Bargh, J. A. (2001). The perception-behavior expressway: Automatic effects of social perception on social behavior. In M. P. Zanna (Ed.), *Advances in experimental social psychology* (Vol. 33, pp. 1–40). San Diego, CA: Academic Press.

Downey, G., & Feldman, S. (1996). Implications of rejection sensitivity for intimate relationships. *Journal of Personality and Social Psychology, 70,* 1327–1343.

Downey, G., Feldman, S., & Ayduk, O. (2000). Rejection sensitivity and male violence in romantic relationships. *Personal Relationships, 7*(1), 45–61.

Downey, G., Freitas, A. L., Michaelis, B., & Khouri, H. (1998). The self-fulfilling prophecy in close relationships: Rejection sensitivity and rejection by romantic partners. *Journal of Personality and Social Psychology, 75*(2), 545–560.

Drigotas, S. M., Rusbult, C. E., Wieselquist, J., & Whitton, S. W. (1999). Close partner as sculptor of the ideal self: Behavioral affirmation and the Michelangelo phenomenon. *Journal of Personality and Social Psychology, 77,* 293–323.

Fazio, R. H., Sanbonmatsu, D. M., Powell, M. C., & Kardes, F. R. (1986). On the automatic activation of attitudes. *Journal of Personality and Social Psychology, 50,* 229–238.

Fiske, A. P. (1991). *Structures of social life: The four elementary forms of human relations: Communal sharing, authority ranking, equality matching, market pricing.* New York: Free Press.

Fiske, A. P. (1992). The four elementary forms of sociality: Framework for a unified theory of social relations. *Psychological Review, 99,* 689–723.

Fiske, A. P. (1995). The cultural dimensions of psychological research: Method effects imply cultural mediation. In P. E. Shrout & S. T. Fiske (Eds.), *Personality research, methods, and theory: A festschrift honoring Donald W Fiske* (pp. 271–294): Hillsdale, NJ, Englandiates.

Fiske, A. P., & Haslam, N. (1996). Social cognition is thinking about relationships. *Current Directions in Psychological Science, 5*(5), 137–142.

Fiske, A. P., Haslam, N., & Fiske, S. T. (1991). Confusing one person with another: What errors reveal about the elementary forms of social relations. *Journal of Personality and Social Psychology, 60,* 656–674.

Fitzsimons, G. M., & Bargh, J. A. (2003). Thinking of you: Nonconscious pursuit of interpersonal goals associated with relationship partners. *Journal of Personality and Social Psychology, 84,* 148–164.

Fraley, R. C., Garner, J. P., & Shaver, P. R. (2000). Adult attachment and the defensive regulation of attention and memory: Examining the role of preemptive and postemptive defensive processes. *Journal of Personality and Social Psychology, 79,* 816–826.

Fraley, R. C., & Shaver, P. R. (1997). Adult attachment and the suppression of unwanted thoughts. *Journal of Personality and Social Psychology, 73,* 1080–1091.

Freud, S. (1958). *The dynamics of transference. Standard edition* (Vol. 12, pp. 99–108). London, England: Hogarth. (Original work published 1912.)

Gillath, O., Mikulincer, M., Fitzsimons, G. M., Shaver, P. R., Schachner, D. A., & Bargh, J. A. (in press). Automatic activation of attachment-related goals. *Personality and Social Psychology Bulletin.*

Glassman, N. S., & Andersen, S. M. (1999). Activating transference without consciousness: Using significant-other representations to go beyond what is subliminally given. *Journal of Personality and Social Psychology, 77,* 1146–1162.

Greenwald, A. G., & Banaji, M. R. (1995). Implicit social cognition: Attitudes, self-esteem, and stereotypes. *Psychological Review, 102*, 4–27.

Greenwald, A. G., McGhee, D. E., & Schwartz, J. L. K. (1998). Measuring individual differences in implicit cognition: The Implicit Associations Test. *Journal of Personality and Social Psychology, 74*, 1464–1480.

Griffin, D. W., & Bartholomew, K. (1994). Models of the self and other: Fundamental dimensions underlying measures of adult attachment. *Journal of Personality and Social Psychology, 67*, 430–445.

Haslam, N., & Fiske, A. P. (1992). Implicit relationship prototypes: Investigating five theories of the cognitive organization of social relationships. *Journal of Experimental Social Psychology, 28*, 441–474.

Hassin, R., Uleman, J. S., & Bargh, J. A. (2005). *The new unconscious*. New York: Oxford University Press.

Hazan, C., & Shaver, P. (1987). Romantic love conceptualized as an attachment process. *Journal of Personality and Social Psychology, 52*, 511–524.

Herr, P. M., Sherman, S. J., & Fazio, R. H. (1983). On the consequences of priming: Assimilation and contrast effects. *Journal of Experimental Social Psychology, 19*, 323–340.

Higgins, E. T. (1987). Self-discrepancy: A theory relating self and affect. *Psychological Review, 94*, 319–340.

Higgins, E. T. (1989). Knowledge accessibility and activation: Subjectivity and suffering from unconscious sources. In J. S. Uleman & J. A. Bargh (Eds.), *Unintended thought* (pp. 75–123). New York: Guilford.

Higgins, E. T. (1996). Knowledge activation: Accessibility, applicability, and salience. In E. T. Higgins & A. W. Kruglanski (Eds.), *Social psychology: Handbook of basic principles* (pp. 133–168). New York: Guilford.

Hinkley, K., & Andersen, S. M. (1996). The working self-concept in transference: Significant-other activation and self-change. *Journal of Personality and Social Psychology, 71*, 1279–1295.

James, W. (1890). *The principles of psychology* (Vol. 1). Cambridge: Harvard University Press.

Klohnen, E. C., Weller, J. A., Luo, S., & Choe, M. (2005). Organization and predictive power of general and relationship-specific attachment models: One for all, all for one? *Personality and Social Psychology Bulletin, 31*, 1665–1682.

Lord, C. G. (1980). Schemas and images as memory aids: Two modes of processing social information. *Journal of Personality and Social Psychology, 38*, 257–269.

Mikulincer, M. (1995). Attachment style and the mental representation of the self. *Journal of Personality and Social Psychology, 69*, 1203–1215.

Mikulincer, M. (1997). Adult attachment style and information processing: Individual differences in curiosity and cognitive closure. *Journal of Personality and Social Psychology, 72*, 1217–1230.

Mikulincer, M. (1998). Adult attachment style and affect regulation: Strategic variations in self-appraisals. *Journal of Personality and Social Psychology, 75*, 420–435.

Mikulincer, M., & Arad, D. (1999). Attachment working models and cognitive openness in close relationships: A test of chronic and temporary accessibility effects. *Journal of Personality and Social Psychology, 77*, 710–725.

Mikulincer, M., Gillath, O., & Shaver, P. R. (2002). Activation of the attachment system in adulthood: Threat-related primes increase the accessibility of mental representations of attachment figures. *Journal of Personality and Social Psychology, 83*(4), 881–895.

Mikulincer, M., Hirschberger, G., Nachmias, O., & Gillath, O. (2001). The affective component of the secure base schema: Affective priming with representations of attachment security. *Journal of Personality and Social Psychology, 81*, 305–321.

Mikulincer, M., Orbach, I., & Iavnieli, D. (1998). Adult attachment style and affect regulation: Strategic variations in subjective self–other similarity. *Journal of Personality and Social Psychology, 75*, 436–448.

Mikulincer, M., & Shaver, P. R. (2004). Security-based self-representations in adulthood: Contents and processes. In W. S. Rholes & J. A. Simpson (Eds.), *Adult attachment: theory, research, and clinical implications* (pp. 159–195). New York, NY: Guilford.

Mikulincer, M., Shaver, P. R., Gillath, O., & Nitzberg, R. A. (2005). Attachment, caregiving, and altruism: Boosting attachment security increases compassion and helping. *Journal of Personality and Social Psychology, 89*, 817–839.

Moors, A., & De Houwer, J. (2006). Automaticity: A theoretical and conceptual analysis. *Psychological Bulletin, 132*, 297–326.

Moretti, M. M., & Higgins, E. (1999). Own versus other standpoints in self-regulation: Developmental antecedents and functional consequences. *Review of General Psychology, 3*(3), 188–223.

Murray, S. L., Holmes, J. G., & Griffin, D. W. (1996). The benefits of positive illusions: Idealization and the construction of satisfaction in close relationships. *Journal of Personality and Social Psychology, 70*, 79–98.

Murray, S. L., Holmes, J. G., & Griffin, D. W. (2000). Self-esteem and the quest for felt security: How perceived regard regulates attachment processes. *Journal of Personality and Social Psychology, 78*(3), 478–498.

Murray, S. L., Holmes, J. G., Griffin, D. W., Bellavia, G., & Rose, P. (2001). The mismeasure of love: How self-doubt contaminates relationship beliefs. *Personality & Social Psychology Bulletin, 27*(4), 423–436.

Murray, S. L., Rose, P., Griffin, D. W., & Bellavia, G. M. (2003). Once hurt, twice hurtful: How perceived regard regulates daily marital interactions. *Journal of Personality and Social Psychology, 84*, 126–147.

Nuttin, J. M. (1985). Narcism beyond Gestalt and awareness: The name letter effect. *European Journal of Social Psychology, 15*, 353–361.

Ogilvie, D. M., & Ashmore, R. D. (1991). Self-with-other representation as a unit of analysis in self-concept research. In R. C. Curtis (Ed.), *The relational self: Theoretical convergencies in psychoanalysis and social psychology* (pp. 282–314). New York: Guilford.

Overall, N. C., Fletcher, G. J. O., & Friesen, M. D. (2003). Mapping the intimate relationship mind: Comparisons between three models of attachment representations. *Personality and Social Psychology Bulletin, 29*, 1479–1493.

Pierce, T., & Lydon, J. E. (2001). Global and specific relational models in the experience of social interactions. *Journal of Personality and Social Psychology, 80*, 613–631.

Pietromonaco, P. R., & Barrett, L. F. (2000). The internal working models concept: What do we really know about the self in relation to others? *Review of General Psychology, 4*, 155–175.

Reis, H. T., & Downey, G. (1999). Social cognition in relationships: Building essential bridges between two literatures. *Social Cognition, 17*(2), 97–117.

Reznik, I., & Andersen, S. M. (2004). Becoming the dreaded self: Diminished self-worth with positive significant others in transference. Unpublished manuscript, New York University.

Reznik, I., & Andersen, S. M. (2005). Agitation and despair in relation to parents: Activating emotional suffering in transference. Unpublished manuscript, New York University.

Rusbult, C. E., & Van Lange, P. A. M. (1996). Interdependence processes. In E. T. Higgins & A. W. Kruglanski (Eds.), *Social psychology: Handbook of basic principles* (pp. 564–596). New York: Guilford.

Schneider, W., & Shiffrin, R. M. (1977). Controlled and automatic human information processing I: Detection, search, and attention. *Psychological Review, 84*, 1–66.

Sedikides, C., Olsen, N., & Reis, H. T. (1993). Relationships as natural categories. *Journal of Personality and Social Psychology, 64*, 71–82.

Shah, J. (2003a). Automatic for the people: How representations of significant others implicitly affect goal pursuit. *Journal of Personality and Social Psychology, 84*, 661–681.

Shah, J. (2003b). The motivational looking glass: How significant others implicitly affect goal appraisals. *Journal of Personality and Social Psychology, 85*, 424–439.

Shoda, Y. & Mischel, W. (1993). Cognitive social approach to dispositional inferences: What if the perceiver is a cognitive social theorist? *Personality and Social Psychology Bulletin, 19*, 574–585.

Simpson, J. A., Rholes, W. S., & Nelligan, J. S. (1992). Support seeking and support giving within couples in an anxiety-provoking situation: The role of attachment styles. *Journal of Personality and Social Psychology, 62*, 434–446.

Strack, F., & Hannover, B. (1996). Awareness of influence as a precondition for implementing correctional goals. In P. M. Gollwitzer & J. A. Bargh (Eds.), *The psychology of action: Linking cognition and motivation to behavior* (pp. 579–596). New York: Guilford.

Sullivan, H. S. (1953). *The interpersonal theory of psychiatry.* Oxford, England: Norton & Co.

Uleman, J. S., & Bargh, J. A. (Eds.). (1989). *Unintended thought.* New York: Guilford Press.

Wegner, D. M., & Bargh, J. A. (1998). Control and automaticity in social life. In D. Gilbert, S. T. Fiske, & G. Lindzey (Eds.), *Handbook of social psychology* (4th ed., Vol. 1, pp. 446–496). New York: McGraw-Hill.

Wilson, T. W., & Brekke, N. (1994). Mental contamination and mental correction: Unwanted influences on judgments and evaluations. *Psychological Bulletin, 116*, 117–142.

Wright, S. C., Aron, A., McLaughlin-Volpe, T., & Ropp, S. A. (1997). The extended contact effect: Knowledge of cross-group friendships and prejudice. *Journal of Personality and Social Psychology, 73*, 73–90.

Wright, S., McLaughlin-Volpe, T., & Brody, S. (2004). Seeking and finding an expanded "me" outside of my ingroup: Outgroup friends and self change. In S. Sinclair & J. Huntsinger (Chairs), *You are who you know: New perspectives on the social basis of the self.* Symposium conducted at the 5th Annual Meeting of the Society for Personality and Social Psychology, Austin, TX.

Yovetich, N. A., & Rusbult, C. E. (1994). Accommodative behavior in close relationships: Exploring transformation of motivation. *Journal of Experimental Social Psychology, 30*(2), 138–164.

Zayas, V., & Shoda, Y. (2005). Do automatic reactions elicited by thoughts of romantic partner, mother, and self relate to adult romantic attachment? *Personality and Social Psychology Bulletin, 31*, 1011–1025.

4

On the Automaticity of Emotion

LISA FELDMAN BARRETT, KEVIN N. OCHSNER, and JAMES J. GROSS

Any emotion, if it is sincere, is involuntary
Mark Twain

*T*he year is 1846. You are a stagecoach driver. All is quiet and peaceful as the red sun sets beyond the horizon, the coach rumbles contentedly along, and sagebrush cast long shadows across the lonesome prairie. Hidden in the shadows, however, is a rattlesnake. Disturbed from its slumber by the horses, the rattler suddenly strikes out, scaring the horses into a fearful, frenzied sprint. Out of control, the stagecoach careens towards the edge of a sheer cliff. First you try to soothe your steeds, but they cannot hear you. Then you try to forcibly rein them in, but their strength is too great. Life itself hangs in the balance as you grimly struggle to control the careening stagecoach.

The distinction between wild stagecoach steed and wily stagecoach driver in many ways mirrors the distinction between feeling and thinking embedded within Western Culture. Emotions are assumed to be primitive, automatic, animalistic entities dwelling within us that the more developed human part of our minds come to know about and control. The notion that feeling is first, fast, and feral traces back to biblical stories of the First Family and their misbegotten emotional impulses to taste that tempting fruit. These ideas about emotion continue in modern-day stories of lovers driven mad with jealousy, businessmen blinded by greed, and widows overcome with grief. As Plato suggested long ago in the Phaedrus, in each of these cases, our emotions, like wild horses, drive us to emotional places we do not deliberately choose to visit and thus must be harnessed and restrained.

In the first section of this chapter, we outline the commonsense view that emotions automatically play themselves out when we encounter certain situations. We describe how this commonsense view – with varying degrees of elaboration and complexity – forms the basis of a consensual view of emotion that pervades much of the scientific inquiry into emotion. We refer to this consensual view as "the modal model" of emotion. In the second section, we argue that although the "modal model" has much to recommend it, mounting evidence suggests that it has several important limitations. In the third section, we argue that the field needs to move beyond a search for entities that conform neatly to our intuitions about what automatic emotions "must" be like. We call for a richer examination of the bottom-up and top-down processes that together give rise to emotion, and suggest that a constraint satisfaction approach may provide the conceptual framework that is needed in order to move beyond the modal model.

FROM COMMON SENSE TO A "MODAL MODEL" OF EMOTION

The Commonsense Approach to Emotion

As common sense has it, emotions are triggered automatically, overcome us, and cause us to act. We yell because we are angry. We cry because we are sad. We jump because we are afraid. Anger, sadness, and fear cause and explain our behavior, just as lightning causes and explains thunder. As the pent up electrical energy of an emotion is discharged, the result is a largely inescapable set of stereotyped outputs that occur in a rapid, involuntary, and automated fashion. Prior knowledge, expectations, beliefs, or any other cognitive input have little impact on the process. You might know that lightning is about to strike, but you can't stop it from happening, and plugging your ears will not keep you from hearing the thunderous blast. As a consequence, emotions such as anger happen *to* you, and overcome you, rapidly overriding whatever else you might have been doing, thinking, and feeling. From a first-person perspective, the conscious experience of emotion (the feeling) is taken as clear evidence that the causal mechanism – the "emotion" – was triggered. Feeling angry is evidence that the anger mechanism has fired. What is more, anger seems to overtake others in much the same way. When observing others, expressive behavior is seen as evidence that an emotion is triggered. The given quality of our own experience, and the way that emotion seems to control others without their awareness, seems to provide proof for the automaticity of emotional responses.

This folk conception of emotion underlies our everyday construal of emotions in self and others. Because we experience instances of anger (or sadness or fear) in ourselves and in others as having a rapid onset and a more or less ballistic trajectory, we believe anger (or sadness or fear) must exist as a primitive entity lying in wait within the brain or body, ready to spring forth automatically and at a moment's notice once the appropriate triggers are present. The commonsense idea of emotions as automatic eruptions is even evident in the criminal justice code, where "passion" is seen as a justifiable defense for violent crime. In the US, the "sudden heat of passion" constitutes adequate provocation that reduces an act of intentional homicide to an offense of voluntary manslaughter (Dressler, 2001, p. 527).

In this view, our emotions are rarely, if ever, the product of controlled, deliberate, and conscious thought. Although it is possible to "think ourselves" into an emotional state, controlled processes typically serve to control, rather than to elicit, emotional responses. Any number of aphorisms admonish us to regulate our feelings either by deliberately thinking differently – "looking on the bright side," "making a silk purse out of a sow's ear," "finding the silver lining in every dark cloud," – or by acting differently – "putting on a happy face," "putting a lid on it," "showing some restraint," "never letting them see you sweat," "getting a grip," or more generally by keeping ourselves from expressing the anger, sadness, or fear that we might feel inside. The very fact that we have to take control to regulate our emotional responses is further evidence for us that they are automatic, and it is precisely because we experience our emotions interfering with our more reasoned responses (that we identify as more essentially "human" in nature) that we experience our emotions as automatic, animalistic, and foreign.

More generally, our experiences of emotions erupting outside of our control, and our sense of agency and effort in shaping them, strongly supports our intuition that there are two fundamentally distinct forms of processing that characterize the human mind: automatic processing (which we share with other animals) and controlled processing (which is most developed in humans). As we will see, virtually every major scientific account of emotion incorporates our intuitions about dual-processing modes in the mind, and specifically our commonsense distinction between automatic elicitation and controlled regulation of emotion.

Two Major Scientific Approaches to Emotion

Dual-process models pervade contemporary psychology (e.g., Barrett, Tugade, & Engle, 2004; Chaiken & Trope, 1999; Devine, 1989; Gilbert, 1991, 1998; Power & Dalgleish, 1997; Schacter, 1997; Sloman, 1996; Smith & DeCoster, 2000; Trope, 1986). A central tenet of such models is that behavior is determined by the interplay of automatic and controlled processing. Models vary in their specifics and emphasis, but all hold that responses to an event begin with the automatic (sometimes called nonconscious, implicit, or heuristic) processing of information. Such processing is assumed to be a default mode, initiated by the simple registration of sensory inputs, which in turn passively activate knowledge structures (called schemas, scripts, or concepts, or even internal goal states) that shape perception and action. Controlled (sometimes called conscious, explicit, or systematic) processing can determine, to a large extent, the degree to which automatic processing is expressed in thoughts, feelings, and behaviors. Controlled processing requires attentional resources, is volitional, is largely goal-driven, and can be used to modulate automatic processes when the outputs they produce conflict with valued goals.

As in other domains in psychology, emotion has proven hospitable ground for dual-process logic (Smith & Neumann, 2005). Indeed, in our view, a dual-process model lies at the heart of much of the scientific theorizing and research dealing with emotion for the past century. This dual-process framework can be summarized in a very simple way in Figure 4.1. Some event or goal-relevant stimulus (usually external, although it could be internal) triggers an emotion mechanism (or set of mechanisms), which, in turn, automatically produces a complex sequence of coordinated changes in the brain and body that constitute an emotional response.

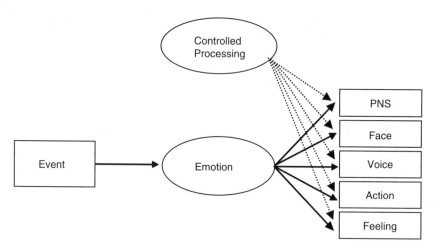

FIGURE 4.1   A dual-process view of emotion. PNS = peripheral nervous system activation.

Substitute for "emotion" any referent for a specific emotion category ("anger", "sadness", "fear", and so on, in English), and you have a model of that emotion. Controlled regulation is thought to occur separately and modulate the extent to which a coordinated emotional response actually manifests in observed behavior.

Within this dual-process framework, two historically distinct (but often complementary) approaches to the study of emotion can be distinguished. One approach has focused on the output side of the emotion-generative process, namely the coordinated expression of complex patterns of behavior that comprise the observable, tangible, and socially impactful component of an emotional response. This has been referred to as the *basic emotion* approach. A second approach has focused on the input side of the emotion-generative process, namely the processing of environmental stimuli that gives rise to the emotional response depicted in Figure 4.1. This has been referred to as the *appraisal* approach. Despite differences in their surface features (for a review, see Scherer et al., 2001), these two approaches share two central assumptions. First, each of these approaches assumes that there are definable kinds of emotion (defined by the brain, or by the deep structure of situations). Second, these approaches assume that emotion generation is dominated by automatic processing (with regulation usually occurring after the fact). Given its ubiquity in the field, we refer to Figure 4.1 as the "modal model" [and in the past have referred to it as the "natural kind model" (Barrett, 2006b) or the "consensual model" of emotional responding (Gross, 1998)]. In the following sections, we describe the role the "modal model" has played in each of these two major approaches.

The Basic Emotion Approach   One of the earliest modern examples of the basic emotion approach can be found in Darwin's (1859/1965) "The Expression of the Emotions in Man and Animals." Darwin's ideas about emotion were infused with commonsense beliefs about how mental states seek expression in, and therefore automatically cause, behaviors. Facial and other behaviors (such as baring the teeth in anger) were seen as vestigial expressions of emotion mechanisms that are homologous in human and nonhuman animals. Darwin focused on a small number of emotions (many of which are now referred to as "basic" emotions), stressing the universality as well as the phylogenetic and ontogenetic continuity of their expressions.

William James (1884, 1890, 1894) famously disagreed with Darwin (and commonsense) as to the correct temporal ordering of the elements in Figure 4.1. Instead of the sequence depicted in Figure 4.1, James argued that an individual's emotional response was best characterized by the sequence: stimulus → physiological response → experience. Notwithstanding this notable difference, James clearly retained the core notion that emotion involved an automatic release of a coordinated set of responses to relevant stimuli (with the embodiment of those responses producing the experience of emotion). As William James himself put it:

> The nervous system of every living thing is but a bundle of predispositions to react in particular ways upon the contact of particular features of the environment . . . The neural machinery is but a hyphen between determinate arrangements of matter outside the body and determinate impulses to inhibition or discharge within its organs . . . Every living creature is in fact a sort of lock, whose wards and springs presuppose special forms of key – which keys however are not born attached to the locks, but are sure to be found in the world near by as life goes on. And the locks are indifferent to any but their own keys. (1884, pp. 190–191).

This quote nicely captures the modern idea of cognitive impenetrability – meaning that emotion circuits fire in an obligatory way once triggered by sensory information about a stimulus, and occur regardless of the context. Onset is rapid, involuntary, and requires little or no attention. Although James concentrated on developing the automatic elicitation side of the emotion equation, he also incorporated the commonsense notion that controlled processes may come into play, such as when we regulate emotion after-the-fact, by limiting its expression. As James saw it: "refuse to express a passion, and it dies." (James, 1884, p. 197).

Later models built more directly on this elicitation-regulation distinction, and further developed the dual-process metaphor for emotion processing. Cannon (1927, 1931) and Bard (1928; Bard & Rioch, 1937), who proposed one of the earliest psychological models of emotion localization in the brain, argued that the emotional part of the brain (in their view, the hypothalamic circuit including the thalamus and hypothalamus) produced responses that could be downregulated by evolutionarily more recent neocortical regions. Papez (1937) similarly argued for top-down cortical regulation of subcortical emotional responses, and MacLean (1949) continued this tradition, positing that the newer "mammalian" part of his triune brain architecture exerted top-down regulatory control of the emotional responses that issued from the older and more primitive "reptilian" and "old mammalian" parts of the brain.

Although concepts such as reptilian and mammalian are no longer part of contemporary basic emotion models, these models have nonetheless retained an emphasis on subcortical structures in the generation of emotion (e.g., Panksepp, 1998). Perhaps the best-known example has been offered by LeDoux (1996), who demonstrated that links between sensory systems and the amygdala are necessary and sufficient for the expression of conditioned fear, but who, along with others, has shown that cortical areas (particularly medial prefrontal cortex) are involved in expressing contextual learning that inhibits the conditioned fear response (Milad & Quirk, 2002; Morgan, Romanski & LeDoux, 1993; Quirk & Gehlert, 2003; Quirk, Likhtik, Pelletier, & Paré, 2003).

A dual-process metaphor can also be clearly seen in the family of models that comprise the modern-day "basic emotion" approach to emotion. Like Darwin and James, basic emotion models focus more on the ways in which emotional responses are automatically elicited. Boiled down to their essential ingredients, these views posit that each kind of "basic" emotion issues from a neural program or circuit, hardwired at birth, homologous with circuits found in nonhuman mammals, that is responsible for an automatic syndrome of hormonal, muscular, and autonomic effects that constitutes the distinctive signature of an emotional response. Although the specific set of "basic" emotions varies somewhat across emotion theorists, there is agreement that specific "basic" emotion mechanisms correspond to English emotion categories (e.g., "fear," "sadness," "disgust," "anger," or "happiness"). This small set of stereotyped, automatic emotion responses are regulated after the fact, usually by means of controlled attentional processes shaped by epigenetic influences, such as context and learning history.

Perhaps the best-known example is Ekman's neurocultural model (Ekman, 1972), which describes emotions as issuing from "affect programs" (Tomkins, 1962) that, once triggered by an eliciting stimulus, direct a complex pattern of coordinated outputs to produce a stereotyped emotional response. Panksepp's (1998; Panksepp et al., 2000) neurobiological model takes its lead more directly from MacLean's (1949) triune brain concept, but is similar, in principle, to the neurocultural model. Panksepp argues for different "basic" emotion systems (seeking/expectancy, rage/anger, fear/anxiety, lust/sexuality, care/nurturance, panic/separation, and play/joy). Each kind of emotion is a separate, inherited, complex reflex that is hardwired at birth and causes a distinctive syndrome of hormonal, muscular, and autonomic effects.

At the core of both Ekman's (1972) and Panksepp's (1998; Panksepp et al., 2000) models is the idea that there is a hardwired set of emotion-specific mechanisms that fire automatically and thereby generate a suite of emotional responses. Over time, however, there has been softening of the emphasis on fixed, hardwired programs that govern emotions from birth. For example, both Ekman and Panksepp acknowledge that there is a greater range of human emotional responding than can be accounted for by a set of basic emotions. Recent developments in the neurocultural model have attempted to account for the complexity and subtlety of emotional life by arguing for families of emotion response (Ekman, 1992), or by suggesting a distinction between "primordial" and "elaborated" emotions (Keltner & Haidt, 2001), where the former are "basic" emotions that produce a stereotyped response signature, and the latter are responses that are more shaped by the norms and social practices within a culture. Both also allow controlled processing to enter the picture, although primarily as a way of regulating the emotion-generative process. In the neurocultural model, culture not only influences the stimuli that trigger emotion programs, it also specifies display rules and regulatory outcomes, so that observed emotional responses display considerable cultural variation, even as the causal mechanisms are hardwired into the brain. Panksepp (1998) also allows for the environment to modulate emotional outputs in the form of cortical control of the basic emotion systems once they have been triggered.

The Appraisal Approach   The dual-process metaphor can also be found in a second family of emotion models, which we refer to collectively as the *appraisal* approach. Appraisal models have been concerned with patterns of cognition that trigger an emotional response. Like the basic emotion approach, many models within the appraisal approach retain the commonsense distinction between automatic elicitation and controlled regulation, although they also incorporate the idea that automatic and controlled cognitive processes (or steps) can interact and give rise to emotional responses. Thus, when appraisal models unpack the input side of Figure 4.1, they typically describe a cognitive logic that involves both automatic and controlled components, although once the emotion is elicited, it is assumed to run automatically to completion.

In these models, emotions are a consequence of how people construe situations. Frijda (1988), one of the best-known and most influential appraisal theorists, calls this the "law of situational meaning." Instead of assuming that a stimulus situation automatically triggers or releases a fixed emotional response (as William James had), appraisal models hold that intervening cognitive processes automatically elicit and determine the quality and intensity of emotional responses. Input an event with a particular meaning, and the result is an emotion of a particular kind. The cognitive processes that compute this meaning, formally known as appraisals, link the external world (an individual's immediate situation) to the internal world (the individual's goals, needs, and concerns). Appraisals diagnose whether the situation in question is relevant to the person's well-being, and if so, identify the nature of that relevance, and trigger an emotion that will maximize the likelihood of producing a functionally effective response consistent with the organism's most central concerns (Kappas, 2001; Smith & Kirby, 2001).

Appraisal models vary in terms of the logic and content of the cognitive judgments that are held to be necessary and sufficient to produce emotional responses. In some models, appraisals describe the way that a situation is experienced, and constitute a descriptive structure of which emotions are felt when; they do not, in and of themselves, indicate the processes by which the meaning is made or arrived at (e.g., Ortony, Clore, & Collins, 1988; Smith & Ellsworth, 1985). In this view, sadness occurs when a situation's meaning involves loss, and fear when the meaning involves danger. Situational analysis, or appraisals, can be determined in any number of ways. A situation's meaning can be determined with associative processing by reinstating an appraisal that derives from a similar situation experienced in the past, or it can be computed on the spot using a rule-based analysis driven by features of the situation and the goals of the person (Clore & Ortony, 2000). Both types of processing can be automatic (Smith & DeCoster, 2000), although on-line computation allows the possibility for more controlled processing.

In other models, appraisals do more than describe the meaning of situations – they are a set of cognitive processes that literally generate an emotional response (e.g., Roseman, Antoniou, & Jose, 1996; Scherer, 1984). Even the appraisal-as-mechanism models differ in which appraisals are seen as necessary and sufficient, which combinations of appraisals elicit particular emotional responses, which categories of emotion are explained, and so on (Roseman & Smith, 2001). They also vary in the fixity of the appraisal process. Some assume that appraisals are made in a specific fixed sequence (e.g., Scherer, 1984, 2001), while others argue for more flexible ordering in appraisal processing (e.g., Frijda, 1986; Roseman et al., 1996), although often it is assumed that particular appraisals (whether a stimulus is pleasant or unpleasant, novel or familiar) come before others that can be more flexibly deployed (e.g., Ellsworth, 1991; Lazarus, 1991). They differ in the extent to which they relax the assumption of cognitive impenetrability (the idea that emotion elicitation is not influenced by factors such as prior knowledge, expectations, beliefs, or any other cognitive input). Appraisal models also differ in whether they consider these rule-based computations to *cause* an emotional response, to *constitute* the response, or to be a *consequence* of emotion processing (cf. Ellsworth & Scherer, 2003; Frijda & Zeelenberg, 2001).

Despite their differences, virtually all appraisal theorists hold that people are continually assessing situations for personal relevance, beginning with an evaluation of whether or not the stimulus is "good for me/bad for me" (Arnold, 1960; Lazarus, 1966; Mandler, 1984; Ortony et al., 1988; Roseman, 1984; Scherer, 1984; Smith & Ellsworth, 1985). The primacy of such an evaluation is consistent with the general idea that we automatically evaluate stimuli (e.g., Bargh, Chaiken, Govender, & Pratto, 1992; Fazio, 2001; Fazio, Sanbonmatsu, Powell, & Kardes, 1986; Ferguson & Bargh, 2004), as well as the specific notion that some aspects of emotional responding – at least those that are related to computing affective valence – are generated automatically (e.g., Berridge & Winkielman, 2003; Cacioppo et al., 1999). Appraisal theorists also hold that different situations that evoke the same appraisal pattern produce the same emotional episode. Each emotion is elicited by a distinctive pattern of appraisals (e.g., Arnold, 1960; Frijda, 1986; Lazarus, 1991; Ortony, Clore, & Collins, 1988; Roseman, 1984; Scherer, 1984; Smith & Ellsworth, 1985), and the pattern of appraisals, rather than a dedicated neural circuit, is responsible for generating the emotional response.

Appraisal models, like basic emotion models, initially retained the automatic elicitation – controlled regulation distinction. Arnold (1960), who was the first contemporary appraisal theorist, assumed that appraisals are an "intuitive and immediate" assessment of the stimulus situation (p. 182). An explicit debate about the importance of the automatic versus controlled processing in emotion generation (Lazarus, 1982; Lazarus & Folkman, 1984; Zajonc, 1980, 1984) refocused attention to the idea that the conceptual processing engendered by appraisal processes can occur automatically, and now most appraisal models incorporate a role for simple, nonconscious appraisals in emotion generation. Even when appraisals occur in response to remembered or imagined events, the cognitive processing involved in the appraisal process is thought to proceed automatically. Particularly in models that propose appraisals as preconditions for activating emotional responses (rather than constituting the responses themselves), appraisals are seen as inputs to the neural circuit view characterized by basic emotion models. Once appraisals have been computed, an emotion is triggered in a way that is very similar to Figure 4.1.

Over time, however, appraisal theorists have shown increasing appreciation for the role of controlled processing in emotion generation, and models have more explicitly relied on the dual-process metaphor that is implicit in basic emotion and early appraisal approaches. For example, Leventhal & Scherer (1987) argued that two kinds of automatic processes generate emotional responses that are modified by a third type of controlled process. An initial sensory-motor level of processing implements a form of biologically prepared perceptual processing driven by innate, unconditioned, hard-wired feature detectors that give rise to reflex-like responses. A second level (thought to mediate the majority of emotional responses) implements schematic processes that automatically match current stimulus patterns to learned stimulus patterns to generate coordinated emotional responses. When these first two types of processes generate a response that is sufficiently intense to enter awareness, consciously guided conceptual-level processes come into play, deploying propositional knowledge to refine emotional responses. Conceptual processing is thought to become ever more automatized (like skill learning) with practice. Many other models similarly suggest that emotions can be generated by some combination of automatic and controlled processing (e.g., Clore & Ortony, 2000; Dalgleish, 2004; Power & Dalgleish, 1997; Smith & Kirby, 2001; Teasdale, 1999; Teasdale & Barnard, 1993; Wells & Matthews, 1994).

In relaxing the assumption of cognitive impenetrability, appraisal models usually allow for the possibility that controlled processing can implement appraisal logic (i.e., the rule-based evaluations that cause the resulting emotional response). The common idea in these models is that various forms of automatic processing (including low-level perceptual processing of stimuli and prior knowledge in the form of schemas) interact with more effortful processing to produce emotional responses (Clark & Isen, 1982; Frijda & Zeelenberg, 2001; Lazarus, 1991). In this way, most appraisal theorists seem to agree that humans play an active role in shaping their information processing, and can exert some control over emotion-generative appraisal processes.

The "Modal Model"

In the past, basic emotion and appraisal approaches have been treated as opposing explanations for emotional responding (Ortony & Turner, 1990; Turner & Ortony, 1992). We believe that despite their differences, both approaches share two intuitively appealing assumptions that can be found in our commonsense ideas about emotion. These common assumptions comprise the core of what we refer to as the "modal model" of emotion. The first of these assumptions is the idea that emotional responses can be characterized as belonging to a small set of discrete categories. The second is the assumption that there is a boundary between the automatic generation of emotion and its controlled regulation after the emotion itself has been triggered.

First, both basic emotion and appraisal accounts focus their attention on explaining a small set of discrete emotions. Although appraisal models acknowledge (at least in principle) the enormous variety in emotional responding and do not assume that particular emotions are basic in any biological way, most models organize emotional responding into the familiar set of discrete categories used by basic emotion theorists. Major research efforts have been directed at identifying the profile of appraisals for a fixed number of discrete emotions (anger, sadness, fear, and so on) that are very similar to the list discussed by basic emotion approaches (e.g., Roseman, 1984, 1991; Smith & Ellsworth, 1985). For example, although Lazarus (1966) initially rejected the idea that there are a limited number of categorically distinct "basic" emotions, he came to view that there are a small number of "relational themes" that correspond to discrete emotions (Lazarus, 1991; Smith & Lazarus, 2001). Similarly, Ortony et al. (1988) discussed a large range of emotional responses, but proposed a hierarchical structure in which some emotions are just more differentiated versions of other emotions. Scherer (2001) suggested that we tend to use basic level categories like "anger" to refer to qualitatively different emotional states, some of which may be "modal" emotions whose appraisal profiles recur with some frequency (Scherer, 1994), whereas other emotions may follow from fluctuations in appraisal profiles that may yield a large number of different emotional responses (e.g., Scherer, 2001).

Second, both basic emotion and appraisal accounts rely heavily on the notion that emotions are generated automatically. Thus, both types of models posit that emotional responses act as an organizing force, "hijacking" the entire system (i.e., disrupting whatever other processes are operative at the time) to deal with the circumstances that elicited the emotion in the first place. Oatley and Johnson-Laird (1987), for example, suggested that basic emotions are internal signals that disrupt ongoing cognitive processing and reset it into specific modes to deal with basic biosocial challenges. Once an emotion is triggered (whether computed by an emotion program or a set of appraisals), there results an inescapable, involuntary, and automated set of synchronized changes in response systems that produce the signature emotional response (like the output side of Figure 4.1).

Both assumptions embodied by the modal model – that there are a small set of different kinds of emotion, and that emotions issue more or less automatically – have guided emotion research for the past century. They have guided the questions that researchers ask, the way that emotional responses are measured, and the interpretation of the data. The resulting research programs have been productive and important. No model is perfect, however, and as we shall see in the next section, there are both theoretical and empirical reasons for a course correction in the way that science approaches the study of emotion.

A CRITICAL EVALUATION OF THE MODAL MODEL

The modal model has been a tremendously valuable organizing force in the field of emotion. The basic emotion approach has helped to define emotion as a topic worthy of study in its own right, facilitating the development of empirical methods for examining facial (e.g., Ekman & Friesen, 1978), vocal (e.g., Scherer, 1986), autonomic (e.g., Cacioppo, Klein, Berntson, & Hatfield, 1993), and central (e.g., Davidson & Irwin, 1999) aspects of emotional responding. It has served as the de facto yardstick against which competing accounts of emotion are evaluated. The appraisal approach has helped to establish the importance of personal relevance and meaning in triggering emotional responses, and has attempted to unpack the notion of ballistic, automatic action programs into a more complicated set of both automatic and controlled processes that together contribute to the generation of an emotional response.

Useful as the modal model has been, however, it is limited and limiting in at least two ways. First, as we describe in more detail below, the modal model privileges a relatively limited number of emotions, leaving large gaps in our understanding of the full spectrum of emotional phenomena in need of explanation. Second, as we see it, the available empirical evidence, guided by a research agenda defined by the modal model, does not uniformly support the core tenets of this model. Specifically, the modal view posits automatic processing mechanisms that do not dovetail neatly with our emerging understanding of the behavioral and biological bases of emotion. As a result, a comprehensive functional architecture for emotion that considers a complete scope of emotional phenomena, and specifies a testable set of functional and neural mechanisms, has, to date, failed to coalesce from this model. In the following sections, we critically consider these two important limitations of the modal model.

Are There a Limited Number of Discrete Kinds of Emotion?

An account of emotion, according to Clore and Ortony (2000, p 32), "needs to do justice to the full richness and range of emotions that comprise human emotional life." The modal model, however, focuses attention on just one part of the larger emotional landscape by considering a small number of kinds of emotion about which we can make inductive discoveries, and which conform to the event → automatic response pattern. In this way, the modal model leads us to restrict our scientific inquiry to characterizing only a fraction of our emotional life. This practice is consistent with the viewpoint held by many emotion researchers that emotions should be defined by species-general aspects. As a field, we ask questions like, "How many emotions are there?" "Which specific pattern of antecedent events, neural activity, physiology, and motor behavior defines each emotion?" and "How do we evoke pure instances of emotion, uncontaminated by contextual influences?" Guided by the modal model, we assume that *kinds* of emotions would reveal themselves if only we could find the right eliciting stimulus or measures (cf. Barrett, 2006b).

Although it is clear that people have experiences that they refer to as anger, sadness, fear, and so on, there is also good evidence that they can experience many other varieties of emotional response as well – responses not readily classifiable as fitting one of the canonical emotion kinds or forms. Variability may be the norm, rather than the exception, and according to some evolutionary biologists, variability is the thing to be explained (Lewinson, 2000). Although movies and novels are replete with examples of full-blown canonical emotion responses, emotion scientists have yet to take an empirical tally of how often these occur in everyday life. It is just assumed that they occur often enough to justify an almost exclusive focus on them empirically. Certainly these stereotyped responses are rarely, if ever, seen in all their glory in the laboratory. What is more, as we describe below, behavior, as well as the physiology that supports it, is more context-sensitive, and linked to the requirements of the situation, than the modal model of emotion would lead us to expect (cf. Barrett, 2006b; Bradley, 2000; Cacioppo, Berntson, Larsen, Poehlmann, & Ito, 2000; Davidson, 1994; Lang, Bradley, & Cuthbert, 1990). Functional demands vary with situations, making it likely that instances of the same emotion can be associated with a range of behaviors (e.g., behaviors associated with fear can range from freezing to vigilance to flight). This observation suggests that there is considerable heterogeneity in emotional responses that might be called fearful (or angry, etc.).

Even putting aside the issue of whether important aspects of human emotional life are neglected by the modal model, there remains the question as to the success of the search for definable patterns of coordinated responses that characterize each kind of emotion. Despite a century of effort, and much to everyone's surprise, there has been little accumulation of evidence to support the hypothesis that emotions represent clearly defined kinds (for a review, see Barrett, 2006b). To appreciate this unexpected outcome, consider a key prediction of the modal model and one of the most compelling ideas in the psychology of emotion: the notion that emotional states have specific and unique patterns of somatovisceral changes.

Although individual studies have reported distinct autonomic correlates for different emotion categories (e.g., Christie & Friedman, 2004; Ekman, Levenson, & Friesen, 1983; Levenson, Ekman, & Friesen, 1990), meta-analytic summaries generally fail to find distinct patterns of peripheral nervous system responses for each basic discrete emotion (Cacioppo et al., 2000). Instead, peripheral nervous system responses configure for conditions of threat and challenge (Quigley, Barrett, & Weinstein, 2002; Tomaka et al., 1993, Tomaka, Blascovich, Kibler, & Ernst, 1997), and for positive versus negative affect (Cacioppo et al., 2000; Lang, Greenwald, Bradley, & Hamm, 1993). What is puzzling here is the gap between common sense (of course different emotions affect my body differently!) and the available physiological findings. Studying the physiological bases of emotion is fraught with challenges (Levenson, 1988), and it is certainly possible that methodological problems are responsible for the impoverished empirical evidence for physiological distinctions among emotions. But it is important to recognize that an equally viable alternative explanation for the lack of consistent findings is that there are, in fact, no clearly demarcated and discrete kinds of emotion that are unambiguously distinguished by patterns of peripheral physiological responses.

This sentiment is reinforced by a similar gap between common intuitions that emotions cause distinctive patterns of expressive behaviors and the relevant empirical data. One of the major research efforts in the basic emotion approach has been concerned with detecting and describing universal facial expressions of emotion (Ekman & Friesen, 1978; Ekman, Friesen, & Ellsworth, 1972; Ekman, Sorenson, & Friesen, 1969; Izard, 1971). This research has yielded evidence that posed facial expressions can be judged with considerably greater than chance accuracy by individuals from a wide range of Western and non-Western cultures (cf. Ekman, 1994; but see Elfenbein & Ambady, 2002). Although perceivers can reliably assign posed facial configurations to discrete emotion categories, alternative explanations for these findings have been offered (cf., Russell, 1994; Russell, Bachorowski, & Fernandez-Dols, 2003), including the idea that perceivers are imposing, rather than detecting, true categorical distinctions in the facial configurations that they rate (Barrett, 2006a). More important, however, is the fact that very limited systematic data exist concerning the *production* (as opposed to the perception) of emotion expressions across cultures. Even within a culture, facial electromyography measurements coordinate around positive versus negative affect (Cacioppo et al., 2000) or intensity of affect (Messinger, 2002), rather than discrete emotion categories per se. More generally, it has been suggested that expressive behaviors in mammals rarely broadcast fixed, encoded messages about the sender's internal state (Fridlund, 1994; Seyfarth & Cheney, 2003), suggesting facial movements and vocal signals may not necessarily "display" information about the sender's emotional state (cf. Russell et al., 2003), even though we perceive them as coordinated "expressions."

Neither is it clear that vocal sounds carry specific information about discrete kinds of emotion (for a review, again see Russell et al., 2003). Listeners also do better than chance at classifying acted portrayals of emotion in vocal cues (Banse & Scherer, 1986; Hess et al., 1988; Johnstone & Scherer 2000; Juslin & Laukka, 2003; Wallbott & Scherer, 1986), but these portrayals do not necessarily have the same acoustic characteristics that are observed in naturally produced vocal expressions (for a discussion, see Bachorowski & Owren, 2003). Furthermore, the acoustic properties of produced vocal cues give clues to a speaker's identity (Edmonson, 1987), indicate his or her arousal level (e.g., Bachorowski 1999; Bachorowski & Owren 1995; Kappas et al., 1991), and are thought to elicit affective responses in listeners (Bachorowski & Owren 2001) more than they give evidence about kinds of emotion per se.

In like fashion, a given instrumental behavioral response need not express a specific kind of emotion. For example, although fear may be associated with freezing, fear is associated with a number of other behaviors, ranging from vigilance to attack (for a review, see Bouton, 2005). The threat (or defense) system is organized so that an animal will engage in different behaviors depending on its psychological distance from a predator (Fanselow, 1994; Fanselow & Lester, 1988). Not only are different behaviors associated with the same emotion category, but one type of behavior can be associated with many categories. For example, varieties of aggressive behavior (e.g., defensive, offensive, predatory) are associated with different types of stimulus situations and are caused by different neural circuitry (Blanchard & Blanchard, 2003).

Evidence from reports of subjective experience also calls into question whether or not there are bounded and distinct kinds of experiences. Not only do people vary greatly in whether or not they distinguish between feelings of anger, sadness, and so on, in reports of subjective experience (Barrett, 1998, 2004; Feldman, 1995), but these reports can be decomposed into more elemental psychological properties, such as valence and arousal. In revealing valence, and to a lesser extent arousal properties, self-reports of experienced emotion produce a similar structure to that which is observed for psychophysiological and behavioral measures of emotion.

Perhaps most important, however, is the finding that physiological, behavioral, and experiential outputs for each emotion category are not as highly intercorrelated as one might expect based on the modal model (Mauss, Wilhelm, & Gross, 2004; for a review, see Bradley & Lang, 2000). Psychophysiologists have long observed weak correlations across response systems (e.g., Weinstein, Averill, Opton, & Lazarus, 1968) and even within the same "response system" (e.g., Lacey, 1967). Recent studies similarly have found modest correlations among measures of emotional responding in the context of fear (Hodgson & Rachman, 1974; Lang, 1988; Rachman, 1984), exhilaration (Ruch, 1995), and surprise (Reisenzein, 2000). Although links between emotion experience and facial behavior have tended to be the strongest (e.g., Adelmann & Zajonc, 1989; Blumberg & Izard, 1991; Rosenberg & Ekman, 1994), even these links are often modest (e.g., Fernández-Dols, Sánchez, Carrera, & Ruiz-Belda, 1997; Fridlund, 1994) and inconsistent (e.g., Casey, 1993; Chovil, 1991; Gross, John, & Richards, 2000; for a meta-analytic review, see Cacioppo et al., 2000). Despite much effort, then, there has been surprisingly little evidence generated for the modal model's prediction of strong response coupling in emotional responding.

As this brief review indicates, physiological, behavioral, and experiential data do not strongly support the notion that there are clearly identifiable discrete kinds of emotion. The accumulating neuroscience evidence echoes this observation, thus far failing to yield strong evidence of dedicated neural circuits for basic emotion categories (Barrett, 2006b). Although there is good evidence that specific behaviors – such as freezing, the baring of fangs or claws, or hair standing on end – each may depend upon specific brainstem and subcortical nuclei (e.g., Panksepp, 1998), there is little evidence to suggest that a single brain structure is responsible for the production of the complete range of behavioral changes that should be associated with any single emotion category (Barbas, 1995; Cavada, Company, Tejedor, Cruz-Rizzolo, & Reinoso-Suarez, 2000). Similarly, many different cortical and subcortical brain systems are capable of modulating physiological and behavioral correlates of emotion, such as heart rate and respiration or freezing, and no single response system appears to be linked exclusively to a single specific emotion (Cacioppo & Gardner, 1999).

Lesion studies suggest that the normal experience and perception of some emotions, such as disgust and fear, may depend critically upon the integrity of particular brain structures – the insula and amygdala, respectively – but expressive deficits following amygdala or insula lesions typically are not absolute, and imaging studies suggest that both of these structures also appear to participate in the generation of other emotions, the perception of other types of stimuli, and may even participate in ostensibly cognitive processes, such as orienting attention, as well (Adolphs & Tranel, 1999; Adolphs, Tranel et al., 1999b; Anderson et al., 2003a,b; Anderson & Phelps, 2000, 2001, 2002; Calder, Lawrence, & Young, 2001; Gallagher & Schoenbaum, 1999; Hamann, Ely, Grafton, & Kilts, 1999; Phan, Wager, Taylor, & Liberzon, 2002). Furthermore, alternative explanations for these findings are rarely explored (e.g., Adolphs, Russell, & Tranel, 1999; for a review, see Barrett 2006b). Meta-analyses of studies examining the neural correlates of anger, sadness, fear, disgust, and happiness (Murphy, Nimmo-Smith, & Lawrence, 2003; Phan et al., 2002) also support the conclusion that no single brain structure is exclusively associated with any single kind of emotion, with the exception of a fear–amygdala correspondence that can be accounted for by alternative explanations (Barrett 2006a,b).[1]

In any view of the neural bases of emotion, it is expected that every individual case of anger (or any other emotion) can be associated with some pattern of neural activity. The important question is whether there are strong and consistent correspondences between particular emotions and particular processing systems in the brain, and to date, such correspondences have yet to be identified. It is possible that a number of methodological and theoretical factors at present limit our ability to draw inferences about the neural bases of emotional responses. These include the facts that the way in which emotions are elicited is not constant across studies (allowing for the possibility that variety in method produces variety in brain activation; see Phan et al., 2002, for evidence), that studies may employ stimuli (such as facial expressions) that to do not elicit strong emotional responses (Ochsner & Barrett, 2001), that little care may be taken to separate emotion generation from emotion regulation, allowing participants, for example, to spontaneously regulate their responses (Cunningham, Raye, & Johnson, 2004), and that measures of multiple channels of emotional response are rarely collected and correlated with brain activation (Ochsner & Barrett, 2001; Ochsner & Gross, 2004).

Even with those caveats in mind, the existing evidentiary base is not supportive of the modal model's core claim that there is a hardwired set of emotion-specific generators. Behavior, experience, or peripheral and central nervous system responses do not show obvious categorical "footprints" for each kind of emotion. It is possible, of course, that kinds of emotion exist and will reveal themselves once scientists find the right eliciting stimuli or employ better measurement tools. Indeed, Skinner claimed that cognitive processes "didn't exist" because they could not be measured reliably, but then psychological science developed better methods, and now such a claim seems preposterous. It seems worth noting, however, that the self-report, behavioral, physiological, and neural evidence are consistent with one another and seem to point to the same conclusion, namely that it may be time to move beyond the modal model.

Is Emotion Generation Automatic?

This second cornerstone of the modal model – namely that emotions are automatically generated – has great intuitive appeal. Indeed, we "see" evidence (or so we think) of highly automatic and stereotyped emotional responses in ourselves, in others, and in non-human animals (such as our dogs and cats). But are our emotions generated automatically as the modal model suggests, leading us this way or that depending upon which emotion has been elicited by a particular context? In general, introspection does not give us privileged information regarding the causal mechanisms that give rise to our behavior (Nisbett & Wilson, 1977; Wilson & Dunn, 2004). Therefore, our experience of emotions as arising unbidden, and then taking us over, does not, in and of itself, constitute evidence that emotion generation is intrinsically automatic.

To be fair, the original definition of automaticity was phenomenological in nature. Automatic processing was characterized by the absence of any subjective experience of control during thought, feeling, and behavior. This idea began with James (1890) and was elaborated by Helmholtz (1925) who clearly described the elements of the subjective experience of automaticity in detail: automatic processing is marked by the absence of any subjective experience of awareness (you are unable to self-reflect on your processing attempts), agency (you do not experience yourself as the agent of your own behavior), effort (you do not experience processing as effortful), and control (you are unaware that automatic processes might be occurring and you are unable to counteract them). By contrast, varieties of controlled processing are defined by the presence of a feeling of awareness, agency, effort, or control.

These ideas were further developed by Bargh (1994), who argued that these four features would be better considered as separate, distinct qualities that can be true of any cognitive process, and can combine in a componential fashion to place processes somewhere along an automatic-controlled continuum. As a result, it is possible to speak of varieties of automatic processing or forms of conditional automaticity, which require a goal to be initiated but run to completion outside of awareness (Bargh, 1989). These essentially phenomenological characteristics continue to dominate the distinction between automatic and controlled processing (e.g., Bargh & Ferguson, 2000), such that *feelings* of control and the *operation* of controlled processes are often confused (Barrett, Tugade, & Engle, 2004).

If we define controlled processing the way that control of attention is defined, as processing that proceeds (either consciously or unconsciously) or is shaped by an internally represented goal state (as opposed to processing that is driven strictly by the stimulus properties of the situation), then evidence from the cognitive literature gives controlled processing a role in phenomena that we typically experience as automatic (Barrett et al., 2004). For example, when goal states affect the processing of information or behavior outside of conscious awareness (e.g., Bargh, Gollwitzer, Lee-Chai, Barndollar, & Troetschel, 2001; Chartrand & Bargh, 1996; Winter & Uleman, 1984), we would call this a form of controlled processing (because attention is being driven by a goal state). The goal itself need not be intended, nor in any way represented in consciousness for controlled processing to proceed. When the goal is intended, or is otherwise conscious, this can result in what social psychologists have called "unintended goal dependent automaticity" – the effects of such processing are unintended and are generally not represented in consciousness (for a discussion, see Bargh, 1989). The idea is that controlled processing can operate even at early perceptual stages, influencing how sensory information is selected, taken in, and processed (for reviews, see Luck & Hillyard, 2000; Posner & DiGirolamo, 2000; Shiffrin, 1988), well before the subjective experience of "seeing," "hearing", or "feeling" an input is generated. This sort of goal-based, controlled attention can "tune" more automatic, stimulus-driven forms of attention, including the ability of a stimulus to capture attention (for a review, see Pashler, Johnston, & Ruthruff, 2001). In current views from cognitive psychology, automatic processing (i.e., that which is stimulus-driven) is often intrinsically influenced by top-down, controlled forms of attention, making it somewhat artificial to separate the two in practice.

In principle, therefore, there need be no correspondence between a conscious feeling of control and the operation of controlled processing in the case of emotion. Indeed, they can be thought of as orthogonal, which means that one cannot be used to indicate when the other is occurring. It is possible, therefore, that controlled processing (as we mean it in this chapter, to refer to goal-dependent processing) may be more central to emotion generation than we have supposed, even though we do not experience any sense of agency or control or intention to generate an emotional response as controlled processes contribute to the formulation of an emotion. For example, if one has the goal of cooperating with another person, one may be less likely to take offense (and get angry) when the person tells an off-color joke than if one has either a competitive interpersonal goal or no specific interaction goal at all. In the view we are advancing, the lack of anger does not result from emotion regulation, but rather, anger may not be generated in the first place.

What does the evidence say regarding automatic emotion generation? Although there is ample anecdotal evidence (including our own first-person experience) for the automaticity of anger, sadness, and so on, there is surprisingly little empirical evidence to support the idea that emotions are inescapable, involuntary sets of synchronized changes in response systems, as depicted in Figure 4.1. Furthermore, when researchers have attempted to elicit discrete instances of emotion in the lab, the methodologies used do not allow clear determination of whether the generation of emotion responses was free from deliberative processing.

One type of methodology involves scripted mood inductions that may include the deliberate use of mental imagery and recall of autobiographical experiences to generate emotions (e.g., Posse et al., 2003; Schneider et al., 1997). In such experiments controlled deliberative processes play a clear role in generating the experiences under investigation (for imaging evidence consistent with this view, see Phan et al., 2002). A second methodology presents participants with film clips thought to elicit a discrete type of feeling such as happiness or sadness (e.g. Gross & Levenson, 1995; Lane, Reiman, Ahern, Schwartz, & Davidson, 1997; Levesque et al., 2003; Reiman et al., 1997). Although participants might report feeling happy or sad in response to such films, they are free to consciously and deliberatively think about and judge film contents, and may even choose to deliberately regulate their responses (Erber, 1996).

Part of the difficulty in determining whether emotions are generated automatically or deliberately is that there is no clear dividing line between automatic and controlled processes, and commonly used experimental methods that typically allow behavioral researchers to distinguish between automatic and deliberative processing may be difficult to employ in the context of emotion. Consider, for example, the fact that one of the most commonly employed means of demonstrating automaticity for a primary task – which in this case would be the generation of an emotion in response to evocative stimulus – is to ask participants to engage in a secondary task that drains attentional resources. If performance on the primary task does not change when participants are placed under "cognitive load," then we can infer that the processes supporting primary task performance are comparatively automatic in as much as they do not require the deliberate application of attention in order to proceed. In the context of emotion, however, even if the underlying processes that generate an emotion are not affected by the secondary task, our ability to measure behavioral correlates of emotion may be obscured: in the presence of a secondary task, self-reports of experience will be difficult to make and may likely change because participants are attending to stimuli relevant to the secondary task; autonomic responses might change because participants are more aroused when doing two things at once; and behavioral responses might change for the same reason.

Another commonly used methodology for evaluating automaticity involves comparing responses to subliminal and supraliminal presentations of stimuli. For investigating questions about emotion generation this methodology may be similarly problematic. At issue are the facts that it is difficult to verify that subliminal presentations resulted in no conscious perception of stimuli, that it is difficult to ask questions about emotional experiences generated by stimuli which participants did not perceive, and that the behavioral effects generated by subliminal presentations often are neither robust nor reliable (Merikle & Reingold, 1998; Pessoa et al., 2006; Phillips et al., 2004).

All told, there is little evidence for completely automatic instances of anger, sadness, fear, and so on. The emotion literature continues to rely on a categorical distinction between automatic and controlled processing that may be problematic, and methodological challenges make it difficult to interpret the existing literature. Some of these problems may be solved by reinterpreting the existing evidence in terms of conditional automaticity, where a given emotional response can be characterized in terms of various automaticity subcomponents, but this would not solve the more general problem that one of the basic postulates of the modal model – signature response patterns for each emotion – is not unambiguously supported by the available empirical evidence. Without such signatures it is difficult, if not impossible, to clearly identify when a given kind of emotion has occurred, and that makes it difficult to develop a cumulative body of scientific knowledge about emotion.

In contrast to the ongoing questions about automatic emotion elicitation, there is ample evidence that a simple form of affective processing – the computation of value and its effects – is largely automatic. Affect can be characterized by hedonic valence (positive–negative, pleasant–unpleasant), and in some models also by degree of activation or felt arousal (Cacioppo & Gardner, 1999; Russell & Barrett,

1999). Various theories suggest that a quick determination of whether a stimulus is good or bad is essential for identifying potential threats and orienting attention to potentially goal-relevant stimuli (LeDoux, 2000; Öhman & Mineka, 2001; Scherer, 2001). Although the representational basis of such valenced evaluations has never been specified precisely, theorists have speculated that valenced information is represented at various levels of the neuroaxis (for discussions, see Barrett, 2006c; Cacioppo & Gardner, 1999; Duckworth et al., 2002; Russell, 2003), including both stimulus–response associations and more abstract, semantic representations. The activation of such representations and their ability to guide or bias perception and action is often referred to as unconscious affect. Unconscious affect is produced by a set of action-oriented affective systems that allows a person to deal with immediate dangers and rewards (Gray, 2004).

Three kinds of behavioral evidence support the idea that people can automatically evaluate stimuli or events for affective value or valence. First, many behavioral studies have found that the subliminal or nonconscious presentation of a valenced stimulus can generate autonomic responses (Esteves, Parra, Dimberg, & Öhman, 1994; Öhman & Mineka, 2001), changes in the activity of facial musculature (Dimberg, Thunberg, & Elmehed, 2000) and behavior (Chen & Bargh, 1999; Mikulincer, Hirschberger, Nachmias, & Gillath, 2001), can bias perception of subsequently presented stimuli in a valence-congruent fashion (Murphy, Monahan, & Zajonc, 1995; Murphy & Zajonc, 1993), and can generate "mystery moods" that are misattributed to other causes (Chartrand et al., in press; Winkielman, Berridge, & Wilbarger, 2005). Second, brief supraliminal presentation of a valenced stimulus facilitates access to valence congruent behavioral responses that seem affective in nature (Chen & Bargh, 1999; Cunningham, Preacher, & Banaji, 2001; Fazio, 2001; Nosek & Banaji, 2001). Third, behavioral and autonomic indices of affective response may implicitly reveal changes in the evaluation of the stimulus not reflected explicitly in conscious experience (Bechara, Damasio, Tranel, & Damasio, 1997; Duckworth et al., 2002; Tranel & Damasio, 1993). Taken together, these findings indicate that stimulus valence may be computed rapidly, and can influence subsequent behavior and experience. It is important to note, however, that these data do not provide a firm foundation for broader claims about whether specific emotions (such as anger, sadness, or fear) are automatically generated.

THE SHAPE OF THINGS TO COME

In the two preceding sections of this chapter, we first examined and then critiqued the core assumptions that have guided emotion research for much of the last century. In this section, we explore the shape of things to come, as emotion research moves beyond the modal model and develops newer models. With neuroscience as their foundation, we expect these newer models to extend well beyond a small set of "basic" emotions, and to avoid the reification of the automatic versus controlled processing distinction, embracing instead an understanding of the intrinsic interplay between top-down (driven by the state of the organism) and bottom-up (stimulus-driven) properties of emotion processing. As a result, any given emotional response may be characterized by the extent to which it is experienced as automatic, or meets the various criteria for conditional automaticity. In our view, these newer models will provide a framework that may lead to different questions, and perhaps to better answers, about what emotions are and how they are generated. In the section that follows, we describe one family of models that we believe may be useful as emotion researchers begin to move beyond the modal model.

Parallel Distributed Processing Models

Parallel distributed processing (PDP) models (also called neural networks or connectionist models) are designed to explain psychological functions by appealing to the manner in which processing is achieved in the brain. PDP models are neurally inspired, meaning that they do not actually attempt to model processing at the level of individual neurons in the brain, but that they are generally consistent with how the brain processes information. Scientists used to conceptualize the brain as a hierarchical set of specialized processing networks, but more recent neuroscience evidence suggests that the brain is a set of distributed, interacting networks. In a PDP model, networks of neuron-like units (called nodes) pass activation to one another in parallel. Nodes in a PDP model can represent information at any level of analysis. For example, in "localist" models, each node represents a type of psychological function or process (e.g., an instance of emotion). In "distributed" models, the psychological function or process is represented by a pattern of activation distributed across a group of nodes. The idea is that multiple brain circuits process different types of inputs in parallel, with the processing in each circuit limiting, shaping, and constraining the way in which the system achieves a single coherent "solution." For the purposes of this chapter, the "solution" is an instance of emotion that suits the particular goals of the individual and constraints of the context.

Early attempts to understand emotion using PDP ideas were inspired by appraisal models, and were therefore firmly grounded in the modal model. Appraisal models made explicit reference to ideas from parallel distributed processing (Scherer, 2001), and nonlinearity and neural network modeling (Frijda & Zeelenberg, 2001). For example, Wehrle & Scherer (2001) used a "black box" computational model that consisted of a set of formulas or algorithms to calculate emotional outputs (e.g., facial or vocal behaviors) on the basis of concrete input parameters (such as a profile of appraisals).

Most of the PDP-inspired models that have been offered to date are "localist" to some extent. For example, Thagard and Nerb (2002) used a "localist" model where particular emotions were nodes within a larger processing system. Other models propose an emotion architecture where behavioral subcomponents of an emotional response (appraisals, physiologic reactions, facial movements, instrumental behaviors, and contextual information) cause an emotion in a way that is similar to what James originally had in mind. One early dynamic system model (Fogel et al., 1992) proposed that components of an emotional response are computed and proceed in parallel fashion and impose mutual constraints on one another to produce an instance of emotion. The result was a self-organizing system that produced the now familiar emotions of anger, sadness, fear, and so on. A more recent dynamic systems model (Lewis, 2005) replaced appraisals, physiologic reactions, and so on, with other components such as arousal, action tendencies, attention orientation, and feeling, but the general idea remained the same: what people usually take to be subcomponents of an emotional response actually have a more causal role in emotion generation. They organize a putative emotion system into coordinated response patterns, thereby causing an emotional response.

A new class of PDP models of emotion with distributed representations more explicitly depicts emotions as emergent phenomena. Distributed models are more neurally plausible than localist models (because the brain uses distributed representations), and they have several important advantages (for a discussion see Queller, 2002). One significant advantage is that a new node or processing unit does not have to be created every time a new instance of emotion is encountered. Instead, activation patterns across a fixed set of units can be altered to represent a new instance. For example, Wagar & Thagard (2004) present a model of core affective responding where collections of nodes represent areas of the brain that are thought to interact to produce a valenced (positive or negative) response. Their model is based on ideas from Damasio's (1994) somatic marker hypothesis. A collection of nodes for the ventral medal prefrontal cortex (VMPFC) directs appraisals of and responses to the situation. A second set of nodes, these representing the amygdala, direct bodily states associated with the current stimulus situation. Together, these nodes compute an initial affective response. Nodes for the hippocampus (coding information about the current context) gate the initial affective information to the nodes representing the nucleus accumbens (NAcc, which directs motor outputs). If the hippocampus allows, the affective signal is passed to the NAcc, which then sends information to nodes for motor/effector sites that then produce context-consistent behavior. The affective signal information is also routed back to the VMPFC and other prefrontal areas to further direct subsequent processing. Although we may not agree with the assumptions this model makes about the functions associated with specific brain systems (see below), we believe that the use of neuroscience data to inform construction of computational models of emotion is an important direction for future work.

A Constraint Satisfaction Approach to Characterizing Emotion

Although initial forays into modeling emotion using PDP networks have taken advantage of some of the properties of parallel distributed networks – for example, the idea that multiple brain circuits process different types of inputs in parallel – they may not yet have realized their full potential. One of the most intriguing properties of PDP networks is the way in which they reach an overall "solution" by taking into account multiple constraints provided by different types of information represented within the network. This process of finding the best fitting solution is known as *constraint satisfaction*. In this section we illustrate some ways in which a constraint satisfaction approach could play an integral role in future models of emotion that take into account current behavioral, physiological, neuropsychological, and imaging work concerning the nature and heterogeneity of emotional responding and move beyond assumptions made by the modal model. A summary of our ideas is presented in Figure 4.2.

A Processing Continuum vs. Categories of Processing Constraint

satisfaction models have been used to account for the same phenomena as traditional dual-process models, including stereotyping (Queller & Smith, 2002), impression formation (Kunda & Thagard, 1996), decision making (Simon & Holyoak, 2002), personality (Shoda, Tiernan, & Mischel, 2002), and the self (Carver & Scheier, 2002). In constraint satisfaction logic, processes are not categorically automatic or controlled. Instead, processes combine in a componential fashion so that a given processing event emerges somewhere along an automatic-controlled continuum, and can be characterized as having some degree of conditional automaticity (for a discussion of conditional automaticity, see Bargh, 1989, 1994). We believe that a constraint satisfaction model of emotional processing that is similar in structure to Wagar & Thagard (2004) holds great promise for the scientific study of emotion.

To illustrate how constraint satisfaction works, we borrow the example of perceiving a tomato from Kosslyn (1995). To see a tomato, your visual system first senses some object out in the world and encodes a set of object properties that constrain what the object might be. Let us say the property red is encoded. At this point, the object could be an apple, a tomato, a strawberry, a flower, a fire engine, a shirt, a book, etc. It cannot, however, be a banana, or any other object that is not red. At the same time, you encode the object as fragrant – this would rule out any object that does not have a fragrant scent (e.g., a fire engine, book, shirt, and so on). You also encode that it is round, ruling out all non-round objects, like flowers and strawberries. When you touch the object, it is soft and pliable, and therefore cannot be an apple. Each object property, or piece of information is a constraint on the way in which the stimulus is perceived, helping narrow down the space of potential objects to the one that most viably satisfies the constraints currently available. Not all sensory features or pieces of information provide constraints on the final processing solution, however. For example, the tomato might have a blemish on its skin, which is a constraint that does not match anything in memory, or that might even resemble best a blemish once seen on an apple.

It is possible that an instance of emotion emerges in a similar fashion, out of processes in the brain that attempt to satisfy and minimize differences between different representational constraints that are simultaneously active in a given instance of processing. That is, the generation of an emotion episode results from a heterogeneous network of bottom-up (stimulus-driven) and top-down (goal or organism-driven) processes that are organized into a coherent interpretation and action plan. All this occurs in parallel, and in real time probably happens in the blink of an eye. The result is an emotional episode that people experience more or less as a gestalt.

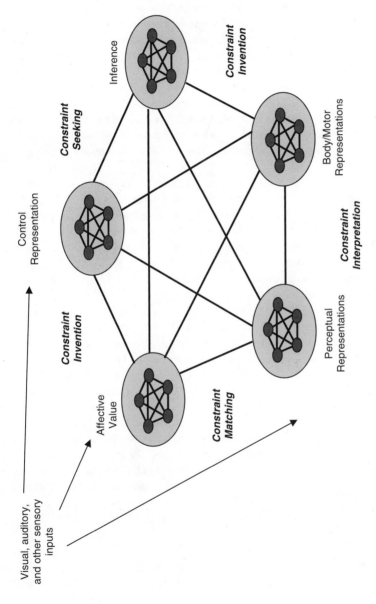

FIGURE 4.2   A constraint satisfaction framework for emotion.

Bottom-up processing in emotion generation Bottom-up processing describes how the sensory properties of the stimulus situation drive neural systems during the generation of emotion. These are processes that compute the initial affective value of a stimulus during stimulus recognition and stimulus identification, and are associated with numerous subcortical and posterior cortical areas of the brain including the amygdala, the ventral striatum, temporal parietal junction, and the hippocampus (located in the medial temporal lobe adjacent to the amygdala). Working together, these bottom-up systems can rapidly ensure responses in a variety of output systems, including those that are typically associated with emotional responding (like autonomic and endocrine changes, voluntary behavior, facial movements, etc.). They function to direct attention to stimuli that require further processing (e.g., Holland & Gallagher, 1999). In addition, outputs computed by bottom-up affective evaluators play an important role in establishing a person's core affective state at a given moment in time (Barrett, 2006a).

Constraint satisfaction can be used to describe two ways in which neural systems can generate emotion bottom-up, driven by aspects of the stimulus input. The first method can be termed *constraint matching*, which occurs when a stimulus first is encountered. The second method can be termed *constraint interpretation*, which follows after a stimulus is recognized via the constraint matching process.

Constraint matching (Kosslyn, 1995) involves matching available sensory inputs with stored unimodal representations in perceptual memory. In the tomato example that we borrowed from Kosslyn (1995), constraint matching proceeds via a number of bottom-up (or stimulus-driven) processes to extract information about shape, color, texture, and size. These features constrain one another during the matching process, leading to stimulus recognition. The result is that the sensory input implicates a single representation in perceptual memory, and the existence of the stimulus is recognized as familiar or not. At this point, the stimulus is not yet associated with a specific name and is not identified as belonging to a specific conceptual category (that is the next step).

Constraint matching is thought to be supported by posterior regions of the brain that represent different types of modality-specific inputs. Information about the spatial location, size, and movement of objects in the "dorsal stream" for visual processing links the occipital and parietal lobes. Information about the identity, form, and visual features of objects (such as facial expressions or body movements) in the "ventral stream" links the occipital and temporal lobes (Kosslyn & Koenig, 1992).

A person begins the initial computation of affective value during the constraint matching process. In the tomato example, this would involve estimating the probability that the stimulus features of this particular tomato predict subsequent threat (e.g., food poisoning) or reward (e.g., satiation of hunger). Affective value is computed with two neural systems that have been implicated in initially evaluating the valence of stimuli and generating appropriate responses in a predominantly stimulus-driven fashion. The centerpiece of the first system is the *amygdala*, shown in numerous studies to be important for rapidly detecting arousing stimuli

(Cunningham, Johnson et al., 2004; Morris, Öhman, & Dolan, 1999; Whalen et al., 1998), recognizing fearful and ambiguously threatening facial expressions (Adams, Gordon, Baird, Ambady, & Kleck, 2003; Adolphs, Baron-Cohen, & Tranel, 2002; Adolphs, Tranel, Damasio, & Damasio, 1994), fear conditioning (LaBar, Gatenby, Gore, LeDoux, & Phelps, 1998; LeDoux, 2000; Phelps et al., 2001), encoding and consolidating affectively charged positive and negative episodic memories (Cahill & McGaugh, 1995; Hamann, Ely, Grafton, & Kilts, 1999), and enhancing perception of arousing stimuli (Anderson & Phelps, 2001). Recent evidence suggests that the amygdala is involved in computing the predictive value of a stimulus (that is, its value in predicting threat or even reward; Kim et al., 2003, 2004).

The second system involved in computing the value of a stimulus involves the *striatum*, especially its ventral portion (known as the ventral striatum), which is important for the anticipation (Knutson, Fong, Adams, Varner, & Hommer, 2001; O'Doherty, Deichmann, Critchley, & Dolan, 2002) and receipt (Delgado, Nystrom, Fissell, Noll, & Fiez, 2000; Elliott, Friston, & Dolan, 2000) of rewarding stimuli with primary or secondary reinforcing properties, as well as learning about the rewarding properties of stimuli in general (Berridge & Robinson, 1998; Schultz, Tremblay, & Hollerman, 2000). More generally, the striatum may be involved in responding to events of immediate motivational significance. Once dopamine marks the salience of an event (such as when dopamine neurons respond strongly to an incoming event; Horvitz, 2000, 2002; Nieoullon & Coquerel, 2003), that event is given privileged access to voluntary motor output systems associated with the striatum and other parts of the basal ganglia.

Although the functional relationship between bottom-up affect encoding systems and perceptual memory systems has not yet been fully worked out and currently is an important topic of research (see e.g., Anderson & Phelps, 2001; George, Driver, & Dolan, 2001), it is clear that affective and perceptual encoding systems can interact in two ways during constraint matching. In some cases – for example those that involve complex perceptual inputs such as photographic images and films that require organization by perceptual representation systems – affect encoding systems may compute an affective value only after perceptual systems have recognized the input. In other cases, however, subcortical inputs from sensory organs to the amygdala and ventral striatum may support the rapid and independent computation of affective value, which can, in turn, constrain further processing in perceptual systems (Anderson, Christoff, Panitz, De Rosa, & Gabrieli, 2003a; Vuilleumier, Armony, Driver, & Dolan, 2003).

Working together, these bottom-up systems can rapidly ensure responses in a variety of output systems, including those that are typically associated with emotional responding (like autonomic and endocrine changes, voluntary behavior, facial movements, etc.). In a sense, these are the systems that produce the unconscious affective response that prepares a person to deal with imminent threat or reward (Gray, 2004). In addition, outputs computed by bottom-up affective evaluators play an important role in establishing a person's core affective state at a given moment in time (Barrett, 2006a). That is, a person's affective state at any given moment is available but not necessarily experienced as feelings of pleasure/displeasure and activation/deactivation.

The second way in which emotions may be generated bottom-up may be termed *constraint interpretation* (Kosslyn, 1995). Constraint interpretation follows after a stimulus is recognized via the constraint matching process. Outputs from unimodal perceptual memory systems and assessments of valence and arousal from affective evaluation systems come together with category information in the conceptual system. As a coherent interpretation of their gestalt is formed, additional conceptual representations about a given object may be activated, including knowledge about the mental – in this case emotional – states likely to arise in conjunction with the object (Barsalou, Niedenthal et al., 2003), what types of situations elicit those emotional states, and so on. The nature of the interpretation formed is represented as what may be termed an attractor state in a neural network, and may depend upon the initial affective salience assigned to the stimulus, the type of emotion knowledge retrieved, what other representations recently have been activated in representational networks (which form additional constraints on the interpretive process), as well as other constraints that influence the overall state at the system, such as that resulting from the prior affective computation (which we think of as "mood") or from processing of the broader situational context. Typically it is the case that the attractor state with the strongest and most coherent representation inhibits all other possible interpretive representations. In that sense, one attractor "wins," and gains access to action planning. In this way, the core affective state resulting from the constraint matching process may evolve into an emotional episode: as conceptual knowledge about objects and emotions is activated, the situational and intentional causal antecedents of the core affective state may be specified, resulting in an emotion episode (for a discussion, see Barrett, 2006a).

Two types of brain systems have been implicated in the representation of conceptual and contextual information that constrains affective computations of the amygdala and ventral striatum in a bottom-up fashion. The first represents explicit, declarative knowledge about the kinds of emotional responses appropriate to a given situation as well as the kinds of behavioral intentions associated with those responses. This type of knowledge has been associated with the temporal parietal junction and the left inferior frontal lobe (Wagner et al., 2001), which may be activated when individuals access contextual knowledge to interpret emotional stimuli (Ochsner, Knierim, et al., 2004; Ochsner, Ray et al., 2004). The second type of system involves the hippocampus (located in the medial temporal lobe adjacent to the amygdala) and plays an essential role in encoding the relationships among multiple modalities of inputs that together comprise a representation of stimuli in their current episodic context (Cohen, Poldrack, & Eichenbaum, 1997; Eichenbaum, Otto, & Cohen, 1992; McClelland, McNaughton, & O'Reilly, 1995). Importantly, the hippocampus helps consolidate these representations in a format that can be flexibly and explicitly retrieved later on. These multimodal representations may provide a constraint on current behavior, registering a match between current and past situational contexts, thereby indicating affordances for certain kinds of appraisal (e.g., knowing that at work, a grimace from your boss means he is not unhappy with you, but with a co-worker). In Figure 4.2, we have depicted conceptual knowledge as perceptual and motor representations, in line with recent research that the conceptual system consists of perceptual, rather than abstract, amodal, symbols (Barsalou, Simmons, Barbey, & Wilson, 2003).

Top-down processing in emotion generation   In some cases, an emotional episode ends when all of the activated constraints are interpreted as a coherent whole and appropriate responses are selected and executed. In many cases, however, a specific emotional response will not emerge. The stimulus context may be ambiguous or impoverished so that information sufficient to coherently interpret an object has not been encoded, or it may happen that multiple competing and closely related interpretations of the inputs are simultaneously activated and it is not possible to easily resolve which interpretation is best suited to the particular circumstance. Goal states that are active at the time of processing provide an internal reason why the network does not easily settle into a single, clear, emotional response. Goal states can be consciously initiated or passively primed by the stimulus environment, but either way, they can bias the final solution by providing additional constraints to the system.

At this point, the system may actively use top-down processes to engage in *constraint seeking* (Kosslyn, 1995). Constraint seeking involves testing hypotheses about the possible meaning of a stimulus input given the activation of ambiguous or competing attractors. In the process of doing so, several brain systems may come into play, each of which is associated primarily with top-down processes involved in the generation of emotion.

The first is the orbital frontal cortex (OFC), which receives multimodal sensory inputs and is robustly interconnected with the amygdala and ventral striatum (Carmichael & Price, 1996; Ongur, Ferry, & Price, 2003). The OFC can be thought to implicitly provide top-down constraints during the generation of emotional responses, implicitly constraining them based on the flexible representations of situation appropriate behavioral goals that have been learned through experience and instrumental action (Ochsner & Gross, 2005). This conclusion is suggested by the fact that OFC neurons rapidly change firing properties (as stimulus-reward mappings change), whereas amygdala and striatal neurons do not (Rolls, 2000; Schoenbaum, Chiba, & Gallagher, 1998), and the fact that OFC lesions render responses to affective stimuli inflexible and situationally inappropriate, as evidenced by impaired social behavior (Beer, Heerey, Keltner, Scabini, & Knight, 2003; Rolls, Hornak, Wade, & McGrath, 1994), impaired extinction of conditioned fear responses (Quirk, Russo, Barron, & Lebron, 2000), an inability to alter stimulus-reward associations (Fellows & Farah, 2003, 2005; O'Doherty, Critchley, Deichmann, & Dolan, 2003; Rolls et al., 1994), and impaired evaluation of the relative costs and benefits of risky decisions (Bechara, 2003).

The second system is the lateral prefrontal cortex (LPFC), generally implicated in the maintenance and manipulation of information (Miller & Cohen, 2001). In the context of emotion, LPFC may play an important role in strategically accessing conceptual memories that aid in the deliberate appraisal of an event's emotional significance (Davidson, Jackson, & Kalin, 2000; Ochsner & Barrett,

2001; Ochsner, Knierim et al., 2004; Ochsner, Ray et al., 2004), such as when one needs to understand the kinds of emotions that might be experienced in a given context or when one tries to understand the current situation in terms of similar ones experienced in the past.

The third system related to top-down emotion generation is the medial prefrontal cortex (MPFC), and especially its dorsal portion (the evolutionary neuro-developmental precursor of lateral prefrontal cortex, to be described next), which plays an essential role in drawing inferences about one's own or other individuals' current affective – or more generally, mental – states (Gallagher, Jack, Roepstorff, & Frith, 2002; Gusnard, Akbudak, Shulman, & Raichle, 2001; Lane, Fink, Chau, & Dolan, 1997; see Gallagher & Frith, 2003 and Ochsner, Knierim, et al., 2004 for reviews). The MPFC has interconnections with autonomic centers (Ongur & Price, 2000), and may provide an interface between higher cognitive representations that are informationally explicit on one hand, and comparatively visceral representations that are not explicit and provide "gut feelings" on the other. MPFC may come into play when one becomes aware of, reflects upon, monitors, and/or labels emotional states, including when emotional understanding requires drawing inferences about one's own behavioral intentions or the intentions of others (Ochsner, Knierim, et al., 2004).

The fourth system involved in constraint seeking is important for signaling when top-down processing is needed. The anterior cingulate cortex, and especially its dorsal portion (dACC), plays an important role in monitoring conflict between competing response tendencies and signaling the need for lateral prefrontal regions to implement control processes that bring performance into line with goals (Botvinick, Braver, Barch, Carter, & Cohen, 2001; Cohen, Botvinick, & Carter, 2000). In the context of emotion, dACC activation may reflect the failure to achieve a single constraint-satisfied interpretation of an emotional stimulus, thereby triggering constraint seeking. dACC then may work hand-in-hand with LPFC to guide the controlled application of emotion knowledge to seek additional information (Ochsner & Gross, 2004, 2005) that may enable the system to settle into a stable attractor state.

The top-down processes that are used to seek information in memory or in the perceptual input may be used to generate emotion in the absence of any external inputs that have affective value. In such cases, *constraint inventing* (Kosslyn, 1995) may be used to generate an emotional response to a situation that otherwise would have been interpreted as fairly neutral. Constraint inventing involves the deliberate construction and maintenance of representations in working memory constructed from information stored in the conceptual system. Although very little research has directly investigated this mode of top-down emotion generation, we recently conducted a study that examined this issue directly. This study is described in the final section below.

Advantages of a Constraint Satisfaction Approach to Emotion

Thus far, we have sketched how an instance of emotion can be thought of as an emergent phenomenon built out of processes that attempt to satisfy and minimize differences between all the different representational constraints simultaneously active in a given context. We envision bottom-up and top-down processes proceeding in parallel, and in real time within fractions of a second. When emotions are generated bottom-up, an emotion is experienced as happening to you, causing you to act and maybe even to feel something. When emotions are generated top-down, you may deliberately instantiate the stimulus and context that triggers bottom-up systems to respond emotionally.

The constraint satisfaction approach that we have outlined shares some features with the modal model. It incorporates the idea from appraisal approaches that an emotional response is launched by the interpretation of what a stimulus situation means to a person at a particular point in time, and that the bottom-up aspects of emotion generation are largely about the evaluation of the stimulus. It also incorporates the idea from basic emotion approaches that emotional behaviors can issue from bottom-up processing. Yet there are also significant differences. The constraint satisfaction approach does not assume that object perception initiates a set of rule-based appraisal processes resulting in a stereo-typed emotional response, although this approach could account for such responses should they occur. Furthermore, emotion-related behaviors are thought to arise both from the early evaluation process and when emotion knowledge is brought to bear during early action planning. There is no requirement, however, that the various emotion-related behaviors (face, voice, body) correspond to one another (although the framework can account for the times when they do).

There are two distinct advantages to a constraint satisfaction approach to emotion. First, not only does it provide a new account of phenomena covered by the modal model, it further allows us to generate hypotheses about emotional phenomena that previously may have been ignored or overlooked. Second, it moves us past the automatic-controlled processing distinction to something that is potentially more useful for finding answers to questions about emotion generation. We briefly consider each issue.

Modeling Heterogeneity in Emotion Representations Unlike the modal model of emotion which attempts to account for a small number of highly conserved emotional kinds, a constraint satisfaction framework predicts considerable heterogeneity in emotion responses in a way that is consistent with what has been observed in the empirical literature. The role of context in emotional responding is enhanced in two ways. First, conceptual knowledge about emotion plays a critical role in the formulation of emotional responses, and it is very likely that such knowledge is highly situation specific (Barrett, 2006a). Recent developments in research on conceptual knowledge in general (e.g., Barsalou, 1999; Barsalou, Simmons, Barbey, & Wilson, 2003) and emotion knowledge in particular (Barsalou, Niedenthal, Barbey, & Ruppert, 2003; Niedenthal et al., 2005) suggest that it consists of situated conceptualizations, such that an instance of an emotion category is constructed in working memory in a way that is tailored to the current situation. Second, representations of remembered contexts interact with current stimulus inputs to generate emotional responses. Although processing driven by stored knowledge allows people to capitalize on what they have learned in prior contexts by reinstating representations of previous emotional configurations, processing within the system can be sculpted by stimulus input guided activation-based processing that would allow an emotion representation (including the action plan) to be sensitive to momentary changes in context.

Interestingly, a constraint satisfaction framework may be able to account not just for heterogeneity in emotional responding, but also for the intuition that there are a few, discrete kinds of emotion. Just as we recognize and categorize physical objects around us, so too we may recognize in ourselves and others instances of core affect and categorize them as instances of emotion (Barrett, 2006a). As described above, through multiple types of constraint satisfaction processes, networks may complete partial inputs. Thus, we may be exposed to only a certain feeling, or a certain behavior, but may "fill in" the rest, making a perceptual inference of emotion.

Moving Beyond the Automatic Versus Controlled Distinction   A constraint satisfaction framework emphasizes the heterogeneity in emotional responding, suggesting that the building blocks of emotional life are something other than a few discrete emotion categories, and treating modal model instances as a special case. This framework also views automatic and controlled processing as tradeoffs within the same system (i.e., as parts of the system that have different functional objectives). In constraint satisfaction logic, processes are not themselves automatic or controlled. Rather, stimulus-driven and goal-based processing combine in a componential fashion so that a given processing event (i.e., an instance of emotion) emerges in a way that can be characterized somewhere along an automatic-controlled continuum, and can be said to have some degree of conditional automaticity (Bargh, 1989, 1994).

If we begin with the assumption that both bottom-up and top-down processes are involved in the generation of an emotional response, we can create experiments to study their interplay in generating emotion that is less or more automatic. It is possible to use a neuroscience methodology – functional magnetic resonance imaging – to examine the relationship between the top-down and the bottom-up generation of emotion characterized by different degrees of conditional automaticity (Ochsner & Gross, 2004; Ochsner et al., 2004). The use of fMRI allows the visualization of functional systems involved in each generative mode to determine whether and how they are similar or different. To generate more automatic emotional responses, participants simply viewed aversive photographs and let themselves respond naturally. To generate emotions in a more controlled fashion, participants viewed neutral photographs and mentally constructed appraisals of the depicted scenes that made them feel negative. For example, when viewing an otherwise neutral photograph of an empty bed, participants could generate a negative appraisal by imagining that a couple who had just slept there were tragically killed in a car crash on the way to work. Relatively automatic generation of negative feelings produced a bilateral activation of the amygdala (known to be important for rapidly encoding the affective properties of stimuli), as well as the right dorsolateral prefrontal cortex (a region known to be important for heightened arousal and sustained attention). By contrast, more controlled instances of negative feeling produced strong activation of left lateral and medial dorsal prefrontal cortex (regions known to be important for cognitive control and verbal · working memory), as well as increased activation of the left amygdala. Importantly, these data suggest that a functional system – the amygdala – typically thought to play a role in the rapid and even automatic generation of responses to affective stimuli, can be recruited using two different methods of generating an emotional experience (in the bottom-up case by encoding the intrinsically negative properties of an aversive image, and in the top-down case by creating a mental representation of these negative properties that did not exist in the real world).

CONCLUDING COMMENT

In this chapter, we have reviewed an intuitively appealing model of emotion that has guided emotion research for the past century. This "modal model" of emotion has served admirably as an initial framework for the field. Using this framework, emotion researchers have developed methods that have yielded a large number of empirical findings. What do these findings tell us about the two core postulates of the modal model? In our view, these findings cast doubt upon the idea that the field of emotion should be solely concerned with discrete kinds of emotion, and upon the idea that emotions typically are generated automatically. How can the field move beyond the modal model? We have suggested that newer models of emotion that are inspired by the idea of parallel distributed processing hold great promise. In particular, we have described a constraint satisfaction approach that we believe makes better contact with the available data than does the modal model, has the potential to handle the heterogeneity in emotional responding that is actually seen, and more generally suggests that automatic and controlled modes of emotional processing differ more in degree than in kind. The ultimate goal, of course, is the elaboration of a model of emotion that accounts for the widest range of clearly specified emotion phenomena possible, in terms of a simple but flexible processing architecture, that fits with and is informed by the known functions and characteristics of brain systems implicated in emotion. With any luck, such models will help us move beyond simple metaphors of emotions as wild animals and towards an understanding of them as rich, multiply determined, and multi-leveled phenomena.

NOTE

1. Alternative explanations for the *fear*–amygdala correspondence include the possibility that fear stimuli (such as facial depictions of fear) differ from other emotional stimuli on features such as novelty (e.g., Schwartz et al., 2003; Wright et al., 2003; Wilson & Rolls, 1993) and uncertainty (Davis & Whalen, 2001; Whalen, 1998; Whalen et al., 1998).

ACKNOWLEDGMENTS

Many thanks to Stephen Kosslyn for his helpful comments on an earlier draft of this chapter. Preparation of this chapter was supported by NSF grants SBR-9727896 and NIMH grant K02 MH001981 to Lisa Feldman Barrett and NIMH grant R01 MH58147 to James Gross.

REFERENCES

Adams, R. B., Jr., Gordon, H. L., Baird, A. A., Ambady, N., & Kleck, R. E. (2003). Effects of gaze on amygdala sensitivity to anger and fear faces. *Science, 300*, 1536.

Adelmann, P. K., & Zajonc, R. B. (1989). Facial efference and the experience of emotion. *Annual Review of Psychology, 40*, 249–280.

Adolphs, R., Baron-Cohen, S., & Tranel, D. (2002). Impaired recognition of social emotions following amygdala damage. *Journal of Cognitive Neuroscience, 14*, 1264–1274.

Adolphs, R., Russell, J. A., & Tranel, D. (1999). A role for the human amygdala in recognizing emotional arousal from unpleasant stimuli. *Psychological Science, 10*, 167–171.

Adolphs, R., & Tranel, D. (1999). Preferences for visual stimuli following amygdala damage. *Journal of Cognitive Neuroscience, 11*, 610–616.

Adolphs, R., Tranel, D., Damasio, H., & Damasio, A. (1994). Impaired recognition of emotion in facial expressions following bilateral damage to the human amygdala. *Nature, 372*, 669–672.

Adolphs, R., Tranel, D., Hamann, S., Young, A. W., Calder, A. J., Phelps, E. A., Anderson, A., Lee, G. P., & Damasio, A. R. (1999b). Recognition of facial emotion in nine individuals with bilateral amygdala damage. *Neuropsychologia, 37*, 1111–1117.

Anderson, A. K., Christoff, K., Panitz, D., De Rosa, E., & Gabrieli, J. D. (2003a). Neural correlates of the automatic processing of threat facial signals. *Journal of Neuroscience, 23*, 5627–5633.

Anderson, A. K., Christoff, K., Stappen, I., Panitz, D., Ghahremani, D. G., Glover, G., Gabrieli, J. D., & Sobel, N. (2003b). Dissociated neural representations of intensity and valence in human olfaction. *Nature Neuroscience, 6*, 196–202.

Anderson, A. K., & Phelps, E. A. (2000). Expression without recognition: contributions of the human amygdala to emotional communication. *Psychological Science, 11*, 106–111.

Anderson, A. K., & Phelps, E. A. (2001). Lesions of the human amygdala impair enhanced perception of emotionally salient events. *Nature, 411*, 305–309.

Anderson, A. K., & Phelps, E. A. (2002). Is the human amygdala critical for the subjective experience of emotion? Evidence of intact dispositional affect in patients with amygdala lesions. *Journal of Cognitive Neuroscience, 14*, 709–720.

Arnold, M. (1960). *Emotion and personality*. New York: Columbia University Press.

Bachorowski J.-A. (1999). Vocal expression and perception of emotion. *Current Directions in Psychological Science, 8*, 53–57.

Bachorowski J.-A., & Owren M. J. (1995). Vocal expression of emotion: Acoustic properties of speech are associated with emotional intensity and context. *Psychological Science, 6*, 219–224.

Bachorowski J.-A., & Owren M. J. (2001). Not all laughs are alike: Voiced but not unvoiced laughter readily elicits positive affect. *Psychological Science, 12*, 252–257.

Bachorowski, J.-A., & Owren, M. J. (2003). Sounds of emotion: The production and perception of affect-related vocal acoustics. *Annals of the New York Academy of Sciences, 1000.* 244–265.

Banse R., & Scherer K. R. (1996). Acoustic profiles vocal emotion expression. *Journal of Personality and Social Psychology, 70,* 614–636.

Barbas, H. (1995). Anatomic basis of cognitive–emotional interactions in the primate prefrontal cortex. *Neuroscience and Biobehavioral Reviews, 19,* 499–510.

Bard, P. (1928). A diencephalic mechanism for the expression of rage with special reference to the sympathetic nervous system. *American Journal of Physiology, 84,* 490–515.

Bard, P., & Rioch, D. M. (1937). A study of four cats deprived of neocortex and additional portions of the forebrain. *Johns Hopkins Hospital Bulletin, 60,* 73–147.

Bargh, J. A. (1989). Conditional automaticity: Varieties of automatic influence in social perception and cognition. In J. S. Uleman, & J. A. Bargh (Eds.), *Unintended thought* (pp. 3–51). New York: Guilford Press.

Bargh, J. A. (1994). The four horsemen of automaticity: Awareness, intention, efficiency, and control in social cognition. In R. S. J. Wyer, & T. K. Srull (Eds.), *Handbook of social cognition, vol. 1: Basic processes; vol. 2: Applications* (2nd ed., pp. 1–40). Hillsdale, NJ: Lawrence Erlbaum Associates.

Bargh, J. A., Chaiken, S., Govender, R., & Pratto, F. (1992). The generality of the automatic attitude activation effect. *Journal of Personality and Social Psychology, 62,* 893–912.

Bargh, J. A., & Ferguson, M. J. (2000). Beyond behaviorism: On the automaticity of higher mental processes. *Psychological Bulletin, 126,* 925–945.

Bargh, J. A., Gollwitzer, P. M., Lee-Chai, A., Barndollar, K., & Troetschel, R. (2001). The automated will: Nonconscious activation and pursuit of behavioral goals. *Journal of Personality and Social Psychology, 81*(6), 1014–1027.

Barrett, L. F. (1998). Discrete emotions or dimensions? The role of valence focus and arousal focus. *Cognition & Emotion, 12,* 579–599.

Barrett, L. F. (2004). Feelings or words? Understanding the content in self-report ratings of experienced emotion. *Journal of Personality and Social Psychology, 87,* 266–281.

Barrett, L. F. (2006a). Solving the emotion paradox: Categorization and the experience of emotion. *Personality and Social Psychology Review, 10,* 20–46.

Barrett, L. F. (2006b). Emotions as natural kinds? *Perspectives on Psychological Science, 1,* 28–58.

Barrett, L. F. (2006c). Valence as a basic building block of emotional life. *Journal of Research in Personality, 40,* 35–55.

Barrett, L. F., Tugade, M. M., & Engle, R. W. (2004). Individual differences in working memory capacity and dual-process theories of the mind. *Psychological Bulletin, 130,* 553–573.

Barsalou, L. W. (1999). Perceptual symbol systems. *Behavioral and Brain Sciences, 22,* 577–609.

Barsalou, L. W., Niedenthal, P. M., Barbey, A., & Ruppert, J. (2003). Social embodiment. In B. H. Ross (Ed.), *The psychology of learning and motivation* (Vol. 41, pp. 43–92). San Diego, CA: Academic Press.

Barsalou, L. W., Simmons, W. K., Barbey, A. K., & Wilson, C. D. (2003). Grounding conceptual knowledge in modality-specific systems. *Trends in Cognitive Sciences, 7,* 84–91.

Bechara, A. (2003). Risky business: Emotion, decision-making, and addiction. *Journal of Gambling Studies, 19,* 23–51.

Bechara, A., Damasio, H., Tranel, D., & Damasio, A. R. (1997). Deciding advantageously before knowing the advantageous strategy. *Science, 275,* 1293–1295.

Beer, J. S., Heerey, E. A., Keltner, D., Scabini, D., & Knight, R. T. (2003). The regulatory function of self-conscious emotion: insights from patients with orbitofrontal damage. *Journal of Personality and Social Psychology, 85,* 594–604.

Berridge, K. C., & Robinson, T. E. (1998). What is the role of dopamine in reward: Hedonic impact, reward learning, or incentive salience? *Brain Research Review, 28,* 309–369.

Berridge, K. C., & Winkielman, P. (2003). What is an unconscious emotion? (The case for unconscious "liking"). *Cognition and Emotion, 17,* 181–211.

Blanchard, D. C., & Blanchard, R. J. (2003). What can animal aggression research tell us about human aggression? *Hormones and Behavior, 44,* 171–177.

Blumberg, S. H., & Izard, C. E. (1991). Patterns of emotion experiences as predictors of facial expressions of emotion. *Merrill-Palmer Quarterly, 37,* 183–197.

Botvinick, M. M., Braver, T. S., Barch, D. M., Carter, C. S., & Cohen, J. D. (2001). Conflict monitoring and cognitive control. *Psychological Review, 108,* 624–652.

Bouton, M. E. (2005). Behavior systems and the contextual control of anxiety, fear, and panic. In L. Feldman Barrett, P. Niedenthal, & P. Winkielman (Eds.), *Emotions: Conscious and unconscious.* New York: Guilford.

Bradley, M. M. (2000). Emotion and motivation. In J. T. Cacioppo & L. G. Tassinary (Eds.), *Handbook of psychophysiology* (2nd ed., pp. 602–642). New York, NY: Cambridge University Press.

Bradley, M. M., & Lang, P. J. (2000). Affective reactions to acoustic stimuli. *Psychophysiology, 37,* 204–215.

Cacioppo, J. T., Berntson, G. G., Larsen, J. T., Poehlmann, K. M., & Ito, T. A. (2000). The psychophysiology of emotion. In M. Lewis, & J. M. Haviland-Jones (Eds.), *Handbook of emotions* (2nd ed., pp. 137–249). New York: Guilford Press.

Cacioppo, J. T., & Gardner, W. L. (1999). Emotions. *Annual Review of Psychology, 50,* 191–214.

Cacioppo, J. T., Gardner, W. L., & Berntson, G. G. (1999). The affect system has parallel and integrative processing components: Form follows function. *Journal of Personality and Social Psychology, 76,* 839–855.

Cacioppo, J. T., Klein, D. J., Berntson, G. G., & Hatfield, E. (1993). The psychophysiology of emotion. In M. Lewis & J.M. Haviland-Jones (Eds.), *Handbook of emotions* (2nd ed., pp. 119–142). New York: Guilford Press.

Cahill, L., & McGaugh, J. L. (1995). A novel demonstration of enhanced memory associated with emotional arousal. *Consciousness and Cognition: An International Journal, 4,* 410–421.

Calder, A. J., Lawrence, A. D., & Young, A. W. (2001). Neuropsychology of fear and loathing. *Nature Review Neuroscience, 2,* 352–363.

Cannon, W. B. (1927). The James-Lange theory of emotions: a critical examination and an alternative theory. *American Journal of Psychology, 39,* 106–124.

Cannon, W. B. (1931). Again the James-Lange and the thalamic theories of emotion. *Psychological Review, 38,* 281–295.

Carmichael, S. T., & Price, J. L. (1996). Connectional networks within the orbital and medial prefrontal cortex of macaque monkeys. *Journal of Comparative Neurology, 371,* 179–207.

Carver, C. S., & Scheier, M. F. (2002). Control processes and self-organization as complementary principles underlying behavior. *Personality and Social Psychology Review, 6,* 304–315.

Casey, R. J. (1993). Children's emotional experience: Relations among expression, self-report, and understanding. *Developmental Psychology, 29,* 119–129.

Cavada, C., Company, T., Tejedor, J., Cruz-Rizzolo, R. J., & Reinoso-Suarez, F. (2000). The anatomical connections of the macaque monkey orbitofrontal cortex. A review. *Cerebral Cortex, 10*, 220–242.

Chaiken, S. E., & Trope, Y. (1999). *Dual-process theories in social psychology*. New York: Guilford Press.

Chartrand, T. L., & Bargh, J. A. (1996). Automatic activation of impression formation and memorization goals: Nonconscious goal priming reproduces effects of explicit task instructions. *Journal of Personality and Social Psychology, 71*, 464–478.

Chartrand, T. L., Bargh, J. A., & van Baaren, R. (in press). Linking automatic evaluation to mood and information processing style: Consequences for experienced affect, information processing, and stereotyping. *Journal of Experimental Psychology: General*.

Chen, M., & Bargh, J. A. (1999). Consequences of automatic evaluation: Immediate behavioral predispositions to approach and avoid the stimulus. *Personality and Social Psychology Bulletin, 25*, 215–224.

Chovil, N. (1991). Social determinants of facial displays. *Journal of Nonverbal Behavior, 15*, 141–154.

Christie, I. C., & Friedman, B. H. (2004). Autonomic specificity of discrete emotion and dimensions of affective space: A multivariate approach. *International Journal of Psychophysiology, 51*, 143–153.

Clark, M. S., & Isen, A. M. (1982). Toward understanding the relationship between feeling states and social behavior. In A. H. Hastorf & A. M. Isen (Eds.), *Cognitive social psychology* (pp. 73–108). New York: Elsevier.

Clore, G. L., & Ortony, A. (2000). Cognition in emotion: Always, sometimes, or never? In R. D. Lane, L. Nadel (Eds.), *Cognitive neuroscience of emotion* (pp. 24–61). London: London University Press.

Cohen, J. D., Botvinick, M., & Carter, C. S. (2000). Anterior cingulate and prefrontal cortex: who's in control? *Nature Neuroscience, 3*, 421–423.

Cohen, N. J., Poldrack, R. A., & Eichenbaum, H. (1997). Memory for items and memory for relations in the procedural/declarative memory framework. *Memory, 5*, 131–178.

Cunningham, W. A., Johnson, M. K., Raye, C. L., Gatenby, J. C., Gore, J. C., & Banaji, M. R. (2004). Separable neural components in the processing of Black and White faces. *Psychological Science, 15*, 806–813.

Cunningham, W. A., Preacher, K. J., & Banaji, M. R., 2001. Implicit attitude measures: consistency, stability, and convergent validity. *Psychological Science, 12*, 163–170.

Cunningham, W. A., Raye, C. L., & Johnson, M. K. (2004). Implicit and explicit evaluation: fMRI correlates of valence, emotional intensity, and control in the processing of attitudes. *Journal of Cognitive Neuroscience, 16*, 1717–1729.

Dalgleish, T. (2004). Editorial. *Behaviour Research & Therapy. Special Festschrift special issue for John Teasdale, 42*(9), 971–974.

Damasio, A. R. (1994). *Descartes' error: Emotion, reason and the human brain*. New York: Grosset/Putnam.

Darwin, C. (1859/1965). *The expression of the emotions in man and animals*. Chicago: University of Chicago Press.

Davidson, R. J. (1994). Complexities in the search for emotion-specific physiology. In P. Ekman & R. J. Davidson (Eds.), *The nature of emotion: Fundamental questions* (pp. 237–242). New York: Oxford University Press.

Davidson, R. J., & Irwin, W. (1999). The functional neuroanatomy of emotion and affective style. *Trends in Cognitive Sciences, 3*, 11–21.

Davidson, R. J., Jackson, D. C., & Kalin, N. H. (2000). Emotion, plasticity, context, and regulation: perspectives from affective neuroscience. *Psychological Bulletin, 126,* 890–909.

Davis, M., & Whalen P. J. (2001). The amygdala: vigilance and emotion. *Molecular Psychiatry, 6,* 13–34.

Delgado, M. R., Nystrom, L. E., Fissell, C., Noll, D. C., & Fiez, J. A. (2000). Tracking the hemodynamic responses to reward and punishment in the striatum. *Journal of Neurophysiology, 84,* 3072–3077.

Dimberg, U., Thunberg, M., & Elmehed, K. (2000). Unconscious facial reactions to emotional facial expressions. *Psychological Science, 11,* 86–89.

Devine P. G. (1989). Stereotypes and prejudice: Their automatic and controlled components. *Journal of Personality and Social Psychology, 56,* 5–18.

Dressler, J. (2001). *Understanding criminal law* (3rd ed.). New York: Matthew Bender.

Duckworth, K. L., Bargh, J. A., Garcia, M., & Chaiken, S. (2002). The automatic evaluation of novel stimuli. *Psychological Science, 13,* 513–519.

Edmonson M. S. (1987). Notes on laughter. *Anthropological Linguist, 29,* 23–33.

Eichenbaum, H., Otto, T., & Cohen, N. J. (1992). The hippocampus – what does it do? *Behavioral and Neural Biology, 57,* 2–36.

Ekman, P. (1972). Universals and cultural differences in facial expressions of emotion. 1971. In J. R. Cole (Ed.), *Nebraska symposium on motivation* (Vol. 19, pp. 207–283). Lincoln: University of Nebraska Press.

Ekman, P. (1992). An argument for basic emotions. *Cognition and Emotion, 6,* 169–200.

Ekman, P. (1994). Strong evidence for universals in facial expressions: A reply to Russell's mistaken critique. *Psychological Bulletin, 115,* 268–287.

Ekman, P., & Friesen. W. V. (1978). *Facial action coding system: A technique for the measurement of facial movement.* Palo Alto, CA: Consulting Psychologists Press.

Ekman, P., Friesen, W. V., & Ellsworth, P. (1972). *Emotion in the human face: Guidelines for research and an integration of findings.* Oxford, England: Pergamon Press.

Ekman, P., Levenson, R. W., & Friesen, W. V. (1983). Autonomic nervous system activity distinguishes among emotions. *Science, 221,* 1208–1210.

Ekman, P., Sorenson, E. R., & Friesen, W. V. (1969). Pan-cultural elements in facial displays of emotion. *Science, 164,* 86–88.

Elfenbein, H. A., & Ambady, N. (2002). On the universality and cultural specificity of emotion recognition, a meta-analysis. *Psychological Bulletin, 128*(2), 203–235.

Elliott, R., Friston, K. J., & Dolan, R. J. (2000). Dissociable neural responses in human reward systems. *Journal of Neuroscience, 20,* 6159–6165.

Ellsworth, P. (1991). Some implications for cognitive appraisal theories of emotion. In K. Strongman (Ed.), *International review of studies of emotion* (Vol. 1, pp. 143–161). New York: Wiley.

Ellsworth, P. C., & Scherer., K. R. (2003). Appraisal processes in emotion. In R. J. Davidson & K. R. Scherer (Eds.), *Handbook of affective sciences* (pp. 572–595). New York: Oxford University Press.

Erber, R. (1996). The self-regulation of moods. In L. L. Martin & A. Tesser (Eds.), *Striving and feeling: Interactions among goals, affect, and self-regulation* (pp. 251–275). Mahwah, NJ: Lawrence Erlbaum Associates.

Esteves, F., Parra, C., Dimberg, U., & Öhman, A. (1994). Nonconscious associative learning: Pavlovian conditioning of skin conductance responses to masked fear-relevant facial stimuli. *Psychophysiology, 31,* 375–385.

Fanselow, M. S. (1994). Neural organization of the defensive behavior system responsible for fear. *Psychonomic Bulletin & Review, 1,* 429–438.

Fanselow, M. S., & Lester, L. S. (1988). A functional behavioristic approach to aversively motivated behavior: Predatory imminence as a determinant of the topography of defensive behavior. In R. C. Bolles & M. D. Beecher (Eds.), *Evolution and learning* (pp. 185–212). Hillsdale, NJ: Lawrence Erlbaum Associates.

Fazio, R. H. (2001). On the automatic activation of associated evaluations: An overview. *Cognition and Emotion, 15*, 115–141.

Fazio, R. H., Sanbonmatsu, D. M., Powell, M. C., & Kardes, F. R. (1986). On the automatic activation of attitudes. *Journal of Personality and Social Psychology, 50*, 229–238.

Feldman, L. A. (1995). Variations in the circumplex structure of emotion. *Personality and Social Psychology Bulletin, 21*, 806–817.

Fellows, L. K., & Farah, M. J. (2003). Ventromedial frontal cortex mediates affective shifting in humans: evidence from a reversal learning paradigm. *Brain, 126*, 1830–1837.

Fellows, L. K., & Farah, M. J. (2005). Different underlying impairments in decision-making following ventromedial and dorsolateral frontal lobe damage in humans. *Cerebral Cortex, 15*, 58–63.

Ferguson, M. J., & Bargh, J. A. (2004). Liking is for doing. The effects of goal pursuit on automatic evaluation. *Journal of Personality and Social Psychology, 87*, 557–572.

Fernández-Dols, J.-M., Sánchez, F., Carrera, P., & Ruiz-Belda, M. A. (1997). Are spontaneous expressions and emotions linked? An experimental test of coherence. *Journal of Nonverbal Behavior Special Issue: The communicative function of facial expressions: I Empirical challenges, 21*, 163–177.

Fogel, A., Nwokah, E., Dedo, J. Y., Messinger, D., Dickson, K. L., Matusov, E., et al. (1992). Social process theory of emotion: A dynamic systems approach. *Social Development, 1*, 122–142.

Fridlund, A. J. (1994). *Human facial expression: An evolutionary view*. San Diego, CA: Academic Press.

Frijda, N. H. (1986). *The emotions*. New York: Cambridge University Press Editions de la Maison des Sciences de l'Homme.

Frijda, N. H. (1988). The laws of emotion. *American Psychologist, 43*, 349–358.

Frijda, N. H., & Zeelenberg, M. (2001). Appraisal: What is the dependent? In K.R. Scherer, A. Schorr, & T. Johnstone, (Eds.), *Appraisal processes in emotion: Theory, methods, research* (pp. 141–155). London: London University Press.

Gallagher, H. L., & Frith, C. D. (2003). Functional imaging of "theory of mind". *Trends Cognitive Science, 7*, 77–83.

Gallagher, H. L., Jack, A. I., Roepstorff, A., & Frith, C. D. (2002). Imaging the intentional stance in a competitive game. *Neuroimage, 16*, 814–821.

Gallagher, M., & Schoenbaum, G. (1999). Functions of the amygdala and related forebrain areas in attention and cognition. *Annals of the New York Academy of Science, 877*, 397–411.

George, N., Driver, J., & Dolan, R. J. (2001). Seen gaze-direction modulates fusiform activity and its coupling with other brain areas during face processing. *Neuroimage, 13*, 1102–1112.

Gilbert, D. T. (1991). How mental systems believe. *American Psychologist, 46*, 107–119.

Gilbert, D. T. (1998). Ordinary personology. In D. T. Gilbert & S. T. Fiske, (Eds.), *The handbook of social psychology* (Vol. 2, 4th ed., pp. 89–150). New York: McGraw-Hill.

Gray, J. (2004). *Consciousness: Creeping up on the hard problem*. New York: Oxford.

Gross, J. J. (1998). The emerging field of emotion regulation: An integrative review. *Review of General Psychology, 2*, 271–299.

Gross, J. J., John, O. P., & Richards, J. M. (2000). The dissociation of emotion expression from emotion experience: A personality perspective. *Personality and Social Psychological Bulletin*, 26, 712–726.

Gross, J. J., & Levenson, R. W. (1995). Emotion elicitation using films. *Cognition and Emotion*, 9, 87–108.

Gusnard, D. A., Akbudak, E., Shulman, G. L., & Raichle, M. E. (2001). Medial prefrontal cortex and self-referential mental activity: relation to a default mode of brain function. *Proceedings of the National Academy of Sciences USA*, 98(7), 4259–4264.

Hamann, S. B., Ely, T. D., Grafton, S. T., & Kilts, C. D. (1999). Amygdala activity related to enhanced memory for pleasant and aversive stimuli. *Nature Neuroscience*, 2, 289–293.

Helmholtz, H. V. (1925). *Treatise on psychological optics*. Menasha, WI: Banta.

Hess U., Scherer K. R., & Kappas, A. (1988). Multichannel communication of emotion: synthetic signal production. In K. Scherer (Ed.), *Facets of emotion: recent research* (pp.161–249). Hillsdale, NJ: Erlbaum.

Hodgson, R., & Rachman, S. (1974). Desynchrony in measures of fear. *Behavior Research and Therapy*, 12, 319–326.

Holland, P. C., & Gallagher, M. (1999). Amygdala circuitry in attentional and representational processes. *Trends in Cognitive Sciences*, 3, 65–73.

Horvitz, J. C. (2000). Mesolimbic and nigrostriatal dopamine responses to salient non-reward events. *Neuroscience*, 96, 651–656.

Horvitz, J. C. (2002). Dopamine, Parkinson's disease, and volition. *Behavioral and Brain Sciences*, 25, 586.

Izard, C. E. (1971). *The face of emotion*. New York: Appleton-Century-Crofts.

James, W. (1884). What is an emotion? *Mind*, 9, 188–205.

James, W. (1890). *The principles of psychology*. New York: Henry Holt.

James, W. (1894). The physical basis of emotion. *Psychological Review*, 1, 516–529.

Johnstone T., & Scherer K. R. (2000). Vocal communication of emotion. In M. Lewis & J. M. Haviland-Jones (Eds.), *Handbook of emotions* (2nd ed., pp. 220–235). New York: Guilford.

Juslin, P. N., & Laukka, P. (2003). Communication of emotions in voal expression and music performance: Different channels, same code? *Psychological Bulletin*, 129, 770–814.

Kappas, A. (2001). A metaphor is a metaphor is a metaphor: Exorcising the homunculus from appraisal theory. In K. R. Scherer, A. Schorr, & T. Johnstone (Eds.), *Appraisal processes in emotion: Theory, methods, research* (pp. 157–172). London: London University Press.

Kappas A. (2002). What facial activity can and cannot tell us about emotions. In M. Katsikitis (Ed.), *The human face: measurement and meaning* (pp. 215–234). Dordrecht: Kluwer.

Kappas, A., Hess, U., & Scherer, K. R. (1991). Voice and emotion. In R. Feldman & B. Rimé (Eds.), *Fundamentals of nonverbal behavior* (pp. 200–238). New York: Cambridge University Press.

Keltner, D., & Haidt, J. (2001). Social functions of emotions. In T. J. Mayne & G. A. Bonanno (Eds.), *Emotions: Currrent issues and future directions*. New York: Guilford Press.

Kim, H., Somerville, L. H., Johnstone, T., Alexander, A., & Whalen, P. J. (2003). Inverse amygdala and medial prefrontal cortex responses to surprised faces. *NeuroReport*, 14, 2317–2322.

Kim, H., Somerville, L. H., Johnstone, T., Polis, S., Alexander, A. L., Shin, L. M., & Whalen,

P. J. (2004). Contextual modulation of amygdala responsivity to surprised faces. *Journal of Cognitive Neuroscience, 16*, 1730–1745.

Knutson, B., Fong, G. W., Adams, C. M., Varner, J. L., & Hommer, D. (2001). Dissociation of reward anticipation and outcome with event-related fMRI. *Neuroreport, 12*, 3683–3687.

Kosslyn, S. M. (1995). Freud returns? In R. L. Solso and D. W. Massarro (Eds.), *The science of the mind: 2001 and beyond* (pp. 90–106). New York: Oxford University Press.

Kosslyn, S. M., & Koenig, O. (1992). *Wetmind: The new cognitive neuroscience*. New York: Free Press.

Kunda, Z., & Thagard, P. (1996). Forming impressions from stereotypes, traits, and behaviors: A parallel constraint-satisfaction theory. *Psychological Review, 103*, 284–308.

LaBar, K. S., Gatenby, J. C., Gore, J. C., LeDoux, J. E., & Phelps, E. A. (1998). Human amygdala activation during conditioned fear acquisition and extinction: a mixed-trial fMRI study. *Neuron, 20*, 937–945.

Lacey, J. I. (1967). Somatic response patterning and stress: Some revisions of activation theory. In M. H. Appley & R. Trumbull (Eds.), *Psychological stress: Issues in research* (pp. 14–37). Englewood Cliffs, NJ: Prentice Hall.

Lane, R. D., Fink, G. R., Chau, P. M., & Dolan, R. J. (1997). Neural activation during selective attention to subjective emotional responses. *Neuroreport, 8*, 3969–3972.

Lane, R. D., Reiman, E. M., Ahern, G. L., Schwartz, G. E., & Davidson, R. J. (1997). Neuroanatomical correlates of happiness, sadness, and disgust. *American Journal of Psychiatry, 154*, 926–933.

Lang, P. J. (1988). Fear, anxiety, and panic: Context, cognition, and visceral arousal. In S. E. Rachman & J. D. Maser (Eds.), *Panic: Psychological perspectives* (pp. 219–236). Hillsdale, NJ: Lawrence Erlbaum Associates.

Lang, P. J., Bradley, M. M., & Cuthbert, B. N. (1990). Emotion, attention, and the startle reflex. *Psychological Review, 97*, 377–395.

Lang, P. J., Greenwald, M. K., Bradley, M. M., & Hamm, A. O. (1993). Looking at pictures: Affective, facial, visceral, and behavioral reactions. *Psychophysiology, 30*, 261–273.

Lazarus, R. S. (1966). *Psychological stress and the coping process*. New York: McGraw-Hill.

Lazarus, R. S. (1982). Thoughts on the relations between emotion and cognition. *American Psychologist, 37*, 1019–1024.

Lazarus, R. S. (1991). *Emotion and adaptation*. Oxford: Oxford University Press.

Lazarus, R. S., & Folkman, S. (1984). *Stress, appraisal and coping*. New York: Springer.

LeDoux, J. E. (1996). *The emotional brain: The mysterious underpinnings of emotional life*. New York: Simon Schuster.

LeDoux, J. E. (2000). Emotion circuits in the brain. *Annual Review of Neuroscience, 23*, 155–184.

Levenson, R. W. (1988). Emotion and the autonomic nervous system: A prospectus for research on autonomic specificity. In H. L. Wagner (Ed.), *Social psychophysiology and emotion: Theory and clinical applications* (pp. 17–42). Oxford, England: John Wiley & Sons.

Levenson, R. W., Ekman, P., & Friesen, W. V. (1990). Voluntary facial action generates emotion-specific autonomic nervous system activity. *Psychophysiology, 27*, 363–384.

Leventhal, H., & Scherer, K. (1987). The relationship of emotion to cognition: A functional approach to a semantic controversy. *Cognition and Emotion, 1*, 3–28.

Levesque, J., Joanette, Y., Mensour, B., Beaudoin, G., Leroux, J. M., Bourgouin, P., & Beauregard, M. (2003). Neural correlates of sad feelings in healthy girls. *Neuroscience, 121*, 545–551.

Lewinson, R. (2000). *The triple helix: Gene, organism, and the environment.* Cambridge, MA: Harvard University Press.

Lewis, M. D. (2005). Bridging emotion theory and neurobiology through dynamic systems modelling. *Behavior and Brain Science, 28,* 169–194.

Luck, S. J., & Hillyard, S. A. (2000). The operation of selective attention at multiple stages of processing: Evidence from human and monkey electrophysiology. In M. S. Gazzaniga (Ed.), *The new cognitive neurosciences* (2nd ed., pp. 687–710). Cambridge, MA: MIT Press.

MacLean, P. D. (1949). Psychosomatic disease and the "visceral brain"; recent developments bearing on the Papez theory of emotion. *Psychosomatic Medicine, 11,* 338–353.

Mandler, G. (1984). *Mind and body: Psychology of emotion and stress.* New York: Norton.

Mauss, I. B., Wilhelm, F. H., & Gross, J. J. (2004). Is there less to social anxiety than meets the eye? Emotion experience, expression, and bodily responding. *Cognition and Emotion, 18,* 631–662.

McClelland, J. L., McNaughton, B. L., & O'Reilly, R. C. (1995). Why there are complementary learning systems in the hippocampus and neocortex: insights from the successes and failures of connectionist models of learning and memory. *Psychological Review, 102,* 419–457.

Merikle, P. M., & Reingold, E. M. (1998). On demonstrating unconscious perception: comment on Draine and Greenwald (1998). *Journal of Experimental Psychology: General, 127,* 304–310.

Messinger, D. S. (2002). Positive and negative: Infant facial expressions and emotions. *Current Directions in Psychological Science, 11,* 1–6.

Mikulincer, M., Hirschberger, G., Nachmias, O., & Gillath, O. (2001). The affective component of the secure base schema: Affective priming with representations of attachment security. *Journal of Personality and Social Psychology, Special Issue, 81,* 305–321.

Milad, M., & Quirk, G. J. (2002). Neurons in medial prefrontal cortex signal memory for fear extinction. *Nature, 240,* 70–74.

Miller, E. K., & Cohen, J. D. (2001). An integrative theory of prefrontal cortex function. *Annual Review of Neuroscience, 24,* 167–202.

Morgan, M. A., Romanski, L. M., & LeDoux, J. E. (1993). Extinction of emotional learning: contribution of medial prefrontal cortex. *Neuroscience Letters, 163,* 109–113.

Morris, J. S., Öhman, A., & Dolan, R. J. (1999). A subcortical pathway to the right amygdala mediating "unseen" fear. *Proceedings of the National Academy of Sciences USA, 96,* 1680–1685.

Murphy, F. C., Nimmo-Smith, I., & Lawrence, A. D. (2003). Functional neuroanatomy of emotions: A meta-analysis. *Cognitive, Affective and Behavioral Neuroscience, 3,* 207–233.

Murphy, S. T., Monahan, J. L., & Zajonc, R. B. (1995). Additivity of nonconscious affect: combined effects of priming and exposure. *Journal of Personality and Social Psychology, 69,* 589–602.

Murphy, S. T., & Zajonc, R. B. (1993). Affect, cognition, and awareness: affective priming with optimal and suboptimal stimulus exposures. *Journal of Personality and Social Psychology, 64,* 723–739.

Niedenthal, P. M., Barsalou, L. W., Winkielman, P., Krauth-Gruber, S., & Ric, F. (2005). Embodiment in attitudes, social perception, and emotion. *Personality and Social Psychology Review, 9,* 184–211.

Nieoullon, A., & Coquerel, A. (2003). Dopamine: A key regulator to adapt action, emotion, motivation and cognition. *Current Opinion in Neurology, 16*, S3–S9.

Nisbett, R. E., & Wilson, T. D. (1977). Telling more than we can know: Verbal reports on mental processes. *Psychological Review, 84*, 231–259.

Nosek, B. A., & Banaji, M. R. (2001). The Go/No-go Association Task. *Social Cognition, 19*, 625–666.

Oatley, K., & Johnson-Laird, P. N. (1987). Towards a cognitive theory of emotions. *Cognition and Emotion, 1*, 29–50.

Ochsner, K. N., & Barrett, L. F. (2001). A multiprocess perspective on the neuroscience of emotion. In T. J. Mayne, and G. A. Bonanno (Eds.), *Emotions: Currrent issues and future directions* (pp. 38–81). New York: Guilford Press.

Ochsner, K. N., & Gross, J. J. (2004). Thinking makes it so: A social cognitive neuroscience approach to emotion regulation. In R. F. Baumeister & K. D. Vohs (Eds.), *Handbook of self-regulation: Research, theory, and applications; handbook of self-regulation: Research, theory, and applications* (pp. 229–255). New York, NY: Guilford Press.

Ochsner, K. N., & Gross, J. J. (2005). The cognitive control of emotion. *Trends in Cognitive Sciences, 9*, 242–249.

Ochsner, K. N., Knierim, K., Ludlow, D., Hanelin, J., Ramachandran, T., & Mackey, S. (2004). Reflecting upon feelings: An fMRI study of neural systems supporting the attribution of emotion to self and other. *Journal of Cognitive Neuroscience, 16*(10), 1748–1772.

Ochsner, K. N., Ray, R. D., Robertson, E. R., Cooper, J. C., Chopra, S., Gabrieli, J. D. E., & Gross, J. J. (2004). For better or for worse: Neural systems supporting the cognitive down- and up-regulation of negative emotion. *Neuroimage, 23*(2), 483–499.

O'Doherty, J., Critchley, H., Deichmann, R., & Dolan, R. J. (2003). Dissociating valence of outcome from behavioral control in human orbital and ventral prefrontal cortices. *Journal of Neuroscience, 23*, 7931–7939.

O'Doherty, J. P., Deichmann, R., Critchley, H. D., & Dolan, R. J. (2002). Neural responses during anticipation of a primary taste reward. *Neuron, 33*, 815–826.

Öhman, A., & Mineka, S. (2001). Fears, phobias, and preparedness: Toward an evolved module of fear and fear learning. *Psychological Review, 108*, 483–522.

Ongur, D., Ferry, A. T., & Price, J. L. (2003). Architectonic subdivision of the human orbital and medial prefrontal cortex. *Journal of Comparative Neurology, 460*, 425–449.

Ongur, D., & Price, J. L. (2000). The organization of networks within the orbital and medial prefrontal cortex of rats, monkeys and humans. *Cerebral Cortex, 10*, 206–219.

Ortony, A., Clore, G. L., & Collins, A. (1988). *The cognitive structure of emotions.* New York: Cambridge University.

Ortony, A., & Turner, T. J. (1990). What's basic about basic emotions? *Psychological Review, 97*, 315–331.

Panksepp, J. (1998). *Affective neuroscience: The foundations of human and animal emotions.* New York: Oxford University Press.

Panksepp, J., LeDoux, J. E., Phelps, E. A., Cacioppo, J. T., Berntson, G. G., Larsen, J. T., et al. (2000). Part II: Biological and neurophysiological approaches to emotion. In M. Lewisand & J. M. Haviland-Jones (Eds.), *Handbook of emotions* (2nd ed., pp. 137–249). New York: Guilford Press.

Papez, J. W. (1937). A proposed mechanism of emotion. *Archives of Neurology and Psychiatry*, 725–743.

Pashler, H., Johnston, J., & Ruthruff, E. (2001). Attention and Performance. *Annual Review of Psychology, 52*, 629–651.

Pessoa, L., Japee, S., Sturman, D., & Ungerleider, L. G. (2006). Target visibility and visual awareness modulate amygdala responses to fearful faces. *Cerebral Cortex, 16,* 366–375.

Phan, K. L., Wager, T., Taylor, S. F., & Liberzon, I. (2002). Functional neuroanatomy of emotion: a meta-analysis of emotion activation studies in PET and fMRI. *Neuroimage, 16,* 331–348.

Phelps, E. A., O'Connor, K. J., Gatenby, J. C., Gore, J. C., Grillon, C., & Davis, M. (2001). Activation of the left amygdala to a cognitive representation of fear. *Nature Neuroscience, 4,* 437–441.

Phillips, M. L., Williams, L. M., Heining, M., Herba, C. M., Russell, T., Andrew, C., et al. (2004). Differential neural responses to overt and covert presentations of facial expressions of fear and disgust. *Neuroimage, 21,* 1484–1496.

Posner, M. I., & DiGirolamo, G. J. (2000). Cognitive neuroscience: origins and promise. *Psychological Bulletin, 126,* 873–889.

Posse, S., Fitzgerald, D., Gao, K., Habel, U., Rosenberg, D., Moore, G. J., & Schneider, F. (2003). Real-time fMRI of temporolimbic regions detects amygdala activation during single-trial self-induced sadness. *Neuroimage, 18,* 760–768.

Power, M., & Dalgleish, T. (1997). *Cognition and emotion: From order to disorder.* Mahwah, NJ: Erlbaum.

Queller, S. (2002). Stereotype change in a recurrent network. *Personality and Social Psychology Review, 6,* 295–303.

Queller, S., & Smith, E. R. (2002). Subtyping versus bookkeeping in stereotype learning and change: Connectionist simulations and empirical findings. *Journal of Personality and Social Psychology, 82,* 300–313.

Quigley, K. S., Barrett, L.F., & Weinstein, S. (2002). Cardiovascular patterns associated with threat and challenge appraisals: Individual responses across time. *Psychophysiology, 39,* 1–11.

Quirk, G. J., & Gehlert, D. R. (2003). Inhibition of the amygdala: key to pathological states? In P. Shinnick-Gallagher, A. Pitkaenen, A. Shekhar, & L. Cahill (Eds.), *The amygdala in brain function: Basic and clinical approaches* (pp. 263–325). New York: New York Academy of Sciences.

Quirk, G. J., Likhtik, E., Pelletier, J. G., & Paré, D. (2003). Stimulation of Medial Prefrontal Cortex Decreases the Responsiveness of Central Amygdala Output Neurons. *Journal of Neuroscience, 23,* 8800–8807.

Quirk, G. J., Russo, G. K., Barron, J. L., & Lebron, K. (2000). The role of ventromedial prefrontal cortex in the recovery of extinguished fear. *Journal of Neuroscience, 20*(16), 6225–6231.

Rachman, S. (1984). *Fear and courage* (2nd ed.). New York: Freeman.

Reiman, E. M., Lane, R. D., Ahern, G. L., Schwartz, G. E., Davidson, R. J., Friston, K. J., et al. (1997). Neuroanatomical correlates of externally and internally generated human emotion. *American Journal of Psychiatry, 154,* 918–925.

Reisenzein, R. (2000). Exploring the strength of association between the components of emotion syndromes: The case of surprise. *Cognition and Emotion, 14,* 1–38.

Rolls, E. T. (2000). The orbitofrontal cortex and reward. *Cerebral Cortex, 10,* 284–294.

Rolls, E. T., Hornak, J., Wade, D., & McGrath, J. (1994). Emotion-related learning in patients with social and emotional changes associated with frontal lobe damage. *Journal of Neurol Neurosurgery Psychiatry, 57,* 1518–1524.

Roseman, I. J. (1984). Cognitive determinants of emotion: A structural theory. *Review of Personality and Social Psychology, 5,* 11–36.

Roseman, I. J. (1991). Appraisal determinants of discrete emotions. *Cognition and Emotion*, 5, 161–200.

Roseman, I. J., Antoniou, A. A., & Jose, P. E. (1996). Appraisal determinants of emotions: Constructing a more accurate and comprehensive theory. *Cognition and Emotion*, 10, 241–277.

Roseman, I. J., & Smith, C. A. (2001). Appraisal theory: Overview, assumptions, varieties, controversies. In K. R. Scherer, A. Schorr, & T. Johnstone (Eds.), *Appraisal processes in emotion: Theory, methods, research* (pp. 3–19). London: London University Press.

Rosenberg, E. L., & Ekman, P. (1994). Coherence between expressive and experiential systems in emotion. *Cognition and Emotion*, 8, 201–229.

Ruch, W. (1995). Will the real relationship between facial expression and affective experience please stand up: The case of exhilaration. *Cognition and Emotion*, 9, 33–58.

Russell, J. A. (1994). Is there universal recognition of emotion from facial expression? A review of the cross-cultural studies. *Psychological Bulletin*, 115, 102–141.

Russell, J. A. (2003). Core affect and the psychological construction of emotion. *Psychological Review*, 110, 145–172.

Russell, J. A., Bachorowski, J.-A., & Fernandez-Dols, J.-M. (2003). Facial and vocal expressions of emotion. *Annual Review of Psychology*, 54, 329–349.

Russell, J. A., & Barrett, L. F. (1999). Core affect, prototypical emotional episodes, and other things called emotion: Dissecting the elephant. *Journal of Personality and Social Psychology*, 76, 805–819.

Schacter, D. L. (1997). The cognitive neuroscience of memory: perspectives from neuroimaging research. *Philosophical Transactions of the Royal Society of London, Series B*, 352, 1689–1695.

Scherer, K. R. (1984). On the nature and function of emotion: A component process approach. In K. R. Scherer and P. Ekman (Eds.), *Approaches to emotion* (pp. 293–317). Hillsdale, NJ: Erlbaum.

Scherer, K. R. (1986). Vocal affect expression: A review and a model for future research. *Psychological Bulletin*, 99, 143–165.

Scherer, K. R. (1994). Toward a concept of "modal emotions". In P. Ekman and R. J. Davidson (Eds.), *The nature of emotion: Fundamental questions*. New York: Oxford University Press.

Scherer, K. R. (2001). Appraisal considered as a process of multilevel sequential checking. In K. R. Scherer, A. Schorr, & T. Johnstone, (Eds.), *Appraisal processes in emotion: Theory, methods, research* (pp. 92–120). London: London University Press.

Scherer, K. R., Schorr, A., & Johnstone, T. (Eds.) (2001). *Appraisal processes in emotion: Theory, methods, research*. London: London University Press.

Schneider, F., Grodd, W., Weiss, U., Klose, U., Mayer, K. R., Nagele, T., & Gur, R. C. (1997). Functional MRI reveals left amygdala activation during emotion. *Psychiatry Research*, 76, 75–82.

Schoenbaum, G., Chiba, A. A., & Gallagher, M. (1998). Orbitofrontal cortex and basolateral amygdala encode expected outcomes during learning. *Nature Neuroscience*, 1, 155–159.

Schultz, W., Tremblay, L., & Hollerman, J. R. (2000). Reward processing in primate orbitofrontal cortex and basal ganglia. *Cerebral Cortex*, 10, 272–284.

Schwartz, C. E., Wright, C. I., Shin, L. M., Kagan, J., Whalen, P. J., McMullin, K. G., & Rauch, S. L. (2003). Differential amygdala response to novel vs. newly familiar neutral faces: A functional MRI probe developed for studying inhibited temperament. *Biological Psychiatry*, 53, 854–862.

Seyfarth, R. M., & Cheney, D. L. (2003). Signalers and receivers in animal communication. *Annual Review of Psychology, 54*, 145–173.

Shiffrin, R. M. (1988). Attention. In R. C. Atkinson, R. J. Herrnstein, G. Lindzey, & R. D. Luce (Eds.), *Stevens' handbook of experimental psychology* (2nd ed., pp. 739–811). New York: Wiley.

Shoda, Y., Tiernan, S., & Mischel, W. (2002). Personality as a dynamical system: Emergence of stability and constancy from intra- and inter-personal interactions. *Personality and Social Psychology Review, 6*, 316–325.

Simon, D., & Holyoak, K. J. (2002). Structural dynamics of cognition: From consistency theories to constraint satisfaction. *Personality and Social Psychology Review, 6*, 283–294.

Sloman, S. A. (1996). The empirical case for two systems of reasoning. *Psychological Bulletin, 119*(1), 3–22.

Smith, C. A., & Ellsworth, P. C. (1985). Patterns of cognitive appraisal in emotion. *Journal of Personality and Social Psychology, 48*, 813–838.

Smith, C. A., & Kirby, L. D. (2001). Toward delivering on the promise of appraisal theory. In K. R. Scherer, A. Schorr, & T. Johnstone, (Eds.), *Appraisal processes in emotion: Theory, methods, research* (pp. 121–138). London: London University Press.

Smith, C. A., & Lazarus, R. S. (2001). Appraisal components, core relational themes, and the emotions. In W. G. Parrott (Ed.), *Emotions in social psychology: Essential readings* (pp. 94–114). Philadelphia, PA: Psychology Press/Taylor & Francis.

Smith, E. R., & DeCoster, J. (2000). Dual-process models in social and cognitive psychology: Conceptual integration and links to underlying memory systems. *Personality and Social Psychology Review, 4*, 108–131.

Smith, E. R., & Neumann, R. (2005). Emotion processes considered from the perspective of dual-process models. In L. F. Barrett, P. Niedenthal, & P. Winkielman (Eds.), *Emotion and Consciousness* (pp. 287–311). New York: Guilford.

Teasdale, J. D. (1999). Multi-level theories of cognition-emotion relations. In T. Dalgleish & M. J. Power (Eds.), *Handbook of cognition and emotion* (pp. 665–681). New York: John Wiley & Sons.

Teasdale, J. D., & Barnard, P. J. (1993). *Affect, cognition, and change: Re-modelling depressive thought*. Hillsdale, NJ: Lawrence Erlbaum Associates.

Tomkins, S. S. (1962). *Affect, imagery, consciousness: Vol. I. The positive affects*. Oxford, England: Springer.

Thagard, P., & Nerb, J. (2002). Emotional gestalts: Appraisal, change, and the dynamics of affect. *Personality and Social Psychology Review, 6*, 274–282.

Tomaka, J., Blascovich, J., Kelsey, R. M., & Leitten, C. L. (1993). Subjective, physiological, and behavioral effects of threat and challenge appraisal. *Journal of Personality and Social Psychology, 65*, 248–260.

Tomaka, J., Blascovich, J., Kibler, J., & Ernst, J. M. (1997). Cognitive and physiological antecedents of threat and challenge appraisal. *Journal of Personality and Social Psychology, 73*, 63–72.

Tranel, D., & Damasio, A. R. (1993). The covert learning of affective valence does not require structures in hippocampal system or amygdala. *Journal of Cognitive Neuroscience, 5*, 79–88.

Trope, Y. (1986). Identification and inferential processes in dispositional attribution. *Psychological Review, 93*, 239–257.

Turner, T. J., & Ortony, A. (1992). Basic emotions: Can conflicting criteria converge? *Psychological Review, 99*, 566–571.

Vuilleumier, P., Armony, J. L., Driver, J., & Dolan, R. J. (2003). Distinct spatial frequency·

sensitivities for processing faces and emotional expressions. *Nature Neuroscience*, 6, 624–631.

Wagar, B. M., & Thagard, P. (2004). Spiking Phineas Gage: A neurocomputational theory of cognitive–affective integration in decision making. *Psychological Review, 111*, 67–79.

Wagner, A. D., Pare-Blagoev, E. J., Clark, J., & Poldrack, R. A. (2001). Recovering meaning: left prefrontal cortex guides controlled semantic retrieval. *Neuron, 31*, 329–338.

Wallbott, H. G., & Scherer, K. R. (1986). Cues and channels in emotion recognition. *Journal of Personality and Social Psychology, 51*, 690–699.

Wehrle, T., & Scherer, K. R. (2001). Towards computational modeling of appraisal theories. In K. R. Scherer, A. Schorr, & T. Johnstone (Eds), *Appraisal theories of emotions: Theories, methods, research* (pp. 350–365). New York: Oxford University Press.

Weinstein, J., Averill, J. R., Opton, E. M., Jr., & Lazarus, R. S. (1968). Defensive style and discrepancy between self-report and physiological indexes of stress. *Journal of Personality and Social Psychology, 10*, 406–413.

Wells, A., & Matthews, G. (1994). *Attention and emotion: A clinical perspective.* Hillsdale, NJ: Lawrence Erlbaum Associates.

Whalen, P. J. (1998). Fear, vigilance and ambiguity: initial neuroimaging studies of the human amygdala. *Current Directions in Psychological Science, 7*, 177–188.

Whalen, P. J., Rauch, S. L., Etcoff, N. L., McInerney, S. C., Lee, M. B., & Jenike, M. A. (1998). Masked presentations of emotional facial expressions modulate amygdala activity without explicit knowledge. *Journal of Neuroscience, 18*, 411–418.

Wilson, T. D., & Dunn, E. W. (2004). Self-knowledge: Its limits, value and potential for improvement. *Annual Review of Psychology, 55*, 493–518.

Wilson, F. A. W., & Rolls, E. T. (1993). The effects of stimulus novelty and familiarity on neuronal activity in the amygdala of monkeys performing recognition memory tasks. *Experimental Brain Research, 93*, 367–382.

Winkielman, P., Berridge, K. C., & Wilbarger, J. (2005). Unconscious affective reactions to masked happy versus angry faces influence consumption behavior and judgments of value. *Personality and Social Psychology Bulletin, 31*, 121–135.

Winter, L., & Uleman, J. S. (1984). When are social judgments made? Evidence for the spontaneousness of trait inferences. *Journal of Personality and Social Psychology, 47*, 237–252.

Wright, C. I., Martis, B., Schwartz, C. E., Shin, L. M., Fischer, H. H., McMullin, K., & Rauch, S. L. (2003). Novelty responses and differential effects of order in the amygdala, substantia and inferior temporal cortex. *Neuroimage, 18*, 660–669.

Zajonc, R. B. (1980). Feeling and thinking: Preferences need no inferences. *American Psychologist, 35*, 151–175.

Zajonc, R. B. (1984). On the primacy of affect. *American Psychologist, 39*, 117–123.

5

The Automaticity of Evaluation

MELISSA J. FERGUSON

*P*eople's ability to assess the evaluative nature of stimuli in their environment has been a central topic of study in psychology throughout the last 100 years (e.g., Allport, 1935; Brendl & Higgins, 1996; Brown, 1998; Eagly & Chaiken, 1993; McGuire, 1969, 1985; Osgood, Suci, & Tannenbaum, 1957; Rosenberg, 1956; Tesser & Martin, 1996; Zajonc, 2001). Although the scholarly questions concerning evaluations have been distinct and wide-ranging, a substantial amount of the work has been conducted using the methodology of direct self-reports (see Himmelfarb, 1993; Krosnick, Judd, & Wittenbrink, 2005). This method entails asking people to overtly describe their attitudes and evaluations, typically by identifying the number along a scale (e.g., a number between 1 and 11) that indicates the degree to which a given stimulus is pleasing or displeasing. In this way, the evaluations, and evaluative processes, that have been examined over the last century can be primarily described as intentionally generated and consciously accessible.

The last 20 years of findings in attitude research stand in stark contrast with this tradition. This research has benefited from advances in methodology that allow the sophisticated, indirect, and subtle measurement of evaluations. This work has demonstrated that in addition to consciously, carefully, and deliberately assessing whether something is good or bad, people also evaluate stimuli nonconsciously and unintentionally upon the immediate perception of the stimuli. In particular, people assess stimuli as positive or negative within half a second after perceiving them, without intending or being aware of such assessments, or even necessarily of the stimuli themselves (e.g., Bargh, Chaiken, Govender, & Pratto, 1992; Fazio, 2001; Fazio, Sanbonmatsu, Powell, & Kardes, 1986; Greenwald, Klinger, & Liu, 1989; Greenwald, McGhee, & Schwartz, 1998; Zajonc, 1980). For instance, people can process whether a face is positive or negative based solely on a subliminal, 2-millisecond presentation of that face on a screen, even while remaining unaware that a face was even presented (e.g., Murphy & Zajonc, 1993; Niedenthal, 1990; Öhman, 1986). The fact that evaluative processes can occur without the perceiver's intention, awareness, or control has led to their characterization as *automatic* (see Bargh, 1994; for evidence of effortlessness, see Hermans, Crombez, & Eelen, 2000).

Interest in the existence and limitations of *automatic evaluation* has especially increased over the last ten years, and has produced a sizable body of empirical findings. For example, *Journal of Personality and Social Psychology* and *Cognition and Emotion* have each devoted journal issues to implicit measures of evaluation in recent years (2001 and 2002 respectively), suggesting the topic's centrality in contemporary research (for reviews see Banaji, 2001; Bassili & Brown, 2005; Blair, 2002; Fazio, 2001; Fazio & Olson, 2003; Musch & Klauer, 2003). The focus on how evaluative processes in particular can operate automatically is part of a broader, developing conceptualization of human cognition as driven by both controlled and automatic processing (e.g., Bargh & Ferguson, 2000; Chaiken & Trope, 1999; Greenwald, & Banaji, 1995; Hassin, Uleman, & Bargh, 2005; Sloman, 1996), as is evidenced by the other chapters in this volume.

The current chapter reviews the research on automaticity in evaluation over the last several decades with a focus on the last ten years. After some initial comments on the terminology in this literature, findings are discussed with regard to the measures that capture automatic attitudes and evaluations, the degree to which such evaluations are contextually independent, the correspondence between evaluations that are generated automatically versus deliberately, the extent to which automatic evaluations can be generated toward novel or unfamiliar stimuli, and the range of downstream consequences of such evaluations on subsequent thinking, feeling, and acting. Lastly, the chapter considers possible underlying cognitive architectures for evaluative processing, some aspects of which are constrained and informed by recent findings.

SOME COMMENTS ON TERMINOLOGY

Before beginning a review of the measures that are used to assess automatic evaluations, some comments on the terminology used in the area seem necessary. The first issue concerns the use of the terms *attitude* and *evaluation*. Although the two terms are often used interchangeably, they may suggest different assumptions about the way in which the construct is represented in memory and generated on perception of a given stimulus. *Attitude* is a longstanding construct in social psychology, and has been defined in dozens of ways over the last century (e.g., Allport, 1935; Doob, 1947; Osgood, Suci, & Tannenbaum, 1957; Sarnoff, 1960; M. B. Smith, Bruner, & White, 1956; Thurstone, 1931). One relatively recent and widely accepted definition comes from Eagly and Chaiken (1993), who define it as a "psychological tendency that is expressed by evaluating a particular entity with some degree of favor or disfavor." This definition depicts the theme of *liking* or *disliking* that is common across many of the definitions.

Over the last twenty years, however, the attitude construct has been increasingly understood as an association in memory between the corresponding object and its evaluation (Fazio, 1986; Fazio, Chen, McDonel, & Sherman, 1982). Because this definition includes an assertion about the representational basis of the construct, it has been highly influential within social cognitive research, which focuses on the processes and representational format that might underlie social psychological constructs (e.g., Kunda, 1999; Moskowitz, 2005). For example, research suggests that the strength of the association between a given object and its corresponding evaluation determines the degree to which that attitude will influence a range of downstream behavior and judgment toward the object (e.g., Fazio, 1989, 1990; Fazio & Williams, 1986; Petty & Krosnick, 1995). From the perspective of much of this research, an *attitude* refers to a stored, summary index of positivity or negativity that is associated with the object representation, and that remains dormant and inert (unchanged) until it is acted upon by independent retrieval processes (Eagly & Chaiken, 1993; Fazio, 1986; Fazio et al., 1982; Fiske & Pavelchek, 1986; for alternative views, see Bassili & Brown, 2005; Duckworth, Bargh, Garcia, & Chaiken, 2002; Ferguson & Bargh, 2002, 2004; Mitchel, Nosek, & Banaji, 2003; Schwarz & Bohner, 2001; Tesser, 1978).

The term *evaluation* also refers to the positive or negative assessment of a stimulus, but has been less formally defined in the literature compared with the term attitude (though see Tesser & Martin, 1996). The use of the term *evaluation* in this literature probably derives in part from the use of the term "automatic evaluation," which describes the act of evaluating a stimulus without intention or awareness (e.g., Bargh, Chaiken, Raymond, & Hymes, 1996; Bargh et al., 1992; Chaiken & Bargh, 1993). Whereas an *attitude* might be assumed to reflect (only) pre-existing evaluative information associated with the object representation, an *evaluation* seems to invoke fewer assumptions about the underlying architectural possibilities. The term *evaluation* denotes the end-product of an evaluative process, which is necessarily on-line and does not explicitly constrain the source(s) of the evaluative information (e.g., Bassili & Brown, 2005; Duckworth et al., 2002; Ferguson & Bargh, 2002, 2004; Gawronski, Walther, & Blank, 2005; Mitchel et al., 2003; Schwarz & Bohner, 2001; Tesser, 1978). That is, the evaluation of any given object might be constructed based on multiple sources of evaluative information, beyond the information associated with the object representation itself (e.g., see Bassili & Brown, 2005). Thus, although the terms *evaluation* and *attitude* are interchangeable based on their similar meaning (i.e., an assessment of positivity or negativity), the former term seems to invoke fewer theoretical implications concerning the potential underlying representational format. Although both terms will appear in the present chapter, it should be noted that the term *attitude* should not imply any particular underlying cognitive architecture. The issue of representation and generation is discussed at the end of the chapter.

It is customary in the literature on automatic evaluation and attitudes to refer to the targets of evaluation as "attitude objects" (e.g., Allport, 1935; Bargh et al., 1992; Fazio, 2001; Fazio et al., 1986; Sarnoff, 1960; M. B. Smith, et al., 1956; Thurstone, 1931). Although the primary definition of the word *object* is "something material that may be perceived with the senses," the use of the term in the attitude literature is based on its secondary meaning of "something mental or physical toward which thought, feeling, or action is directed" (Merriam-Webster, 2005). In other words, it can denote anything that is discriminable, or a subject of thought (Eagly & Chaiken, 1993). This can include concrete inanimate (e.g., fruit, bottle) as well as animate stimuli (e.g., people, animals), event and issues (e.g., abortion, death penalty), and abstract notions and values (e.g., liberty, freedom).

As Thurstone (1931) noted, an attitude refers to the "affect for or against a *psychological* object" (p. 261; italics added).

Another source of potential confusion about the terminology in this area concerns the measures that are used to assess attitudes in an implicit fashion (these measures are discussed in more detail in the following section). Some controversy exists about whether the dissociation between attitudes that are measured implicitly versus explicitly (e.g., see Blair, 2002; Dovidio, Kawakami, Johnson, & Howard, 1997; Fazio & Olson, 2003) reflects two distinct underlying attitude constructs (i.e., an implicit versus explicit attitude; Devine, 1989; Wilson, Lindsey, & Schooler, 2002) or merely differences in the way in which one underlying construct is measured (Brendl, Markman, & Messner, 2001; Fazio, Jackson, Dunton, & Williams, 1995; Fazio & Olson, 2003). Because there is as yet no definitive answer as to whether the two kinds of measures tap the same (e.g., Fazio & Olson, 2003), related (e.g., Hofmann, Gawronski, Gschwendner, Le, & Schmitt, 2005; Nosek, 2005), or independent constructs (e.g., Wilson et al., 2000), some theorists have cautioned against referring to implicitly measured attitudes as "automatic attitudes," or "implicit attitudes", which gives the impression that an attitude measured implicitly is distinct from one measured explicitly (see De Houwer, 2006; Fazio & Olson, 2003). In this chapter, the terms "automatic attitudes" and "implicit attitudes" will be used with the proviso that they should not imply any assumptions about the qualitative distinction between such attitudes and those attitudes measured explicitly. The issue of whether differences between implicitly and explicitly measured attitudes reflect substantive versus merely methodological differences is discussed in a subsequent section.

Finally, the measures that are used to assess automatic evaluations are typically referred to as "implicit" (Banaji, 2001; Greenwald & Banaji, 1995) because they assess the attitude indirectly or covertly, that is, without asking the respondent to report her or his attitude. This is an important difference from the traditional, explicit, and direct way in which attitudes have been measured throughout the past century (e.g., Himmelfarb, 1993; Krosnick et al., 2005). However, as some have noted (see De Houwer, 2006; Fazio & Olson, 2003), the term *implicit* is used in cognitive psychology to describe an influence of past experience that cannot be recalled, regardless of effort and intention (Roediger, 1990; Squire & Kandel, 1999; Tulving & Craik, 2000). This definition of the term may not accurately describe the way in which attitudes are measured in social psychology as there is typically no evidence that participants who are completing the "implicit" measures are unable to access their evaluations of the pertinent stimuli. Thus, it should be noted that there are some differences in the way in which the term *implicit* is used across social and cognitive psychology.

EVIDENCE FOR AUTOMATIC EVALUATION

Psychologists have traditionally measured attitudes by directly asking people how they feel toward certain people, groups, objects, issues, and concepts (see Albarracín, Johnson, & Zanna, 2005). For example, initial attempts to assess people's attitudes toward stigmatized groups often involved asking respondents to report their agreement with stark statements such as "Black people are generally not as smart as Whites" (McConahay, 1986). Given the rise over the second half of the twentieth century in social pressures for equal treatment and egalitarian behavior toward all people irrespective of their group membership(s) (e.g., McConahay, 1986; Myers, 1993), researchers began to suspect that people might be reluctant to openly admit intergroup negativity (see also Dovidio, Mann, & Gaertner, 1989; Jones & Sigall, 1971; Katz & Hass, 1988). To circumvent this reluctance, researchers devised more subtle attempts to gauge a person's attitudes, and these efforts led to the development of implicit attitude measures. In the present section, the implicit measures of attitudes that are predominant in contemporary research are described (for other contemporary implicit attitude measures see De Houwer, 2003; De Houwer & Eelen, 1998; Dovidio, Kawakami, Johnson, & Howard, 1997; Koole, Dijksterhuis, & van Knippenberg, 2001; Nosek & Banaji, 2001; Payne, Cheng, Govorun, & Stewart, 2005; von Hippel, Sekaquaptewa, & Vargas, 1997).

Evaluative Priming Paradigm

In 1986, Fazio and colleagues published the first article suggesting that people's evaluations or attitudes toward stimuli are automatically activated from memory on the mere perception of the stimuli. Fazio et al. (1986) modified a semantic priming paradigm that was originally developed to examine automatic and controlled processing in semantic memory (Logan, 1980; Meyer & Schvaneveldt, 1971; Neely, 1976, 1977; Posner & Snyder, 1975; Shiffrin & Schneider, 1977). Neely (1977) was interested in testing whether the perception of a stimulus leads to the automatic activation in memory of knowledge semantically related to that stimulus. To explore this question, Neely constructed a series of prime–target pairs that were or were not semantically related, and assessed whether the perception of a prime stimulus, such as *BIRD*, led to faster responses to semantically related targets, such as *ROBIN*, compared with when the preceding prime was a nonsense stimulus (*XXX*). Faster responses to the target *ROBIN* when it was preceded by the prime *BIRD* (versus *XXX*) would suggest that semantically related knowledge about birds (including knowledge about robins) was automatically activated and allowed faster encoding of related targets. Neely (1977) found that when the stimulus onset asynchrony (SOA) between the prime and target was shorter than 500 ms, knowledge semantically related to the prime stimulus was indeed activated regardless of the perceiver's intentions and strategic processing (see also Meyer & Schvanevedlt, 1971; Posner & Snyder, 1975).

Fazio and colleagues were interesting in testing whether the perception of a stimulus also led to the automatic activation of *evaluative* information about that stimulus, along with other semantically related information. To do so, Fazio et al. (1986) constructed prime–target pairs that were unrelated semantically, except for sharing (or not sharing) a positive or negative valence (e.g., sunshine-wonderful, death-excellent). Based on the research by Neely (1977), Fazio et al. (1986) used a brief SOA (300 ms) in the paradigm to ensure that any effect of the primes on the speed of responses to targets would reflect nonstrategic and unintentional (i.e., automatic) processing. In three experiments, participants were faster to respond to the target adjectives when the targets and primes shared (versus did not share) the same valence. Fazio et al. concluded that this *evaluative priming effect* suggested that the evaluative information about primes was automatically activated, and then allowed faster encoding and responding to similarly evaluative targets. This evaluative priming paradigm thus provided the first evidence that evaluative information about stimuli (i.e., attitudes, evaluations) is automatically activated on perception of those stimuli.

The evaluative priming effect has since been replicated numerous times using a variety of experimental stimuli and response tasks. For example, the effect has emerged when the prime stimuli consist of lexical primes (e.g., Bargh et al., 1992; Fazio et al., 1986), pictures (Giner-Sorolla, Garcia, & Bargh, 1999), and odors (Hermans, Baeyens & Eelen, 1998). Although much of the research in this area has used an evaluation response task ("Is this target word positive or negative?"), the effect has also emerged when participants are asked to pronounce the targets (Bargh et al., 1996; Duckworth, Bargh, Garcia, & Chaiken, 2002; Glaser & Banaji, 1999; Hermans, De Houwer, & Eelen, 1994), or generate a speeded motor response task to the primes alone (Chen & Bargh, 1999; Duckworth et al., 2002; Wentura, 2000).

There has been considerable debate concerning the generality of the effect across stimuli (i.e., whether attitude strength moderates automatic attitude activation; Castelli, Zogmaister, Smith, & Arcuri, 2004; Chaiken & Bargh, 1993; Fazio, 1993) and response tasks (e.g., Klauer & Musch, 2003; Wentura, 1999, 2000), as well as possible underlying mechanisms and boundary conditions of the effect (e.g., Fazio, 2001; Ferguson & Bargh, 2003; Klauer & Musch, 2003; Klauer & Stern, 1992; Klinger, Burton, & Pitts, 2000; Wentura, 1999). Nevertheless, much of this debate has centered on the consequences of automatic evaluations once they have been generated; the evidence that evaluations are automatically generated is considerable and largely noncontroversial.

The evaluative priming paradigm has been used as an implicit attitude measure (e.g., Fazio et al., 1995; Ferguson & Bargh, 2004; Wittenbrink, Judd, & Park, 1997, 2001). Researchers have used versions of this paradigm to assess participants' automatic evaluation of a particular set of prime stimuli by investigating how the perception of the primes influences subsequent responses to positive versus negative adjectives, compared to some comparison set of prime stimuli. If participants respond faster to positive versus negative adjectives after a given prime stimulus (compared to a control prime stimulus), then one can assume that the participants generated a positive evaluation of that prime. If, on the other hand, participants respond faster to negative versus positive adjectives, one can conclude that they exhibited a negative evaluation of the prime stimulus (e.g., Fazio et al., 1995; Ferguson & Bargh, 2004; Wittenbrink et al., 2001). For instance, it is possible to measure whether participants automatically generate a positive or negative evaluation of a Black face by seeing whether the perception of the face prime facilitates their subsequent responses to unrelated positive versus negative adjectives.

Implicit Association Test (IAT)

In 1998, Greenwald and colleagues published an article describing the Implicit Association Test (IAT; Greenwald, McGhee, & Schwartz, 1998). This measure assesses the degree to which people implicitly associate a class of objects with pleasant versus unpleasant stimuli (Greenwald et al., 1998; for reviews see Fazio & Olson, 2003; Greenwald & Nosek, 2001; Nosek & Banaji, Chapter 6 of this volume). In this task, participants are asked to perform two sorting tasks that are counterbalanced. If researchers want to gauge participants' automatic attitudes toward women versus men, for example, one sorting task would be to press a certain response key if the stimulus that appears on the computer screen is a member of the category "female names" (e.g., *Linda*) or a member of the positively valenced category "flowers" (e.g., *daffodil*). Participants are asked to press a different response key if the stimulus is a member of the category "male names" (e.g., *Frank*) or a member of the negatively valenced category "bugs" (e.g., *roach*). The second sorting task is a reversal of the first one, and participants are asked to group female names with bugs, and male names with flowers. Researchers can then assess via response latencies and error data the relative ease of the two sorting tasks in order to infer whether participants are faster to group female names with flowers versus bugs, compared to male names. If it is generally easier to group female names with flowers, then it is assumed that participants more strongly associate women (versus men) with positive versus negative information.

Research on the IAT has now yielded an extraordinary amount of data, particularly through its implementation on the worldwide web (see Nosek, Banaji, & Greenwald, 2002). For example, researchers have investigated self-esteem (Greenwald & Farnham, 2000), prejudice (e.g., Ashburn-Nardo, Voils, & Monteith, 2001; Blair, Ma, & Lenton, 2001; McConnell & Leibold, 2001), social identity (Greenwald et al., 2002), gender bias in mathematics (Nosek, Banaji, & Greenwald, 2002), and personality traits (e.g., Jordan, Spencer, & Zanna, 2003; Marsh, Johnson, & Scott-Sheldon, 2001). Although researchers are still clarifying the precise nature of the associations captured by the IAT (e.g., what kinds of behavior they predict, their external and predictive validity; see Hofmann et al., 2005; Karpinski & Hilton, 2001; Mierke & Klauer, 2003; Nosek, Greenwald, & Banaji, 2005; Olson & Fazio, 2004), the IAT has proven highly effective in implicitly tapping the relative ease with which people associate certain stimuli with evaluative information.

There are some differences between the IAT and the evaluative priming paradigm in terms of why they are considered implicit measures. The automaticity of evaluations captured by the evaluative priming paradigm is assumed because the SOA normally used in the paradigm (less than 500 ms) is too brief a period to allow strategic, intentional processing (Neely, 1976, 1977). In addition, participants are never asked to explicitly evaluate the prime stimuli, so their evaluations are necessarily spontaneous, especially in paradigms in which participants are not asked to explicitly evaluate the target stimuli (see Bargh et al., 1996). Finally, the evaluative priming effect has emerged even when the primes are presented subliminally (e.g., Ferguson, Bargh, & Nayak, 2005; Greenwald et al., 1989; Murphy & Zajonc,

1993; Niedenthal, 1990), demonstrating that the activation of evaluative information does not require participants' awareness of the stimuli or their intention to evaluate.

In comparison, the associations captured by the IAT are considered implicit primarily because participants are not aware that their attitudes toward the stimuli are being measured, and also because they are instructed to respond as quickly as possible, thereby minimizing strategic processing. Nevertheless, whereas associations captured by the IAT can be considered implicit (i.e., indirect; see Fazio & Olson, 2003), the extent to which they rely on strategic processing is not yet clear. For example, there is some evidence that the evaluations captured by the IAT are subject to more controlled processing than those measured by an evaluative priming paradigm (see Sherman, Presson, Chassin, Rose, & Koch, 2003). Indeed, the complexity of the classification task of the IAT (sorting the target stimuli according to two orthogonal dimensions) is greater than that of the evaluation decision task or lexical decision task typically used in the evaluative priming paradigm (sorting the stimuli according to one dimension), and thus perhaps necessarily invokes greater processing demands.

One interesting area of research concerns the application of process dissociation procedures to various tasks (PDP; Jacoby, 1992, 1997; Jacoby, Yonelinas, & Jennings, 1997; see also Conrey, Sherman, Gawronski, Hugenberg, & Groom, 2005; Sherman, in press). The process dissociation framework assumes that any measurement task will capture aspects of both automatic and controlled processing – in other words, no response is *process pure* in that it results from only one kind of processing. For example, when there is no conflict between a correct response and automatic tendencies on a trial in a task, controlled and automatic processes will work together in synchrony to produce the response. However, when automatic tendencies and the correct response are in opposition, the two types of processes will be working against one another to produce the response. PDP involves the computation of estimates for each type of processing, and then the identification of the relative contribution of each to a pattern of responses (for more detail on process dissociation procedures, see Payne & Stewart, Chapter 7 in this volume). Researchers have begun to apply process dissociation techniques to implicit attitude measures (e.g., Payne, 2001; Payne, Jacoby, & Lambert, 2005; Sherman, 2005), and this will potentially shed light on the relative influence of automatic versus controlled processing across the various measures.

Brain Imaging Methodologies

Brain imaging methodologies represent a new direction in the study of implicit evaluation. Researchers have begun to use these techniques both to gather evidence for implicit evaluation, and also to investigate the particular brain areas implicated in automatic versus strategic evaluation (e.g., Amodio, Harmon-Jones, & Devine, 2003; Cunningham, Johnson, Gatenby, Gore, & Banaji, 2003; Ito & Cacioppo, 2000; Phelps, O'Connor, Cunningham, Funayama, Gatenby, Gore, & Banaji, 2000). Ito and Cacioppo (2000), for example, asked participants to categorize a series of social (e.g., a photograph of a couple embracing; mourners at a graveside) and nonsocial (e.g., chocolate bar; littered beach) stimuli. Participants were asked to categorize the stimuli according to a non-evaluative dimension (i.e., "Were people present or absent?"), and while they were doing so their event-related brain potentials (ERP) were recorded. Even though participants were not explicitly relying on evaluative information to complete the categorization task, there was increased electroencephalographic activity when the stimuli suggested an evaluative inconsistency (negative stimulus in a positive context, or the reverse), suggesting their unintended sensitivity to the evaluative dimension.

Cunningham et al. (2003) have recently reported data that suggest which brain regions are involved in implicit evaluative processing. Participants underwent functional magnetic resonance imaging (fMRI) while they were asked to explicitly assess famous names along an evaluative ("good or bad?") or non-evaluative ("past or present fame?") dimension. The findings suggest greater amygdala activity for negative famous names relative to positive famous names, regardless of whether the task was evaluative or not. These data suggest that participants assessed the evaluative implications of the stimuli unintentionally while they were focused on a non-evaluative dimension. Other research as well has found that the amygdala is particularly active in response to negative stimuli (e.g., LeDoux, 2000; Phelps, O'Connor, Gatenby, Gore, Grillon, & Davis, 2001; Zald & Pardo, 1997), even when the negative stimuli are nonconsciously processed (e.g., Cunningham, Johnson, Raye, Gatenby, Gore, & Banaji, 2004; Morris, Öhman, & Dolan, 1998).[1]

Research on brain imaging during evaluative processing also suggests that different brain regions are implicated in evaluative processing depending on the demands of the evaluative task. Whereas the amygdala and right inferior prefrontal cortex (PFC) tend to be more active in response to negatively versus positively valenced stimuli, regardless of whether the perceiver is intentionally evaluating the stimuli (e.g., see Cunningham et al., 2003), activity in the medial and ventrolateral PFC is greater when participants are explicitly making evaluative judgments about the stimuli, especially when the stimuli are evaluatively complex. This suggests that more evaluatively complex information might demand greater deliberate evaluative processing (Cunningham et al., 2003; Cunningham, Raye, & Johnson, 2004). Data from research using brain imaging techniques have converged with behavioral evidence to suggest that automatic evaluation is a pervasive, constant, and spontaneous activity, and at the same time suggest that intentional and unintentional evaluative processing may each depend on different neural substrates.

THE INFLUENCE OF CONTEXT ON AUTOMATIC EVALUATION

Contextual Independence

One of the central questions guiding research on automatic evaluation over the past five years has been the degree to which such evaluations are stable across time and contexts. Initially, the attitudes and evaluations captured by implicit measures were embraced as potentially reliable indices precisely because they were assumed to be independent of the context in which they were measured (e.g., Banaji, 2001; Bargh, 1999; Bargh et al., 1992; Bargh et al., 1996; Devine, 1989; Fazio et al, 1995; Greenwald et al., 1998; Wilson & Hodges, 1992; Wilson et al., 2000), unlike the contextual influences inherent in explicit attitude measurement (see Banaji, 2001; Fazio et al., 1995; Schwarz & Bohner, 2001). In particular, because implicit measures can assess participants' evaluations without their awareness, participants were assumed to be unable to strategically edit or modify their responses. Accordingly, those studying socially sensitive topics such as prejudice toward groups began to rely on implicit (versus explicit) attitude measures in order to obtain a clearer index of people's socially undesirable thoughts and feelings (e.g., Bargh, 1999; Devine, 1989; Fazio et al., 1995; Swanson, Rudman, & Greenwald, 2001).

The assumptions of independence were bolstered by findings suggesting that while participants' responses on explicit measures showed little or no negativity toward traditionally stigmatized groups, their automatic reactions were considerably more negative (e.g., Devine, 1989; Fazio et al., 1995; Greenwald et al., 1998). For example, Fazio et al. (1995) demonstrated that even though some participants' automatically activated attitudes toward Blacks were negative, their explicitly reported attitudes toward Blacks as assessed by the Modern Racism Scale (MRS; McConahay, 1986) were highly positive. The reactivity of the MRS was demonstrated in a different study when participants reported less prejudice when the experimenter was Black versus White (Fazio et al., 1995, study 3). Theorists speculated that whereas people's desire to avoid appearing prejudiced prompts them to edit and modify (i.e., hide) their true feelings on explicit measures, no such modification is possible on the implicit measures and thus their true feelings are captured (though see Arkes & Tetlock, 2004; Banaji, Nosek, & Greenwald, 2004).

Initial presumptions of contextual independence and stability were also supported by the early findings from the evaluative priming paradigm. Researchers noted the consistency between items that were explicitly evaluated and those that were spontaneously evaluated (e.g., Bargh et al., 1992). For example, Bargh et al. (1992) gathered normative data on the prime stimuli used in their studies, and found that participants' automatic evaluations largely corresponded with the normative, explicit ratings of the respective objects. In other words, objects that had been explicitly classified as positive (e.g., puppy, sunshine) did in fact seem to facilitate response latencies to positive versus negative adjectives, relative to objects that had been classified as negative (e.g., death, cockroach). The signature evaluative priming effect therefore inherently depended on some degree of correspondence between implicit and explicit evaluations.

Contextual dependence

As research on the two types of attitude measures accumulated, evidence began to emerge that implicitly measured attitudes were often weakly correlated or completely unrelated to attitudes measured explicitly (e.g., Greenwald & Banaji, 1995; Fazio et al., 1995; Karpinski & Hilton, 2001; though see Cunningham, Preacher, &

Banaji, 2001; McConnell & Leibold, 2001; Wittenbrink, Judd, & Park, 1997). Although some degree of disconnect between the two types of measures was expected given the differences in the nature of the measures, a complete lack of correspondence worried researchers, and some questioned the construct validity of implicitly measured attitudes and evaluations (see Banaji, 2001 for a discussion). If implicit measures were tapping people's "true" attitudes and preferences, then they should at least partially correspond with related measures under some circumstances, in line with basic conventions regarding convergent and criterion validity. This concern provoked considerable research efforts at examining the stability and contextual independence of implicitly measured attitudes and the relation between implicit and explicit measures in general (e.g., for a review see Blair et al., 2001; Brauer, Wasel, & Niedenthal, 2000; Dovidio, Kawakami, & Beach, 2001; Fazio & Olson, 2003).

The findings from this research activity suggest a host of contextual influences on implicitly measured evaluations and attitudes, contrary to the initial assumptions of contextual independence. Specifically, findings suggest that the direction and strength of an automatic evaluation of a given object vary depending on the type of recently activated, or repeatedly learned, object-relevant information (e.g., Barden, Maddux, Petty, & Brewer, 2004; Dasgupta & Greenwald, 2001; Karpinski & Hilton, 2001; Livingston & Brewer, 2002; Lowery, Hardin, & Sinclair, 2001; Mitchell et al., 2003; Wittenbrink et al., 2001). For example, researchers found that participants displayed significantly less negative automatic evaluations toward group members who are commonly targets of prejudice after being exposed to pro-elderly stimuli (Karpinski & Hilton, 2001), exemplars of well-liked African-Americans and disliked White people (Dasgupta & Greenwald, 2001, Experiment 1), or presentations of a movie clip of an African-American family enjoying themselves at a picnic (Wittenbrink et al., 2001, Experiment 1).

Recent work has suggested that automatic evaluations are also influenced by the type of goal or objective that the perceiver is currently pursuing (e.g., Ferguson & Bargh, 2004; Lowery et al., 2001; Moors & De Houwer, 2001; Moors, De Houwer, & Eelen, 2004; Sherman et al., 2003, study 2) as well as by the perceiver's chronic motivations (Maddux, Barden, Brewer, & Petty, 2005). For example, Lowery et al. (2001) found that participants who completed the IAT under the direction of a Black (versus White) experimenter exhibited significantly reduced negative attitudes toward Blacks, demonstrating that automatic attitude measures may be susceptible to social influence pressures. Mitchell et al. (2003) recently demonstrated that automatic evaluations are also dependent on participants' categorization goal as they encounter the respective objects. For example, Mitchell et al. (2003) selected Black targets who were liked athletes, and White targets who were disliked politicians. When participants were instructed to classify the Black and White targets in an IAT in terms of career, African-American exemplars were more easily associated with positively (versus negatively) valenced stimuli compared with when they were classified in terms of race. These findings together show that different contextual parameters, such as objectives and instructions, can influence the type of information that is activated with regard to the object(s) of interest.

Automatic evaluations are also influenced by whether the perceiver has satisfied her or his current goal regarding those objects (Ferguson & Bargh, 2004; Sherman et al., 2003). In research by Ferguson and Bargh (2004), participants who were currently pursuing a goal (or not) completed an evaluative priming paradigm that measured their automatic evaluations of objects that varied in their relevance to the goal. The results suggest that objects that were relevant to the goal were automatically evaluated as most positive when the perceiver was still pursuing the goal versus had already completed it. For example, participants who were thirsty implicitly evaluated the highly thirst-relevant objects (e.g., water, juice) as most positive, compared with the other objects (e.g., chair, table), and the participants who had just quenched their thirst. These findings demonstrate that automatic evaluations are sometimes prospective with regard to the utility of the objects, and are not always solely a function of recent experience with the objects. As such, the findings are in accord with the classic notion that attitudes are functionally tied to the perceiver's current motivational priorities (e.g., Cacioppo, Priester, & Berntson, 1993; Chen & Bargh, 1999; Katz, 1960; Lewin, 1935; Pratkanis et al., 1989; Rosenberg, 1956; Wentura, Rothermund, & Bak, 2000).

People's chronic goals can also influence automatic evaluations. Maddux et al. (2005) recently showed that the impact of contextual cues on participants' automatic evaluations of Blacks depended on participants' chronic motivation to avoid being prejudiced. Those participants low in this motivation exhibited negative automatic evaluations toward Blacks in contexts that were threatening (e.g., a prison cell) compared to nonthreatening (e.g., a church), which is consistent with previous research (Wittenbrink et al., 2001). In contrast, however, those participants high in the motivation to avoid being prejudiced actually showed less negative evaluations of Blacks in the threatening context, compared with other participants overall and also with high-motivation participants in the nonthreatening context. Interestingly, these participants' less negative evaluations resulted from an inhibition of negative information in the threatening condition. This work suggests that people's chronic motivations can determine the way in which they respond to contextual cues regarding the nature of the evaluated stimuli (see also Moskowitz, Gollwitzer, Wasel, & Schaal, 1999).

Compatibility of Findings on Independence versus Dependence

Given the array of findings over the last five years suggesting the contextual dependence of automatic evaluation, how is it possible that early work suggested stability and contextual independence? First, none of the initial experiments on automatic attitude activation manipulated the nature of object-relevant, recently activated information (e.g., Bargh et al., 1992; Bargh et al., 1996; Fazio et al., 1986). In other words, it may be that given a default context (i.e., one in which there is no manipulation of preceding, object-relevant information), the perception of the word *dentist*, for example, may automatically and explicitly evoke a negative evaluation much of the time for most participants. Yet, this does not preclude the possibility that the accessibility of positive dentist-related information (e.g., a prestigious profession) would lead to a positive automatic evaluation of *dentist* (Ferguson & Bargh, 2003). Furthermore, the objects that were used in the early studies were strongly normatively positive (e.g., gift) or negative (e.g., poison), compared to the more evaluatively ambiguous attitude objects that have been studied in more recent articles (e.g., African-American faces; Fazio et al., 1995). The more an object is associated in memory with evaluatively divergent information, the more likely the object will be automatically evaluated in different ways across time and situations.

Initial research on implicitly measured attitudes also rarely examined individual objects as the dependent variable. Most often the dependent variables of interest consisted of groups of positive and negative attitude objects, and groups of positive and negative target words (e.g., see Bargh et al., 1992, 1996; Fazio et al., 1986) and five or six objects typically comprised each valence group. Because of this grouping, it may be that although the intensity or even direction of the attitude for each object varied to some extent, when grouped together with others the group remained positive or negative. This method of grouping can hide the fluctuations of the evaluations of individual objects.

Although research over the last five years clearly demonstrates that both implicit and explicit attitudes are contextually dependent, recent research suggests that the two types of measurements are not equivalently sensitive to the same set of factors. For instance, one interesting area of recent research suggests that implicit attitudes may not reflect certain situational influences that are easily integrated into explicit attitudes. For example, Gawronski and colleagues have argued that whereas explicit attitudes are sensitive to dissonance pressures, implicit attitudes are not (see Gawronski et al., 2005; Gawronski & Strack, 2004). In a recent set of experiments, Gawronski and Strack (2004) demonstrated that people who had written a counterattitudinal essay under low perceived situational pressure exhibited more pro-issue explicit attitudes than those who had written it under high perceived pressure, in line with the classic findings by Festinger and colleagues (e.g., Festinger, 1957; Festinger & Carlsmith, 1957). However, there was no difference in participants' implicit attitudes across the situational pressure conditions, suggesting that such attitudes might not represent the (potentially nonconscious; Liberman, Ochsner, Gilbert, & Schacter, 2001) cognitive restructuring that occurs in dissonance-inducing situations (see also Kruglanski & Klar, 1987). Further research continues to explore the parameters of contextual influence on such evaluations, and also the degree to which such influence compares and contrasts to the contextual dependence of explicit measures.

COMPATIBILITY OF AUTOMATICALLY VERSUS DELIBERATELY ACTIVATED EVALUATIONS

The issue of whether automatic evaluations correspond with those that are generated more deliberately has been of central interest since the advent of implicit attitude measures. As mentioned in the earlier section on contextual dependence, initial findings suggested a dissociation between attitudes assessed by these two types of measurements, particularly in the area of prejudice (e.g., Banaji &

Hardin, 1996; Blair & Banaji, 1996; Bosson, Swann, & Pennebaker, 2000; Devine, 1989; Dovidio et al., 1997; Fazio et al., 1995; Hofmann et al., 2005; Greenwald et al., 1998). This dissociation was originally interpreted as possible evidence that implicit measures were capturing the negative feelings that participants were not willing to express on explicit measures (e.g., Fazio et al., 1995). Since this work, however, research suggests that these two types of measures can sometimes provide compatible attitudes, especially if the error inherent in each type of measure is controlled (Cunningham, Nezlek, Banaji, 2004; Cunningham, Preacher, & Banaji, 2001).

Moreover, instead of asking *whether* explicit attitudes are consistent with implicit attitudes, the focus of research has moved toward asking *when* such consistency will emerge (see Devine, 2001; Fazio & Olson, 2003). To this end, researchers have identified moderators of the relationship between explicitly and implicitly measured attitudes (e.g., see Dovidio et al., 1997; Fazio et al., 1995; Hofmann et al., 2005; Nosek, 2005). The social stigmatization of the objects seems to be one important moderator, which is why the evidence of dissociation has emerged mostly in the area of prejudice. When respondents are concerned about the social desirability of their attitudes, they may edit their explicitly reported attitudes, which might result in the dissociation between those attitudes and their automatically activated ones (e.g., Fazio et al., 1995; Greenwald et al., 1998).

The strength of the attitude is also assumed to moderate whether explicit and implicit measures will be in agreement (e.g., Fazio, 1986, 1993; Krosnick & Petty, 1995). When the association between the object and its respective evaluation is strong, the attitude should be more likely to be automatically activated on the mere perception of the object. This should mean that the attitude will be more likely (than a weak attitude) to become spontaneously activated and influential on explicit judgments and behavior, and this in turn should lead to greater correspondence between implicit and explicit measures of that attitude (see also Fazio, 2001).

Nosek (2005) recently reported two additional moderators of the relationship between attitudes assessed by these two types of measurements. One concerns the dimensionality of the respective attitude objects, or, in other words, whether the object is considered to be bipolar or unipolar (e.g., see Pratkanis, 1989). A dimension is referred to as bipolar when one end of the dimension represents the acceptance of the object and the other represents the rejection of the object. For example, attitudes toward the death penalty presumably lie along a bipolar continuum in that acceptance (or support) of the death penalty necessarily means that the person does not reject (or disagree with) the death penalty. A dimension that is unipolar, on the other hand, represents simply more or less positivity toward the object, and can be orthogonal to one's negativity toward the object (see Cacioppo & Gardner, 1999; Larsen, McGraw, & Cacioppo, 2001). Nosek (2005) proposed that because bipolar attitudes tend to be more consistent across time and structured in a simpler manner compared with unipolar attitudes (see Judd and Kulik, 1980), there should be more consistent explicit–implicit relations for bipolar versus unipolar attitudes, and the data supported this prediction.

Additionally, Nosek (2005) proposed that the distinctiveness of the attitude objects should moderate the relations between implicit and explicit attitude measures. Distinctiveness here refers to the degree to which one's own attitude differs from the perceived norm. To the extent that one's attitude is highly distinctive (e.g., one might not like chocolate even though the vast majority of people do), she or he is likely to be more aware of the attitude, and may therefore express it more consistently. As such, highly distinctive attitudes should show greater consistency across implicit and explicit measures, and this hypothesis was also supported by the findings.

The research in this area also addresses the question of whether attitudes that are measured implicitly are substantively distinct from those measured explicitly. Researchers differ in terms of whether they believe that inconsistency in implicit–explicit relations suggests two different underlying constructs (e.g., Dovidio et al., 1997; Greenwald & Banaji, 1995; Wilson et al., 2000), two related but distinct constructs (Cunningham et al., 2001; Gawronski et al., 2005; Greenwald & Farnham, 2000; Nosek, 2005), or one construct that can be measured in different manners (Fazio & Olson, 2003). Whereas the first two views assume that implicit and explicit attitudes are based on nonoverlapping or partially overlapping evaluative information, the one-construct perspective assumes that only the expression of the construct differs depending on the type of measurement. One may modify one's (automatic) attitude if he or she has the motivation and opportunity to do so, but should be drawing on approximately the same evaluative information in either case (see Fazio & Olson, 2003). The question of whether inconsistency between implicit and explicit measures reflects differences in representational format necessarily depends on one's assumptions about the cognitive architecture that might enable evaluative processing. This issue is discussed in more detail in a subsequent section.

DEVELOPMENT OF AUTOMATIC EVALUATIONS

Is it possible to automatically evaluate an object that one has never seen before (and cannot easily categorize)? Although the development of automatic evaluations has generally been understudied (though see Betsch, Plessner, Schwieren, & Gütig, 2001; Duckworth et al., 2002; Olson & Fazio, 2001), theory concerning automatic evaluations as well as notions about information processing in general assume that underlying responses must be repeatedly enacted over time in order to operate automatically (Bargh, 1984, 1990; Fazio, 1986; Shiffrin & Dumais, 1981; Smith & Lerner, 1986). In a classic example, Shiffrin and Schneider (1977) demonstrated that participants had to be trained on over 1,000 trials in order to be able to automatically perceive a given target (e.g., "C") in differently sized arrays of distracters (but see Smith & Lerner, 1986).

The assumption that automatic evaluations in particular require some experience with the respective objects is inherent in the dominant view of attitude representation and organization in memory (Fazio 1986, 1990, 2001). Fazio and others have asserted that an attitude consists of evaluative information (positivity or negativity) associated with the object representation in memory within an associative network organization (see Eagly & Chiaken, 1993; Fazio, 1986, 1990, 2001). From this perspective, attitude strength is a function of the strength of the association between the evaluative information and the object representation. A strong attitude will have a stronger link, or association, compared to a weaker attitude. Fazio and colleagues have argued that only those objects with strong, associated attitudes should be automatically evaluated (Fazio et al., 1986). This assertion implies that only objects that have been strongly (repeatedly) evaluated in the past will be able to be evaluated automatically, and in accord with this Fazio and colleagues have manipulated the strength of attitudes in experiments by varying how often participants repeat their evaluations of the objects (e.g., Fazio & Williams, 1986; Roskos-Ewoldsen & Fazio, 1992; Smith, Fazio, & Cejka, 1996). The assumption that automatic evaluations require some previous experience with the respective objects implies that people might be unable to automatically evaluate novel or unfamiliar attitude objects. That is, if people are encountering an object for the first time (and the object is not easily categorizable), they have likely not yet developed an association between the object representation (which may itself be only partially formed) and evaluative information (i.e., an attitude).

The claim that automatic evaluations are slow to develop is also in accord with the assertion that they are slow to change in the face of new object information or experience. For example, researchers have argued that the evaluations or attitudes that are activated automatically from memory are slow to form and change, and are generally resistant to persuasive efforts (e.g., Wilson & Hodges, 1992; Wilson, Lindsey, & Schooler, 2000). In their model of dual attitudes (i.e., implicit and explicit), Wilson et al. (2000) argued that although the generation and expression of explicit attitudes are highly contingent on the context at the time of measurement (e.g., recently activated memories, the perceiver's goals and strategic concerns, etc.), implicit attitudes are assumed to be unchanging and resistant. For instance, they asserted that "Explicit attitudes change relatively more easily whereas implicit attitudes, like old habits, change more slowly. Attitude change techniques often change explicit but not implicit attitudes" (p. 4). This claim of rigidity is also consistent with efforts at changing automatic attitudes through extensive training regimens (e.g., Karpinski & Hilton, 2001; Kawakami, Dovidio, Moll, Hermsen, & Russin, 2000; Rudman, Asmore, & Gary, 2001).

The view that automatic evaluations might be restricted to familiar objects, and resistant to new information about the respective objects, is also in accord with the contention in social and cognitive psychology that the integration of recently acquired evaluative information requires conscious effort (e.g., Bargh, 1984, 1990; Jastrow, 1906; Schneider & Fisk, 1982; Shiffrin & Dumais, 1981; Shiffrin & Schneider, 1977; Smith & Lerner, 1986; but see Dijksterhuis, 2004; Gollwitzer, 1996, 1999). Assuming that the evaluation of unfamiliar objects requires some (novel) integration of evaluative information, this claim implies that people should be unable to evaluate such objects without conscious awareness and deliberation (e.g., Wilson & Hodges, 1992; cf. Bargh, 1999; Duckworth et al., 2002). Explicit attitude measures, on the other hand, ostensibly allow more complex integrations of object-relevant and novel information.

There have been several interesting articles over the last five years that directly address assumptions regarding the development of automatic evaluations. For instance, Duckworth et al. (2002) found that participants were able to automatically evaluate unfamiliar abstract art drawings and novel Turkish words. Participants automatically evaluated as positive the stimuli that had been explicitly classified as positive by a separate group of participants, and their automatic evaluations also tended to correlate with the explicit ratings of the negative stimuli. Importantly, these findings demonstrate that people can evaluate objects for which they do not have pre-existing object representations in memory, and can do so "on the fly," or within a fraction of a second after perceiving them.

Olson and Fazio (2001) addressed the development of implicit attitudes, and examined whether they might emerge as a result of the implicit detection of co-variation between a novel attitude object and valenced stimuli. In this research, participants watched a series of images and words appear in a seemingly random order on a computer screen, and were asked to press a key whenever a particular object appeared. Embedded in the images that appeared were pairings of a novel attitude object (a Pokemon character) with either positively (e.g., picture of a sundae) or negatively (e.g., picture of a cockroach) valenced stimuli. (Participants did not have to respond to any of these stimuli.) Results demonstrate that participants were unaware of the co-variation, and reported (explicit) attitudes in line with the conditioning procedure. In a different experiment that included the same conditioning procedure, participants also exhibited implicit attitudes as measured by the IAT in line with the conditioning procedure. This research demonstrates that people unintentionally and seemingly nonconsciously can form both explicit and automatic attitudes (see also De Houwer, Baeyens, & Field, 2005; De Houwer, Thomas, & Baeyens, 2001; Martin & Levy, 1978; Walther, Nagengast, & Trasselli, 2005).

In an intriguing series of experiments, Betsch et al. (2001) addressed a similar question, and examined whether people's evaluations are sensitive to recently encountered valenced information about the corresponding objects, even when that information is learned passively and without the intention to evaluate the objects. Betsch et al. predicted that participants' evaluations would reflect the *sum* of the valenced information rather than the *average*. Participants watched a series of ads appear on a computer screen while saying aloud the share returns from five companies that scrolled across the top of the screen. Participants' focal task was to remember the information in the ads and they were led to believe that the share information was meant as a distraction from the focal task. They were presented with 75 total pieces of return information (15 per share) and watched a total of 60 ads. At the end of the task, they were asked to evaluate the shares, and their evaluations did in fact reflect the summed returns, rather than the average. This research demonstrates that people absorb even complex evaluative information about objects without intending to do so, and that the evaluative information accumulates in a summative manner, contrary to predictions from models of cognitive integration.

Recent work by Castelli and colleagues (Castelli et al., 2004) suggests that people can implicitly evaluate recently encountered stimuli even when they cannot remember the details of the stimuli that led them to their initial evaluations.

Participants who learned about target persons described as child molesters later implicitly evaluated those people as negative even when they could not accurately recall whether the people were described as child molesters or as belonging to a more benign category (e.g., teachers). Castelli et al. discuss how this work challenges the assumption that implicit evaluations reflect summary indices associated with object representations in memory. Instead, they suggest that implicit evaluations might be better understood as being generated by a connectionist system that naturally incorporates contextual information in an integrative and online fashion, and can handle dissociations between explicit and implicit memory (see also Bassili & Brown, 2005; Ferguson & Bargh, 2003; Mitchell et al., 2003). This issue is revisited later in the chapter.

The notion that people can quickly and spontaneously generate evaluative assessments of stimuli in their environment is consistent with a long history of research in experimental learning where a wide variety of animals are able to learn fear responses after one exposure to the threatening stimulus (e.g., for a review see LeDoux, 2000). For example, after rats were shocked once while exploring a particular caged environment, they subsequently exhibited fear responses when placed back into the same cage. Such one-trial fear learning has obvious adaptive advantages and has been demonstrated in worms, flies, rats, monkey, and humans. Animals that are able to avoid making the same mistake twice, with other animals, plants, or dangerous elements of any kind, clearly possess an evolutionary advantage. This research is consistent with work showing that people are able to evaluate novel objects on the basis of little information, and with relative ease and little deliberation.

Also in accord with the recent findings by Castelli et al. (2004), work in cognitive science on implicit memory also suggests that people can retain implicit memories of negative or threatening people even if their explicit memory fails them (e.g., Squire & Kandel, 1999; Squire, 1992). For example, Squire and Kandel (1999) described the classic example of a person with anterograde amnesia who is introduced to a new person who unexpectedly shocks the amnesiac's hand with a hand buzzer as they are shaking hands. After leaving the room, several minutes later the amnesiac reports that she has no memory of the shocker. However, the amnesiac demonstrates that she must have retained implicit evaluative memory when she later refuses to shake the shocker's hand, presumably on the basis of the earlier negative experience (see also Gazzaniga & Heatherton, 2003). This type of work coincides with much research on implicit memory (e.g., Squire, 1992), and suggests that people might be able to implicitly evaluate stimuli for which there is no (accessible) explicit memory or even very limited previous experience, contrary to longstanding notions about the repetition needed for automatic responses to develop (Bargh, 1984, 1990; Fazio, 1986; Shiffrin & Dumais, 1981; Shiffrin & Schneider, 1977; Smith & Lerner, 1986). This work is also inconsistent with the assumption that evaluations are automatically generated via the activation of the respective object representation in memory (see Fazio, 1986, 1993, 2001).

CONSEQUENCES OF AUTOMATIC EVALUATION

In addition to questions concerning the contextual dependence and development of automatic attitudes, a fundamental question in this area concerns the downstream consequences of such attitudes for thinking, feeling, and acting. What are the consequences of automatic evaluations for the evaluated stimuli themselves as well as for unrelated stimuli? This question has been of utmost importance in this area of research for two central reasons. The first is that the way in which automatic evaluations influence processing of subsequently encountered stimuli might suggest important constraints on the underlying architecture (see below).

The second reason is that, as previously mentioned, researchers have sought substantive evidence that implicitly measured attitudes or evaluations represent hypothetical constructs that influence real behavior. Indeed, the area of explicit attitudes underwent its most intense period of scrutiny and criticism after Wicker (1969) published his now famous paper criticizing the lack of correspondence between explicit attitudes and the actual behaviors the attitudes were supposed to predict (see also LaPiere, 1934; Schuman & Johnson, 1976; Thurstone, 1928). As a result, researchers have carefully studied this question with regard to automatic evaluations, and there has been considerable recent work on this topic in the last five years (see Fazio & Olson, 2003).

There are two streams of research concerning the consequences of automatic evaluations. The first concerns the immediate implications of an evaluative act itself for the subsequent processing of stimuli that are related or unrelated to the originally evaluated object. That is, what are the implications of such fleeting generations of positivity or negativity, if any? The second stream of research concerns the degree of predictive utility of these kinds of evaluations. In other words, do such evaluations possess criterion and predictive validity such that a positive automatic evaluation of a stimulus predicts approach behaviors toward that stimulus in other situations?

Immediate Consequences

For Evaluated Objects Themselves   Researchers have argued that automatic evaluations are functional because they quickly afford the perceiver with valuable information about how to behave toward the evaluated objects (e.g., Chen & Bargh, 1999; Duckworth et al., 2002; Fazio, 1989; Ferguson & Bargh, 2002, 2004; Lang, Bradley, & Cuthbert, 1990; LeDoux, 1996; Öhman, 1986; Pratkanis, Breckler, & Greenwald, 1989; Roskos-Ewoldsen & Fazio, 1992). This functional argument presupposes a strong link between the evaluation of an object and immediate approach versus avoidance behavioral tendencies toward that object, and several lines of research support this supposition. For example, a series of studies suggests that the automatic evaluation of an object influences extension or flexion arm movements in line with the nature of the particular evaluation. Chen and Bargh (1999) asked participants to either push a lever away from them (extension) when they saw a word appear on the computer screen in front of them, or pull the lever toward them (flexion). When participants were pushing the lever

away from them, they were significantly faster to do so when the stimuli on the screen were negative in valence (e.g., *poison*) compared to positive in valence (e.g., *puppy*). Participants were also significantly faster to pull the lever toward them when the stimuli were positive versus negative. In line with a functional view of automatic evaluations, this suggests that positivity is associated with approach arm movements whereas negativity is associated with avoidance arm movements (see also Duckworth et al., 2002).

There is a large body of work outside of the automatic evaluation literature that suggests that the quick and unintentional evaluation of stimuli has implications for judgment and decision-making concerning those stimuli. Although these studies do not typically use implicit evaluation measures, they nevertheless suggest that the spontaneous affective assessment of an object has a range of consequences for how the perceiver reacts toward that object. For example, recent work suggests that the way in which a perceiver spontaneously evaluates an object influences her or his recognition of the stimulus (Monin, 2003). Monin argued that people misattribute the positivity of a stimulus as evidence for its familiarity, and thereby commit the so-called *Warm Glow* heuristic. Across a series of experiments, people were significantly more likely to falsely recognize novel stimuli if the stimuli were attractive or positive in valence versus unattractive, neutral, or negative in valence. Although Monin did not ensure that the initial evaluations of the stimuli were automatic in nature, they were unprompted and thus the findings constitute preliminary evidence that spontaneous evaluations of stimuli can influence unrelated recognition judgments about the stimuli themselves.

Other findings provide additional evidence that automatic evaluations of stimuli influence "real world" judgment and decision-making concerning those stimuli (e.g., Damasio, 1999, 2001; Epley & Caruso, 2004) as well as moral judgments about events related to the respective stimuli (e.g., Haidt, 2001, 2003). Work by Damasio and colleagues, for instance, suggests that the way in which people affectively and immediately react to stimuli serves as an important signal for how they should behave toward the stimuli (see Damasio, 1999). According to Damasio's framework, after people experience the affective consequences of certain stimuli (e.g., eating sugar feels good), they learn to anticipate the emotional consequences of stimuli without necessarily re-experiencing those emotional consequences. Once people have learned that eating sugar is pleasurable, for instance, stimuli that have previously preceded or co-varied with that feeling (e.g., candy) become spontaneously and quickly evaluated as positive. This evaluative reaction allows the perceiver to react to the stimulus (in this case, probably approach it) without having to first re-experience the positive emotion. Such pre-emptive appraisals afford people extra time to prepare to secure or avoid the stimulus, and such preparation undoubtedly leads to greater success in obtaining or avoiding it. From Damasio's perspective then, contrary to the traditional viewpoint of affect biasing or interfering with otherwise rational judgment and decision-making, quick affective reactions provide information that is essential for adaptively making decisions and performing actions toward those stimuli (see Damasio, 1994, 1999, 2001; Fazio, Blascovich, & Driscoll, 1992; Frank, 1988, 2003, Zajonc, 1980).

In a related line of work, Haidt and colleagues (Greene & Haidt, 2002; Haidt,

2001, 2003) have argued that the immediate affective assessment of an event forms the basis for reasoning about the morality of that event. In opposition to classic models of moral reasoning in which affect is incidental, disruptive, or peripheral to the moral judgment, Haidt (2001, 2003) argues that people first experience an inevitable affective reaction to a behavior or action based on learned cultural norms (their "moral intuition"), and then attempt to justify their assessment of the action as moral according to various post hoc reasons. In this model, people's immediate affective reactions to events, behaviors, and people form the basis upon which subsequent judgments are formed, even outside of people's intention and awareness. For example, Haidt has argued that people who are given the hypothetical scenario of a brother and sister having sex together under select circumstances base their moral judgment of the scenario on the way in which they (usually negatively) affectively react to it, and try to generate various deliberate reasons that will explain their judgment (Haidt, 2001; see also Nisbett & Wilson, 1977). According to this framework, the reasons for a moral judgment are post hoc, and derive from the immediate affective reactions to the event under consideration.

Together, the research described above suggests that the way in which people automatically evaluate objects in their environment has various consequences for how they subsequently judge and behave toward those objects. This recent work suggests, for instance, that when people spontaneously evaluate a person as negative, they may be more likely to engage in subtle avoidance behaviors and judge the person along more negative dimensions than if they had first evaluated the person in a more positive manner. Clearly, even though automatic evaluative acts last only a fraction of a second and occur without the person's intention or awareness, they have a host of downstream outcomes that can influence how people see and understand the world around them.

For Unrelated Objects Does an evaluative act have consequences for how people process subsequent, unrelated stimuli? The literature on evaluative priming suggests that the automatic evaluation of a stimulus does enable faster responding to subsequent, similarly valenced stimuli, even if there is otherwise no relation between the evaluated object and the target (e.g., for a review see Musch & Klauer, 2003). But beyond effects on the speed of responding to subsequent stimuli, does the automatic evaluation of an object influence the way in which people interpret and understand completely unrelated objects?

The automatic evaluation of clearly valenced stimuli seems to influence evaluative judgments about different stimuli (e.g., Muphy & Zajonc, 1993; Niedenthal, 1990; Stapel, Koomen, & Ruijs, 2002). For instance, Murphy and Zajonc (1993) demonstrated that subliminal presentations of smiling or frowning cartoon faces led to respectively more positive or negative evaluations of novel Chinese characters. Stapel et al. (2002) recently expanded on this research by showing that the effects of subliminally presented cartoon face stimuli on judgments of affect in subsequent target cartoon faces depended on the presentation time of the subliminally presented prime stimuli. Whereas stimuli presented very briefly (30 ms) tended to have diffuse effects on stimuli, stimuli presented for relatively longer durations (100 ms) tended to have more circumscribed effects. This research together suggests that clearly valenced stimuli such as smiling faces can influence people's subsequent perception of emotion as well as their liking judgments of novel stimuli. But are effects of automatic evaluation for unrelated stimuli limited to liking judgments?

Early research on impression formation argues against any effect of evaluative primes on nonliking judgments about unrelated stimuli. In particular, research by Higgins, Rholes, and Jones (1977) on the consequences of trait priming on person judgment demonstrated that primes only influenced judgments when they were applicable – that is, related to the behavior that was relevant to the judgments. For example, participants primed with the trait prime *neat* were not more likely to later judge Donald's ambiguously reckless behaviors as adventurous, even though *neat* and *adventurous* share the same (positive) valence. This led Higgins et al. to conclude that inapplicable primes do not influence nonliking judgments, a sentiment that has been reinforced by numerous studies since then (e.g., Bargh, Bond, Lombardi, & Tota, 1986; Devine, 1989; Erdley & D'Agostino, 1988; Higgins, 1996), and referred to by some as an axiom in priming research (see Stapel and Koomen, 2000).

However, recent studies suggest that there are circumstances under which the evaluation of inapplicable trait primes does influence person judgments. Croizet and Fiske (2000) conducted a conceptual replication of Higgins et al. (1977) but induced some participants to feel like experts in social judgment. Croizet and Fiske (2000) replicated the findings of Higgins et al. only with those participants not induced to feel like experts, and found an effect of the inapplicable primes for those who did feel like experts. Croizet and Fiske (2000) speculated that the feeling of expertise might have lowered the threshold of usability of activated knowledge for these participants relative to the default situation (see Higgins, 1996).

Stapel and Koomen (2000) have also conducted research concerning this issue and found that trait primes that are extremely valenced and broad (e.g., *bad*) can influence judgments about unrelated behavior while moderately valenced and or narrow trait terms (e.g., *frugal*) do not. This suggests that certain traits might be sufficiently strong and valenced to influence subsequent unrelated trait judgments. For example, while the prime *good* should lead people to interpret an ambiguously adventurous behavior as adventurous (rather than reckless), the prime *frugal* should have no effect.

Other recent work suggests that automatic evaluations have broad implications for subsequently encountered, unrelated stimuli. Whereas research by Stapel and Koomen (2000) and Croizet and Fiske (2000) suggests that certain trait terms can influence subsequent unrelated person judgments if participants have a certain goal or if the trait terms are broad and evaluatively extreme, recent findings suggest that the automatic evaluation of positive and negative everyday nouns (e.g., movies, germs) can influence a range of judgments about unrelated stimuli (Ferguson et al., 2005). In a series of experiments, the automatic evaluation of subliminally presented nouns influenced how participants subsequently interpreted words, categorized people and objects, and rendered explicit personality judgments about people. For example, participants were asked to classify a series of people (e.g., Bill Clinton; Mike Tyson) and items (e.g., chocolate; vodka) according to the word that seemed to best capture the object. Each object was presented with two possible words that differed in valence; for example, vodka was presented with the words "hangover" and "party" and Bill Clinton was presented with the words "politician" and "adulterer". The results demonstrated that the valence of the subliminally presented (yet unrelated) primes influenced the descriptions that participants chose as best capturing the objects. Those primed with positive primes were significantly more likely to associate the subsequent objects with the positive descriptions compared to those primed with control primes and negative primes.

The above findings suggest that automatic evaluations have potentially long-ranging implications because they have the ability to influence the explicit interpretations and judgments about subsequently encountered but semantically unrelated stimuli. This means that quick evaluative acts can influence the way in which people see, understand, and act toward the evaluated stimuli, as well as toward completely unrelated but temporally close stimuli. Any ambiguous object that is encountered immediately after an evaluative act can be potentially disambiguated in line with the valence of the initial evaluated object, even when there is no relation between the two.

General Processing Effects Some recent findings suggest that the automatic evaluation of stimuli can also influence people's mood, which can then influence stereotyping effects in accord with how explicitly manipulated mood typically does so. Chartrand, Bargh, & van Baaren (in press) demonstrated that participants subliminally primed with positive words reported significantly more experienced positive affect than those primed with negative words. In addition, those who reported a positive mood were significantly more likely to stereotype on an implicit measure. These findings suggest that a series of automatic evaluative acts of the same valence can induce mood states, with all the downstream implications of such an affective state (e.g., Forgas, 2000, 2001; Martin, & Clore, 2001; Ortony, Clore, & Collins, 1988). Furthermore, because automatic evaluations occur without the perceiver's awareness or intention, the reasons for such moods would be difficult for the perceiver to identify.

Correspondence

The second area of research that speaks to the consequences of automatic evaluations concerns their predictive validity. As previously mentioned, a traditionally central research question concerning automatic evaluations is their ability to predict people's behavior, either toward the evaluated stimuli themselves, or toward similar stimuli (e.g., Arkes & Tetlock, 2004; Banaji, 2001; Banaji et al., 2004; Dovidio, Kawakami, & Gaertner, 2002; Fazio & Olson, 2003; Kawakami & Dovidio, 2001; Lambert et al., 2005). From this perspective, people's automatic evaluations can be conceptualized as indices of how they will behave toward some related object in the future.

One of the first articles to establish the predictive validity of automatic evaluations was conducted by Fazio and colleagues (Fazio et al., 1995). The findings showed correspondence between people's automatic evaluations of Black faces, and behaviors toward a Black experimenter. In particular, across a series of studies, the negativity of participants' automatic evaluations of Blacks predicted participants' subsequent, nonverbal behaviors with a Black experimenter (as judged by the experimenter). In addition, participants' automatic evaluations also predicted some of their opinions about the well-publicized (at the time) trial of police brutality against Rodney King. Subsequent research has confirmed the correspondence (McConnell & Liebold, 2001) between people's automatic evaluations of Blacks as measured by the IAT and their nonverbal behavior toward a Black person.

Research by Nosek et al. (2002) also supports some degree of correspondence between people's automatic evaluations of objects and their performance in domains related to those objects. Participants' implicitly measured attitudes toward math, as assessed by the IAT, predicted their scores on the scholastic aptitude test (SAT). These findings strongly suggest that the degree to which people implicitly associate a certain object with positive versus negative words indicates their behaviors toward that object at different times and in unrelated circumstances. This work suggests the criterion validity of such attitudes, at least in some domains.

Researchers in this area have speculated that whereas explicitly measured attitudes might best predict deliberate and conscious behaviors, implicitly measured attitudes might ultimately predict those behaviors that are primarily driven by automatic processing (e.g., Blair, 2002; Dovidio, Kawakami, & Gaertner, 2002; Dovidio et al., 1997; Kawakami & Dovidio, 2001; Lambert et al., 2005). For example, researchers have frequently assessed the extent to which implicitly measured attitudes predict nonverbal (i.e., difficult to control; see Fazio & Olson, 2003) behavior toward a Black target person (though see Lambert et al., 2005), and have sometimes found that implicit attitudes predict such behaviors better than explicitly measured constructs.

Researchers are continuing to examine the predictive capacity of automatic evaluations, and also the boundary conditions for any effects (e.g., Lambert et al., 2005). For example, some have noted that the predictive validity of automatically activated attitudes might depend on various explicit motivational variables under some circumstances (Fazio & Olson; 2003; Nosek, 2005), such as the motivation to modify or edit responses on explicit measures (e.g., Dunton & Fazio, 1997; Plant & Devine, 1998). The automatic attitudes of those who report low motivation to avoid prejudice might predict a variety of more overt and deliberate behaviors compared with the attitudes of those who report higher motivation. From this perspective, the predictive validity of automatic attitudes might ultimately depend both on the motivations of the perceiver and the obviousness of the behaviors.

THE GENERATION AND REPRESENTATION OF AUTOMATIC EVALUATIONS

The previous review of findings on automatic evaluation suggests several constraints for the presumed representation and generation of evaluative information in memory. The findings suggest that automatic evaluations are contextually dependent, correspond with explicit attitudes under some circumstances, can be generated in response to unfamiliar stimuli, and have a host of implications for subsequent thinking, feeling, and action. The dominant perspective of how attitudes are generated and represented in memory is first described, and then an alternative perspective is considered. There is then a consideration of whether the recent findings can differentiate between the dominant and alternative views of how evaluations are represented and generated.

Single-Tag Perspective

How are automatic evaluations generated? What do implicit attitude measures capture in terms of what is stored in memory? The predominant theoretical model over the last two decades of how attitudes are represented and generated has been articulated by Fazio (1986, 1989, 1993, 2001; see also Fiske & Pavelchak, 1986). Fazio and others have asserted that the attitudes that are captured by evaluative priming paradigms reflect evaluative summary information that is associated in memory with the corresponding object representation (e.g., Bargh et al., 1992; Eagly & Chaiken, 1993; Fazio, 2001; Fazio et al., 1986, 1995; Fiske & Pavelchak, 1986; Wilson et al., 2000). This summary evaluative index is ostensibly formed by repeated experience with the object (see Shiffrin & Schneider, 1977), and the strength of the attitude is proportional to the strength of the association between the evaluative information and the object representation. In line with typical instantiations of associative networks (see Quillian, 1968; Collins and Loftus, 1975), when the object is perceived, its corresponding representation is activated, and activation then spreads along the associative links to semantically related information, including evaluative information. Much of the research on the automatic activation of evaluations is based on the supposition that many objects are associated in memory with a positive or negative summary index, or "tag" (e.g., Bargh et al., 1992, 1996; Fazio et al., 1986; Fiske & Pavelchak, 1986).

From the single-tag perspective, a given object is associated in memory with a stored, summary evaluation of that object and, importantly, this is what is measured in an attitude implicit measure (plus measurement error). In other words, this suggests that what is measured by an implicit attitude measure is a 1-to-1 mapping of the observed response to the stored attitude toward that object in memory (plus measurement error). According to this framework, assuming a perfect measure, it is possible to directly measure the evaluative summary index associated in memory with a given attitude object.

This perspective is most closely aligned with classic, so-called localist, symbolic models of memory that often presuppose associative networks in which isolated nodes represent individual constructs, exemplars, or features of an object (e.g.,

Anderson, 1983; Anderson & Bower, 1973; Collins & Loftus, 1975). These nodes are interconnected according to the degree of (semantic) relation between the nodes, with activation spreading along these links automatically on perception of an object (e.g., Meyer & Schvaneveldt, 1971;.Neely, 1976, 1977; Posner & Snyder, 1975; Shiffrin & Schneider, 1977). Such models have been referred to as "file-drawer" models of memory, and have guided research and theory in social psychology for decades (e.g., see Carlston & Smith, 1996; Fazio, 1986; Hastie, 1980; Smith, 1996, 1997; Srull, 1981, 1983).

The single-tag perspective has been unquestionably essential in guiding a social cognitive analysis of how evaluative information can be automatically activated in memory on perception of the corresponding objects. Furthermore, this perspective, with its emphasis on the importance of the strength of the association between the object representation and the attitude, paved the way for process-oriented research on the mediating role of attitude accessibility in attitude–behavior relationships (e.g., Bassili, 1996; Fazio et al., 1986; Fazio & Williams, 1986; Roskos-Ewoldsen & Fazio, 1992; Smith, Fazio, & Cejka, 1996).

Constructive Perspective

In recent years, a variety of alternatives to the single-tag perspective have emerged (e.g., Bassili & Brown, 2005; Duckworth et al., 2002; Ferguson & Bargh, 2003; Gawronski et al., 2005; Greenwald, 1990; Livingston & Brewer, 2002; Mitchell et al., 2003; Smith, 1997, 2000). These approaches can all be considered "constructive" in that they assume that any given evaluation measured by an implicit test signifies a composite of evaluative information, rather than a single, stored, pre-existing summary index. In this way, although such a composite would necessarily rely on stored evaluative information as the elements of the computation, any given evaluation of an object would be constructed on the fly, across multiple sources of information that are contextually specific. Numerous researchers have argued that explicitly rendered evaluations are constructed in this fashion (e.g., Rosenberg, 1956; Salancik & Conway, 1975; Schwarz & Bohner, 2001; Tesser, 1978; Zaller, 1992), and this possibility has begun to be applied to implicitly measured evaluations (Bassili & Brown, 2005; Blair, 2002; Duckworth et al., 2002; Ferguson & Bargh, 2003; Livingston & Brewer, 2002; Mitchell et al., 2003).

This constructive view is consistent with the notion that most attitude objects are associated in memory with a complex array of different kinds of information (e.g., Abelson, 1976, 1981; Barsalou, 1992; Bower, 1981; Carlston, 1994; Fishbein & Ajzen, 1975; Fiske & Pavelchak, 1986; Schank & Abelson, 1977; Smith, 1992; Smith & Zarate, 1992). With the additional assumption that some of the associated object memories can differ in their evaluative implications, this notion suggests that explicitly and implicitly measured attitudes will vary depending on the chronic and temporary factors in place at the time of measurement. Indeed, recent work on the contextual dependence of automatic evaluations suggests that given such an organization of evaluative information, evaluations that are measured implicitly are contingent on the evaluative profile of the most accessible attitude object memories (e.g., Dasgupta & Greenwald, 2001; Wittenbrink et al., 2001).

According to this view, a 1-to-1 mapping of the stored evaluative information in memory to the observed response (e.g., in an implicit measure) is impossible, even assuming a flawless measurement technique. Instead, any given object is evaluated based on an integration of evaluative information across multiple sources, regardless of how the object is ultimately categorized. In this way, the observed response on an implicit attitude measure does not reflect a stored, pre-existing evaluative tag associated with a category or object (see Livingston & Brewer, 2002), but instead reflects a computation performed by an evaluative system, across numerous representations such as multiple categories and exemplars that relate to the object in various ways (see Bassili & Brown, 2005; Castelli et al., 2004; Duckworth et al., 2002; Ferguson & Bargh, 2003; Fiedler, 1996; Schwarz & Bohner, 2001; Smith, 1997, 2000).

What kind of architecture would underlie a constructive process? In principle, a constructive process is consistent with the traditional "file-drawer" model of memory in which concepts are represented by nodes, and the nodes are interconnected according to semantic similarity (e.g., see Smith, 1996). In these types of models, representations are inert and static when not activated, and are periodically manipulated by processes such as encoding, storage, and retrieval (see Anderson, 1983). It would be theoretically possible for an integrative or constructive process to take place across numerous single-tag representations, although the process by which such a computation would occur is not clear, and would require additional assumptions from the single-tag perspective.

In contrast, the possibility of integrative processing across various sources of evaluative information is directly predicted by parallel distributed processing models of memory (e.g., Anderson & Rosenfeld, 1988; Bassili & Brown, 2005; Bechtel & Abrahamsen, 1991; Carlston and Smith, 1996; Masson, 1991, 1995; Smith, 1996, 1997; Smith & DeCoster, 1999). Models of connectionist systems include the assertion that every observable response (explicit or implicit) is the result of a transitive state of the mind, wherein all representations are potentially implicated or contributive (e.g., Smith, 1996; Smolensky, 1989). This would suggest that an attitude reflects the current state of activation within a connectionist system (e.g., Gawronski et al., 2005; Smith, 1996), and would be influenced by multiple elements of information pertaining to the current physical and psychological circumstances of the perceiver. For instance, in order to provide evidence that (explicit) attitudes are sometimes sensitive to the context, Wilson et al. (2000) stated that "Most parallel distributed processing models assume that mental representations are highly sensitive to the current context, because aspects of the context always influence the pattern of activation that determines mental representation" (pp. 3; also see Arieli, Sterkin, Grinvald, & Aertsen, 1996). A construction across multiple sources of evaluative information would be highly compatible with the assumptions of connectionist systems (see also Eiser, Fazio, Stafford, & Prescott, 2003; Fiedler, 1996; Mitchell et al., 2003).

Do the Recent Findings Suggest a Single-Tag or Constructive Process?

Evidence of Contextual Dependence To what degree does the recent evidence for the contextual dependence of automatic evaluations support the single-tag versus constructive perspective? According to the single-tag perspective, variability in the automatic evaluation of an object across contexts could be due to the object being implicitly categorized in different ways across situations. The assumption here would be that almost every category is associated with an evaluative tag, and the evaluation of the object would depend on how it is categorized. This would be consistent with the single-tag claim that a stored, unitary summary index is what is being captured by the implicit measure (plus measurement error).

One critical problem with the single-tag perspective, however, is that it does not address or explain inhibitory processes at work during automatic evaluative processing. Although the vast majority of research on automatic evaluation has addressed only the degree to which facilitatory processes underlie such evaluations, recent work on contextual dependence suggests that both inhibitory and facilitatory processing can be involved (Ferguson & Bargh, 2004; Maddux et al., 2005). For example, in research by Maddux et al. (2005), participants high in the motivation to avoid prejudice exhibited significantly more inhibition of negative information when perceiving an African-American in a threatening context. And, in work by Ferguson and Bargh (2004), the effect of a current goal state on automatic evaluations sometimes involved the inhibition of negativity and the facilitation of positivity associated with the object. These findings are difficult to reconcile with a model that posits that a single summary tag is activated in response to the perception of the object. Namely, the possibility that positive and negative evaluative information associated with the object in memory can be facilitated and inhibited simultaneously (depending on the valence of the information) suggests that objects are associated with more than just one summary tag (see also Cacioppo & Gardner, 1999; Larsen et al., 2001).

In contrast to the single-tag perspective, the findings regarding the situational influences on automatic evaluation are directly consistent with a constructive view of how evaluations are generated. A constructive model would naturally allow for contextual influence – the essence of such a model is that the evaluation of any given object depends on the evaluative profile of the object memories, and other relevant memories, activated at the time of encountering the object. This means that the evaluation of an object might vary across time and contexts according to the degree to which the object is stored in memory with information that is evaluatively complex (i.e., not uniform), and the circumstances of the situation.

Furthermore, the findings regarding inhibitory processing in automatic evaluation could be accounted for by a perspective that assumes a constructive, integrative process across multiple sources of information. Specifically, such a perspective would assume that different sources of evaluative information might be implicated on perception of the respective object – while some types of information might be made more accessible, other types might become less accessible (i.e., inhibited).

These various effects could influence the computation that ultimately determines the final positive or negative (approach or avoid) response.

It should be noted that a constructive approach would not necessarily preclude high stability of implicit attitudes across time and situations (cf. Wilson et al., 2000). Assuming that an implicit attitude represents a combination of pieces of evaluative information related to the object and context, stability should emerge to the degree that the object is associated with mostly univalent memories, and is associated also with univalent contextual memories. For example, one's memories concerning puppies might be almost uniformly positive, and the contextual memories that are associated with puppies might also tend to be positive. If this is the case, then one might expect the automatic reaction to the word *puppy* to be relatively stable across time, assuming little measurement error (e.g., Bargh et al., 1992, 1996; Fazio et al., 1986). This approach would assume that stability should increase to the extent that the object is associated with differently valenced object and contextual memories.

It is important to note that even though the evidence of contextual dependence seems to support a constructive approach, it does not necessarily speak to the issue of the type of architecture that would underlie such a model. Again, although connectionist models have been more often formalized and modeled to account for specific phenomena compared to associative networks (see Smith, 1997), and also routinely predict inhibitory processing, it might be the case that a symbolic associative network could be bootstrapped in terms of accounting for the recent findings in this area.

Evidence of Compatibility between Explicit and Implicit Measures

Findings concerning the consistency of explicit and implicit attitudes are not exclusively supportive of either the single-tag or constructive approaches to attitude representation and generation. For example, findings suggesting a dissociation could be explained by the single-tag perspective based on the notion that a different attitude is being measured in each case (see Wilson et al., 2000). With additional time and deliberation, a person who is automatically classified (and evaluated) solely by race, for example, might upon further reflection be classified and evaluated according to profession, or personality (see Brewer, 1988; Fiske & Neuberg, 1990; Kunda, 1999). The categories might be associated with different summary tags, which would lead to the dissociation between the attitude measures (Wilson et al., 2000).

Findings suggesting a dissociation between implicit and explicit attitudes could also be easily explained by the constructive approach. Just as the additional deliberation in explicit measures might lead to a different categorization than during an implicit measure, the same additional deliberation might influence the way in which evaluative information is constructed. For example, the reflection and introspection that is possible during an explicit measure would undoubtedly allow the activation of additional evaluative information about the object itself as well as the context in which the object is encountered. This additional reflection could change the array of information contributing to the current pattern of activation within a connectionist system.

Although the findings regarding implicit–explicit relations do not discriminate between the single-tag and constructive approaches, they have inspired researchers to claim that different processes underlie explicit versus implicit measures (Gawronski & Strack, 2004; Gawronski et al., 2005; Strack & Deutsch, 2004). In line with dual-process models of social information processing (e.g., Chaiken & Trope, 1999; Kahneman, 2003; Lieberman, Gaunt, Gilbert, & Trope, 2002; Sloman, 1996; Smith & DeCoster, 1999), Gawronski and colleagues have argued that while implicit attitudes are based on associative evaluations, explicit attitudes are based on propositional evaluations. Associative evaluations are those that are automatically activated in response to the perception of a stimulus, and do not reflect the person's endorsement of the evaluation. Such evaluations can be generated via connectionist frameworks, and, as such, naturally incorporate contextual information. Explicit evaluations, on the other hand, reflect more deliberate, rule-based processing that is itself based on momentarily activated associative evaluations. The rule-based processing though allows for the assessment of the "truth value" of the evaluative information – propositional evaluations only emerge if they are formally endorsed by the perceiver. In line with this perspective, research is actively examining the degree to which explicit and implicit attitudes differ in terms of whether they reflect endorsed evaluations (e.g., Olson & Fazio, 2004).

Evidence of Evaluations of Novelty   What does the evidence that automatic evaluation occurs for novel stimuli indicate for the organization and generation of evaluative information in memory? Although the single-tag perspective does not formally predict such effects (see Fazio, 1989, 2001; Wilson et al., 2000), it is not in principle contradictory with such findings. For example, one could surmise that novel objects are quickly classified into the most appropriate, preexisting category (e.g., an unfamiliar abstract art image might be classified into the pre-existing category "colorful abstract art designs") and then acquire whatever stored, summary evaluative tag is associated with that category. Although this model would break down for objects that are not immediately classifiable, one could argue that there are no objects in existence that would not be immediately categorized, albeit in a perhaps mistaken or temporary manner (see Kunda, 1999).

The evidence concerning novelty is consistent with a constructive account (e.g., Duckworth et al., 2002; Ferguson & Bargh, 2003). Findings showing that people can automatically evaluate novel or unfamiliar stimuli suggest the ability to integrate evaluative information from numerous, familiar aspects or features in order to generate an evaluative reaction to the unfamiliar object. In this way then, a person who encounters a strange animal while on vacation (e.g., a quakka on Rottnest Island in Western Australia), for example, might integrate evaluative information from familiar features (e.g., although looks like a big rat, seems gentle like a bunny, and no growling, squinted eyes, or bared teeth that would suggest an imminent attack), and immediately and unintentionally evaluate the novel animal as positive.

In sum, although researchers have argued that the automatic evaluation of novel objects indicates that people integrate evaluative information across more familiar features (e.g., Duckworth et al., 2002), these recent findings cannot ultimately discriminate between the possibility that novel objects are categorized into familiar groups and then acquire the stored, summary tag associated with that group, versus are evaluated according to a computation across multiple relevant exemplars and categories. Both perspectives remain valid at this point.

Evidence of Consequences of Automatic Evaluations Research concerning the consequences of automatic evaluations has traditionally informed discussions of the possible organization of evaluative information in memory (for a review see Musch & Klauer, 2003). In particular, findings concerning the immediate consequences of the automatic evaluation of an object for both related and unrelated stimuli directly address a debate about how evaluative information might be organized in memory. Whereas some researchers have asserted that the automatic evaluation of an object leads to the increased accessibility of a valence construct (positive or negative; see Fazio 2001) or all similarly valenced memories ("spreading activation" accounts; Bargh et al., 1996; Ferguson et al., 2005), others have argued that such accessibility effects do not occur ("response competition" accounts; e.g., see Klauer & Musch, 2003; Klinger, Burton, & Pitts, 2000; Wentura, 1999). These two perspectives on what happens after an automatic evaluative act necessarily presuppose different organizations of evaluative memory. Whereas "spreading activation" accounts assume that evaluative information is interconnected just on the basis of valence (though perhaps not literally as in an associative network), response competition accounts would make no such assertion.

This debate is ongoing, and in fact there is evidence that supports both "spreading activation" accounts (e.g., Ferguson et al., 2005) as well as response competition accounts (e.g., see Klauer & Musch, 2003; Klinger, Burton, & Pitts, 2000; Wentura, 1999). This suggests that both accounts might ultimately hold considerable explanatory power under various circumstances, and possibly for data gathered from particular paradigms (see Fazio, 2001). Further research on the varied consequences of an automatic evaluative act on subsequent judgment, feeling, and behavior will undoubtedly proffer implications for how evaluative information is represented and organized in memory.

Reconciliation Based on evidence gathered so far, it is not yet possible to definitively resolve the arguably most central issues concerning automatic evaluation. The first of course is how an evaluation is generated, and whether it reflects the activation of a stored, unitary summary index associated with the object representation, or a constructive process across multiple sources of evaluative information. Although the evidence concerning contextual dependence and novelty seems most consistent with the idea of a constructive model, there is no definitive way of establishing this as of yet.

The second issue is much broader, and concerns the question of whether memory consists of localist, symbolic systems, connectionist systems, or some combination of both (e.g., see Marcus, 2001). This tension between possible cognitive architectures is driving a considerable amount of research in contemporary cognitive science, and the jury is still out on which framework is best supported by data and theory (see Fodor, 2000; Marcus, 2001; Pinker, 1997; Plotkin, 1997). At the least, there is evidence that the associative network models that have dominated theory and research in social cognition for the last 30 years are beginning to wane in popularity (see Carlston & Smith, 1996; Smith, 1996, 1997, 2000), and some researchers in social psychology have begun to assert the advantages of connectionist frameworks for explaining social psychological phenomena (e.g., Bassili & Brown, 2005; Eiser et al., 2003; Ferguson & Bargh, 2003, 2004; Mitchell et al., 2003).

CONCLUSION

Research in social psychology over the last three decades, and in particular over the last five to ten years, has provided considerable insight into the nature of automatic evaluation. In particular, this work suggests that people tend to evaluate a wide array of both novel and familiar stimuli, without necessarily intending or being aware of such evaluations. Evaluations that are automatically generated tend to be highly sensitive to the context in which the person encounters the respective stimuli, and also seem to be distinct from more deliberate, conscious appraisals. Finally, even though the positivity or negativity that is activated in response to an object is fleeting, it nevertheless has various consequences for subsequent judgment, emotion, and behavior. Although these characteristics have considerably expanded an understanding of automatic evaluation, many unanswered questions remain. The most important among these would seem to be the way in which evaluative information is represented in memory and generated on perception of a given object. Future research on the boundary conditions and moderating variables underlying contextual-dependence, implicit-explicit relations, novel evaluations, and criterion and predictive validity will undoubtedly shape the answers to such questions over the upcoming years.

NOTE

1. Recent research has suggested that the amygdala is activated more in response to positive versus neutral stimuli (e.g., Hamann & Mao, 2002; Liberzon, Phan, Decker, & Taylor, 2003; Zald, 2003), and thus might be specialized for processing intense stimuli rather than solely negative stimuli (see Cunningham, Raye, & Johnson, 2004).

ACKNOWLEDGMENTS

Preparation of this chapter was supported in part by grants R03-MH067877 and R03-MH73629 from the National Institute of Mental Health (NIMH).

REFERENCES

Abelson, R. P. (1976). Script processing in attitude formation and decision making. In J. S. Carroll & J. W. Payne (Eds.), *Cognition and social behavior* (pp. 33–45). Hillsdale, NJ: Erlbaum.

Abelson, R. P. (1981). Psychological status of the script concept. *American Psychologist, 36,* 715–729.

Albarracín, D., Johnson, B. T., & Zanna, M. P. (2005). *The handbook of attitudes.* Mahwah, NJ: Erlbaum.

Allport, G. W. (1935). Attitudes. In C. Murchison (Ed.), *Handbook of social psychology* (pp. 798–844). Worcester, MA: Clark University Press.

Amodio, D. M., Harmon-Jones, E., & Devine, P. G. (2003). Individual differences in the activation and control of affective race bias as assessed by startle eyeblink responses and self-report. *Journal of Personality and Social Psychology, 84,* 738–753.

Anderson, J. A., & Rosenfeld, E. (1988). *Neurocomputing: Foundations of research.* Cambridge, MA: MIT Press.

Anderson, J. R. (1983). *The architecture of cognition.* Cambridge, MA: Harvard University Press.

Anderson, J. R., & Bower, G. H. (1973). *Human associative memory.* Washington, DC: Winston and Sons.

Anderson, N. H. (1974). Cognitive algebra: Integration theory applied to social attribution. In L. Berkowitz (Ed.), *Advances in experimental social psychology* (Vol. 7, pp. 1–101). New York: Academic Press.

Arieli, A., Sterkin, A., Grinvald, A., & Aertsen, A. (1996). Dynamics of ongoing activity: Explanation of the large variability in evoked cortical responses. *Science, 273,* 1868–1871.

Arkes, H. R., & Tetlock, P. E. (2004). Attributions of implicit prejudice, or "Would Jesse Jackson 'fail' the Implicit Association Test?". *Psychological Inquiry, 15,* 257–278.

Ashburn-Nardo, L., Voils, C. I., & Monteith, M. J. (2001). Implicit associations as the seeds of intergroup bias: How easily do they take root? *Journal of Personality and Social Psychology, 81,* 789–799.

Banaji, M. R. (2001). Implicit attitudes can be measured. In H. L. Roediger, J. S. Nairne, I. Neither & A. Surprenant (Eds.), *The nature of remembering: Essays in honor of Robert G. Crowder* (pp. 117–150). Washington, DC: American Psychological Association.

Banaji, M. R., & Hardin, C. D. (1996). Automatic stereotyping. *Psychological Science, 7*(3), 136–141.

Banaji, M. R., Nosek, B. A., & Greenwald, A. G. (2004). No place for nostalgia in science: A response to Arkes and Tetlock. *Psychological Inquiry, 15,* 279–310.

Bargh, J. A. (1984). Automatic and conscious processing of social information. In R. S. Wyer Jr. & T. K. Srull (Eds.), *Handbook of social cognition* (Vol. 3, pp. 1–43). Hillsdale, NJ: Erlbaum.

Bargh, J. A. (1990). Auto-motives: Preconscious determinants of social interaction. In E. T. Higgins & R. M. Sorrentino (Eds.), *Handbook of motivation and cognition: Foundations of social behavior* (Vol. 2, pp. 93–130). New York, NY: Guilford Press.

Bargh, J. A. (1994). The Four Horsemen of automaticity: Awareness, efficiency, intention, and control in social cognition. In R. S. Wyer, Jr. & T. K. Srull (Eds.), *Handbook of social cognition* (2nd ed., pp. 1–40). Hillsdale, NJ: Erlbaum.

Bargh, J. A. (1999). The cognitive monster. In S. Chaiken & Y. Trope (Eds.), *Dual process theories in social psychology* (pp. 361–382). New York: Guilford Press.

Bargh, J. A., Bond, R. N., Lombardi, W. J., & Tota, M. E. (1986). The additive nature of chronic and temporary sources of construct accessibility. *Journal of Personality and Social Psychology, 50,* 869–878.

Bargh, J. A., Chaiken, S., Govender, R., & Pratto, F. (1992). The generality of the automatic attitude activation effect. *Journal of Personality and Social Psychology, 62,* 893–912.

Bargh, J. A., Chaiken, S., Raymond, P., & Hymes, C. (1996). The automatic evaluation effect: Unconditional automatic attitude activation with a pronunciation task. *Journal of Experimental Social Psychology, 32,* 104–128.

Bargh, J. A., & Ferguson, M. J. (2000). Beyond behaviorism: On the automaticity of higher mental processes. *Psychological Bulletin, 126,* 925–945.

Barsalou, L. W. (1992). *Cognitive psychology: An overview for cognitive scientists.* Hillsdale, NJ: Erlbaum.

Barden, J., Maddux, W. W., Petty, R. E., & Brewer, M. B. (2004). Contextual moderation of racial bias: The impact of social roles on controlled and automatically activated attitudes. *Journal of Personality and Social Psychology, 87,* 5–22.

Bassili, J. N. (1996) The "how" and "why" of response latency measurement in survey research. In N. Schwarz & S. Sudman (Eds.), *Answering questions: Methodology for determining cognitive and communicative processes in survey research* (pp. 319–346). San Francisco, CA: Jossey-Bass Publishers.

Bassili, J. N., & Brown, R. D. (2005). Implicit and explicit attitudes: Research, Challenges, and theory. In D. Albarracín, B. T. Johnson & M. P. Zanna (Eds.), *The handbook of attitudes* (pp. 543–574). Mahwah, NJ: Erlbaum.

Bechtel, W., & Abrahamsen, A. (1991). *Connectionism and the mind: An introduction to parallel processing in networks.* Oxford, England: Basil Blackwell.

Betsch, T., Plessner, H., Schwieren, C., & Gütig, R. (2001). I like it but I don't know why: A value-account approach to implicit attitude formation. *Personality and Social Psychology Bulletin, 27,* 242–253.

Blair, I. (2002). The malleability of automatic stereotypes and prejudice. *Personality and Social Psychological Review, 6,* 242–261.

Blair, I. V., & Banaji, M. R. (1996). Automatic and controlled processes in stereotype priming. *Journal of Personality and Social Psychology, 70,* 1142–1163.

Blair, I. V., Ma, J. E., & Lenton, A. P. (2001). Imagining stereotypes away: The moderation of implicit stereotypes through mental imagery. *Journal of Personality and Social Psychology, 81,* 828–841.

Bosson, J. K., Swann, W. B., Jr., & Pennebaker, J. (2000). Stalking the perfect measure of implicit self-esteem: The blind men and the elephant revisited? *Journal of Personality & Social Psychology, 79,* 631–643.

Bower, G. H. (1981). Mood and memory. *American Psychologist, 36,* 129–148.

Brauer, M., Wasel, W., & Niedenthal, P. M. (2000). Implicit and explicit components of prejudice. *Review of General Psychology, 4,* 79–101.

Brendl, C. M., & Higgins, E. T. (1996). Principles of judging valence: What makes events positive or negative? *Advances in Experimental Social Psychology, 28,* 95–160.

Brendl, C. M., Markman, A. B., & Messner, C. (2001). How do indirect measures of evaluation work? Evaluating the inference of prejudice in the Implicit Association Test. *Journal of Personality and Social Psychology, 81,* 760–773.

Brewer, M. B. (1988). A dual process model of impression formation. In T. K. Srull & R. S. Wyer (Eds.), *Advances in social cognition* (Vol. 1, pp. 1–36). Hillsdale, NJ: Erlbaum.

Brown, J. D. (1998). *The self.* New York: McGraw-Hill.

Cacioppo, J. T., & Gardner, W. L. (1999). Emotion. *Annual Review of Psychology, 50*, 191–214.

Cacioppo, J. T., Priester, J. R., & Berntson, G. G. (1993). Rudimentary determinants of attitudes: II. Arm flexion and extension have differential effects on attitudes. *Journal of Personality and Social Psychology, 65*, 5–17.

Carlston, D. E. (1994). Associated systems theory: A systematic approach to the cognitive representation of persons and events. In R. S. Wyer (Ed.) *Advances in social cognition: Vol. 7. Associated systems theory* (pp. 1–78). Hillsdale, NY: Erlbaum.

Carlston, D. E., & Smith, E. R. (1996). Principles of mental representation. In E. T. Higgins, & A. W. Kruglanski (Eds.), *Social psychology: Handbook of basic principles* (pp. 184–210). New York, NY: Guilford Press.

Castelli, L., Zogmaister, C., Smith, E. R., & Arcuri, L. (2004). On the automatic evaluation of social exemplars. *Journal of Personality and Social Psychology, 86*, 373–387.

Chaiken, S., & Bargh, J. A. (1993). Occurrence versus moderation of the automatic attitude activation effect: Reply to Fazio. *Journal of Personality and Social Psychology, 64*, 759–765.

Chaiken, S., & Trope, Y. (1999). *Dual-process theories in social psychology.* New York: Guilford Press.

Chartrand, T. L., Bargh, J. A., & van Baaren, R. (in press). Linking automatic evaluation to mood and information processing style: Consequences for experienced affect, information processing, and stereotyping, *Journal of Experimental Psychology: General.*

Chen, M., & Bargh, J. A. (1999). Consequences of automatic evaluation: Immediate behavioral predispositions to approach and avoid the stimulus. *Personality and Social Psychology Bulletin, 25*, 215–224.

Collins, A. M., & Loftus, E. F. (1975). A spreading-activation theory of semantic processing. *Psychological Review, 82*, 407–428.

Conrey, F. R., Sherman, J. W., Gawronski, B., Hugenberg, K., & Groom, C. (2005). Separating multiple processes in implicit social cognition: The Quad-Model of implicit task performance. *Journal of Personality and Social Psychology, 89*, 469–487.

Croizet, J. C., & Fiske, S. T. (2000). Moderation of priming by goals: Feeling entitled to judge increases judged usability of evaluative primes. *Journal of Experimental Social Psychology, 36*, 155–181.

Cunningham, W. A., Johnson, M. K., Gatenby, J. C., Gore, J. C., & Banaji, M. R. (2003). Neural components of social evaluation. *Journal of Personality and Social Psychology, 85*, 639–649.

Cunningham, W. A., Johnson, M. K., Raye, C. L., Gatenby, J. C., Gore, J. C., & Banaji, M. R. (2004). Separable neural components in the processing of Black and White faces. *Psychological Science, 15*, 806–813.

Cunningham, W. A., Nezlek, J. B., & Banaji, M. R. (2004). Implicit and explicit ethnocentrism: Revisiting the ideologies of prejudice. *Personality and Social Psychology Bulletin, 30*, 1332–1346.

Cunningham, W. A., Preacher, K. J., & Banaji, M. R. (2001). Implicit attitude measures: Consistency, stability, and convergent validity. *Psychological Science, 12*, 163–170.

Cunningham, W. A., Raye, C. L., & Johnson, M. K. (2004). Implicit and explicit evaluation: fMRI correlates of valence, emotional intensity, and control in the processing of attitudes. *Journal of Cognitive Neuroscience, 16*, 1717–1729.

Damasio, A. R. (1994). *Descartes' error: Emotion, reason and the human brain.* Putnam: New York.

Damasio, A. R. (1999). *The feeling of what happens: Body and emotion in the making of consciousness.* Orlando, FL: Harcourt.

Damasio, A. R. (2001). Fundamental feelings. *Nature, 413,* 781.

Dasgupta, N., & Greenwald, A. G. (2001). On the malleability of automatic attitudes: Combating automatic prejudice with images of liked and disliked individuals. *Journal of Personality and Social Psychology, 81,* 800–814.

Devine, P. G. (1989). Stereotypes and prejudice: Their automatic and controlled components. *Journal of Personality and Social Psychology, 56,* 5–18.

Devine, P. G. (2001). Implicit prejudice and stereotyping: How automatic are they? Introduction to the special section. *Journal of Personality and Social Psychology, 81,* 757–759.

Dijksterhuis, A. (2004). I like myself but I don't know why: Enhancing implicit self-esteem by subliminal evaluative conditioning. *Journal of Personality and Social Psychology, 86,* 345–355.

Doob, L. W. (1947), The behavior of attitudes. *Psychological Review, 51,* 135–156.

Dovidio, J. F., Kawakami, K., & Beach, K. R. (2001). Implicit and explicit attitudes: Examination of the relationship between measures of intergroup bias. In R. Brown & S. L. Gaertner (Eds.), *Blackwell handbook of social psychology* (Vol. 4, Intergroup Relations, pp. 175–197). Oxford, UK: Blackwell.

Dovidio, J. F., Kawakami, K., & Gaertner, S. L. (2002). Implicit and explicit prejudice and interracial interaction. *Journal of Personality and Social Psychology, 82,* 62–68.

Dovidio, J. F., Kawakami, K., Johnson, C., & Howard, B. (1997). On the nature of prejudice: Automatic and controlled processes. *Journal of Experimental Social Psychology, 33,* 510–540.

Dovidio, J. F., Mann, J., & Gaertner, S. L. (1989). Resistance to affirmative action: The implications of aversive racism. In F. A. Blanchard & F. J. Crosby (Eds.), *Affirmative action in perspective* (pp. 83–102). New York: Springer Verlag.

Duckworth, K. L., Bargh, J. A., Garcia, M., & Chaiken, S. (2002). The automatic evaluation of novel stimuli. *Psychological Science, 13,* 513–519.

Dunton, B. C., & Fazio, R. H. (1997). An individual difference measure of motivation to control prejudiced reactions. *Personality and Social Psychology Bulletin, 23,* 316–326.

Eagly, A. H., & Chaiken, S. (1993). *The psychology of attitudes.* Fort Worth, TX: Harcourt Brace Jovanovich College.

Eiser, J. R., Fazio, R. H., Stafford, T., & Prescott, T. J. (2003). Connectionist simulation of attitude learning: Asymmetries in the acquisition of positive and negative evaluations. *Personality and Social Psychology Bulletin, 29* 1121–1235.

Epley, N., & Caruso, E. M. (2004). Egocentric ethics. *Social Justice Research, 17,* 171–187.

Erdley, C. A., & D'Agostino, P. R. (1988). Cognitive and affective components of automatic priming effects. *Journal of Personality and Social Psychology, 54,* 741–747.

Fazio, R. H. (1986). How do attitudes guide behavior? In R. M. Sorrentino & E. T. Higgins (Eds.), *Handbook of motivation and cognition: Foundations of social behavior* (pp. 204–243). New York: Guilford.

Fazio, R. H. (1989). On the power and functionality of attitudes: The role of attitude accessibility. In A. R. Pratkanis, S. J. Breckler & A. G. Greenwald (Eds.), *Attitude structure and function* (pp. 153–179). Hillsdale, NJ: Erlbaum.

Fazio, R. H. (1990). Multiple processes by which attitudes guide behavior: The MODE model as an integrative framework. In M. P. Zanna (Ed.), *Advances in experimental social psychology* (Vol. 23, pp. 75–109). New York: Academic Press.

Fazio, R. H. (1993). Variability in the likelihood of automatic attitude activation: Data re-analysis and commentary on Bargh, Chaiken, Govender, and Pratto (1992). *Journal of Personality and Social Psychology, 64,* 753–758, 764–765.

Fazio, R. H. (2001). On the automatic activation of associated evaluations: An overview. *Cognition and Emotion, 14,* 1–27.

Fazio, R. H., Blascovich, J., & Driscoll, D. M. (1992). On the functional value of attitudes: The influence of accessible attitudes upon the ease and quality of decision making. *Personality and Social Psychology Bulletin, 18,* 388–401.

Fazio, R. H., Chen, J., McDonel, E. C., & Sherman, S. J. (1982). Attitude accessibility, attitude-behavior consistency and the strength of the object-evaluation association. *Journal of Experimental Social Psychology, 18,* 339–357.

Fazio, R. H., Jackson, J. R., Dunton, B. C., & Williams, C. J. (1995). Variability in automatic activation as an unobtrusive measure of racial attitudes. A bona fide pipeline? *Journal of Personality and Social Psychology, 69,* 1013–1027.

Fazio, R. H., & Olson, M. A. (2003). Implicit measures in social cognition research: Their meaning and use. *Annual Review of Psychology, 54,* 297–327.

Fazio, R. H., Sanbonmatsu, D. M., Powell, M. C., & Kardes, F. R. (1986). On the automatic activation of attitudes. *Journal of Personality and Social Psychology, 50,* 229–238.

Fazio, R. H., & Williams, C. J. (1986). Attitude accessibility as a moderator of the attitude-perception and attitude-behavior relations: An investigation of the 1984 presidential election. *Journal of Personality and Social Psychology, 51,* 505–514.

Ferguson, M. J., & Bargh, J. A. (2002). Sensitivity and flexibility: Exploring the knowledge function of automatic attitudes. In L. F. Barrett & P. Salovey (Eds.), *The wisdom in feeling: Psychological processes in emotional intelligence* (pp. 383–405). New York: Guilford Press.

Ferguson, M. J., & Bargh, J. A. (2003). The constructive nature of automatic evaluation. In J. Musch & K. C. Klauer (Eds.), *The psychology of evaluation: Affective processes in cognition and emotion* (pp. 169–188). Hillsdale, NJ: Erlbaum.

Ferguson, M. J., & Bargh, J. A. (2004). Liking is for doing: Effects of goal pursuit on automatic evaluation. *Journal of Personality and Social Psychology, 88,* 557–572.

Ferguson, M. J., Bargh, J. A., & Nayak, D. (2005). After-affects: How automatic evaluations influence the interpretation of unrelated, subsequent stimuli. *Journal of Experimental Social Psychology, 41,* 182–191.

Festinger, L. (1957). *A theory of cognitive dissonance.* Stanford, CA: Stanford University Press.

Festinger, L., & Carlsmith, J. M. (1959). Cognitive consquences of forced compliance. *Journal of Abnormal and Social Psychology, 58,* 203–210.

Fiedler, K. (1996). Explaining and simulating judgment biases as an aggregation phenomenon in probabilistic, multiple-cue environments. *Psychological Review, 103,* 193–214.

Fishbein, M., & Ajzen, I. (1975). *Belief, attitude, intention, and behavior: An introduction to theory and research.* Reading, MA: Addison-Wesley.

Fiske, S. T., & Neuberg, S. L. (1990). A continuum of impression formation, from category-based to individuating processes: Influences of information and motivation on attention and interpretation. In M. P. Zanna (Ed.), *Advances in experimental social psychology* (Vol. 23, pp. 1–74). New York: Academic Press.

Fiske, S. T., & Pavelchak, M. A. (1986). Category-based versus piecemeal-based affective responses: Development in schema-triggered affect. In R. M. Sorrentino & E. T. Higgins (Eds.), *Handbook of motivation and cognition: Foundations of social behavior* (pp. 167–203). New York: Guilford.

Fodor, J. (2000). *The mind doesn't work that way.* Cambridge, MA: MIT Press.

Forgas, J. P. (2000). *Feeling and thinking: Affective influences on social cognition*. New York: Cambridge University Press.

Forgas, J. P. (2001). *The handbook of affect and social cognition*. Mahwah, NJ: Erlbaum.

Frank, R. H. (1988). *Passions within reason: The strategic role of the emotions*. W. W. Norton.

Frank, R. H. (2003). Introducing moral emotions into models of rational choice. In A. S. R. Manstead, N. H. Frijda & A. H. Fischer (Eds.), *Feelings and emotions: The Amsterdam symposium*. New York: Cambridge University Press.

Gawronski, B., & Strack, F. (2004). On the propositional nature of cognitive consistency: Dissonance changes explicit, but not implicit attitudes. *Journal of Experimental Social Psychology, 40*, 535–542.

Gawronski, B., Walther, E., & Blank, H. (2005). Cognitive consistency and the formation of interpersonal attitudes: Cognitive balance affects the encoding of social information. *Journal of Experimental Social Psychology, 41*, 618–626.

Gazzaniga, M. S., & Heatherton, T. F. (2003). *The psychological Science: Mind, brain, and behavior*. New York: W. W. Norton.

Giner-Sorolla, R., Garcia, M. T., & Bargh, J. A. (1999). The automatic evaluation of pictures. *Social Cognition, 17*, 76–96.

Glaser, J., & Banaji, M. R. (1999). When fair is foul and foul is fair: Reverse priming in automatic evaluation. *Journal of Personality and Social Psychology, 77*, 669–687.

Gollwitzer, P. M. (1996). The volitional benefits of planning. In P. M. Gollwitzer & J. A. Bargh (Eds.), *The psychology of action: Linking cognition and motivation to behavior* (pp. 287–312). New York, NY: Guilford Press.

Gollwitzer, P. M. (1999). Implementation intentions: Strong effects of simple plans. *American Psychologist, 54*, 493–503.

Greene, J., & Haidt, J. (2002). How (and where) does moral judgment work? *Trends in Cognitive Science, 6*, 517–523.

Greenwald, A. G. (1990). What cognitive representations underlie social attitudes? *Bulletin of the Psychonomic Society, 28*, 254–260.

Greenwald, A. G., & Banaji, M. R. (1995). Implicit social cognition: Attitudes, self-esteem, and stereotypes. *Psychological Review, 102*, 4–27.

Greenwald, A. G., Banaji, M. R., Rudman, L. A., Farnham, S. D., Nosek, B. A., & Mellott, D. S. (2002). A unified theory of implicit attitudes, stereotypes, self-esteem, and self-concept. *Psychological Review, 109*, 3–25.

Greenwald, A. G., & Farnham, S. D. (2000). Using the Implicit Association Test to measure self-esteem and self-concept. *Journal of Personality and Social Psychology, 79*, 1022–1038.

Greenwald, A. G., Klinger, M. R., & Liu, T. J. (1989). Unconscious processing of dichoptically masked words. *Memory and Cognition, 17*, 35–47.

Greenwald, A. G., McGhee, D. E., & Schwartz, J. L. K. (1998). Measuring individual differences in implicit cognition: The Implicit Association Test. *Journal of Personality and Social Psychology, 74*, 1464–1480.

Greenwald, A. G., & Nosek, B. A. (2001). Health of the Implicit Association Test at age 3. *Zeitschrift für Experimentelle Psychologie, 48*, 85–93.

Haidt, J. (2001). The emotional dog and its rational tail: A social intuitionist approach to moral judgment. *Psychological Review, 108*, 814–834.

Haidt, J. (2003). The moral emotions. In R. J. Davidson, K. R. Scherer & H. H. Goldsmith (Eds.), *Handbook of affective sciences* (pp. 852–870). Oxford: Oxford University Press.

Hamann, S., & Mao, H. (2002). Positive and negative emotional verbal stimuli elicit activity in the left amygdala. *Neuroreport, 13,* 15–19.

Hassin, R. R., Uleman, J. S., & Bargh, J. A. (2005). *The new unconscious.* [a sequel to Uleman & Bargh's *Unintended thought,* 1989]. New York: Oxford University Press.

Hastie, R. (1980). Memory for behavioral information that confirms or contradicts a personality impression. In R. Hastie, et al. (Eds.), *Person memory: The cognitive basis of social perception* (pp. 155–177). Hillsdale, NJ: Erlbaum.

Hermans, D., Baeyens, F., & Eelen, P. (1998). Odours as affective processing context for word evaluation: A case of cross-modal affective priming. *Cognition and Emotion, 12,* 601–613.

Hermans, D., Crombez, G., & Eelen, P. (2000). Automatic attitude activation and efficiency: The fourth horseman of automaticity. *Psychologica Belgica, 40,* 3–22.

Hermans, D., De Houwer, J., & Eelen, P. (1994). The affective priming effect: Automatic activation of evaluative information in memory. *Cognition and Emotion, 8,* 515–533.

Higgins, E. T. (1996). Knowledge activation: Accessibility, applicability, and salience. In E. T. Higgins & A. W. Kruglanski (Eds.), *Social psychology: Handbook of basic principles* (pp. 133–168). New York: Guilford.

Higgins, E. T., Rholes, W. S., & Jones, C. R. (1977). Category accessibility and impression formation. *Journal of Experimental Social Psychology, 13,* 141–154.

Himmelfarb, S. (1993). The measurement of attitudes. In A. H. Eagly, & S. Chaiken (Eds.), *The psychology of attitudes* (pp. 23–84). Fort Worth, TX: Harcourt Brace Jovanovich College.

Hofmann, W., Gawronski, B., Gschwendner, T., Le, H., & Schmitt, M. (2005). A meta-analysis on the correlation between the Implicit Association Test and explicit self-report measures. *Personality and Social Psychology Bulletin, 31,* 1369–1385.

De Houwer, J. (2003). The extrinsic affective Simon task. *Experimental Psychology, 50,* 77–85.

De Houwer, J. (2006). What are implicit measures and why are we using them? In R. W. Wiers & A. W. Stacy (Eds.), *The handbook of implicit cognition and addiction* (pp. 11–28). Thousand Oaks, CA: Sage Publishers.

De Houwer, J., Baeyens, F., & Field, A. P. (2005). *Associative learning of likes and dislikes.* Hove: Psychology Press.

De Houwer, J., & Eelen, P. (1998). An affective variant of the Simon paradigm. *Cognition and Emotion, 8,* 45–61.

De Houwer, J., Thomas, S., & Baeyens, F. (2001) Associative learning of likes and dislikes: A review of 25 years of research on human evaluative conditioning. *Psychological Bulletin, 127,* 853–869.

Ito, T. A., & Cacioppo, J. T. (2000). Electrophysiological evidence of implicit and explicit categorization processes. *Journal of Experimental Social Psychology, 36,* 660–676.

Jacoby, L. L. (1992). A process dissociation framework: Separating automatic from intentional uses of memory. *Journal of Memory and Language, 30,* 513–541.

Jacoby, L. L. (1997). Invariance in automatic influences of memory: Toward a user's guide for the process-dissociation procedure. *Journal of Experimental Psychology: Learning, Memory and Cognition, 24,* 3–26.

Jacoby, L. L., Yonelinas, A. P., & Jennings, J. (1997). The relation between conscious and unconscious (automatic) influences. A declaration of independence. In J. Cohen & J. W. Schooler (Eds.), *Scientific approaches to consciousness* (pp.13–47). Mahweh, NJ: Erlbaum.

Jastrow, J. (1906). *The subconscious.* Boston, MA: Houghton-Mifflin.

Jones, E. E., & Sigall, H. (1971). The bogus pipeline: A new paradigm for measuring affect and attitude. *Psychological Bulletin, 76,* 349–364.

Jordan, C. H., Spencer, S. J., & Zanna, M. P. (2003). "I love me . . . I love me not": Implicit self-esteem, explicit self-esteem, and defensiveness. In S. J. Spencer, S. Fein, M. P. Zanna & J. M. Olson (Eds.). *Motivated social perception: The Ontario symposium* (Vol. 9, pp. 117–145). Mahwah, NJ: Erlbaum.

Judd, C. M., & Kulik, J. A. (1980). Schematic effects of social attitudes on information processing and recall. *Journal of Personality and Social Psychology, 38,* 569–578.

Kahneman, D. (2003). A perspective on judgment and choice: Mapping bounded rationality. *American Psychologist, 58,* 697–720.

Karpinski, A., & Hilton, J. L. (2001). Attitudes and the implicit association test. *Journal of Personality and Social Psychology, 81,* 774–788.

Katz, D. (1960). The functional approach to the study of attitudes. *Public Opinion Quarterly, 24,* 163–204.

Katz, I., & Hass, R. G. (1988). Racial ambivalence and American value conflict: Correlational and priming studies of dual cognitive structures. *Journal of Personality and Social Psychology, 55,* 893–905.

Kawakami, K., & Dovidio, J. F. (2001). Implicit stereotyping: How reliable is it? *Personality and Social Psychology Bulletin, 27,* 212–225.

Kawakami, K., Dovidio, J. F., Moll, J., Hermsen, S., & Russin, A. (2000). Just say no (to stereotyping): Effects of training in the negation of stereotypic associations on stereotype activation. *Journal of Personality and Social Psychology, 78,* 871–888.

Klauer, K. C., & Musch, J. (2003). Affective priming: Findings and theories. In K. C. Klauer & J. Musch (Eds.), *The psychology of evaluation: Affective processes in cognition and emotion* (pp. 7–50). Mahwah, NJ: Erlbaum.

Klauer, K. C., & Stern, E. (1992). How evaluations guide memory-based judgments: A two-process model. *Journal of Experimental Social Psychology, 28,* 186–206.

Klinger, M. R., Burton, P. C., & Pitts, G. S. (2000). Mechanisms of unconscious priming: I. Response competition, not spreading activation. *Journal of Experimental Psychology: Learning, Memory, and Cognition, 26,* 441–455.

Koole, S. K., Dijksterhuis, A., & van Knippenberg, A. (2001). What's in a name: Implicit self-esteem. *Journal of Personality and Social Psychology, 80,* 614–627.

Krosnick, J. A., Judd, C. M., & Wittenbrink, B. (2005). The measurement of attitudes. In D. Albarracín, B. T. Johnson & M. P. Zanna (Eds.), *The handbook of attitudes* (pp. 21–76). Mahwah, NJ: Erlbaum.

Krosnick, J. A., & Petty, R. E. (1995). Attitude strength: An overview. In R. E. Petty and J. A. Krosnick (Eds.), *Attitude strength: Antecedents and consequences.* Hillsdale, NJ: Erlbaum.

Kruglanski, A. W., & Klar, Y. (1987). A view from a bridge: Synthesizing the consistency and attribution paradigms from a lay epistemic perspective. *European Journal of Social Psychology, 17,* 211–241.

Kunda, Z. (1999). *Social cognition.* Cambridge, MA: MIT Press.

Lambert, A., J., Payne, B. K., Ramsey, S., & Shaffer, L. M. (2005). On the predictive validity of implicit attitude measures: The moderating effect of perceived group variability. *Journal of Experimental Social Psychology, 41,* 114–128.

Lang, P. J., Bradley, M. M., & Cuthbert, B. N. (1990) Emotion, attention, and the startle reflex. *Psychological Review, 97,* 377–395.

LaPiere, R. T. (1934). Attitudes vs. actions. *Social Forces, 13,* 230–237.

Larsen, J. T., McGraw, P., & Cacioppo, J. T. (2001). Can people feel happy and sad at the same time? *Journal of Personality and Social Psychology, 81,* 684–696.

LeDoux, J. (1996). *The emotional brain*. New York: Touchstone.

LeDoux, J. E. (2000) Emotion circuits in the brain. *Annual Review Neuroscience, 23*, 155–184.

Levey, A. B., & Martin, I. (1975). Classical conditioning of human "evaluative" responses. *Behaviour Research and Therapy, 13*, 221–226.

Lewin, K. (1935). *A dynamic theory of personality*. New York: McGraw-Hill.

Liberzon, I., Phan, K. L., Decker, L. R., & Taylor, S. F. (2003). Extended amygdala and emotional salience: A PET investigation of positive and negative affect. *Neuropsychopharmacology, 28*, 726–733.

Lieberman, M. D., Gaunt, R., Gilbert, D. T., & Trope, Y. (2002). Reflection and reflexion: A social cognitive neuroscience approach to attributional inference. *Advances in Experimental Social Psychology, 34*, 199–249.

Lieberman, M. D., Ochsner, K. N., Gilbert, D. T., & Schacter, D. L. (2001). Do amnesics exhibit cognitive dissonance reduction? The role of explicit memory and attention in attitude change. *Psychological Science, 12*, 135–140.

Livingston, R. W., & Brewer, M. B. (2002). What are we really priming? Cue-based versus category-based processing of facial stimuli. *Journal of Personality and Social Psychology, 82*, 5–18.

Logan, G. D. (1980). Attention and automaticity in Stroop and priming tasks: Theory and data. *Cognitive Psychology, 12*, 523–553.

Lowery, B. S., Hardin, C. D., & Sinclair, S. (2001). Social influence on automatic racial prejudice. *Journal of Personality and Social Psychology, 81*, 842–855.

Maddux, W. W., Barden, J., Brewer, M. B., & Petty, R. E. (2005). Saying no to negativity: The effects of context and motivation to control prejudice on automatic evaluative responses. *Journal of Experimental Social Psychology, 41*, 19–35.

Marcus, G. F. (2001). *The algebraic mind: Integrating connectionism and cognitive science*. Cambridge, MA: MIT Press.

Marsh, K. L., Johnson, B. T., & Scott-Sheldon, L. A. J. (2001). Heart versus reason in condom use: Implicit versus explicit attitudinal predictors of sexual behavior. *Zeitschrift für Experimentelle Psychologie, 48*, 161–175.

Martin, L. L., & Clore, G. L. (2001). *Theories of mood and cognition: A user's guidebook*. Mahwah, NJ: Erlbaum.

Martin, I., & Levey, A. B. (1978). Evaluative conditioning. *Advances in Behaviour Research and Therapy, 1*, 57–102.

Masson, M. E. J. (1991). A distributed memory model of context effects in word identfication. In D. Besner, & G. W. Humphreys (Eds.), *Basic processes in reading* (pp. 233–263). Hillsdale, NJ: Erlbaum.

Masson, M. E. J. (1995). A distributed memory model of semantic priming. *Journal of Experimental Psychology: Learning, Memory, and Cognition, 21*(1), 3–23.

McConahay, J. (1986). Modern racism, ambivalence, and the Modern Racism scale. In J. Dovidio (Ed.), *Prejudice, discrimination, and racism* (pp. 91–125). San Diego, CA: Academic Press.

McConnell, A. R., & Leibold, J. M. (2001). Relations among the Implicit Association Test, discriminatory behavior, and explicit measures of racial attitudes. *Journal of Experimental Social Psychology, 37*, 435–442.

McGuire, W. J. (1969). The nature of attitudes and attitude change. In G. Lindzey & E. Aronson (Eds.), *Handbook of social psychology* (2nd ed., Vol. 3, pp. 136–314). Reading, MA: Addison-Wesley.

McGuire, W. J. (1985). Attitudes and attitude change. In G. Lindzey & E. Aronson (Eds.),

Handbook of social psychology (3rd ed., Vol. 2, pp. 233–346). New York: Random House.

Meyer, D. E., & Schvaneveldt, R. W. (1971). Facilitation in recognizing pairs of words: Evidence of a dependence between retrieval operations. *Journal of Experimental Psychology, 90*, 227–234.

Mierke, J., & Klauer, K. C. (2003). Method-specific variance in the Implicit Association Test. *Journal of Personality and Social Psychology, 85*, 1180–1192.

Mitchell, J. P., Nosek, B. A., & Banaji, M. R. (2003). Contextual variations in implicit evaluation. *Journal of Experimental Psychology: General, 132*, 455–469.

Monin, B. (2003). The warm glow heuristic: When liking leads to familiarity. *Journal of Personality and Social Psychology, 85*(6), 1035–1048.

Moors, A., & De Houwer, J. (2001). Automatic appraisal of motivational valence: Motivational affective priming and Simon effects. *Cognition and Emotion, 15*, 749–766.

Moors, A., De Houwer, J., & Eelen, P. (2004). Automatic stimulus-goal comparisons: Evidence from motivational affective priming studies. *Cognition and Emotion, 18*, 29–54.

Morris, J. S., Öhman, A., & Dolan, R. J. 1998. Conscious and unconscious emotional learning in the human amygdala. *Nature, 393*, 467–470.

Moskowitz, G. B. (2005). *Social cognition: Understanding self and others.* New York: Guilford Press.

Moskowitz, G. B., Gollwitzer, P. M., Wasel, W., & Schaal, B. (1999). Preconscious control of stereotype activation through chronic egalitarian goals. *Journal of Personality and Social Psychology, 77*, 167–184.

Murphy, S. T., & Zajonc, R. B. (1993). Affect, cognition, and awareness: Affective priming with suboptimal and optimal stimuli. *Journal of Personality and Social Psychology, 64*, 723–739.

Musch, J., & Klauer, K. C. (2003). *The psychology of evaluation: Affective processes in cognition and emotion.* Mahwah, NJ: Erlbaum.

Myers, D. G. (1993). *Social psychology* (4th ed). Columbus, OH: McGraw-Hill.

Neely, J. H. (1976). Semantic priming and retrieval from lexical memory: Evidence for faciliatory and inhibitory processes. *Memory and Cognition, 4*, 648–654.

Neely, J. H. (1977). Semantic priming and retrieval from lexical memory: Roles of inhibitionless spreading activation and limited-capacity attention. *Journal of Experimental Psychology: General, 106*, 225–254.

Niedenthal, P. M. (1990). Implicit perception of affective information. *Journal of Experimental Social Psychology, 26*, 505–527.

Nisbett, R., & Wilson, T. (1977). Telling more than we can know: Verbal reports on mental processes. *Psychological Review, 84*, 231–259.

Nosek, B. A. (2005). Moderators of the relationship between implicit and explicit evaluation. *Journal of Experimental Psychology: General, 134*, 565–584.

Nosek, B. A., & Banaji, M. R. (2001). The go/no-go association task. *Social Cognition, 19*(6), 625–666.

Nosek, B. A., Banaji, M. R., & Greenwald, A. G. (2002). Math=Me, Me=Female, therefore Math is not equal to me. *Journal of Personality and Social Psychology, 83*, 44–59.

Nosek, B. A., Greenwald, A. G., & Banaji, M. R. (2005). Understanding and using the Implicit Association Test: II. Method variables and construct validity. *Personality and Social Psychology Bulletin, 31*, 166–180.

Öhman, A. (1986). Face the beast and fear the face: Animal and social fears as prototypes for evolutionary analysis of emotion. *Psychophysiology, 23*, 123–145.

Olson, M. A., & Fazio, R. H. (2001). Implicit attitude formation through classical conditioning. *Psychological Science, 12*, 413–417.

Olson, M. A., & Fazio, R. H. (2004). Reducing the influence of extra-personal associations on the Implicit Association Test: Personalizing the IAT. *Journal of Personality and Social Psychology, 86*, 653–667.

Ortony, A., Clore, G. L., & Collins, A. (1988). *The cognitive structure of emotions*. Cambridge, UK: Cambridge University Press.

Osgood, C. E., Suci, G. J., & Tannenbaum, P. H. (1957). *The measurement of meaning*. Chicago: University of Illinois Press.

Payne, B. K. (2001). Prejudice and perception: The role of automatic and controlled processes in misperceiving a weapon. *Journal of Personality and Social Psychology, 81*, 181–192.

Payne, B. K., Cheng, C. M., Govorun, O., & Stewart, B. (2005). An inkblot for attitudes: Affect misattribution as implicit measurement. *Journal of Personality and Social Psychology, 89*, 277–293.

Payne, B. K., Jacoby, L. L., & Lambert, A. J. (2005). Attitudes as accessibility bias: Dissociating automatic and controlled processes. In R. R. Hassin, J. S. Uleman & J. A. Bargh (Eds.), *The new unconscious* (pp. 393–420). New York: Oxford University Press.

Petty, R. E., & Krosnick, J. A. (1995). *Attitude strength: Antecedents and consequences*. Hillsdale, NJ: Erlbaum.

Phelps, E. A., O'Connor, K. J., Cunningham, W. A., Funayama, E. S., Gatenby, J. C., Gore, J. C., & Banaji, M. R. (2000). Performance on indirect measures of race evaluation predicts amygdala activation. *Journal of Cognitive Neuroscience, 12*, 729–738.

Phelps, E. A., O'Connor, K. J., Gatenby, J. C., Grillon, C., Gore, J. C. & Davis, M. (2001). Activation of the human amygdala to a cognitive representation of fear. *Nature Neuroscience, 4*, 437–441.

Pinker, S. (1997). *How the mind works*. New York: W. W. Norton.

Plant, E. A., & Devine, P. G. (1998). Internal and external motivation to respond without prejudice. *Journal of Personality and Social Psychology, 75*, 811–832.

Plotkin, H. (1997). *Evolution in mind*. London: Allen Lane, Penguin, UK.

Posner, M. I., & Snyder, C. R. R. (1975). Attention and cognitive control. In R. L. Solso (Ed.), *Information processing and cognition: The Loyola symposium* (pp. 55–85). Hillsdale, NJ: Erlbaum.

Pratkanis, A. R. (1989). The cognitive representation of attitudes. In A. R. Pratkanis, S. J. Breckler, & A. G. Greenwald (Eds.), *Attitude structure and function* (pp. 71–98). Hillsdale, NJ: Erlbaum.

Pratkanis, A. R., Breckler, S. J., & Greenwald, A. G. (1989). *Attitude structure and function*. Hillsdale, NJ: Erlbaum.

Quillian, M. R. (1968). Semantic memory. In M. Minsky (Ed.), *Semantic information processing* (pp. 216–270). Cambridge, MA: MIT Press.

Roediger, H. L. (1990). Implicit memory: Retention without remembering. *American Psychologist, 45*(9), 1043–1056.

Rosenberg, M. J. (1956). Cognitive structure and attitudinal affect. *Journal of Abnormal and Social Psychology, 53*, 367–372.

Roskos-Ewoldsen, D. R., & Fazio, R. H. (1992). On the orienting value of attitudes: Attitude accessibility as a determinant of an object's attraction of visual attention. *Journal of Personality and Social Psychology, 63*, 198–211.

Rudman, L. A., Ashmore, R. D., & Gary, M. L. (2001). "Unlearning" automatic biases: The malleability of implicit stereotypes and prejudice. *Journal of Personality and Social Psychology, 81*, 856–868.

Salancik, G. R., & Conway, M. (1975). Attitude inferences from salient and relevant cognitive content about behavior. *Journal of Personality and Social Psychology*, *32*, 829–840.

Sarnoff, I. (1960). Psychoanalytic theory and social attitudes. *Public Opinion Quarterly*, *24*, 251–279.

Schank, R. C., & Abelson, R. P. (1977). *Scripts, plans, goals, and understanding: An inquiry into human knowledge structures.* Hillsdale, NJ: Erlbaum.

Schneider, W., & Fisk, A. D. (1982). Degree of consistent training: Improvements in search performance and automatic process development. *Perception and Psychophysics*, *31*, 160–168.

Schuman, H., & Johnson, M. P. (1976). Attitudes and behavior. *Annual Review of Sociology*, *2*, 161–207.

Schwarz, N., & Bohner, G. (2001). The construction of attitudes. In A. Tesser & N. Schwarz (Eds.), *Blackwell handbook of social psychology: Intraindividual processes* (Vol. 1, pp. 436–457). Oxford, UK: Blackwell.

Sherman, J. W. (in press). On building a better process model: It's not only how many, but which ones and by which means. *Psychological Inquiry.*

Sherman, J. W. (2005). Automatic and controlled components of implicit stereotyping and prejudice. *Psychological Science Agenda*, *19*(3), Fazio & P. Brinol (Eds.), *Attitudes: Insights from the new wave of implicit measures.*

Sherman, S. J., Presson, C. C., Chassin, L., Rose, J. S., & Koch, K. (2003). Implicit and explicit attitudes toward cigarette smoking: The effects of context and motivation. *Journal of Social and Clinical Psychology*, *22*, 13–39.

Shiffrin, R. M., & Dumais, S. T. (1981). The development of automatism. In J. R. Anderson (Ed.), *Cognitive skills and their acquisition* (pp. 111–140). Hillsdale, NJ: Erlbaum.

Shiffrin, R. M., & Schneider, W. (1977). Controlled and automatic human information processing: II. Perceptual learning, automatic attending, and a general theory. *Psychological Review*, *84*, 127–190.

Sloman, S. A. (1996). The empirical case for two systems of reasoning. *Psychological Bulletin*, *119*, 3–22.

Smith, E. R. (1992). The role of exemplars in social judgment. In L. L. Martin and A. Tesser (Eds.), *The construction of social judgment* (pp. 107–132). Hillsdale, NJ: Erlbaum.

Smith, E. R. (1996). What do connectionism and social psychology offer each other? *Journal of Personality and Social Psychology*, *70*, 893–912.

Smith, E. R. (1997). Preconscious automaticity in a modular connectionist system. In R. S. Wyer (Ed.), *Advances in social cognition* (Vol. 10, pp. 181–202). Mahway, NJ: Erlbaum.

Smith, E. R. (2000, February). Connectionist representation of evaluation. Paper presented at the meeting of the *Society for Personality and Social Psychology*, Nashville, TN.

Smith, E. R., & DeCoster, J. (1999). Associative and rule-based processing: A connectionist interpretation of dual-process models. In S. Chaiken, & Y. Trope (Eds.), *Dual-process theories in social psychology* (pp. 323–336). New York: Guilford Press.

Smith, E. R., Fazio, R. H., & Cejka, M. A. (1996). Accessible evaluations influence categorization of multiply categorizable objects. *Journal of Personality and Social Psychology*, *71*, 888–898.

Smith, E. R., & Lerner, M. (1986). Development of automatism of social judgments. *Journal of Personality and Social Psychology*, *50*, 246–259.

Smith, E. R., & Zarate, M. A. (1992). Exemplar-based model of social judgment. *Psychological Review*, *99*, 3–21.

Smith, M. B., Bruner, J. S., & White, R. W. (1956). *Opinions and personality*. New York: Wiley.

Smolensky, P. (1989). Connectionist modeling: Neural computation/mental connections. In L. Nadel (Ed.), P. Culicover, L. A. Cooper & R. M. Harnish (Assoc. Eds.), *Neural connections, mental computation* (pp. 49–67). Cambridge, MA: MIT Press/Bradford.

Squire, L. R. (1992). Memory and the hippocampus: A synthesis from findings with rats, monkeys, and humans. *Psychological Review, 99*, 195–231.

Squire, L. R., & Kandel, E. R. (1999). *Memory: From mind to molecules*. New York: Scientific American Library.

Srull, T. K. (1981). Person memory: Some tests of associative storage and retrieval models. *Journal of Experimental Psychology: Human Learning and Memory, 7*, 440–463.

Srull, T. K. (1983). The role of prior knowledge in the acquisition, retention, and use of new information. In R. P. Bagozzi & A. M. Tybout (Eds.), *Advances in consumer research* (Vol 10, pp. 572–576). Ann Arbor, MI: Association for Consumer Research.

Stapel, D. A., & Koomen, W. (2000). How far do we go beyond the information given?: The impact of knowledge activation on interpretation and inference. *Journal of Personality and Social Psychology, 78*, 19–37.

Stapel, D. A., Koomen, W., & Ruijs, K. (2002). The effects of diffuse and distinct affect. *Journal of Personality and Social Psychology, 83*, 60–74.

Strack, F., & Deutsch, R. (2004). Reflection and impulse as determinants of "conscious" and "unconscious" motivation. In J. P. Forgas, K. Williams, & S. Laham (Eds.), *Social motivation: Conscious and unconscious processes*. Cambridge, UK: Cambridge University Press.

Swanson, J. E., Rudman, L. A., & Greenwald, A. G. (2001). Using the Implicit Association Test to investigate attitude–behaviour consistency for stigmatised behaviour. *Cognition and Emotion, 15*, 207–230.

Tesser, A. (1978). Self-generated attitude change. In L. Berkowitz (Ed.), *Advances in experimental social psychology* (Vol. 11, pp. 289–338). New York: Academic Press.

Tesser, A., & Martin, L. (1996). The psychology of evaluation. In E. T. Higgins, & A. W. Kruglanski (Eds). *Social psychology: Handbook of basic principles* (pp. 400–432). New York: Guilford Press.

Thurstone, L. L. (1928). Attitudes can be measured. *American Journal of Sociology, 33*, 529–554.

Thurstone, L. L. (1931). Measurement of social attitudes. *Journal of Abnormal and Social Psychology, 26*, 249–269.

Tulving, E., & Craik, F. I. M. (2000). *Handbook of memory*. Oxford: Oxford University Press.

von Hippel, W., Sekaquaptewa, D., & Vargas, P. (1995). On the role of encoding processes in stereotype maintenance. *Advances in Experimental Social Psychology, 27*, 177–254.

Walther, E. (2002). Guilty by mere association: Evaluative conditioning and the spreading evaluation effect. *Journal of Personality and Social Psychology, 82*, 919–924.

Walther, E., Nagengast, B., & Trasselli, C. (2005). Evaluative conditioning in social psychology: Facts and speculations. *Cognition and Emotion, 19*, 175–196.

Wentura, D. (1999). Activation and inhibition of affective information: Evidence for negative priming in the evaluation task. *Cognition and Emotion, 13*, 65–91.

Wentura, D. (2000). Dissociative affective and associative priming effects in the lexical decision task: *Yes* versus *no* responses to word targets reveal evaluative judgmental tendencies. *Journal of Experimental Psychology: Learning, Memory, and Cognition, 26,* 456–469.

Wentura, D., Rothermund, K., & Bak, P. (2000). Automatic vigilance: The attention grabbing power of approach- and avoidance-related social information. *Journal of Personality and Social Psychology, 78,* 1024–1037.

Wicker, A. W. (1969). Attitude versus actions: The relationship of verbal and overt behavioral responses to attitude objects. *Journal of Social Issues, 25*(4), 41–78.

Wilson, T. D., & Hodges, S. D. (1992). Attitudes as temporary constructions. In A. Tesser & L. Martin (Eds.), *The construction of social judgment* (pp. 37–65). Hillsdale, NJ: Erlbaum.

Wilson, T. D., Lindsey, S., & Schooler, T. Y. (2000). A model of dual attitudes. *Psychological Review, 107,* 101–126.

Wittenbrink, B., Judd, C. M., & Park, B. (1997). Evidence for racial prejudice at the implicit level and its relationship with questionnaire measures. *Journal of Personality and Social Psychology, 72,* 262–274.

Wittenbrink, B., Judd, C. M., & Park, B. (2001). Spontaneous prejudice in context: Variability in automatically activated attitudes. *Journal of Personality and Social Psychology, 81,* 815–827.

Zajonc, R. B. (1980). Feeling and thinking. Preferences need no inferences. *American Psychologist, 35,* 151–175.

Zajonc, R. (2001). Mere exposure: A gateway to the subliminal. *Current Directions in Psychological Science, 10,* 224–228.

Zald, D. H. (2003). The human amygdala and the emotional evaluation of sensory stimuli. *Brain Research Reviews, 41,* 88–123.

Zald, D. H., & Pardo, J. V. (1997). Olfaction, emotion and the human amygdala: Amygdala activation during aversive olfactory stimulation. *Proceedings of the National Academy of Sciences, 94,* 4119–4124.

Zaller, J. (1992). *The nature and origins of mass opinion.* Cambridge, UK: Cambridge University.

6

The Implicit Association Test at Age 7: A Methodological and Conceptual Review

BRIAN A. NOSEK, ANTHONY G. GREENWALD, and
MAHZARIN R. BANAJI

*A*mong earthly organisms, humans have a unique propensity to introspect or look inward into the contents of their own minds, and to share those observations with others. With the ability to introspect comes the palpable feeling of "knowing," of being objective or certain, of being mentally in control of one's thoughts, aware of the causes of one's thoughts, feelings, and actions, and of making decisions deliberately and rationally. Among the noteworthy discoveries of 20th century psychology was a challenge posed to this assumption of rationality. From the groundbreaking theorizing of Herbert Simon (1955) and the mind-boggling problems posed by Kahneman, Slovik, and Tversky (1982) to striking demonstrations of illusions of control (Wegner, 2002), the paucity of introspection (Nisbett and Wilson, 1977), and the automaticity of everyday thought (Bargh, 1997), psychologists have shown the frailties of the minds of their species.

As psychologists have come to grips with the limits of the mind, there has been an increased interest in measuring aspects of thinking and feeling that may not be easily accessed or available to consciousness. Innovations in measurement have been undertaken with the purpose of bringing under scrutiny new forms of cognition and emotion that were previously undiscovered and especially by asking if traditional concepts such as attitude and preference, belief and stereotype, self-concept and self-esteem can be rethought based on what the new measures reveal.

These newer measures do not require introspection on the part of the subject. For many constructs this is considered a valuable, if not essential, feature of measurement; for others, avoiding introspection is greeted with suspicion and skepticism. For example, one approach to measuring math ability would be to ask "how good are you at math?" whereas an alternative approach is to infer math ability via a performance on a math skills test. The former requires introspection to assess the relevant construct, the latter does not. And yet, the latter is accepted as a measure of math ability, and is even preferred to one requiring self-assessment.

When the target construct concerns a preference, stereotype, or identity rather than performance, issues about interpretation turn out to be more complex than those involving performance, such as on tests of ability (memory, concept formation) where there is an assumed correct answer. For some, the dismissal of introspection as relevant to the assessment of such constructs is difficult. Attitudes, stereotypes, and identity appear to be wound so tightly to subjective thoughts and feelings that "asking" seems to be the most persuasive of probes. "I know how I feel" and "Don't tell me how I feel" are not just expressions in inter-personal communication – they are assumed by psychologists who accept such an epistemological stance.

In the last few years, one measure in particular, the Implicit Association Test (IAT), has spurred discussion among both experts and nonexperts – about its mechanisms, scope, interpretation, and political implications. In this chapter, we review the main issues that are debated and provide our best assessment of its current status.

Implicit Cognition Building on the implicit–explicit distinction in memory (Roediger, 1990; Schacter, Bowers, & Booker, 1989), Greenwald and Banaji proposed a general distinction for implicit cognition. They defined an implicit construct as "the introspectively unidentified (or inaccurately identified) trace of past experience that mediates R" where R refers to the category of responses that are assumed to be influenced by that construct (Greenwald & Banaji, 1995, p. 5). Greenwald and Banaji applied that general definition to social psychology's most central constructs – attitudes, stereotypes, and self-esteem. They noted that implicit cognition could reveal associative information that people were either unwilling or unable to report. In other words, implicit cognition could reveal traces of past experience that people might explicitly reject because it conflicts with values or beliefs, or might avoid revealing because the expression could have negative social consequences. Even more likely, implicit cognition can reveal information that is not available to introspective access even if people were motiv-ated to retrieve and express it (see Wilson, Lindsey, & Schooler, 2000, for a similar theoretical distinction for the attitude construct specifically). Such information is simply unreachable in the same way that memories are sometimes unreachable, not just in amnesic patients but in every person.

For many constructs such as memory, attitudes, stereotypes, self-concept, self-esteem, personality, and knowledge, the implicit–explicit taxonomy has not just helped to organize existing theory and empirical evidence, but has also broadened the construct beyond introspective limits. For example, while few definitions of attitude mentioned introspective access as a necessary feature, until the 1980s attitude measurement largely proceeded as if the very definition of attitude relied on an assumption that attitudes were consciously available (Greenwald & Banaji, 1995).

Implicit Measurement   Whatever the value of the implicit–explicit distinction, in practice the distinction has been rather loosely applied to organize a heterogeneous set of assumed cognitive mechanisms. The term *implicit* has come to be applied to measurement methods that avoid requiring introspective access, decrease the mental control available to produce the response, reduce the role of conscious intention, and reduce the role of self-reflective, deliberative processes. The next generation of research in implicit cognition will likely revise the simple implicit–explicit distinction and introduce a more refined taxonomy that better reflects the heterogeneity of cognitive processes that are collectively termed *implicit*. In this chapter, we do not tackle these issues. Instead, we spotlight a particular method and summarize the evidence for its reliability, validity, interpretation, and proper use.

The Implicit Association Test (IAT)   The focus of this review is on the Implicit Association Test (IAT; Greenwald, McGhee, & Schwartz, 1998). In the seven years since its initial publication, the IAT has been applied in a diverse array of disciplines including social and cognitive psychology (Fazio & Olson, 2003; Greenwald & Nosek, 2001), clinical psychology (de Jong, Pasman, Kindt, & van den Hout, 2001; Teachman, Gregg, & Woody, 2001), developmental psychology (Baron & Banaji, 2006; Dunham, Baron, & Banaji, in press), neuroscience (Cunningham, Johnson, Raye, Gatenby, Gore, & Banaji, 2004; Phelps et al., 2000; Richeson et al., 2003), market research (Maison, Greenwald, & Bruin, 2001), and health psychology (Teachman, Gapinski, Brownell, Rawlins, & Jeyaram, S., 2003). The wide range of application provides an ample research literature from which to review the features, strengths, and limitations of the IAT for continued research of implicit cognition. The present review can be seen as an "age 7" follow-up to Greenwald and Nosek's (2001) review of the IAT "at age 3" with added attention to general issues of interpretation and application of this tool for scientific research.

The IAT is a method for indirectly measuring the strengths of associations among concepts. The task requires sorting of stimulus exemplars from four concepts using just two response options, each of which is assigned to two of the four concepts. The logic of the IAT is that this sorting task should be easier when the two concepts that share a response are strongly associated than when they are weakly associated.

Table 6.1 presents a schematic describing a typical IAT design for the assessment of association strengths between categories of *men* and *women* and attributes of *good* and *bad*. The IAT consists of seven phases, some of which are practice tasks to acquaint subjects with the stimulus materials and sorting rules. The critical phases of the IAT involve simultaneous sorting of stimulus items representing four concepts (*men, women, good, bad*) with two response options. In one critical phase (B3 and B4 in the example), items representing *men* and *good* (e.g., male faces and words such as wonderful, glorious) receive one response, and items representing the concepts *women* and *bad* (e.g., female faces and words such as terrible, horrible) receive the alternative response. In the second critical phase (B6 and B7 in the example), items representing the concepts *women* and *good* are sorted with one response, and items representing the concepts *men* and *bad*

TABLE 6.1   Sequence of Blocks in the Implicit Association Test (IAT) Measuring Gender Evaluations

Block	No. of trials	Items assigned to left-key response	Items assigned to right-key response
B1	20	Faces of females	Faces of males
B2	20	Pleasant words	Unpleasant words
B3	20	Female faces + Pleasant words	Male faces + Unpleasant words
B4	40	Female faces + Pleasant words	Male faces + Unpleasant words
B5	40	Faces of males	Faces of females
B6	20	Male faces + Pleasant words	Female faces + Unpleasant words
B7	40	Male faces + Pleasant words	Female faces + Unpleasant words

Notes: A trial is defined as the time from the onset of a single stimulus to the correct categorization of that stimulus. Trials in which an error is made require the participant to correct the error before proceeding. Blocks B3, B4, B6, and B7 alternate trials presenting a pleasant or unpleasant word with trials presenting a male or female face. If all of the stimuli were from the same modality (e.g., words), then items and labels from one response dimension (men/women) would be presented in a distinct font (color or type) from the items and labels from the other dimension (pleasant/unpleasant). In most IAT applications, the sorting rules in blocks B1, B3, B4 are counterbalanced with B5, B6, B7 between subjects.

are sorted with the alternative response. For subjects who possess stronger associations of positive evaluation with females compared to males, the second sorting task should be much easier than the first. Likewise, subjects who possess stronger associations of positive evaluation with males compared to females should find the first sorting task to be easier than the second. Ease of sorting can be indexed both by the speed of responding (faster responding indicating stronger associations) and the frequency of errors (fewer errors indicating stronger associations).

In this chapter, we describe the IAT's procedural details, along with evidence for its validity as a measure of association strengths. Also, a variety of threats to validity are identified and correctives are suggested. Finally, we review some of the critical issues concerning the interpretation of IAT effects and some reflections on proper use of its potential applications.

INTERNAL VALIDITY

This section reviews issues concerning the internal validity of the IAT, including: the selection and design of stimulus materials such as category labels and exemplars, procedural features such as the order and length of response blocks, a review of the known extraneous influences on the IAT and potential correctives for those influences if they are available, suggested analytic procedures for the IAT, a review of evidence for the IAT's internal consistency and test–retest reliability, and a review of evidence concerning the fakeability of IAT performance.

Materials

The critical materials of an IAT are four categories defined by category labels (e.g., *men, women, good, bad*) and stimulus items that serve as exemplars for those categories (e.g., male and female faces, and words with good or bad meaning). In most IAT designs, the four categories represent two contrasted pairs, sometimes distinguished as target concepts (e.g., *men–women*) and attribute (e.g., *good–bad*) dimensions.[1] The two dimensions usually define the two nominal features that are of direct interest and create the contrasting identification tasks – e.g., "what is the gender?" for category items, and "what is the evaluation?" for attribute items (Greenwald, Nosek, Banaji, & Klauer, 2005). The IAT effect is a comparative measure of the combined association strengths of two associative pairs (*men* with *good, women* with *bad*) contrasted with strengths of two other associative pairs (*men* with *bad, women* with *good*). In the present case, the resulting score has a relatively simple interpretation as an implicit measure of relative preference for men compared to women.

Design of an IAT requires selecting category labels that define the concepts of interest and stimulus items to represent those concepts. There are some important factors to consider in the selection of these materials.

Ensure that the Category Membership of Stimulus Items is Clear and Used for Categorization
The subjects' primary task in the IAT is to identify the category membership of stimulus items as quickly as possible. Each stimulus item must be identifiable as representing just one of the four categories, e.g., *men* or *women* for gender, and *good* or *bad* for evaluation. If the category membership of a stimulus item is difficult to identify or confounded with multiple categories, then subjects may be unable to categorize accurately, or may attempt to complete the task with sorting rules different from those intended for the design.

Task confusion can be reduced by providing multiple cues for identifying the relevant nominal feature of any given stimulus item, so that items clearly represent one and only one of the four categories. For example, confounds between dimensions should be avoided (Steffens & Plewe, 2001). In the current example, using "gendered" *good* and *bad* items such as "nurturing" and "aggressive" could introduce confusion about whether to categorize the items on the basis of gender or evaluation. Also, the distinctiveness of nominal dimensions is enhanced if different stimulus modalities are used, such as faces for gender and words for evaluation, or by using distinct colors or fonts such as gender words in green and evaluation words in white. Finally, strictly alternating response trials between nominal dimensions creates a predictable pattern for the switching between the relevant feature judgments. As an added benefit, alternating trials maximizes task switches, which appear to be important contributors to IAT effects (Klauer & Mierke, 2005).

Another important aspect of exemplar selection is to ensure that stimulus items are categorized on the basis of the intended nominal feature rather than an irrelevant stimulus feature. In other words, it should be difficult to distinguish the two categories of a single nominal dimension (e.g., men or women) using any characteristic except the nominal feature (gender). If the categories *men* and *women* were comprised of Black male and White female faces respectively, category membership would be clear, but subjects could sort items based on race (irrelevant) or gender (relevant). Likewise, if all of the *good* words were more than 10 letters and the *bad* words were less than 5, subjects could sort them based on evaluative meaning or length.

Other Stimulus Characteristics   Stimulus items can be presented as words, pictures, sounds, or in a combination of modalities. Generating stimulus items requires balancing the competing demands of creating an accurate representation of the superordinate category, and avoiding exemplars that are only weakly representative of the category. Nosek, Greenwald, and Banaji (2005) observed that the magnitude and reliability of IAT effects were relatively unaffected by the number of stimulus items per category, except that effects were somewhat weaker when only a single exemplar per category was used. Stimulus sets should contain only items that clearly belong to the target category and, as a group, represent the intended category in a fashion appropriate for research purposes – for example, not representing a distinct subset of a category (e.g., fruit juices) when the larger category (e.g., soft drinks) is of interest.

Categories in the IAT are constructed as contrasting pairs (*men–women*, *good–bad*). The resulting IAT score is a relative measure of associations between categories (Greenwald et al., 1998). Whereas the IAT measures relative association strengths involving four categories (*men* with *good* and *women* with *bad* compared to *men* with *bad* and *women* with *good*), one might reasonably be interested in measuring the association of evaluations with men alone (*men* with *good* versus *men* with *bad*). However, as a relative measure, the IAT is not as useful for measuring associations toward single targets (Nosek et al., 2005). The relative measurement feature of the IAT constrains its proper application and interpretation. As a consequence, the selection of comparison categories is of critical importance in design. For research efforts in which single category assessments are of particular interest, a different measure of associations should be considered such as the Go/No-Go Association Task (Nosek & Banaji, 2001) or the Extrinsic Affective Simon Task (De Houwer, 2003).

Procedural Design

Greenwald, Nosek, and Banaji (2003) summarized a standard IAT procedure that requires rapid sorting of exemplars representing two concept categories (*men* and *women*) and two attribute categories (*good* and *bad*) into their nominal categories with a set of seven response blocks (see Table 6.1): (B1) 20 trials sorting the two target concepts with the same two keys – e.g., "males" with the "e" key, "females" with the "i" key; (B2) 20 trials sorting good and bad words using two response keys

– e.g., "good" words with the "e" key, "bad" words with the "i" key; (B3) 20 trials sorting items from all four categories with the same two keys alternating by trial between concept and attribute items – e.g., males and good with "e", females and bad with "i"; (B4) 40 trials with the same sorting rule as B3; (B5) 20 trials of sorting the concept categories with the reverse key mapping from B1 – i.e., "males" with "i" key and "females" with "e" key; (B6) 20 trials sorting items from all four categories with the opposite key pairings from B3 and B4 – i.e., females and good with "e" key, males and bad with "i" key; and (B7) 40 trials with same sorting rule as B6. Blocks B3, B4, B6, and B7 comprise the critical data of the task.

In most IAT studies, half of the sample completes the task in the order above, and the other half completes the task with B1, B3, B4 switched with B5, B6, B7. Nosek et al. (2005) proposed changing B5 to 40 response trials as a standard corrective for a persistent extraneous influence of task order (see next section). A comparison of average latency between the first combined sorting condition (B3, B4) and the second (B6, B7) is taken to reveal the relative association strengths between the concepts and attributes. In other words, participants who find it easier to sort men with good (and women with bad) compared to sorting men with bad (and women with good) are said to implicitly prefer males to females.

There are some additional procedural factors that are important and are applied across all response blocks. For each block, the category labels appear on the top left and right of the computer screen to remind participants of the response key mapping rules. When stimulus items are incorrectly categorized, an error indication appears (often a red "X" immediately below the stimulus item) and the subject is obliged to fix the error by hitting the correct response key before continuing to the next trial. The interval between occurrence of one trial's response and presentation of the following trial's stimulus – the intertrial interval (ITI) – is typically short, although usually not less than 150 ms. Greenwald et al. (1998) reported that use of longer ITIs (up to 750 ms) had no appreciable effect on IAT measures. A relatively short ITI (250 ms may be most often used) allows the measure to be obtained rapidly.

The IAT has been used with procedural variations, usually without any attempt to collect data to discriminate alternate versions. The virtues of the procedure as described here are that it has received very widespread use, achieves satisfactory reliability, and can be administered in just five minutes. Nevertheless, there may be circumstances in which it would be advantageous to alter these procedures. For example, extra practice blocks or trials may be essential for populations that are unfamiliar or unskilled with computers or speeded responding (e.g., the elderly or young children).

Extraneous Influences

Some procedural and person factors that have been shown to have little or no influence on IAT measures include: whether a particular category is assigned to the left or right response key (Greenwald et al., 1998), whether the response–stimulus interval (ITI) was as low as 150 milliseconds or as high as 750 milliseconds

(Greenwald et al., 1998), whether there is wide variation in the familiarity of stimulus items comprising the attitude object categories (Dasgupta, Greenwald, & Banaji, 2003; Dasgupta, McGhee, Greenwald, & Banaji, 2000; Ottaway, Hayden, & Oakes, 2001; Rudman, Greenwald, Mellot, & Schwartz, 1999), and whether subjects were right or left-handed (Greenwald & Nosek, 2001).

On the other hand, there are several extraneous influences that can obscure the measurement of association strengths with the IAT. Procedural and analytic innovations may reduce some of these undesired influences. The following paragraphs summarize the known extraneous influences on the IAT. Empirically identified correctives are offered where available.

Order of Combined Tasks   The influence of the order of combined tasks mentioned in the previous section is the most commonly observed extraneous factor (Greenwald & Nosek, 2001). Performance of the first combined pairing (B3, B4) tends to interfere with performance of the second (B6, B7). As a consequence, IAT effects are slightly biased toward indicating that the associations drawn upon in the first-performed combined task are stronger than those drawn upon in the second-performed task. Nosek et al. (2005) observed that using 40 response trials in B5 instead of 20 significantly reduced the influence of this extraneous factor. Consequently, increasing the number of trials in B5 is a recommended procedure. In addition, counterbalancing the task order helps to identify and enables statistical removal of the biasing effects of this influence.

Cognitive Fluency   Another extraneous influence is the individual difference in average response latency, or cognitive fluency. Subjects who perform the task more slowly overall tend to show larger IAT effects than those who perform more quickly (Greenwald et al., 2003; McFarland & Crouch, 2002). This is a common nuisance factor for response latency data. Greenwald and colleagues (2003) introduced a scoring algorithm (D) that, among other improvements, reduces the influence of this factor (see also Cai, Sriram, Greenwald, & McFarland, 2004). The scoring algorithm is introduced in the next section. Researchers may also introduce content-irrelevant response latency tasks to provide a cognitive fluency factor that could possibly be used as the basis for a covariance adjustment.

A particular form of cognitive fluency, task-switching ability, or the facility for switching between judgment tasks (e.g., gender or evaluation) has been extensively examined in the IAT (Mierke & Klauer, 2001, 2003). As with overall speed of responding, the D scoring algorithm appears to significantly reduce the extraneous influence of this factor (Back, Schmukle, & Egloff, 2005; Mierke & Klauer, 2003).

Subject Age   Perhaps related to effects of variations in cognitive fluency, older subjects tend to show larger IAT effects than younger subjects (Greenwald & Nosek, 2001; Hummert, Garstka, O'Brien, Greenwald, & Mellott, 2002), especially when the original scoring algorithm (Greenwald et al., 1998) is used. The improved scoring algorithm suggested by Greenwald and colleagues (2003) reduces this relationship between age and IAT scores.

Experience with the IAT   Effect magnitudes with the IAT tend to decline with repeated administrations (Greenwald & Nosek, 2001; Greenwald et al., 2003). The D scoring algorithm reduces the influence of this factor, but IAT experience should not be ignored either in designs that use multiple IATs in a single session or that use repeated IAT measures in longitudinal studies with multiple testing sessions. An additional corrective for such designs is to include a control IAT for comparison purposes that is not expected to change as a function of the manipulation or intervention (e.g., Teachman & Woody, 2003).

Order of Measures   It is possible that the order in which self-report and IAT measures are completed affects IAT performance as well as self-report. For example, performing self-report measures first may increase the accessibility of some cognition and affect subsequent IAT performance. Likewise, an IAT that reveals an unexpected association may influence ensuing self-report. The actual effects of task order are not fully understood, though the accumulated evidence suggests that effects in typical circumstances are minimal. In a meta-analysis of IAT studies, Hofmann, Gawronski, Gschwendner, Le, and Schmidt (2005) found no effect of order. And, in experimental manipulations of task order, little to no effect of task order was observed in large web-based samples reported by Nosek et al., 2005. Even so, it is reasonable to suppose that some manipulations of task order will influence IAT effects (see Nosek et al., 2005). A reasonable procedural guideline is to counterbalance order of IAT and self-report measures in the absence of reasons for using just a single order.

Analysis

Greenwald and colleagues (2003) evaluated a variety of candidate scoring algorithms on a wide range of psychometric criteria (sensitivity to known influences, correlations with parallel self-report measures, internal consistency, and resistance to extraneous procedural influences) on very large Internet samples. The best performing algorithm (D) strongly outperformed the conventional scoring procedures and was recommended by Greenwald and colleagues (2003). The D algorithm has since been shown to have additional psychometric benefits over the conventional scoring procedures (Back, et al., 2005; Cai, et al., 2004; Mierke & Klauer, 2003).

The algorithm recommended by Greenwald et al., (2003) has the following steps for IAT designs in which subjects must correct errant responses before continuing: (1) use data from Blocks 3, 4, 6, and 7 (see Table 6.1); (2) eliminate trials with latencies > 10,000 ms; (3) eliminate subjects for whom more than 10% of trials have latencies < 300 ms; (4) compute one standard deviation for all trials in Blocks 3 and 6, and another standard deviation for all trials in Blocks 4 and 7; (5) compute means for trials in each of the four blocks (Blocks 3, 4, 6, 7); (6) compute two difference scores (one between 3 and 6 and the other between 4 and 7), subtracting what is intended to represent the high (positive) end of the measure from the block containing associations representing the low end; (7) divide each difference score by its associated standard deviation from Step 4; and (8) average the two quotients from Step 7.[2]

Reliability

A persistent challenge for implicit measures is to achieve substantial internal consistency and test–retest reliability. For example, some evaluative priming measures show weak internal consistency (e.g., split-half $r = .06$, Olson & Fazio, 2003; see also Bosson, Swann, and Pennebaker, 2000; Fazio & Olson, 2003). Early variants of the Go/No-go Association Task (GNAT) show relatively weak reliability when its signal detection method variation is used (average split-half $r = .20$; Nosek & Banaji, 2001). In a direct comparison, the IAT outperformed the Extrinsic Affective Simon Task (EAST $\alpha = .19, .24, .19$; IAT $\alpha > .75$; Teige, Schnabel, Banse, & Asendorpf, 2004). Part of the IAT's acceptance as an implicit measure may be attributable to its achieving greater reliability than other latency-based implicit measures.

Internal Consistency The IAT has displayed satisfactory internal consistency, which is relatively rare for latency-based measures. For example, Bosson et al. (2000) observed a split-half internal consistency for the self-esteem IAT of $r = .69$ compared to r values of $-.05$ to $.28$ for other latency-based implicit self-esteem measures. Internal consistency estimates (split-half correlations or alphas) for the IAT measures tend to range from .7 to .9 (Greenwald & Nosek, 2001; Schmukle & Egloff, 2004).

Test–Retest Reliability Another form of measurement consistency is test–retest reliability – the consistency of measurement over time. High test–retest correlations should occur to the extent that the IAT is a trait measure rather than a state measure. If the IAT is state-dependent, then test–retest reliability may be low even when internal consistency estimates are high. Egloff, Schmukle, and colleagues have conducted the most thorough tests of internal consistency and test–retest reliability of IAT measures (Egloff, Schwerdtfeger, & Schmukle, 2005; Schmukle & Egloff, 2004, 2005). Figure 6.1 is based on a summary table of IAT test–retest studies contained in Schmukle and Egloff (2004) and including a few additional studies. The x-axis presents the time, in days, between two administrations of the IAT, and the y-axis is the correlation between the two tests. Across studies, the IAT shows stable test–retest reliability (median $r = .56$) that varies little with retest interval. Two qualifications of this conclusion are (1) only one study has examined test–retest reliability with more than a 1 month gap (1 year; Egloff et al., 2005); and (2) Figure 6.1 combines data from a variety of tasks (anxiety, racial attitudes, extroversion) – possible variation in test–retest reliability by content domain is undetermined (Schmukle & Egloff, 2005). Even so, the effect of time between tests on test–retest reliability is unaffected by the presence of the outlier study. Schmukle and Egloff (2004) concluded that the IAT has satisfactory test–retest reliability while also showing evidence of both trait-specific variation (an individual difference that is stable across time) and occasion-specific variation.

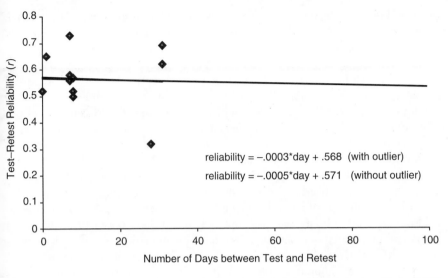

FIGURE 6.1   Test–retest reliability for the Implicit Association Test (IAT) by number of days between test and retest. Adapted from Egloff et al. (2005) with additional studies included. Data points represent Banse et al. (2001); Bosson et al. (2000); Cunningham et al. (2001); Dasgupta & Greenwald (2001); Egloff et al. (2005); Egloff & Schmukle (2002); Greenwald & Farnham (2000); Schmukle & Egloff (2004); and Steffens & Buchner (2003). Outlier data point appears at 379 days with an *r* of .47.

Fakeability

All psychological measures attempt to assess some aspect of mental content. This typically requires the willingness of the respondent to be assessed, and the honest efforts of the respondent to answer accurately or otherwise follow instructions. Direct measures make the meaning of the response plain, and allow the respondent to straightforwardly determine the response content. Indirect methods attempt to reduce the likelihood of deliberate faking by obscuring what is being measured, how it is being measured, or limiting the ability to control the response content. In this regard, implicit measures comprise a subset of indirect methods.

Investigations of IAT fakeability across multiple content domains, including shyness, extraversion, moral identity, attitudes toward flowers versus insects, attitudes toward sexual orientation, and attitudes toward racial groups, collectively suggest that the IAT is much less fakeable than self-report, the IAT is not very fakeable when subjects are given only abstract instructions to do so (e.g., "try not to appear shy"), and that two factors – experience with the IAT and explicit instructions about how to control IAT scores – increase fakeability (Asendorpf, Banse, & Mucke, 2002; Asendorpf, Banse, & Schnabel, 2006; Banse, Seise, & Zerbes, 2001; Egloff & Schmukle, 2002; Kim, 2003; Perugini & Leone, 2004; Steffens, 2004). Also, the IAT often reveals associations that subjects do not endorse, or would prefer not to reveal, suggesting that it is resistant to deliberate alteration in practice. For example, many White subjects show a consistent implicit preference for Black relative to White despite an explicit desire not to do so, and many Black subjects do not show an implicit preference for Black relative to White despite an explicit desire to do so (e.g., Nosek, Banaji, & Greenwald, 2002).

The fact that IAT measures are often only weakly correlated with self-reported attitudes suggests that deliberate faking may not be substantial under typical study conditions. Even so, this role of faking in IAT performance deserves further attention. Another fertile, but untapped question in this area is whether faking, when it does occur, can be empirically distinguished from honest task performance. It is possible that algorithms could be designed to distinguish actual from faked IAT data.

The issue of faking is related to the possibility that subjects could attempt to exert cognitive control in order to either suppress or overcome their automatic associations. This type of control may not be faking in the sense of trying to create a false impression (i.e., people may genuinely reject their automatically activated thoughts), but it suggests that cognitive control may mask automatic associations that are otherwise activated. In other words, response alternation in the IAT might occur by deliberate alteration of the task procedures, but may also occur through deliberate effort to alter one's mind. For example, Akalis and Banaji (2004) have shown that instructions to "think good thoughts" or "think compassionately" reduce bias toward overweight persons and in a novel group context. Conrey and colleagues have developed a promising multinomial model for parceling the various controlled and automatic cognitive processes that contribute to IAT effects (Conrey, Sherman, Gawronski, Hugenberg, & Groom, 2005). This modeling approach has the virtue of highlighting the fact that the IAT, like all tasks, is not process pure, and that the component processes involved in IAT effects such as automatic influences and efforts to overcome bias may be distinguishable through sophisticated experimental and statistical methods.

CONSTRUCT VALIDITY

This section reviews evidence for the construct validity of the IAT, focusing on the relationship between the IAT and other implicit measures, the relationship between the IAT and parallel self-report measures, the predictive validity of the IAT, evidence for independent variable influences on the IAT, and evidence concerning the development of IAT effects in children.

The Relationship between the IAT and Other Implicit Measures

The IAT is one of a diverse family of measures that are referred to as *implicit*. In one of the few investigations comparing multiple measures, Bosson, Swann, and Pennebaker (2000) observed weak relations among seven implicit measures of self-esteem, including the IAT (r values ranged from −.14 to .23). Also, a number of studies have compared the IAT with variations of evaluative priming and found weak relations (Bosson et al., 2000; Marsh, Johnson, & Scott-Sheldon, 2001; Olson & Fazio, 2003; Sherman, Presson, Chassin, Rose, & Koch, 2003).

There are two factors that appear to contribute to the observation of weak relations among implicit measures. First, implicit measures often demonstrate relatively weak reliability compared to other forms of psychological measurement. Reliability of measures set upper limits on their possible correlations with other measures. For example, the maximum, meaningful correlation that can be observed between a measure with reliability of .10 and a measure with perfect reliability (1.0) is .32, which is estimated by calculating the product of the square roots of the two reliability coefficients (Nunnally & Bernstein, 1994, p. 241). If the second measure's reliability is .50 instead of perfect, the maximum observable correlation is only .22. It is not uncommon for response-latency-based measures to show reliabilities well below .50. For example, Bosson and colleagues (2000) reported internal consistencies (α values) for the IAT, supraliminal priming, subliminal priming, and stroop of .88, −.16, .49, and −.38 respectively. Further, of the response latency methods, only the IAT showed test–retest reliability greater than r = .25 (IAT test–retest r = .69; Bosson et al., 2000). In sum, the relations among implicit measures (and between implicit measures and other variables) will be underestimated to the extent that they are unreliably assessed.

When unreliability is accounted for in models, stronger relations emerge. Cunningham, Preacher, and Banaji (2001) used structural equation modeling to estimate disattenuated correlations between implicit measures and observed correlations ranging from .53 to .77 between two versions of a racial attitude IAT and a response window evaluative priming measure. Also, Nosek and Banaji (2001) observed a disattenuated correlation of .55 between the IAT and the GNAT.

While some of this weak relationship among implicit measures is surely attributable to low reliability, the relations may also reflect heterogeneity of cognitive processes that contribute to the various measures. The term *implicit* has become widely applied to measurement methods for which subjects may be unaware of what is being measured, unaware of how it is being measured, or unable to control their performance on the measure. Identification of the cognitive processes that contribute to different measures will promote a more nuanced description and categorization of methods based on the particular processes that they engage.

Some research efforts have identified relevant differences in measurement methods to clarify the relations among implicit measures (e.g., Brauer, Wasel, & Niedenthal, 2000; Olson & Fazio, 2003). Olson and Fazio (2003), for example, commented on the fact that evaluative priming allows spontaneous categorization of target concepts (primes), while the IAT constrains concept categorization to a particular feature of the stimulus items (e.g., the race of face). In support of this spontaneous versus constrained process distinction, a variation of the priming measure that encouraged subjects to categorize primes in racial terms showed stronger correspondence with the IAT than did the more typical priming procedure.[3]

The Relationship between the IAT and Self-Report

Some of the first research efforts with the IAT emphasized the distinctiveness of implicit and explicit cognition in finding weak to absent relations between implicit measures, like the IAT, and self-report (Greenwald et al., 1998). More recent research has shown that, in some cases, the IAT and self-report can be strongly related (Greenwald et al., 2003; Hofmann et al., 2005; Nosek et al., 2002; Nosek, 2005). At the most extreme, a large Internet sample of data measuring preferences for Al Gore relative to George Bush revealed a disattenuated correlation of .86 with an explicit measure of candidate preference (Greenwald et al., 2003). In a meta-analysis of IAT and self-report correlations, Hofmann and colleagues (2005) reported an average r of .24, and in an investigation of 57 different content domains, Nosek (2005) reported an average correlation of .37 (when similar data were subjected to structural equation modeling, the disattenuated r was .46; Nosek & Smyth, in press).[4]

Convergent and Discriminant Validity

The realization that the IAT and self-report are related introduces important questions about whether they measure distinct constructs. In a multitrait-multimethod (MTMM) investigation of the IAT and self-report across seven attitude domains, Nosek and Smyth (in press) found strong evidence for both convergent and discriminant validity – IAT attitude measures were related to their corresponding self-report measure and not measures of other traits. Further, using structural equation modeling, this MTMM investigation revealed that the best-fitting models represented the IAT and self-report as related but distinct constructs, rather than as a single attitude construct, even after accounting for common method variance in both measures (Nosek & Smyth, in press; see also Cunningham, Nezlek, & Banaji, 2004). This extends similar findings for individual constructs such as Greenwald and Farnham (2000) for self-esteem, and Cunningham et al. (2001) for racial attitudes. Finally, Nosek (2005) reported evidence that the relationship between the IAT and self-report is moderated by multiple interpersonal (self-presentation, perceived distinctiveness from the norm) and intrapersonal (e.g., evaluative strength) features of attitudes.

Predictive Validity

Evidence for the predictive validity of the IAT is emerging from a wide variety of domains. As already reviewed, IAT scores are predictive of self-report attitudes and the strength of that relationship is moderated by multiple factors (Hofmann et al., 2005; Nosek, 2005). Poehlman, Uhlmann, Greenwald, and Banaji (2004) recently compiled 61 studies with 86 individual effect sizes to show the predictive validity of the IAT when perceptual, judgment, and action processes were examined as criterion variables. From the meta-analysis the authors draw two main conclusions. In studies that involve some measure of discrimination toward a social group, both explicit and IAT measures predict behavior but the IAT does a superior job of prediction (mean $r_{IAT} = .25$, mean $r_{self-report} = .13$). In studies that measure brand preferences or political candidate preferences, both IAT and explicit measures predict the outcome, but explicit measures do a superior job of prediction (mean $r_{IAT} = .40$, mean $r_{self-report} = .71$).

Malleability and Development

Conceptions of automaticity have often emphasized its consistency and inflexibility. This feature of automaticity has undergone a slow revision with the realization that automaticity is conditional and malleable on features of the present context (Gilbert & Hixon, 1991; Kahneman & Treisman, 1984; Macrae, Bodenhausen, Milne, Thorn, & Castelli, 1997; Wittenbrink, Judd, & Park, 2001). Evidence for conditional automaticity in implicit cognition has blossomed in recent years in investigations of the malleability of attitudes, identity, and beliefs (Blair, 2002; Blair, Ma, & Lenton, 2001; Dasgupta & Asgari, 2004; Dasgupta & Greenwald, 2001; Ferguson & Bargh, 2003; Florack, Bless, & Piontkowski, 2003; Foroni & Mayr, 2005; Lowery, Hardin, & Sinclair, 2001; Mitchell, Nosek, & Banaji, 2003; Richeson & Ambady, 2003; Richeson & Nussbaum, 2004; Rudman, Ashmore, & Gary, 2001; Teachman & Woody, 2003; Wittenbrink et al., 2001). For example, Lowery and colleagues (2001) demonstrated that implicit racial bias, measured by the IAT and subliminal priming, was substantially weaker when the experiment was administered by an African-American compared to a Caucasian American. Likewise, Foroni and Mayr (2005) showed that attitudes toward flowers relative to insects differed as a function of reading a short story about "dangerous" or "good" flowers.

Development of Implicit Cognition   Baron and Banaji (2006) devised a child friendly version of the IAT, called the Ch-IAT (available at *www.people.fas.harvard.edu/~banaji*). Using this version, children as young as age 4 have been tested on race and gender attitudes. Grouping White participants into three categories of age 6, age 10, and adults, Baron and Banaji (2006) found that the IAT race attitude remains constant across the three age groups. Explicit attitudes toward Black Americans change systematically with 10-year-olds reporting lower race bias than 6-year-olds and adults showing no race bias at all. Dunham, Baron, and Banaji (in press) have also studied Japanese children and adults in a small town of approximately 6000 residents, and found that children prefer their own group (Japanense) compared to both Whites and Blacks, whereas adult Japanese show less liking of Japanese when contrasted with Whites than when contrasted with Blacks. The origins of bias, and implicit cognition more generally, are likely to become a more active area of research for those interested in the early stages of social category knowledge, preference formation, and the extent to which such categories are or are not "essential" and part of core knowledge begin to incorporate implicit measurement into their research.

Malleability and Fakeability   There is an intriguing contrast between findings that relatively simple situational manipulations can result in shifts in automatic evaluations, and findings that spontaneous faking of IAT effects is not so easy. Consider, for example, Kim's (2003) observation that instructing subjects to fake the race attitude IAT resulted in no difference in effects compared to a control group, whereas Lowery et al. (2001) showed a dramatic shift in automatic racial evaluations just by varying the race of the experimenter. Even more dramatically, Foroni and Mayr (2005) had participants complete a flower–insect attitude IAT twice, once after reading a "pro-flowers" story and once after receiving one of three task manipulations: read a brief fantasy story about dangerous flowers and valuable insects following a nuclear war; instructions to associate insects with negative and flowers with positive; or instructions that the IAT is a lie-detector and that they should try to deceive it by pretending that they dislike flowers and like insects. Only the first of these three conditions elicited less positivity toward flowers relative to insects compared to the control condition. Remarkably, this suggests that it is easier to shift IAT effects through indirect means like telling a story than through a request to deliberately alter the effects. This demonstration underscores the malleability of automatic cognition, and suggests limitations of the involvement of deliberative processes in producing that malleability.

INTERPRETATION OF IAT EFFECTS

This section considers some of the interpretive issues that regularly arise in relation to IAT effects, including the IAT as a relative measure of association strengths, the influence of stimulus items versus category labels on IAT effects, whether IAT effects should be considered more accurate or "real" than self-report, and the cognitive processes and neurological correlates of IAT effects.

Relative Measurement

A prior section pointed out that the IAT is a relative measure of association strengths (Greenwald et al., 1998). Some researchers have attempted to circumvent this procedural constraint of the IAT by applying analytic methods designed to measure absolute associations that analyze response latencies for only those trials in which an exemplar from just one of the two target concepts was presented (e.g., Baccus, Baldwin, & Packer, 2004; Gemar, Segal, Sagrati, & Kennedy, 2001; de Jong et al., 2001). For example, in an attitude IAT contrasting Black faces from White faces, response latencies to categorizing Black faces might be extracted from the two conditions in an effort to measure liking for Blacks irrespective of evaluations of Whites. However, the individual response trials in the IAT are not independent events, and these analytic methods do not isolate single associations from the IAT (Nosek et al., 2005).

Another approach for measuring absolute associations with the IAT is to contrast the target category (e.g., self) with a neutral category (e.g., furniture, middle, animals, shapes). This type of application assumes that the neutral contrasting category contributes no meaningful variability to measurement and thus results in a score that can be interpreted as an absolute assessment of the target concept (e.g., Jajodia & Earlywine, 2003; Sherman et al., 2003). This approach is viable to the extent that the contrasting category is truly neutral and produces no meaningful variability in measurement. While this type of contrast category selection may reduce meaningful variability contributed by the contrast, it is not ideal for measuring single associations because of the strong assumptions that are required for interpretation.

Another strategy that has been used to measure single associations with the IAT is a "one category" variation (Karpinski & Steinman, in press; Wigboldus, 2004). In this version of the IAT, only three categories are used instead of four (one target concept and two attribute concepts). The two critical conditions of the task involve categorizing two sets of concepts with one response and one concept with the alternate response (e.g., *Black+bad* to the left, *good* to the right; then *bad* to the left and *Black+good* to the right). The simplicity of this approach is appealing. However, our own parameter testing with this IAT variant suggested a substantial threat to internal validity (Nosek & Banaji, 1997). Some subjects appeared to spontaneously or deliberately simplify the task to search for items belonging to the unpaired attribute category and accept or reject all items based on this concept exclusively (i.e., if *bad* hit the key, otherwise hit the other key), thus reducing attention to the nominal features of the (single) target concept items included in the task. Perhaps additional procedural innovations to the one-category task can reduce these threats to internal validity, but those innovations have not yet emerged.

A final alternative for measuring single associations is to avoid the IAT altogether and instead use a measure that is designed to assess them. Two measures that may provide this flexibility include the Go/No-go Association Task (Nosek & Banaji, 2001) and the Extrinsic Affective Simon Task (De Houwer, 2003). The psychometric properties of these new measures are not as well understood as the IAT, so their usefulness as measurement methods remains to be determined.

Attitudes toward Stimulus Items or Category Labels

A feature that clearly differentiates the IAT from its implicit cousin, evaluative priming (Fazio, Sanbonmatsu, Powell, & Kardes, 1986; Wittenbrink et al., 1997), is that the IAT requires explicit categorization of target stimuli into superordinate concepts. In sequential priming measures, primed concepts are not necessarily explicitly categorized and, in some cases, may not even be consciously perceived (Draine & Greenwald, 1998). The IAT requires that the subject explicitly categorize stimulus items into a specified superordinate category. This difference may have important effects on measurement such that participants may idiosyncratically categorize items in sequential priming procedures, but must arrive at a specific categorization for IAT performance (Olson & Fazio, 2003).

This distinctive procedural feature has produced interest in the extent to which IAT effects are influenced by the superordinate categories defined by the category labels, and the individual features of the stimulus exemplars. Some researchers have assumed that the IAT effects are purely a result of stimulus features (Brendl, Markman, & Messner, 2001; Mitchell, 2004), and others have concluded that IAT effects are determined largely by the category labels (De Houwer, 2001; Fazio & Olson, 2003).

The available evidence suggests that the answer is in between. Category labels appear to be critical for constraining the interpretation of the stimulus items. At the same time, the stimulus items, as a set, can affect the construal of the target category (Govan & Williams, 2004; Mitchell, et al., 2003; Nosek et al., 2005; Steffens & Plewe, 2001). For example, males' automatic association between romantic fantasies and their partner varied as a function of whether the romantic fantasies were sexualized stimulus items (e.g., vixen) or not (e.g., Cinderella; Rudman & Heppen, 2003, Studies 2 and 3). Also, in a Gay–Straight attitude IAT, changing just two stimulus items in the "Gay people" category from representations of gay women to gay men resulted in stronger pro-straight preferences in the latter compared to the former representation (Nosek et al., 2005). Finally, the importance of the category labels for constraining interpretation of stimulus items is made plain by unpublished parameter testing from our laboratories in which math and arts stimulus items were replaced with meaningless symbols (X's and O's; Nosek & Banaji, 1997). Instructing subjects on the proper interpretation of the symbols (X means math, O means arts) was sufficient to elicit IAT effects consistent with "real stimuli" IATs.

In sum, IAT design requires careful attention to the selection of both category label and stimulus items. Category labels are clearly of great importance for the IAT, but the stimulus exemplars can nevertheless influence the construal of those categories. Stimulus exemplars can aid in the definition of the superordinate category (e.g., whether gay people refers to gay men, lesbians, or both).

Does the IAT Reveal Cognitions that are More "True" or "Real" than Self-Report?

A rarely asserted interpretation of the IAT is that it might serve as a lie-detector, revealing associations that are more "real", "true", or accurate than self-report. Our review of the IAT literature has not found any article that endorsed this position, but we did find a number of articles that criticized users of the IAT for espousing that position, either incorrectly attributing the lie-detector view to the originators of the IAT, or attributing the view without supporting citation (e.g., Arkes & Tetlock, 2004; Gehring, Karpinski, & Hilton, 2003; Karpinski & Hilton, 2001).

To the extent that the IAT assesses implicit cognition as defined by Greenwald and Banaji (1995) and discussed in the opening section of this paper, it reveals associations that an individual may not want to report, and may not be aware of possessing. So, the IAT and self-report can differ because: the individual is unaware of the implicitly measured associations, and uses introspection to generate a unique explicit response; the individual is aware of the implicitly measured associations, but genuinely rejects them as not conforming to his or her belief system and so reports a distinct explicit response; or the individual is aware of the implicit associations, but chooses to report an alternative explicit response due to social concern about the acceptability of such a response. Only the third case would fit with the conception of detecting a deliberate hiding of privately endorsed evaluations. In all three cases, implicit and explicit assessments may have separate predictive utility, which would indicate that both are "real" measures.

If the IAT measured only associations that fit into the third category above, then the notion of a lie-detector might have merit. However, the evidence is clearly against such an understanding of the IAT. Some of those who complete an IAT that reveals something undesirable (e.g., racial bias) are surprised by the result and may have feelings of guilt (Monteith, Ashburn-Nardo, Voils, & Czopp, 2002; Monteith, Voils, & Ashburn-Nardo, 2001). The IAT clearly should not be regarded simply as a measure of the constructs assessed by self-report, but with all self-presentation concern removed. Self-presentation (for genuine or deceptive reasons) is just one of a variety of factors that moderate the relationship between implicit and explicit measures (Nosek, 2005).

A second way in which IAT results might be considered more "real" than self-report is in the ability of each to predict psychological outcomes. If the IAT is consistently superior in outcome prediction, then it might be considered more "real" with regard to its superior predictive validity. However, in a meta-analysis of predictive validity Poehlman et al. (2004) reported that the IAT and self-report each have domains of superior predictive validity.

In sum, it does not appear useful to classify the IAT or self-report as having distinguishable degrees of access to *reality* or *truth*. Each is a real assessment – one is intended to measure products of introspection, the other is not.

What Processes are Involved in IAT Effects?

Process Models   The IAT has enjoyed a period of sustained empirical use during which its creators, developers, and users have remained relatively calm about the absence of an established cognitive model of performance at the task that generates the IAT measure. There have been a few notable attempts to interpret at least portions of the cognitive processes involved in performing the IAT (Brendl, Markman, & Messner, 2001; Conrey et al., 2005; Greenwald, Nosek, Banaji, & Klauer, 2005; Hall, Mitchell, Graham, & Lavis, 2003; De Houwer, 2001; Mierke & Klauer, 2001, 2003; Olson & Fazio, 2003; Rothermund & Wentura, 2001, 2004). The points that seem well established are that the IAT involves representations at the level of categories more strongly than those at the level of the category's exemplars (esp. De Houwer, 2001), and that the difficulty of switching between the IAT's two discrimination tasks when two concepts assigned to the same key are weakly associated contributes substantially to a slowing of performance that plays an important role in the measure (esp. Mierke & Klauer, 2001).

Having a more comprehensive model of the IAT's performance would likely benefit research using the IAT, possibly by affording greater efficiencies in administration, by suggesting design changes that would increase the IAT's construct validity as a measure of association strength, or by making further progress toward developing effective non-relative measures of association strength. Because there are now several laboratories working on various aspects of deciphering the cognitive mechanisms of the IAT, it may be reasonable to expect important progress in this area before the IAT reaches age 10.

Neurological Correlates of IAT Effects   The first social cognitive neuroscience study involving the IAT (Chee, Sriram, Soon, & Lee, 2000) identified brain regions engaged when subjects were immersed in performing the IAT itself. This is an interesting way to motivate the question of the mechanism underlying the IAT because we already have information on the processes that particular brain regions are involved in. The most satisfactory evidence from this study is the finding that the regions that are active during the IAT procedure are similar if not isomorphic with those involved in the Stroop task: the anterior cingulate, ventrolateral prefrontal cortex (PFC), and dorsolateral PFC.

Phelps et al. (2000) compared the IAT to amygdala activation, a brain region associated with fear or negative emotional responding, by having participants view Black and White faces while being scanned, making an L or R judgment on each face. Relative Black > White activation was found to be correlated with an IAT measure of race bias and a Black > White startle eyeblink response. No such correlations were observed using the Modern Racism Scale.

Cunningham et al. (2005) showed that the correlation between the imaging data and the IAT is much stronger when the faces are presented subliminally than supraliminally. These data also gave signs of a dampening down of the subcortical response to Black faces in those who showed greater dorsolateral PFC, ventrolateral PFC, and anterior cingulated cortex, regions known to be involved in inhibition, conflict resolution, and control. Such evidence provides converging support for the idea that IAT performance is connected to the response of an early detection emotion module whose activity is also likely to be consciously controlled via activity in regions that kick in later based on more deliberative thought.

Are the Associations Measured by the IAT Available to Introspection?   The literature on the IAT appears to reach consensus that the IAT bypasses introspective access, and that IAT effects are influenced by automatic processes (though the degree to which the IAT is influenced by automatic processes is still uncertain). To what extent does the IAT capture those associations that are not available to introspection (Fazio & Olson, 2003)? That is, in what sense (if any) can IAT effects be said to reflect cognitive processes that exist outside of awareness?

It is certainly the case that subjects can be aware of their performance on the IAT after completing it (Ashburn-Nardo et al., 2001) and possibly as they are completing it. Also, it is clear from subject reports that some (though not all) are aware of what the task is intended to measure while they are performing it. However, neither of these senses of awareness address whether introspection is involved in producing the end result that is the IAT score.

The question of self-awareness is difficult to answer definitively because it is not possible to assess the contents of one's awareness except through self-report. Any null result could mean that the questions were not posed appropriately. Even so, the evidence suggests that the IAT can measure associations that can escape some layers of awareness. For many content domains, subjects (including the authors of this paper) were genuinely surprised by the outcome of their IAT performance. In many cases, the task performance seems so distant from expectation (presumably based on introspection) that subjects rapidly generate alternative explanations for the result that are external to the person and are often known to be incorrect, such as appeal to known-incorrect hypotheses about the order in which combined tasks were done, the sides on which stimuli were located, handedness, individual differences in hand–eye coordination, and the familiarity of stimulus items.

In controlled investigations, Mitchell et al. (2003) gave subjects experience with the IAT and then asked them to predict their performance for a novel domain. Predictions were unrelated to actual performance. Finally, in unpublished studies from our laboratories, subjects with and without IAT experience, and with and without background information about the IAT, have consistently failed to predict task performance.

Justifiable Applications of the IAT

The accumulated evidence for the construct and predictive validity of the IAT in assessing individual differences shows that it is thriving as a research tool and will likely continue to do so. The IAT's successes have also prompted interest in applying it in diagnostic and selection settings. Such potential applications should be approached cautiously with careful attention to acceptable interpretations of IAT effects. The known malleability of the IAT implies that its predictive validity is moderated by situational variables. Further, the known potential for controlled processes to override automatic processes suggests that increased controlled processing can impair the IAT's predictive correlations. Finally, the fact that the IAT and self-report both have spheres of superior predictive validity indicates that the IAT is not properly interpreted as a lie-detector or as revealing something more *true* or more *real* than self-report.

Until understanding of the IAT's predictive validity develops further, it is premature to use the IAT as a diagnostic indicator for conclusions that have important, direct, and personal consequences – for example, as a device for selection for employment. Applications that reach beyond what can be justified by available evidence may backfire by producing public or professional reactions that can retard the orderly progress of discovery.

The IAT's best current applications are in education, where it has been used to afford insight into automatic associative processes that are introspectively inaccessible. The IAT is also beginning to be used as a clinical diagnostic tool. The IAT's psychometric properties are currently adequate for this type of clinical use in research settings. However, for more sensitive diagnostic tasks it is more appropriate – pending further research development – to treat the IAT as a useful adjunct to diagnosis than to treat it as a self-sufficient procedure. This is not to disparage the compelling evidence for the validity of the IAT, but to point out that there is still much to learn before its appropriate applications are known.

CONCLUSION

In its seventh year, the IAT is showing a rapid growth in maturity with a solid base of evidence for its internal, construct, and predictive validity. Still, there are many issues unresolved about the nature of the IAT, and its potential for revealing disquieting aspects about human minds. With the vigorous ongoing research programs testing the limits of the IAT from many directions, the IAT is a tool worthy of continued scrutiny. As research in implicit cognition continues to grow and age, insights with the IAT may even lead to progeny that will reach beyond the IAT's own capabilities.

NOTES

1. The concept–attribute designation is not always true for the IAT. More generally, the IAT involves measurement of associations among four concepts.

2. A nearly equivalent alternative for IAT designs in which errant trials are not corrected by the subject has the following steps: (1) use data from Blocks 3, 4, 6, and 7 (see Table 6.1); (2) eliminate trials with latencies > 10,000 ms; (3) eliminate subjects for whom more than 10% of trials have latencies < 300 ms; (4) compute the mean of correct latencies for each of the four blocks; (5) replace each error latency with the block mean from Step 4 + a 600 millisecond error penalty; (6) compute one standard deviation for all trials in Blocks 3 and 6, and another standard deviation for all trials in Blocks 4 and 7; (7) compute means for trials in each of the four blocks (Blocks 3, 4, 6, 7); (8) compute the two difference scores; (9) divide each difference score by its associated standard deviation from Step 6; and (10) average the two quotients from Step 9. Table 4 in Greenwald et al. (2003) was confusing, with Steps 5 and 6 above being presented in reverse order for this form of the algorithm. The consequences of switching the order of Steps 5 and 6 (SD calculated with or without error corrected trials) are very minor, but the present algorithm has the advantage of creating specific boundary conditions [−2, +2] of possible IAT D scores (Nosek & Sriram, in press; Sriram, Greenwald, & Nosek, 2006).

3. While plausible, the definitiveness of this finding is tempered by the fact that the typical and modified versions of the evaluative priming procedure also had different reliabilities (typical priming split-half $r = .04$; "category" priming split-half $r = .39$). Taking those values, which probably underestimate the reliability of the whole measure, the maximum possible correlations with the IAT (split-half $r = .53$) in that study were just $r = .15$ for the typical priming measure and $r = .45$ for the category priming measure.

4. The difference between the Hofmann et al. (2005) meta-analysis and the Nosek (2005) finding can be understood by noting the difference in domains examined. Hofmann et al. examined the existing literature, which has a heavy emphasis on content domains that are likely to elicit weak correlations (e.g., racial attitudes) whereas Nosek sampled attitudes across a wide variety of domains, many of which showed moderate to substantial correlations.

ACKNOWLEDGMENTS

This research was supported by the National Institute of Mental Health (Grants MH-41328, MH-01533, MH-57672, and MH-68447) and the National Science Foundation (Grants SBR-9422241 and SBR-9709924).

REFERENCES

Akalis, S., & Banaji, M. R. (2004). Modification of the IAT effect via compassion. Unpublished data, Harvard University.

Arkes, H., & Tetlock, P. E. (2004). Attributions of implicit prejudice, or "Would Jesse Jackson 'fail' the Implicit Association Test?" *Psychological Inquiry, 15*(4), 257–278.

Asendorpf, J. B., Banse, R., & Mucke, D. (2002). Double dissociation between implicit and explicit personality self-concept: The case of shy behavior. *Journal of Personality and Social Psychology, 83,* 380–393.

Asendorpf, J. B., Banse, R., & Schnabel, K. (2006). Employing automatic approach and avoidance tendencies for the assessment of implicit personality self-concept. *Experimental Psychology, 53*(1), 69–76.

Ashburn-Nardo, L., Voils, C., & Monteith, M. (2001). Implicit associations as the seeds of intergroup bias: How easily do they take root? *Journal of Personality and Social Psychology, 81*(5), 789–799.

Baccus, J. R., Baldwin, M. W., & Packer, D. J. (2004). Increasing implicit self-esteem through classical conditioning. *Psychological Science, 15*(7), 498–502.

Back, M. D., Schmukle, S. C., & Egloff, B. (2005). Measuring task-switching ability in the Implicit Association Test. *Experimental Psychology, 52*(3), 167–179.

Banse, R., Seise, J., & Zerbes, N. (2001). Implicit attitudes toward homosexuality: Reliability, validity, and controllability of the IAT. *Zeitschrift fur Experimentelle Psychologie, 48,* 145–160.

Bargh, J. A. (1997). The automaticity of everyday life. In R. S. Wyer, Jr. (Ed). *Advances in Social Cognition* (Vol. 10, pp. 1–61). Mahwah, NJ: Erlbaum.

Baron, A. S., & Banaji, M. R. (2006). The development of implicit attitudes: Evidence of race evaluations from ages 6 and 10 and adulthood. *Psychological Science, 17*(1), 53–58.

Blair, I. V. (2002). The malleability of automatic stereotypes and prejudice. *Personality and Social Psychology Review, 6,* 242–261.

Blair, I. V., Ma, J., & Lenton, A. P. (2001). Imagining stereotypes away: The moderation of automatic stereotypes through mental imagery. *Journal of Personality and Social Psychology, 81,* 828–841.

Bosson, J. K., Swann, W. B., & Pennebaker, J. W. (2000). Stalking the perfect measure of implicit self-esteem: The blind men and the elephant revisited? *Journal of Personality and Social Psychology, 79,* 631–643.

Brauer, M., Wasel, W., & Niedenthal, P. (2000). Implicit and explicit components of prejudice. *Review of General Psychology, 4,* 79–101.

Brendl, C. M., Markman, A. B., & Messner, C. (2001). How do indirect measures of evaluation work? Evaluating the inference of prejudice in the Implicit Association Test. *Journal of Personality and Social Psychology, 81*(5), 760–773.

Cai, H., Sriram, N., Greenwald, A. G., & McFarland, S. G. (2004). The Implicit Association Test's D measure can minimize a cognitive skill confound: Comment on McFarland and Crouch (2002). *Social Cognition, 22*(6), 673–684.

Chee, M. W. L., Sriram, N., Soon, C. S., & Lee, K. M. (2000). Dorsolateral prefrontal cortex and the implicit association of concepts and attributes. *Neuroreport: For Rapid Communication of Neuroscience Research, 11*(1), 135–140.

Conrey, F. R., Sherman, J. W., Gawronski, B., Hugenberg, K., & Groom, C. (2005). Beyond automaticity and control: The quad-model of behavioral response. *Journal of Personality and Social Psychology, 89*(4), 469–487.

Cunningham, W. A., Johnson, M. K., Raye, C. L., Gatenby, J. C., Gore, J. C., & Banaji, M. R. (2004). Separable neural components in the processing of black and white faces. *Psychological Science, 15*(12), 806–813.

Cunningham, W. A., Preacher, K. J., & Banaji, M. R. (2001). Implicit attitude measures: Consistency, stability, and convergent validity. *Psychological Science, 12*(2), 163–170.

Cunningham, W. A., Nezlek, J. B., & Banaji, M. R. (2004). Implicit and explicit ethnocentrism: Revisiting the ideologies of prejudice. *Personality and Social Psychology Bulletin, 30*(10), 1332–1346.

Dasgupta, N., & Asgari, S. (2004). Seeing is believing: Exposure to countersterotypic women leaders and its effect on the malleability of automatic gender stereotyping. *Journal of Experimental Social Psychology, 40*, 642–658.

Dasgupta, N., & Greenwald, A. G. (2001). On the malleability of automatic attitudes: Combating automatic prejudice with images of admired and disliked individuals. *Journal of Personality and Social Psychology, 81*(5), 800–814.

Dasgupta, N., Greenwald, A. G., & Banaji, M. R. (2003). The first ontological challenge to the IAT: Attitude or mere familiarity? *Psychological Inquiry, 14*(3&4), 238–243.

Dasgupta, N., McGhee, D. E, Greenwald, A. G., & Banaji, M. R. (2000). Automatic preference for White Americans: Eliminating the familiarity explanation. *Journal of Experimental and Social Psychology, 36*, 316–328.

Draine, S. C., & Greenwald, A. G. (1998). Replicable unconscious semantic priming. *Journal of Experimental Psychology: General, 127*(3), 286–303.

Dunham, Y., Baron, A., & Banaji, M. (in press). From American city to Japanese village: A cross-cultural investigation of implicit race attitudes. *Child Development.*

Egloff, B., & Schmukle, S. C. (2002). Predictive validity of an Implicit Association Test for measuring anxiety. *Journal of Personality and Social Psychology, 83*, 1441–1455.

Egloff, B., Schwerdtfeger, A., & Schmukle, S. C. (2005). Temporal stability of the Implicit Association Test – anxiety. *Journal of Personality Assessment, 84*(1), 82–88.

Fazio, R. H., & Olson, M. A. (2003). Implicit measures in social cognition research: Their meaning and use. *Annual Review of Psychology, 54*, 297–327.

Fazio, R. H., Sanbonmatsu, D. M., Powell, M. C., & Kardes, F. R. (1986). On the automatic activation of attitudes. *Journal of Personality and Social Psychology, 50*(2), 229–238.

Ferguson, M. J., & Bargh, J. A. (2003). The constructive nature of automatic evaluation. In Musch, J., & Klauer, K. C. (Eds). *The Psychology of Evaluation: Affective Processes in Cognition and Emotion* (pp. 169–188). Mahwah, NJ: Lawrence Erlbaum Associates.

Florack, A., Bless, H., & Piontkowski, U. (2003). When do people accept cultural diversity? Affect as determinant. *International Journal of Intercultural Relations, 27*, 627–640.

Foroni, F., & Mayr, U. (2005). The power of a story: New, automatic associations from a single reading of a short scenario. *Psychonomic Bulletin and Review, 12*(1), 139–144.

Gehring, W. J., Karpinski, A., & Hilton, J. L. (2003). Thinking about interracial interactions. *Nature Neuroscience*, 6(12), 1241–1243.

Gemar, M. C., Segal, Z. V., Sagrati, S., & Kennedy, S. J. (2001). Mood-induced changes on the Implicit Association Test in recovered depressed patients. *Journal of Abnormal Psychology*, 110(2), 282–289.

Gilbert, D. T., & Hixon, J. G. (1991). The trouble of thinking: Activation and application of stereotypic beliefs. *Journal of Personality and Social Psychology*, 60, 509–517.

Govan, C. L., & Williams, K. D. (2004). Reversing or eliminating IAT effects by changing the affective valence of the stimulus items. *Journal of Experimental Social Psychology*, 40(3), 357–365.

Greenwald, A. G., & Banaji, M. R. (1995). Implicit social cognition: Attitudes, self-esteem, and stereotypes. *Psychological Review*, 102(1), 4–27.

Greenwald, A. G., & Farnham, S. D. (2000). Using the Implicit Association Test to measure self-esteem and self-concept. *Journal of Personality and Social Psychology*, 79(6), 1022–1038.

Greenwald, A. G., McGhee, D. E., & Schwartz, J. L. K. (1998). Measuring individual differences in implicit cognition: The Implicit Association Test. *Journal of Personality and Social Psychology*, 74(6), 1464–1480.

Greenwald, A. G., & Nosek, B. A. (2001). Health of the Implicit Association Test at age 3. *Zeitschrift für Experimentelle Psychologie*, 48, 85–93.

Greenwald, A. G., Nosek, B. A., & Banaji, M. R. (2003). Understanding and using the Implicit Association Test: I. An improved scoring algorithm. *Journal of Personality and Social Psychology*, 85(2), 197–216.

Greenwald, A. G., Nosek, B. A., Banaji, M. R., & Klauer, K. C. (2005). Validity of the salience asymmetry interpretation of the IAT: Comment on Rothermund and Wentura (2004). *Journal of Experimental Psychology: General*, 134(3), 420–425.

Hall, G., Mitchell, C., Graham, S., & Lavis, Y. (2003). Acquired equivalence and distinctiveness in human discrimination learning: Evidence for associative mediation. *Journal of Experimental Psychology: General*, 132(2), 266–276.

Hofmann, W., Gawronski, B., Gschwendner, T., Le, H., & Schmitt, M. (2005). A meta-analysis on the correlation between the Implicit Association Test and explicit self-report measures. *Personality and Social Psychology Bulletin*, 31(10), 1369–1385.

De Houwer, J. (2001). A structural and process analysis of the Implicit Association Test. *Journal of Experimental Social Psychology*, 37, 443–451.

De Houwer, J. (2003). The extrinsic affective Simon task. *Experimental Psychology*, 50(2), 77–85.

Hummert, M. L., Garstka, T. A., O'Brien, L. T., Greenwald, A. G., & Mellott, D. S. (2002). Using the implicit association test to measure age differences in implicit social cognitions. *Psychology and Aging*, 17(3), 482–495.

Jajodia, A., & Earleywine, M. (2003). Measuring alcohol expectancies with the implicit association test. *Psychology of Addictive Behaviors*, 17(2), 126–133.

de Jong, P. J., Pasman, W., Kindt, M., & van den Hout, M. A. (2001). A reaction time paradigm to assess (implicit) complaint-specific dysfunctional beliefs. *Behaviour Research and Therapy*, 39(1), 101–113.

Kahneman, D., & Treisman, A. (1984). Changing views of attention and automaticity. In R. Parasuraman & D. R. Davies (Eds.), *Varieties of attention* (pp. 29–61). San Diego, CA: Academic Press.

Kahneman, D., Slovic, P., & Tversky, A. (1982). Judgment under uncertainty: Heuristics and biases. New York: Cambridge University Press.

Karpinski, A., & Hilton, J. L. (2001). Attitudes and the implicit association test. *Journal of Personality and Social Psychology, 81,* 774–788.

Karpinksi, A., & Steinman, R. B., (in press). The single category implicit association test as a measure of implicit social cognition. *Journal of Personality and Social Psychology.*

Kim, D. Y. (2003). Voluntary controllability of the Implicit Association Test (IAT). *Social Psychology Quarterly, 66,* 83–96.

Klauer, K. C., & Mierke, J. (2005). Task-set inertia, attitude accessibility, and compatibility-order effects: New evidence for a task-set switching account of the Implicit Association Test effect. *Personality and Social Psychology Bulletin, 31,* 208–217.

Lowery, B. S., Hardin, C. D., & Sinclair, S. (2001). Social influence effects on automatic racial prejudice. *Journal of Personality and Social Psychology, 81,* 842–855.

Macrae, C. N., Bodenhausen, G. V., Milne, A. B., Thorn, T. M. J., & Castelli, L. (1997). On the activation of social stereotypes: The moderating role of processing objectives. *Journal of Experimental Social Psychology, 33,* 471–489.

Maison, D., Greenwald, A. G., & Bruin, R. (2001). The Implicit Association Test as a measure of implicit consumer attitudes. *Polish Psychological Bulletin, 32*(1), 61–69.

Marsh, K. L., Johnson, B. T., & Scott-Sheldon, L. A. (2001). Heart versus reason in condom use: Implicit versus explicit attitudinal predictors of sexual behavior. *Zeitschrift für Experimentelle Psychologie, 48*(2), 161–175.

McFarland, S. G., & Crouch, Z. (2002). A cognitive skill confound on the Implicit Association Test. *Social Cognition, 20*(6), 483–510.

Mierke, J., & Klauer, K. C. (2001). Implicit association measurement with the IAT: Evidence for effects of executive control processes. *Zeitschrift für Experimentelle Psychologie, 48*(2), 107–122.

Mierke, J., & Klauer, K. C. (2003). Method-specific variance in the Implicit Association Test. *Journal of Personality and Social Psychology, 85*(6), 1180–1192.

Mitchell, C. J. (2004). Mere acceptance produces apparent attitude in the Implicit Association Test. *Journal of Experimental Social Psychology, 40*(3), 366–373.

Mitchell, J. A., Nosek, B. A., & Banaji, M. R. (2003). Contextual variations in implicit evaluation. *Journal of Experimental Psychology: General, 132*(3), 455–469.

Monteith, M. J., Ashburn-Nardo, L., Voils, C. I., & Czopp, A. M. (2002). Putting the brakes on prejudice: On the development and operation of cues for control. *Journal of Personality and Social Psychology, 83*(5), 1029–1050.

Monteith, M. J., Voils, C. I., & Ashburn-Nardo, L. (2001). Taking a look underground: Detecting, interpreting, and reacting to implicit racial biases. *Social Cognition, 19*(4), 395–417.

Nisbett, R. E., & Wilson, T. D. (1977). Telling more than we can know: Verbal reports on mental processes. *Psychological Review, 84*(3), 231–259.

Nosek, B. A. (2005). Moderators of the relationship between implicit and explicit evaluation. *Journal of Experimental Psychology: General, 134,* 565–584.

Nosek, B. A., & Banaji, M. R. (1997). Initial parameter testing of the Implicit Association Test. Unpublished data.

Nosek, B. A., & Banaji, M. R. (2001). The go/no-go association task. *Social Cognition, 19*(6), 625–666.

Nosek, B. A., Banaji, M. R., & Greenwald, A. G. (2002). Harvesting intergroup implicit attitudes and beliefs from a demonstration Web site. *Group Dynamics, 6*(1), 101–115.

Nosek, B. A., Greenwald, A. G., & Banaji, M. R. (2005). Understanding and using the Implicit Association Test: II. Method variables and construct validity. *Personality and Social Psychology Bulletin, 31*(2), 166–180.

Nosek, B. A., & Smyth, F. L. (in press). A multitrait-multimethod validation of the Implicit Association Test: Implicit and explicit attitudes are related but distinct constructs. *Experimental Psychology*.

Nosek, B. A., & Sriram, N. (in press). Faulty assumptions: A comment on Blanton, Jaccard, Gonzales, and Christie. *Journal of Experimental Social Psychology*.

Nunnally, J. C., & Bernstein, I. H. (1994). *Psychometric theory*. New York: McGraw-Hill.

Olson, M. A., & Fazio, R. H. (2003). Relations between implicit measures of prejudice: What are we measuring? *Psychological Science, 14*(6), 636–639.

Ottaway, S. A., Hayden, D. C., & Oakes, M. A. (2001). Implicit attitudes and racism: Effects of word familiarity and frequency on the implicit association test. *Social Cognition, 19*(2), 97–144.

Perugini, M., & Leone, L. (2004). Individual differences in moral decision making: Validation of an implicit measure of morality. Unpublished manuscript.

Phelps, E. A., O'Connor, K. J., Cunningham, W. A., Funayama, E. S., Gatenby, J. C., Gore, J. C., & Banaji, M. R. (2000). Performance on indirect measures of race evaluation predicts amygdala activation. *Journal of Cognitive Neuroscience, 12*(5), 729–738.

Poehlman, T. A., Uhlmann, E., Greenwald, A. G., & Banaji, M. R. (2004). Understanding and using the Implicit Association Test: III. Meta-analysis of predictive validity. Manuscript submitted for publication.

Richeson, J. A., & Ambady, N. (2003). Effects of situational power on automatic racial prejudice. *Journal of Experimental Social Psychology, 39*(2), 177–183.

Richeson, J. A., Baird, A. A., Gordon, H. L., Heatherton, T. F., Wyland, C. L., Trawalter, S., & Shelton, J. N. (2003). An fMRI investigation of the impact of interracial contact on executive function. *Nature Neuroscience, 6*(12), 1323–1328.

Richeson, J. A., & Nussbaum, R. J. (2004). The impact of multiculturalism versus color-blindness on racial bias. *Journal of Experimental Social Psychology, 40*(3), 417–423.

Roediger, H. L. (1990). Implicit memory: Retention without remembering. *American Psychologist, 45*(9), 1043–1056.

Rothermund, K., & Wentura, D. (2001). Figure-ground asymmetries in the Implicit Association Test (IAT). *Zeitschrift für Experimentelle Psychologie, 48*(2), 94–106.

Rothermund, K., & Wentura, D. (2004). Underlying processes in the Implicit Association Test (IAT): Dissociating salience from associations. *Journal of Experimental Psychology: General, 133*(2), 139–165.

Rudman, L. A., Ashmore, R. D., & Gary, M. L. (2001). "Unlearning" automatic biases: The malleability of implicit prejudice and stereotypes. *Journal of Personality and Social Psychology, 81*(5), 856–868.

Rudman, L. A., Greenwald, A. G., Mellott, D. S., & Schwartz, J. L. K. (1999). Measuring the automatic components of prejudice: Flexibility and generality of the Implicit Association Test. *Social Cognition, 17*(4), 437–465.

Rudman, L. A., & Heppen, J. B. (2003). Implicit romantic fantasies and women's interest in personal power: A glass slipper effect? *Personality and Social Psychology Bulletin, 29*(11), 1357–1370.

Schacter, D. L., Bowers, J., & Booker, J. (1989). Intention, awareness, and implicit memory: The retrieval intentionality criterion. In S. Lewandowsky, J. C. Dunn & K. Kirsner (Eds.), *Implicit memory: Theoretical issues* (pp. 47–65). Hillsdale, NJ: Erlbaum.

Schmukle, S. C., & Egloff, B. (2004). Does the Implicit Association Test for assessing anxiety measure trait and state variance? *European Journal of Personality, 18*, 483–494.

Schmukle, S. C., & Egloff, B. (2005). A latent state-trait analysis of implicit and explicit personality measures. *European Journal of Psychological Assessment, 21*(2), 100–107.

Sherman, S. J., Presson, C. C., Chassin, L., Rose, J. S., & Koch, K. (2003). Implicit and explicit attitudes toward cigarette smoking: The effects of context and motivation. *Journal of Social and Clinical Psychology, 22*, 13–39.

Simon, H. A. (1955). A behavioral model of rational choice. *Quarterly Journal of Economics, 69*, 99–118.

Sriram, N., Greenwald, A. G., & Nosek, B. A. (2006). Scale invariant contrasts of response latency distributions. Unpublished manuscript.

Steffens, M. C. (2004). Is the Implicit Association Test immune to faking? *Experimental Psychology, 51*(3), 165–179.

Steffens, M. C., & Buchner, A. (2003). Implicit Association Test: Separating transsituationally stables and variable components of attitudes toward gay men. *Experimental Psychology, 50*(1), 33–48.

Steffens, M. C., & Plewe, I. (2001). Items' cross-category associations as a confounding factor in the Implicit Association Test. *Zeitschrift für Experimentelle Psychologie, 48*, 123–134.

Teachman, B. A., Gregg, A. P., & Woody, S. R. (2001). Implicit associations for fear-relevant stimuli among individuals with snake and spider fears. *Journal of Abnormal Psychology, 110*(2), 226–235.

Teachman, B. A., & Woody, S. R. (2003). Automatic processing in spider phobia: Implicit fear associations over the course of treatment. *Journal of Abnormal Psychology, 112*(1), 100–109.

Teachman, B. A, Gapinski, K. D., Brownell, K. D., Rawlins, M., & Jeyaram, S. (2003). Demonstrations of implicit anti-fat bias: The impact of providing causal information and evoking empathy. *Health Psychology. 22*(1), 68–78.

Teige, S., Schnabel, K., Banse, R., & Asendorpf, J. B. (2004). Assessment of multiple implicit self-concept dimensions using the Extrinsic Affective Simon Task (EAST). Unpublished manuscript.

Wegner, D. M. (2002). *The illusion of conscious will*. Cambridge, MA: Bradford Books.

Wigboldus, D. (2004). Single-target implicit associations. Unpublished manuscript.

Wilson, T. D., Lindsey, S., & Schooler, T. Y. (2000). A model of dual attitudes. *Psychological Review, 107*(1), 101–126.

Wittenbrink, B., Judd, C. M., & Park, B. (1997). Evidence for racial prejudice at the implicit level and its relationship with questionnaire measures. *Journal of Personality and Social Psychology, 72*(2), 262–274.

Wittenbrink, B., Judd, C. M., & Park, B. (2001). Spontaneous prejudice in context: Variability in automatically activated attitudes. *Journal of Personality and Social Psychology, 81*(5), 815–827.

7

Automatic and Controlled Components of Social Cognition: A Process Dissociation Approach

B. KEITH PAYNE and BRANDON D. STEWART

*I*n a famous description of unintended behavior, William James (1890) noted that, "Very absent-minded persons in going to their bedroom to dress for dinner have been known to take off one garment after another and finally to get into bed, merely because that was the habitual issue of the first few movements when performed at a later hour," (p. 115). This kind of absent-mindedness, or something like it, will probably strike most readers as all too familiar. Compare this with a description by the neurologist Francois Lhermitte of a patient nearly a century later. When shown into a bedroom, the patient "immediately began to get undressed. He got into bed, pulled the sheet up to his neck, and prepared to go to sleep," (Lhermitte, 1986, p. 338). We can be sure that this behavior is more exceptional than James' absent-mindedness, because the bedroom belonged to Lhermitte.

The patient had a massive surgical lesion of the left frontal lobe, a brain region critical for strategic planning and control of actions. This and other similar patients suffered from what Lhermitte termed "environmental dependency syndrome." Although their behaviors were coordinated and complex (not simple reflexes), they were under the control of the environment to a striking extent. They behaved in accord with whatever environmental cues caught their eye. In one demonstration, upon noticing that a syringe had been laid out, a patient picked it up and began to give the neurologist an injection. The reader is not told whether the injection was carried out. In another, even more macabre investigation, the patient was led to a table where a pistol and some bullets had been placed. Without pause or comment, he picked up the pistol, pulled back the magazine, and loaded it. At this point we read, "The experiment was then stopped," (p. 338). These were not the momentary lapses of voluntary control that we all experience, but profound absences. Lhermitte described it as a disorder of autonomy.

No less intriguing are the struggles of individuals with alien hand syndrome.

Because of damage to the frontal lobes or the corpus callosum connecting left and right hemispheres, these patients experience "autonomous" actions by one or more limbs. The actions are autonomous in the sense that the patient cannot voluntarily control them, nor do they experience the behaviors (nor even the limb itself) as their own. Like Lhermitte's patients, the "alien" actions are usually triggered by environmental cues. For example, patients may experience a "struggle between the hands as each attempts to answer the telephone," or even more drastically, "one hand tried to turn left when the other hand tried to turn right while driving a car," (Doody & Jankovic, 1992; p. 807). Marchetti and Della Sala (1998) report a patient who, "at dinner, much to her dismay saw her left hand taking some fish bones from the leftovers and putting them into her mouth," (p. 196).

These bizarre conditions seem so strange because they are dissociations between functions that usually work seamlessly together, with intentions reining in the automatic when it goes astray. Dissociations are so informative because so much can be learned about the structure of a system from where its fault lines lie. When a crystalline icicle shatters on the floor it comes apart in remarkably regular patterns, very different from the shattering of an egg. Their inner organization reveals itself in the ways they come apart. Neurologists have been studying dissociations caused by anatomical lesions for more than a century. Neurological dissociations have more recently attracted the attention of social psychologists for their potential to shed light on the control of complex thought processes such as those involved in social behavior (e.g. Bargh, 2005; Beer et al., 2003; Wegner, 2002).

Although anatomical dissociations map out these fault lines in vivid detail, dissociations in the behavior of healthy men and women can be just as informative. One way to find the seams between the intentionally controlled and the uncontrolled is to compare explicit and implicit tasks. Amnesiac patients, for example, show profound deficits when tested using explicit memory tests, which ask the person to intentionally retrieve a memory. Yet when tested with implicit memory tests, their performance shows effects of past experience without the intent to remember or the feeling of remembering (Shimamura, 1986). But it is not just amnesiac patients who show this difference. Normal healthy college students also show dissociations between implicit and explicit memory tests (Jacoby & Dallas, 1981). Factors that affect performance on one kind of test often have no impact on the other (see Roediger & McDermott, 1993). With the help of implicit and explicit tasks, researchers can probe the distinctions between mental processes without relying on rare, unfortunate cases of brain damage. They can infer the inner structures without waiting for them to crack. The fact that healthy men and women show dissociations between intentional and unintentional aspects of behavior forces us to ask about the fault lines in ordinary thought. Do we all have little disorders of autonomy? In some ways, we shall see, the answer is yes.

The cases reviewed here are all dissociations between intentional and unintentional processes, each at different levels of analysis. The dissociations become increasingly subtle, but no less intriguing as we zoom in from the macro scale to the micro. Lhermitte's frontal patients showed a dissociation at the level of the *whole person*. Most people act with intentional control most of the time, but these patients did not. Cases of alien hand represent dissociations within a person, but between limbs. One hand is under voluntary control, and the other is not. At a still finer grain are dissociations between tasks. The same person acts differently on the two tasks because the tasks draw on different processes.

We can zoom in further. This chapter focuses on a process dissociation approach – a technique for separating intentional and unintentional contributions to the same behavior performed by the same person at the same time. Imagine that a man is walking toward you on the street. Although you do not recognize him, you have a bad feeling about him and decide to cross the street. If you had been able to intentionally retrieve the fact that you saw him yesterday on a wanted poster, you would have had an even better basis for your decision, and might have hurried faster, or called the police afterward. But even without being able to remember the poster, the vague sense of threat can also guide your response. Here intentional and unintentional forms of learning could both feed into the response, in varying degrees. The fact that you can have one without the other illustrates that they are separable. Just as lesion studies allow dramatic dissociations based on anatomy, the process dissociation approach seeks to separate intentional and unintentional influences, even though they normally operate together.

The goal of this chapter is to overview the logic behind the process dissociation approach, what it measures, and what it does not. We will describe some of the many different topics where process dissociation has been used, and the kinds of insights it can provide for social psychology. Along the way, we will discuss the assumptions that must be met to properly use the procedure, and we will see how this way of thinking about the automatic–controlled distinction compares and contrasts with other prominent approaches. Although the procedure was developed in the context of memory research (Jacoby, 1991; Jacoby, Toth, & Yonelinas, 1993) we will focus on applications outside of pure memory research, emphasizing instead social cognition and behavior. Interested readers are referred to Jacoby (1998) for an overview of the procedure as developed in memory research and Yonelinas (2002) for a theoretical review of dual-process theories of memory using process dissociation and related methods.

PROCESS DISSOCIATION IN SOCIAL COGNITION

A study by Hense, Penner, and Nelson (1995) marked a point of departure from pure memory research to social memory. We will use this experiment to illustrate how process dissociation can be used to study social memory distortions. Participants were asked to remember a list of traits that described elderly or young individuals. Each trait was stereotypical for either old or young people. After studying the traits, participants were asked to recall the traits that described the older and younger target persons under two sets of instructions. In the *inclusion* condition, participants were asked to respond with the trait they had studied or, if they could not remember the trait, respond with the first word that came to mind. In this condition, responses can be driven by either intentionally retrieved memories or by automatic forms of memory that cause certain thoughts to come to mind more readily. In the inclusion condition intentional and unintentional forms of memory work in concert. In the *exclusion* condition, participants were asked to respond with a new trait that was *not* studied. If they remembered having studied a trait, they could successfully avoid reporting it. However, if they failed to consciously remember a trait, but it unintentionally came to mind, they would be likely to report it. This condition pits intentional and unintentional forms of memory against each other.

By comparing performance in inclusion and exclusion conditions, the influence of intentional and unintentional uses of memory can be estimated. To the extent that a person responds with the correct trait when they try to, but also withholds it when they try to, memory is under intentional control. Because in this paradigm subjective awareness of the memory is the basis for controlling memory reports, consciousness of the memory can also be inferred. But to the extent that past experience influences performance *regardless* of what participants are trying to do, they are being unintentionally influenced by memory. Jacoby and colleagues have termed this the "logic of opposition." The equations for estimating these influences will be discussed in a later section.

Hense and colleagues found that stereotypical traits had a selective influence on the unintentional use of memory without affecting controlled recollection. Stereotype-consistent traits such as slow and frail came to mind easily and biased memory reports whether they were trying to retrieve them or trying not to retrieve them. Consciously controlled memory was affected by a divided attention task, but this was independent of the stereotyping effect.

This study revealed an important dissociation. Within the single activity of remembering traits, intentional and unintentional forms of memory both fed into responses. Automatic influences reflected participants' own stereotypes. In contrast, consciously controlled memory was affected by divided attention. This study helped to characterize the mechanisms behind stereotypical memory biases that have been known for years (for a review see Stangor & McMillan, 1992). Social psychology has a tradition of emphasizing dissociations between underlying processes that would seemingly go together. Devine's (1989) important demonstration that the automatic activation of stereotypes could be dissociated from their use provides a clear example in the domain of stereotyping. Whereas Devine contrasted results from a priming task with results from self-report measures, the study by Hense and colleagues (1995) contrasted two aspects of a single act of remembering.

Even within the same task, intentional and unintentional uses of memory operate very differently. Using a memory paradigm in which race stereotypes could bias memory, we have explored the ways that components of memory are related to subjective experience (Payne, Jacoby, & Lambert, 2004). We found that people's subjective sense of confidence in their memories was well-attuned to recollection. When they were consciously recollecting the past, they expected to be right, and they usually were. When they had no recollection, they expected to be wrong, and they usually were. But confidence was not at all tuned in to the automatic influences of stereotypes on memory. When conscious memory failed, feelings of confidence gave no clues about whether an automatic bias was at work. This asymmetry of subjective awareness has important consequences for avoiding stereotypical biases.

In one condition of the study we required participants to answer every memory question, whether they remembered the correct answer or not. In the other condition, we instructed participants to answer only if they believed their answer to be correct. What effect did the freedom to choose have on memory reports? That depended on what aspect of memory is looked at. When it came to overall accuracy, the freedom to choose helped memory. Because subjective confidence was well-tuned to recollection, participants were able to avoid answering questions they would get wrong, and they chose to answer those items they were likely to get correct.

But the story was very different when it came to the influence of stereotypes. Memory reports were biased toward stereotype-consistent memory errors. But critically, the pattern of stereotype-consistent bias was just as strong when participants were allowed to choose as when they were required to answer every question. When it came to recollection, as in many areas of life, awareness bestowed control. But when stereotypes came readily to mind, Jamal was likely to become an athlete, and Walter was likely to become a politician independent of intent, independent of subjective experience, and independent of the choice to keep quiet.

These studies moved from basic memory research to social memory biases. But the process dissociation procedure can also be used in contexts completely unrelated to memory. Imagine now that the person approaching on the street looks like a suspect and you are a police officer. The suspect pulls an object from his pocket. What should you do? This was the decision facing four police officers on February 4, 1999 when they confronted Amadou Diallo outside his apartment in New York City. Their decision turned out to be wrong. Diallo was killed despite being unarmed and having nothing to do with the crime the officers were investigating. The case sparked public outrage and charges of racism because Diallo was Black. However, as in so many instances in daily life, there was no "control group" to gauge the impact of race. Since that incident, many similar cases have been reported in the national press. Many inside and outside of law enforcement have asked themselves, "What would I do in that situation?" We have used the process dissociation procedure to study what people actually do in that kind of split-second decision situation.

To see how process dissociation can be informative here, consider the different possible scenarios that might confront the officer. In one scenario, a Black suspect pulls a gun. Here, the "correct" response (at least for the purposes of our thought experiment) is to "shoot." That response might come about from two routes. One is an intentionally controlled response, in which you shoot because you mean to shoot. The second route is an unintentional or automatic response evoked by race stereotypes about the suspect. Because intentional and unintentional processes are working together here, we cannot tell them apart. Now consider a different scenario, in which the Black suspect holds only a wallet (as, in fact, Diallo held). Here an intentionally controlled response would be to not shoot. But an automatic response based on racial stereotypes might still lead one to pull the trigger. To the extent that a person systematically shoots despite not intending to, we know that an unintentional process is at work. But to the extent that a person shoots when they mean to, and not otherwise, we know that they are in control.

Our laboratory has conducted a number of studies examining these sorts of scenarios. We have used a simple procedure in which the faces of Black and White individuals are flashed on a computer screen just before pictures of handguns and hand tools are shown. All of the pictures are presented long enough to see clearly and all of the items are easy to identify. We show pairs of objects on the screen and ask participants to respond by pressing a "gun" key or a "tool" key as quickly as possible. Across many studies, we have found a clear and consistent tendency to mistakenly respond "gun" when a Black face is flashed. That tendency increases as participants are rushed to respond faster and faster (Payne, 2001; Payne, Lambert, & Jacoby, 2002).

The similarity of this task to other implicit measures makes it tempting to think of the bias as an "automatic effect." That way of thinking about it is consistent with the task dissociation approach, in which implicit tasks are identified with automatic processes and explicit tasks are identified with controlled processing. But that way of thinking overlooks the possibility of both automatic and controlled processes feeding into responses.

To reveal the distinct processes seamlessly guiding responses, we compared responses when automatic and controlled processes were acting in concert versus when they were opposed. When both automatic and controlled processes pointed to the "gun" response (an inclusion condition), the probability of a gun response was .75. This can be formalized as the sum of controlled processing and automatic processing when control fails: Control + Automatic × (1 − Control). Because the values here are probabilities, the absence of an event can be easily expressed as (1 − the probability of that event). On Black–tool trials where automatic stereotyping would lead to a "gun" response but controlled responding would lead to a "tool" response, participants still responded "gun" with a probability of .37. This represents the tendency for an automatic bias to drive responses in the absence of control: Automatic × (1 − Control).

To estimate how much of this behavior was due to intentional control, we took the difference in performance when both automatic and controlled processes favored a response, versus when automatic but not controlled processes favored it. This gives a control estimate of .38 (= .75 − .37).[1] It is important to notice that control, as conceptualized here, is not a reaction to a stereotypical thought. It is not thought suppression or an after-the-fact editing of responses. It is the ability to focus attention, thought, and action on goal-relevant behaviors independent of automatic distractions. If control were a perfect 1.0, actions would be determined completely by intentions. In this experiment the value was much lower, allowing for other factors to unintentionally influence behavior. With simple constraints like speeded responding, it is not difficult to see momentary disorders of autonomy crippling good intentions.

To estimate the automatic effect of stereotyping we looked at how often participants responded in line with the stereotype even when they intended to respond otherwise (.37). Although this value reflects an unintentional process, it is an underestimate because it is the joint probability that an automatic process was at work *and* that control failed. The more control a person exerts, the more this value underestimates the automatic stereotyping effect. Under the assumption that automatic and controlled processes are independent, we can correct for this underestimation, dividing by the probability that control has failed ($1 - .38 = .62$). This yields an automatic estimate of .60.

Using this procedure, we found that requiring fast responses dramatically reduced control, compared to a group that responded at their own pace. But fast responding had no effect on the automatic process, as we would expect because automatic processes operate quickly and require little capacity. On the other hand, the automatic estimate was affected by the Black versus White faces. The automatic tendency toward "gun" responses was higher on Black compared to White trials.

These dissociations are important because they enhance our ability to answer questions about how unintended racial biases influence people. When studying how stereotypes have their effects, a commonly asked question is, "is it an automatic or a controlled effect?" And a common way to test that question is to impose a cognitive load, to rush responding, or look for motivational differences. If cognitive load, rushed responding, or low motivation interferes with the effect, it is inferred to be resource dependent and therefore likely controlled. In contrast, if these variables have no effect (or increase the stereotyping effect), it is inferred that the effect is automatic, because it is not dependent on the investment of cognitive resources.

Even a relatively "simple" behavior is complex. It is difficult to find any behavior that does not include some amalgam of processes with automatic features and controlled features (Bargh, 1989). It therefore becomes important to separate complex behaviors into more basic components. The process dissociation approach shifts the question from "automatic *or* controlled?" to "what combination of automatic *and* controlled?" The focus changes from labeling a phenomenon to taking apart its component processes. Importantly, process dissociation also provides a measurement model for quantifying and summarizing those components.

This new question becomes particularly interesting when automatic and controlled components behave in different ways. We have uncovered several variables that all impact or correlate with people's judgments in the weapon scenarios. Each of these selectively affects either automatic stereotyping or intentional control. For instance, we recently investigated the effects of self-regulation depletion on stereotyping (Govorun & Payne, 2006). Based on prior findings that exerting self-control in one domain reduces self-regulation in a subsequent context (Muraven & Baumeister, 2000), we predicted that the depletion group would show reduced intentional control. We assigned one group to perform a boring but attention-demanding Stroop color naming task for a continuous 15 minute period. Following this tedious task, participants completed the weapon identification task as described above. The control group performed the Stroop task for only 30 seconds, and then went on to the weapon task unfatigued. As predicted, the depleted group showed poorer control, but no differences in automatic stereotyping. For individuals with a stereotypical automatic bias, this reduction in control resulted in more stereotypical false "gun" responses. For these individuals, automatic stereotypes were left unopposed by intentional control.

Compare that manipulation with another one intended to influence stereotyping, a blatant warning that the weapon identification task measures racial stereotyping and that they should be careful to avoid stereotyping. Ironically, warned participants showed a more stereotypical pattern of mistakes than a control group (Payne, Lambert, & Jacoby, 2002). Was this because the ability to control responses was diminished, or because the warning made race accessible to the point that it increases the automatic impact of stereotypes? Our results suggest the latter – a blatant warning increased stereotyping via increasing automatic bias, having no effect on control.

From a distance, the warning study and the ego depletion study appear very similar. Compared to control groups, both warning about race stereotypes and depleting self-regulatory strength increased stereotyping as measured by errors. But these two superficially similar effects were driven by different mechanisms (see also Lambert, Payne, Jacoby, Shaffer, Chasteen, & Khan, 2003). In the warning study, stereotyping increased by boosting the automatic activation of stereotypic associations. In the depletion study, stereotyping increased by reducing control over behaviors.

The two studies we just described suggest a rather pessimistic outlook, because both manipulations increased stereotyping rather than decreasing it. It is worth considering, from both practical and scientific points of view, how stereotyping can be decreased below the baseline level of our control participants. Process dissociation allows us to track how the automatic and controlled components of behavior mediate that change. Stereotypical responding could be reduced either by reducing automatic bias or by increasing intentional control.

A recent study tested the utility of concrete action plans in overcoming the automatic impact of race stereotypes (Stewart & Payne, 2006). Previous work has shown that concrete action plans linking a specific environmental cue to an action can help people carry out their intentions more effectively (Gollwitzer, 1999). When applied to stereotypical weapon judgments, that idea might take the form of "when I see a Black person, I will respond 'tool'." However, this kind of plan would just replace one bias with another. We wanted to find out whether the action phase could be used to generate a thought that would counteract the influence of the stereotype without creating a new bias. To that end, we asked participants in one condition to form a plan so that whenever they saw a Black person, they would "think safe." In fact, that simple plan reduced the effect of stereotypes, compared to a control group who were asked to "think quickly" when they saw a Black person.

Did this simple treatment reduce stereotyping by increasing control or reducing automatic influences? Across three studies, we found that the thought-plan reduced the automatic influence of race, without altering intentional control. Moreover, the plan took effect in the first several trials, suggesting that it was very efficient and did not require extensive practice as other methods of altering automatic biases may (e.g. Kawakami et al., 2000).

SOME WAYS TO THINK ABOUT AUTOMATIC AND CONTROLLED ESTIMATES

The meanings of the estimates generated by process dissociation depend on the kind of behavior that is being analyzed. In all of the studies reviewed so far, the automatic estimates represented unintentional influences of stereotypes. But as we moved from memory studies to perceptual judgments, the meanings of the controlled estimate changed more dramatically. In the memory studies, the controlled component was recollection: a consciously controlled use of memory. Having full access to the context and the details of an event allowed participants to use or not to use whatever came to mind. These shifts in the interpretations of process estimates are unavoidable, because people control their behavior in different ways depending on what they are doing.

In the weapon judgment studies, what is the best way to characterize the processes underlying intentional control? Concretely, the controlled component reflected the ability to respond based on one set of information (the features of the target items) and not another (racial stereotypes). Seen in this light, the weapon task is similar to other compatibility tasks such as the Stroop color naming task. In that task, subjects try to name the ink colors of words while ignoring the word itself. When the word is a color word, it becomes very difficult to name an ink if it is incompatible with the word meaning (e.g. the word red in green ink). In fact, in the Govorun and Payne study, performance on the Stroop task was significantly correlated with the controlled (but not the automatic) estimate from the weapons task.

Executive Function and the Control of Bias

The Stroop task and similar interference tasks are usually understood as measures of executive control – the ways people direct their information processing and actions to keep them consistent with their goals. Executive control is believed to include subprocesses including selection of relevant information, inhibition of interfering information, and maintenance of the currently pursued goal (Baddeley, 1986; Kane, Bleckley, Conway, & Engle, 2001). The analogy between the weapon judgment scenario and the Stroop task suggests that control in the weapons task has something to do with devoting selective attention to one stream of inputs, while blocking out another.

A recent study supports this suggestion. Payne (2005) used an antisaccade task to test the idea that control in the weapons task relies on the executive processes of selective attention. The antisaccade is a well-established measure of attentional control often used in cognitive and neuroscience studies (Everling & Fischer, 1998). Think back to the last time you were in the middle of a talk or lecture, and someone mistakenly opened the door only to sheepishly realize that they were in the wrong place. Try as we might to concentrate on the matters at hand, it is incredibly difficult not to turn and look at the interloper. The reason is that the orienting reflex which compels us to attend to new items in our surroundings is highly automatic. The ability to intentionally override such automatic reflexes has been used to measure executive control. The antisaccade task asks participants to avoid looking at an item that flashes abruptly on a computer screen. A distracting item (e.g. a red circle) appears on one side of the screen, and a target (e.g. a letter to be identified) flashes on the other side a fraction of a second later. Looking away from the distracter will enhance identification of the target, but looking at the distracter will interfere.

Research from our lab showed that performance on an antisaccade task was correlated with the controlled component, but not the automatic component, in the weapon judgment task (Payne, 2005). In contrast, the automatic estimate was correlated with two measures of implicit race attitudes, the implicit association test and evaluative priming. This dissociation reveals two very different kinds of processes that normally blend imperceptibly together as people make a single decision. The answer to the question "how would I act in that situation?" has at least two parts. The first depends on a person's automatic reactions to Black individuals. The second depends on the person's ability to engage executive control, that is, to keep their thoughts and actions on track rather than being swayed by accessible but inappropriate information.

These studies illustrate a range of processes that might be measured using process dissociation methods. Other research has found creative applications of the procedure outside of both memory and stereotyping. As one illustration, Fitzsimons and Williams (2000) used a modification of the process dissociation procedure to investigate the *mere measurement effect*. The mere measurement effect is the finding that simply asking a person about how likely they are to perform a behavior in the future actually increases the likelihood that they will perform that behavior (Morwitz, Johnson, & Schmittlein, 1993; Sherman, 1980). Fitzsimons and Williams (2000, study 1) asked one group of participants how likely they would be to choose a new brand of candy bar, whereas the control group was not asked about the candy bar. The mere measurement effect suggests that the group who was asked would be more likely to choose the candy bar than the control group. In addition to the intent question, participants were given information suggesting that they were more or less likely to actually receive the candy bar if they chose it. This manipulation was intended to manipulate the self-interest of participants. A rational (in the sense of self-interested) analysis would suggest that participants should be more likely to choose the candy bar when informed that they were likely to get the candy bar. By crossing the measurement of intent with the self-interest information, this study created conditions in which the mere measurement effect was congruent with self-interest, and conditions in which it was incongruent with self-interest.

This study showed that, indeed, participants asked about their likely choice more often chose the candy bar. Using a modified model based on the logic of process dissociation, these researchers separated two components of the effect. One component reflected how strongly the intent question influenced choice regardless of self-interest (akin to the automatic component in the other studies discussed here). The other component reflected the extent to which choices were guided by the self-interest. This is related to the controlled component we have discussed, but because the procedure pitted self-interest against the mere measurement effect, this component reflected self-interested decision-making. The intent question influenced choices largely irrespective of whether it was consistent with self-interest or not, an effect driven by the automatic component.

From the studies reviewed here, it is clear that the process dissociation procedure is not limited to measuring recollection and familiarity in the context of memory research where it was developed. Although extensions beyond memory research are a relatively new endeavor, the procedure is flexible, and can be adapted to any number of topics. The key to this flexibility is that process dissociation represents a general framework for thinking about intentional and unintentional processes. The basic logic of placing intended and unintended influences in concert and in opposition in order to disentangle them can be implemented across many, many domains.

It is important to note that the meaning of the processes measured depends entirely on the task being studied. Phrased another way, the meaning of the estimates depends on what processes are placed in concert and in opposition with each other. If implicit and explicit influences of memory are arranged in this way, the procedure can yield estimates of implicit and explicit memory. If automatic stereotyping and executive control are arranged in this way, the procedure can estimate these processes, and so on. As these contrasts illustrate, the logic of opposition creates a conceptual and methodological way to think about many different kinds of factors that might influence people either intentionally or regardless of intent. Nevertheless, it is often tempting to think of the automatic and controlled components as having fixed meanings, based on other prominent process distinctions that have been made in social cognition. In the following section we compare the process dissociation approach to some of these commonly invoked dimensions of automatic and controlled processing, highlighting the similarities and differences.

Invariants and Particulars

Given all the different uses to which one might put the procedure, one might wonder if there is anything that the different automatic or controlled processes have in common (see Moors & De Houwer, Chapter 1 of this volume). Yet there appear to be certain properties consistently attached to controlled components, and certain properties attached to automatic components, across the many different domains. For example, the controlled component in memory studies requires attention, and is disrupted by distraction (Hense et al., 1995; Sherman et al., 2003). The controlled component in weapon identification studies requires time, and is disrupted by rushed responding (Payne et al., 2002). Control in the weapon studies is also influenced by motivations. Higher motivation to control prejudice is associated with more intentional control during judgments (Payne, 2005; Amodio et al., 2004). In contrast to these results for intentional control, these same studies show that the automatic estimate appears unaffected by divided attention, occurs rapidly, and is not associated with motivations. Readers may have noticed that these are the defining characteristics usually invoked to distinguish automatic and controlled processing in general (Bargh, 1989; Posner & Snyder, 1975; Shiffrin & Schneider, 1977).

This is no accident. The fact that these properties remain attached to automatic and controlled estimates regardless of the specific task suggests something interesting. It suggests that regardless of *what* one intends to do, it is the constraining of behavior to intent that requires resources, time, and motivation. On the other hand, it is being pushed along regardless of intent that is quick, effortless, and easy, perhaps regardless of what force is doing the pushing.

In this light, the relationship between the process dissociation framework and other commonly studied forms of automatic and controlled behavior becomes clearer. To bring this relationship more sharply into focus, we will consider as examples two dual-process distinctions prominent in social psychology. The first is deliberative reasoning versus shallow heuristic-based reasoning. The second is the distinction between implicit and explicit attitudes. These distinctions form the crux of more than one prominent dual-process theory aimed at explaining why, when, or how automatic and controlled aspects of cognition combine to drive behavior. Each distinction could potentially be illuminated by a process dissociation approach, once it is understood what assumptions must be made and how process estimates could map on to these distinctions.

The contrast between deliberative reasoning and shallow inferences based on heuristics is at the heart of many dual-process theories (Chaiken, 1980; Fazio, 1990; Petty & Cacioppo, 1986). The process dissociation estimates discussed thus far in the context of memory and weapon identification studies seem far removed from this distinction. However, the conceptual approach can be applied here just as in these other areas of study. Perhaps the most closely related research is the work of Fitzsimons and Williams (2000) described above. In their studies they placed self-interest and the mere measurement effect in concert and in opposition to tease apart their separate contributions. It is easy to imagine other situations where careful thought would lead to one kind of outcome, and heuristics would lead to another. Here the two processes would be set in opposition. It is just as easy to imagine an experimental arrangement in which careful thought and heuristics would lead to the same response, thereby setting up an in-concert condition.

In fact, this kind of paradigm is routinely used in studies of attitudes and persuasion, although it may not be framed in these terms. A common procedure for studying the processes of attitude change is to manipulate argument strength. The assumption is that when people are thinking carefully they will be more persuaded by strong than weak arguments. This manipulation is sometimes crossed with a heuristic or cue, such as the number of arguments used or the attractiveness of the source making the arguments. The assumption is that when people are processing shallowly, they are more likely to be persuaded by these simple cues.

When argument strength and heuristic cues are fully crossed, the design creates some conditions in which both deliberate thinking and heuristic thinking would lead to agreement or disagreement with the message (i.e. the strong argument, positive cue cell and the weak argument, negative cue cell). Also created are conditions in which deliberative and heuristic thinking would lead to different outcomes (i.e., the strong argument, negative cue cell and the weak argument, positive cue cell). Because deliberative thinking and heuristic-based thinking can be arranged in this way, they can potentially be separated and quantified using the process dissociation approach. One estimate would represent the contribution of deliberate reasoning and the other would represent the contribution of heuristic reasoning. As in any new application of a model, validation tests would need to be performed to test whether the assumptions of the process dissociation procedure match the properties of the attitude change paradigm. The broader point is that process dissociation does not fix the meanings of the automatic and controlled estimates. It is instead a way to think about and quantify the contributions of different processes, as needed to answer specific questions.

In the studies of race biases in memory and perceptual identification described in the previous section, the automatic estimate can be said to reflect implicit attitudes or stereotypes. Implicit attitudes are commonly contrasted with explicit attitudes, which are the attitudes people overtly express when directly asked. However, in the studies described, automatic biases were contrasted not with explicit attitudes, but with the ability to intentionally control responses. By this approach an implicit attitude is the evaluation that drives responses when intentional control fails. For some purposes, however, researchers wish to separate implicit attitudes from explicit attitudes.

The typical way of separating implicit and explicit attitudes is by comparing an implicit measure and an explicit measure. If an outcome behavior correlates with an implicit measure but not an explicit measure, it is said to be the product of implicit or automatic processes. If a behavior correlates with an explicit measure but not an implicit measure, it is said to be the product of controlled processes. However, many different factors vary between implicit and explicit measures beyond automaticity and control. For example, how should one compare reaction times in word pairings to Likert scales? Even if they are standardized to the same scale, should they be interpreted in the same ways? What if one measure is more reliable or sensitive than the other? Early findings that implicit and explicit measures of attitudes toward the same topics tended to correlate weakly, if at all, led to a great deal of theorizing about whether implicit and explicit attitudes represent separate constructs (e.g., Fazio & Olson, 2003; Wilson, Lindsey, & Schooler, 2000). In our view, there are many reasons to expect the relationship between implicit and explicit measures to be weakened, even if they are tapping the same construct. Before we are able to fully address this issue of single versus separate constructs, it will be important to deal with other factors such as reliability (which tends to be lower for implicit measures; see Cunningham, Preacher, & Banaji, 2001) and the difficulties of comparing vastly different types of behavior on implicit versus explicit tasks.

Because of these limitations to the *task* dissociation approach, we have pursued a complementary approach within the *process* dissociation framework. It may be possible to design experiments in which intentional and unintentional contributions estimated from the same behavior represent explicit and implicit attitudes. If so, this would allow intentional and unintentional aspects of attitudes to be compared on the same scale and within the same task, overcoming the problems of comparing across radically different measures. We next describe a newly developed method for measuring attitudes implicitly within the task dissociation framework, and then explore how that method might be expanded for a process dissociation analysis.

We have known for years that people sometimes misattribute their evaluative reactions from one source to another source (Dutton & Aron, 1974; Schwarz & Clore, 1983). For example, Murphy and Zajonc (1993) showed that flashing pleasant and unpleasant images before presenting an ambiguous Chinese pictograph influenced the way people evaluated the pictographs. In this study, the outcome of interest was not response times, but how pleasant or unpleasant participants found the pictographs. When the prime was pleasant, participants found the pictograph more pleasant; when the prime was unpleasant, participants found the pictograph less pleasant.

Although this effect has been widely known for more than a decade, there is an important implication that has gone unnoticed: This misattribution produces an indirect measure of individuals' attitudes toward the primes. If a particular prime item systematically causes participants to evaluate an ambiguous pictograph positively, it suggests a positive attitude toward the prime item. In the original Murphy and Zajonc (1993) procedure, the primes only affected judgments of the pictographs when they were flashed too briefly to be consciously identified. However, with some modifications to the procedure, we were able to produce strong misattributions even when the primes were plainly visible, and even when participants were blatantly warned against being influenced by them (Payne, Cheng, Govorun, & Stewart, 2005).

Using this modified procedure (which we refer to as an affect misattribution procedure), we found that the kinds of misattributions people made when primed with pictures of George W. Bush and John Kerry strongly predicted their explicitly rated attitudes toward the candidates ($r = .65$) and who they intended to vote for ($r = .58$). We expected high implicit–explicit correspondence in this domain because people are well aware of their political attitudes and quite willing to express them. In this case, whatever variance in the two measures did not overlap may have been caused by the problems of comparing across two very different kinds of measures.

In another study, we replaced the pictures of Bush and Kerry with pictures of White and Black young men who were judged as appearing prototypical of their respective groups. For people who had a negative affective reaction when presented with a Black person, we expected this reaction to be reflected in their judgments of the pictographs. As expected, we found a pattern of in-group favoritism on the task. White subjects showed a strong pattern of misattributions implying more favorable attitudes toward the White photos than the Black photos. In contrast, Black participants showed the opposite pattern. These patterns of misattributions persisted despite blatant warnings against being influenced by the primes. They also correlated with explicit ratings of attitudes toward Blacks and

Whites as groups ($r = .58$). However, this relationship was moderated by people's motivations to respond without prejudice. Among those who lacked such motivation, their implicit and explicit measures correlated very strongly. However, among individuals who were highly motivated to avoid prejudice, the relationship was much weaker. This was because highly motivated people expressed highly positive attitudes toward Blacks on the self-report measure, but still showed negativity toward Blacks on the implicit measure.

So far, these results are exactly what one would expect based on previous research comparing implicit and explicit attitude measures, except in two respects. The first is that the correlations are larger than most findings reported. The second is that the misattribution measure produced much higher reliability than most implicit measures, and equal to many explicit measures (average Cronbach's *alpha* = .88). Although the kinds of responses compared in these studies (pleasantness judgments about pictographs and favorability ratings of individuals or groups) are not as discordant as comparing reaction times and rating scales, they were still not directly comparable.

Consider now a modification of the affect misattribution procedure consisting of two phases. One phase is identical to the procedure already described: participants judge pictographs as pleasant or unpleasant and are instructed *to avoid* being influenced by the primes of Black and White photos. In the second phase, participants see the same item pairs, but this time they are instructed to ignore the pictographs and evaluate their reactions to the prime photos themselves as pleasant or unpleasant. The first phase measures attitudes toward the prime items indirectly, through their unintended effects on judgments of the pictographs. The second phase measures attitudes toward the prime items directly. In the first phase, participants are trying not to express any evaluation of the primes. In the second phase, they are trying to express their evaluation of the primes. The stimuli and judgment scale are held constant; the only factor that varies is participants' intentions. With the stimuli and judgment scale held constant, we are in a position to make direct comparisons between the two conditions. We could then use the first phase as an implicit measure of racial attitudes, and the second phase as an explicit measure.

We do not need to stop with this comparison. The second phase of the task is not only an explicit measure of attitudes toward the primes – it is also an *inclusion* condition. The ways people judge the pleasantness may be a product of both intentional and unintentional evaluative influences. The first phase is not only an implicit measure, but it is also an *exclusion* condition. Judgments of the pictographs are only influenced by evaluations of the primes when people's intentions to avoid their influence fail. By comparing these two conditions, we can estimate how much control each person has over whether they express a particular evaluation, and we can estimate what evaluation is revealed when control fails.

As part of validating this procedure, we have to validate some assumptions that are made when carrying out the process dissociation analysis. In the next section, we outline those assumptions that are made by any application of process dissociation, and place them in the context of other models and alternative assumptions that may be made.

Assumptions and Alternatives

All mathematical models make assumptions in order to relate actual data to formal equations. When applying the process dissociation framework in a new context, it is important to be clear about those assumptions. One assumption of process dissociation is that the controlled and automatic processes at work exert similar influences in inclusion and exclusion conditions. In other words, the two processes should exert as much influence together in the inclusion condition as they exert against each other in the exclusion condition. It is important to avoid the misinterpretation that automatic and controlled estimates should be numerically equal across experimental conditions, or to each other. If the estimates logically had to equal some particular value, we would not need to do the experiment or compute the estimates from data. Instead, it means that the automatic and controlled processes in question play the same roles in inclusion and exclusion conditions.

The second assumption, which has been discussed more widely, is that automatic and controlled processes are independent of each other (for discussions of the independence assumption in memory research, see Curran and Hintzman, 1995; 1997; Jacoby, Begg, & Toth, 1997; Jacoby & Shrout, 1997). Whether this assumption is met depends on the experimental paradigm that is being used. In some cases, automatic and controlled processes could be positively or negatively correlated with each other, which would violate the independence assumption. Because we cannot directly observe the processes, we must indirectly test whether the processes are likely to be independent or dependent. The most common way to do this is to look for dissociations, or selective effects on one or both estimates. The logic is that if automatic and controlled processes are independent, then it should be relatively easy to find variables that affect one but not the other. If the independence assumption is badly violated, then automatic and controlled processes would strongly covary with each other. As a result, it would be difficult to find variables that affect one process without affecting the other.

Much of our work has been focused on examining selective effects on automatic and controlled components in the weapon identification procedure. For example, Payne (2001) found a double dissociation between the two processes. Prime pictures of Black and White faces affected the automatic component but not the controlled component. In contrast, speeded responding affected the controlled component but not the automatic component. Further, racial attitudes correlated selectively with the automatic component. Lambert and colleagues (2003) found that anxiety over an impending public discussion reduced the controlled component without affecting the automatic component. The study described above by Govorun and Payne (2006) showed that ego depletion influenced the controlled component but not the automatic component. Finally, the study by Stewart and Payne (2006) described above showed that specific action plans could affect the automatic component without changing the controlled component.

These dissociations would not be expected if the independence assumption were violated in the weapon identification task. However, for some tasks, or under some conditions, it is always possible to violate one's assumptions. Researchers will be most familiar with these considerations in the context of common statistical tests. It is widely understood that different statistical tests make different assumptions. For example, analysis of variance (ANOVA) assumes a dependent variable that is at least an interval scale, a normally distributed dependent variable, and homogeneity of variance across different conditions, among other things. If an assumption is violated slightly (e.g., a slightly skewed distribution) the resulting biases are usually small. If an assumption is violated badly (for example, distributions are heavily skewed) it is often a good idea to choose a different test that does not depend on the problematic assumption. Just as the failure of an assumption in a particular study does not invalidate the ANOVA technique in general, studies showing that an assumption of process dissociation has been violated do not invalidate the general method. Instead, other methods may be more appropriate in a particular context.

Several other methods are sometimes used as alternatives to process dissociation. These include the task dissociation method (comparing explicit and implicit measures), signal detection theory, and multinomial models. Although they may not be explicitly stated, each of these approaches also involves assumptions which may be violated. Let us take first the task dissociation method. Although this method does not use a mathematical model, it still makes some assumptions. By using an implicit task to measure automatic or unconscious processes, and an explicit task to measure controlled or conscious processes, the task dissociation approach makes the tacit assumption that each measure is process-pure. That is, one assumes that the measures differ only on the dimension of interest to the researcher. If the two tasks differ in ways other than the explicit/implicit dimension, then any different results on explicit versus implicit tasks could be because of those other (confounded) features.

The psychological processes behind implicit tasks (such as reaction times to classify words) and those behind explicit tasks (such as endorsing complex propositional statements) are very different. As a result, the assumption that implicit and explicit tasks differ only on the dimension of interest is not likely to be commonly met. Both process dissociation and task dissociation methods make assumptions to relate observed data to unobserved theoretical ideas. In the case of process dissociation, those assumptions are made explicit, whereas in the task dissociation method they often remain unstated.

A second alternative approach is signal detection theory (SDT). Signal detection theory assumes that perceivers are natural statisticians, who make decisions about world events in the way that researchers decide whether to reject a null hypothesis (Tanner & Swets, 1954). A decision about what one is perceiving or how to respond is treated as a problem of detecting a signal in a noisy environment. Perceivers have a certain amount of evidence, and they select a criterion (similar to the conventional use of $p < .05$ in psychology research) that marks off how strong the evidence has to be before they will accept that a signal is present. Given a pattern of correct responses and errors, signal detection theory can separate *sensitivity* (the ability to discriminate when a signal is actually present or absent) from *bias* (a tendency to respond as if a signal is present whether it is or not). Signal detection theory is mute on issues of automatic versus intentionally controlled behavior, and its development predated the current interest in automaticity. Nonetheless, signal detection analyses are sometimes preferred to process dissociation on the belief that SDT makes fewer assumptions.

That belief is mistaken. Signal detection theory makes some of the same assumptions as process dissociation, and some that are different. For instance, SDT also makes an independence assumption. It assumes that sensitivity and bias are independent in the same way that process dissociation assumes that controlled and automatic components are independent. Signal detection also assumes normal distributions of evidence strength, and equal variances. Beyond statistical assumptions, signal detection makes substantive assumptions about the way humans process information. For instance, it assumes that decisions are made on the basis of a single continuum of evidence. There is no allowance for qualitatively different kinds of evidence. Process dissociation, in contrast, treats intentional control and automatic biases as qualitatively different processes feeding into behavior. Like ANOVA, both models make assumptions that may be more or less suitable in a given context.

Finally, multinomial models have a great deal in common with process dissociation. A multinomial model posits a branching tree of unobserved cognitive processes, leading eventually to behavioral responses (Riefer & Batchelder, 1988). For example, Klauer and Wegener (1998) developed a model to study the effects of stereotypic expectations on memory. In this model, participants attempt to remember whether they witnessed a given action. If so, they attempt to remember who performed the action. If they cannot remember who performed the action, they may remember the social category to which the actor belonged. And if they cannot remember the social category, they may guess the category on the basis of stereotypes, and so on. Using the pattern of correct and incorrect memory responses, a computer algorithm is used to estimate the best-fitting values for each process. In this way, the degree of memory and guessing at each stage can be estimated, and the model can be tested statistically to see how well it fits the data (see also Conrey et al., 2005).

Multinomial models are sometimes presented as alternatives to a process dissociation approach. However, it is probably more accurate to think of process dissociation and multinomial models as two specific cases of a general family of models. Both make similar assumptions. Both are aimed at separating unobservable psychological processes that give rise to observed behavior. Process dissociation uses algebra to estimate the cognitive processes involved, whereas multinomial models use a computer algorithm. However, the relatedness of the models can be seen in the fact that the process dissociation model can be represented and estimated as a multinomial model with two process parameters (automatic and controlled components; Jacoby, 1998; Payne, Jacoby, & Lambert, 2005).

A multinomial model may have any number of parameters, in any number of combinations. This is both a strength and a weakness. It is a strength because it allows flexibility in exploring various theoretical models. However, the more parameters a model has, the more it is likely to fit any given set of data, even an incorrect one. As the number of parameters increases, the possible ways to combine those parameters increases exponentially (do people attempt to remember social category only after memory for the person fails, or do they first remember the category and then the person?). There are often many different models that could fit the data equally well. It is important when using this approach to have strong a priori theoretical predictions to avoid choosing an arbitrary model or capitalizing on chance.

Despite these caveats, multinomial models as well as task dissociations, signal detection, and process dissociation all provide valuable tools for taking apart the complex patterns in social behavior into simpler, more digestible parts. Social psychologists know a lot about how knowledge structures and prior experience guide our reactions. Those procedures we know a lot about tend to seem harmless, whereas less familiar ones tend to seem more menacing. As we shift from the comfortable ANOVA and task dissociation methods toward signal detection theory, which is less frequently seen in social psychology, many readers may feel less sure. And as we look closely at multinomial models and process dissociation, there will probably be more unease. The methods seem foreign, the assumptions seem difficult. All of these tools make assumptions, and there is variability in how nervous these assumptions make us. But the difficulty in many cases is not so much with the methods and assumptions as with the newness of these tools for social psychologists. The costs of making assumptions must be gauged against the potential gains in knowledge generated by using these tools. In our view, the evidence reviewed here shows that potential to be high.

CONCLUSION

We began this chapter by exploring the startling ways that brain damage can fragment mental events that normally flow silently together. At a finer grain of analysis, comparison of implicit and explicit tasks reveals the same kinds of fissures in normal healthy persons. Social psychological research on automaticity (Bargh & Ferguson, 2000), willed behavior (Wegner, 2002), and implicit cognition (Greenwald & Banaji, 1995) is humbling, because it suggests that disorders of autonomy may not be such rare conditions after all. They can be captured in little slips and subtle lapses that are made and forgotten every day. We may have a little more in common with some lesion patients than we thought. But how much? Process dissociation helps tally up the lapses, giving a number to something as gossamer as goals, intent, and will.

NOTE

1. The values of process estimates here differ by .02–.03 from the values reported in Payne (2001) because a statistical correction was applied to the data in that article to correct for extreme values prior to calculating estimates. Here we have used the raw data for the sake of clarity.

REFERENCES

Amodio, D. M., Harmon-Jones, E., Devine, P. G., Curtin, J. J., Hartley, S. L., & Covert, A. E. (2004). Neural signs for the detection of unintentional race bias. *Psychological Science, 15*, 225–232.

Baddeley, A. D. (1986). *Working memory*. London: Oxford University Press.

Bargh, J. A. (1989). Conditional automaticity: Varieties of automatic influences in social perception and cognition. In J. S. Uleman & J. A. Bargh (Eds.) *Unintended thought* (pp. 3–51). New York: Guilford.

Bargh, J. A. (2005). Bypassing the will: Towards demystifying behavioral priming effects. In R. Hassin, J. Uleman & J. Bargh (Eds.), *The new unconscious*. Oxford, UK: Oxford University Press.

Bargh, J. A., & Ferguson, M. J. (2000). Beyond behaviorism: On the automaticity of higher mental processes. *Psychological Bulletin, 126*, 925–945.

Beer, J. S., Heerey, E. H., Keltner, D., Scabini, D., & Knight, R. T. (2003). The regulatory function of self-conscious emotion: Insights from patients with orbitofrontal damage. *Journal of Personality and Social Psychology, 85*, 594–604.

Chaiken, S. (1980). Heuristic versus systematic information processing and the use of source versus message cues in persuasion. *Journal of Personality and Social Psychology, 39*, 752–766.

Conrey, F. R., Sherman, J. W., Gawronski, B., Hugenberg, K., & Groom, C. (2005). Separating multiple processes in implicit social cognition: The Quad-Model of implicit task performance. *Journal of Personality and Social Psychology, 89*, 469–487.

Cunningham, W. A., Preacher, K. J., & Banaji, M. R. (2001). Implicit attitude measures: Consistency, stability, and convergent validity. *Psychological Science, 12*, 163–170.

Curran, T., & Hintzman, D. L. (1995). Violations of the independence assumption in process dissociation. *Journal of Experimental Psychology: Learning, Memory, and Cognition, 21*, 531–547.

Curran, T., & Hintzman, D. L. (1997). Causes and consequences of correlations in process dissociation. *Journal of Experimental Psychology: Learning, Memory, and Cognition, 23*, 496–504.

Devine, P. G. (1989). Stereotypes and prejudice: Their automatic and controlled components. *Journal of Personality and Social Psychology, 56*, 5–18.

Doody, R. S., & Jankovic, J. (1992). The alien hand and related signs. *Journal of Neurology, Neurosurgery, and Psychiatry, 55*, 806–810.

Dutton, D. G., & Aron, A. P. (1974). Some evidence for heightened sexual attraction under conditions of high anxiety. *Journal of Personality and Social Psychology, 30*, 510–517.

Everling, S., & Fischer, B. (1998). The antisaccade: A review of basic research and clinical studies. *Neuropsychologia, 36*, 885–899.

Fazio, R. H. (1990). Multiple processes by which attitudes guide behavior: The MODE model as an integrative framework. In M. P. Zanna (Ed.), *Advances in experimental social psychology* (Vol. 23, pp. 75–109). New York: Academic Press.

Fazio, R. H., & Olson, M. A. (2003). Implicit measures in social cognition research: Their meaning and uses. *Annual Review of Psychology, 54*, 297–327.

Fitzsimons, G. J., & Williams, P. (2000). Asking question can change choice behavior: Does it do so automatically or effortfully? *Journal of Experimental Psychology: Applied, 6*, 195–206.

Gollwitzer, P. M. (1999). Implementation intentions: Strong effects of simple plans. *American Psychologist, 54*, 493–503.

Govorun, O., & Payne, B. K. (2006). Ego depletion and prejudice: Separating automatic and controlled components. *Social Cognition, 24*, 111–136.

Greenwald, A. G., & Banaji, M. R. (1995). Implicit social cognition: Attitudes, self-esteem, and stereotypes. *Psychological Review, 102*, 4–27.

Hense, R. L., Penner, L. A., & Nelson, D. L. (1995). Implicit memory for age stereotypes. *Social Cognition, 13*, 399–415.

Jacoby, L. L. (1991). A process dissociation framework: Separating automatic from intentional uses of memory. *Journal of Memory and Language, 30*, 513–541.

Jacoby, L. L. (1998). Invariance in automatic influences of memory: Toward a user's guide for the process-dissociation procedure. *Journal of Experimental Psychology: Learning, Memory, and Cognition., 24*, 3–26.

Jacoby, L. L., Begg, I. M., & Toth, J. P. (1997). In defense of functional independence: Violations of assumptions underlying the process-dissociation procedure? *Journal of Experimental Psychology: Learning, Memory, and Cognition, 23*, 484–495.

Jacoby, L. L., & Dallas, M. (1981). On the relationships between autobiographical memory and perceptual learning. *Journal of Experimental Psychology: General, 110*, 306–340.

Jacoby, L. L., & Shrout, P. E. (1997). Toward a psychometric analysis of violations of the independence assumption in process dissociation. *Journal of Experimental Psychology: Learning, Memory, and Cognition, 23*, 505–510.

Jacoby, L. L., Toth, J. P., & Yonelinas, A. P. (1993). Separating conscious and unconscious influences of memory: Measuring recollection. *Journal of Experimental Psychology: General, 122*, 139–154.

James, W. (1890). *Principles of psychology*. New York: Holt.

Kane, M. J., Bleckley, M. K., Conway, A. R. A., & Engle, R. W. (2001). A controlled-attention view of working-memory capacity. *Journal of Experimental Psychology: General, 130*, 169–183.

Kawakami, K., Dovidio, J. F., Moll, J., Hermsen, S., & Russin, A. (2000). Just say no (to stereotyping): Effects of training in the negation of stereotypic associations on stereotype activation. *Journal of Personality and Social Psychology, 78*, 871–888.

Klauer, K. C., & Wegener, I. (1998). Unraveling social categorization in the "Who said what?" paradigm. *Journal of Personality and Social Psychology, 75*, 1155–1178.

Lambert, A. J., Payne, B. K., Jacoby, L. L., Shaffer, L. M., Chasteen, A. L., & Khan, S. K. (2003). Stereotypes as dominant responses: On the "social facilitation" of prejudice in anticipated public contexts. *Journal of Personality and Social Psychology, 84*, 277–295.

Lhermitte, F. (1986). Human autonomy and the frontal lobes. Part II: Patient behavior in complex and social situations: The "environmental dependency syndrome." *Annals of Neurology, 19*, 335–343.

Marchetti, C., & Della Sala, S. (1998). Disentangling the alien hand and anarchic hand. *Cognitive Neuropsychiatry, 3,* 191–207.

Morwitz, V. G., Johnson, E., & Schmittlein, D. (1993). Does measuring intent change behavior? *Journal of Consumer Research, 20,* 46–61.

Muraven, M., & Baumeister, R. F. (2000). Self-regulation and depletion of limited resources: Does self-control resemble a muscle? *Psychological Bulletin, 126,* 247–259.

Murphy, S. T., & Zajonc, R. B. (1993). Affect, cognition, and awareness: Affective priming with optimal and suboptimal stimulus exposures. *Journal of Personality and Social Psychology, 64,* 723–739.

Payne, B. K. (2001). Prejudice and perception: The role of automatic and controlled processes in misperceiving a weapon. *Journal of Personality and Social Psychology, 81,* 181–192.

Payne, B. K. (2005). Conceptualizing Control in Social Cognition: How executive control modulates the expression of automatic stereotyping. *Journal of Personality and Social Psychology, 89,* 488–503.

Payne, B. K., Cheng, C. M., Govorun, O., & Stewart, B. D. (2005). An inkblot for attitudes: Affect misattribution as implicit measurement. *Journal of Personality and Social Psychology, 89,* 277–293.

Payne, B. K., Jacoby, L. L., & Lambert, A. J. (2004). Memory monitoring and the control of stereotype distortion. *Journal of Experimental Social Psychology, 40,* 52–64.

Payne, B. K., Jacoby, L. L., & Lambert, A. J. (2005). Attitudes as accessibility bias: Dissociating automatic and controlled components. In R. Hassin, J. Bargh, & J. Uleman, (Eds.), *The new unconscious.* Oxford, UK: Oxford University Press.

Payne, B. K., Lambert, A. J., & Jacoby, L. L. (2002). Best laid plans: Effects of goals on accessibility bias and cognitive control in race-based misperceptions of weapons. *Journal of Experimental Social Psychology, 38,* 384–396.

Petty, R. E., & Cacioppo, J. T. (1986). *The Elaboration Likelihood Model of persuasion.* New York: Academic Press.

Posner, M. I., & Snyder, C. R. R. (1975). Attention and cognitive control. In R. L. Solo (Ed.), *Information processing and cognition: The Loyola symposium* (pp. 55–85). Hillsdale, NJ: Erlbaum.

Riefer, D. M., & Batchelder, W. H. (1988). Multinomial modelling and the measurement of cognitive processes. *Psychological Review, 95,* 318–339.

Roediger, H. L., & McDermott, K. B. (1993). Implicit memory in normal human subjects. In H. Spinnler & F. Boller (Eds.), *Handbook of neuropsychology* (Vol. 8, pp. 63–131). Amsterdam: Elsevier.

Schwarz, N., & Clore, G. L. (1983). Mood, misattribution, and judgments of well-being: Informative and directive functions of affective states. *Journal of Personality and Social Psychology, 45,* 513–523.

Sherman, S. J. (1980). On the self-erasing nature of errors of prediction. *Journal of Personality and Social Psychology, 39,* 340–350.

Sherman, J. W., Groom, C. J., Ehrenberg, K., & Klauer, K. C. (2003). Bearing false witness under pressure: Implicit and explicit components of stereotype-driven memory distortions. *Social Cognition, 21,* 213–246.

Shiffrin, R., & Schneider, W. (1977). Controlled and automatic human information processing: II. Perceptual learning, automatic attending, and a general theory. *Psychological Review, 84,* 127–190.

Shimamura, A. P. (1986). Priming effects in amnesia: Evidence for a dissociable memory function. *Quarterly Journal of Experimental Psychology: Human Experimental Psychology, 38,* 619–644.

Stangor, C., & McMillan, D. (1992). Memory for expectancy-congruent and expectancy-incongruent information: A review of the social and social developmental literatures. *Psychological Bulletin, 111*, 42–61.

Stewart, B. D., & Payne, B. K. (2006). Counterstereotypical thought plans reduce automatic stereotyping. Manuscript submitted for publication.

Tanner, W. P., & Swets, J. A. (1954). A decision making theory of visual detection. *Psychological Review, 61*, 401–409.

Wegner, D. M. (2002). *The illusion of conscious will*. Cambridge, MA: MIT Press.

Wilson, T. D., Lindsey, S., & Schooler, T. Y. (2000). A model of dual attitudes. *Psychological Review, 107*, 101–126.

Yonelinas, A. P. (2002). The nature of recollection and familiarity: A review of 30 years of research. *Journal of Memory and Language, 46*, 441–451.

Author Index

Chapters by contributors denoted in **bold** type.

A

Aarts, H., 1, 2, 4, **51–131**, 51, 52, 56, 57, 77, 78, 80, 85, 89, 90, 92, 95, 96, 97, 98, 99, 100, 101, 103, 104, 105, 106, 107, 108, 109, 110, 112, 113, 114
Abelson, R. P., 95, 244
Abrahamsen, A., 245
Adams, C. M., 197
Adams, R. B., Jr., 197
Adelmann, K. A., 64
Adelmann, P. K., 186
Adolphs, R., 187, 197
Aertson, A., 245
Agnew, C. R., 141
Ahern, G. L., 189
Ajzen, I., 244
Akalis, S., 276
Akbudak, E., 200
Albarracín, D., 222
Alexander, A., 197
Alley, T. R., 61
Allport, G. W., 65, 219, 220, 221
Alon, A., 21
Ambady, N., 85, 92, 185, 197, 279
Amodio, D. N., 226
Andersen, S. M., 2, 5, **133–172**, 134, 137, 138, 146, 148, 149, 151, 152, 155, 156, 157, 159, 162
Anderson, A. K, 187, 197
Anderson, C. A., 81
Anderson, J. A., 245
Anderson, J. R., 12, 15, 20, 104, 107, 244
Anderson, M. C., 109
Andrews, C., 190
Antoniou, A. A., 180
Arad, D., 143, 146, 147
Arcuri, L., 224, 235, 236, 245
Arielli, A., 245
Arkes, H. R., 228, 241, 282
Arkin, R., 68

B

Baars, B. J., 31, 33, 37, 39, 40, 115
Baccus, J. R., 139, 280
Bachorowski, J.-A, 185
Back, M. D., 272, 273
Bacon, P. L., 141
Baddeley, A. D, 15, 32, 301
Baeyens, F., 224, 235
Bailenson, J. N., 74
Baird, A. A., 197, 267
Bak, P., 230
Baldwin, M. W., 134, 138, 139, 140, 143, 149, 151, 152, 155, 280
Banaji, M. R., 3, 7, 40, 77, 135, 191, 197, 220, 221, 222, 223, 224, 225, 226, 227, 228, 229, 231, 232, 233, 236, 241, 242, 244, 245, 250, **265–292**, 266, 267, 269, 270, 271, 272, 273, 274, 275, 276, 277, 278, 279, 280, 281, 282, 283, 284, 285, 286, 305, 311
Bandura, A., 96
Banfield, J. F., 80
Banse, R., 185, 274, 275

A

Armony, J. L., 197
Arnold, M., 180
Aron, A., 134, 140, 141, 154, 162, 306
Aron, E. N., 140, 141, 154
Aronson, J., 92, 93
Asch, S. E., 83
Asendorpf, J. B., 274, 275
Asgari, S., 279
Ashburn-Nardo, L., 225, 283, 284
Ashmore, R. D., 134, 234, 279
Ashton-James, C., 73
Atkinson, J. W., 108
Auman, C., 92
Averill, J. R., 186
Aydemir, A., 40
Ayduk, O., 144, 157

Ernst, J. M., 184
Estes, Z., 84, 89, 90
Esteves, F., 191
Etcoff, N. L., 197, 203
Eubanks, J., 81
Evans, A. C., 63
Everling, S., 301

F

Fadiga, L., 54, 60
Fanselow, M. S., 185
Farah, M. J., 199
Farnham, S. D., 225, 233, 275, 278
Fazio, F., 63
Fazio, R. H., 7, 12, 86, 135, 164, 180, 191, 219, 220, 221, 222, 223, 224, 225, 226, 228, 229, 230, 231, 232, 233, 234, 235, 236, 237, 238, 241, 242, 243, 244, 245, 247, 248, 249, 250, 267, 274, 276, 277, 281, 283, 284, 304, 305
Fehr, B., 134, 143, 151
Feldman, L. A., 186
Feldman, S., 143, 144, 146, 151, 157
Fellows, L. K., 199
Ferguson, M. J., 7, 100, 180, 188, **219–264**, 220, 221, 224, 225, 229, 230, 231, 236, 240, 244, 245, 246, 248, 249, 250, 279, 311
Fernandez-Dols, J.-M., 185, 186
Fernandez-Duque, D., 16
Ferraro, R., 74
Ferry, A. T., 199
Festinger, L., 231
Fiedler, K., 82, 245
Field, A. P., 235
Fiez, J. A., 197
Fink, G. R., 200
Finkel, E. A., 76
Fischl, B., 34
Fischbach, A., 95, 104
Fischer, B., 301
Fischer, H. H., 203
Fishbein, M., 244
Fisk, A. D., 21, 234
Fiske, A. P., 145, 147
Fiske, S. T., 1, 7, 59, 77, 87, 147, 221, 240, 243, 243, 244, 247
Fissell, C., 197
Fitzgerald, D., 189
Fitzsimons, G. J., 103, 302, 304
Fitzsimons, G. M., 2, 5, 101, 102, 103, **133–172**, 139, 155, 156, 161
Fleck, S., 84, 87, 90
Fletcher, G. J. O., 143
Florack, A., 279

Fockenberg, D. A., 70
Fodor, J., 14, 250
Fogassi, L., 54, 60
Fogel, L. A., 192
Folkman, S., 180
Fong, G. W., 197
Forgas, J. P., 241
Foroni, F., 279, 280
Forster, K. I., 108
Förster, J., 85, 109
Fournet, M., 78, 82, 83
Fox, E., 39
Fraley, R. C., 158, 162
Francolini, C. M., 16
Frank, R. H., 238
Freitas, A. L., 160
Freud, S., 137
Fridlund, A. J., 185, 186
Friedman, B. H., 184
Friedman, R. S., 85, 95, 99, 104
Friesen, M. D., 143
Friesen, W. V., 183, 184, 185
Frijda, N. H., 179, 180, 181, 192
Friston, K. J., 189, 197
Frith, C.D., 114, 200
Froming, W. J., 76, 80
Fujita, K., 85, 92
Funayama, E. S., 226, 267, 284

G

Gabrieli, J. D., 187, 197, 198, 200
Gaertner, S. L., 223, 241, 242
Galanter, E., 28, 95, 107, 110
Gallagher, H. L., 196, 200
Gallagher, M., 187, 199
Gallese, V., 54, 60
Ganellen, R. J., 76, 80
Gao, K., 189
Gapinsky, K. D., 267
Garcia, M., 191, 221, 224, 233, 234, 235, 238, 244, 245, 248, 249
Gardner, W. L., 141, 180, 186, 190, 191, 232, 246
Garner, J. P., 158
Gartska, T. A., 272
Gary, M. L., 234, 279
Gatenby, J. C., 197, 226, 227, 267, 284
Gati, I., 39
Gaunt, R., 248
Gawronski, B., 3, 221, 222, 225, 226, 231, 232, 233, 244, 245, 248, 273, 276, 278, 283, 286, 310
Gazzaniga, M. S., 236
Geen, R. G., 99, 101

Subject Index

Page entries for main headings that have subheadings refer only to general aspects of that topic.
Page entries for tables are denoted in **bold**.
Page entries for figures are denoted in *italic*.